Ironclad Captain

Seth Phelps in uniform

Ironclad

Seth Ledyard Phelps

Captain

& the U.S. Navy, 1841–1864

Jay Slagle

With a Foreword by Edwin C. Bearss

The Kent State University Press

Kent, Ohio, & London, England

©1996 by The Kent State University Press,

Kent, Ohio 44242

ALL RIGHTS RESERVED

Library of Congress Catalog Card Number 96-12755

ISBN 0–87338–550–0

Manufactured in the United States of America

05 04 03 02 01 00 99 98 97 96   5 4 3 2 1

Library of Congress Cataloging-in-Publication Data

Slagle, Jay, 1946–

Ironclad captain : Seth Ledyard Phelps and the U. S. Navy,
1841–1864 / Jay Slagle ; with a foreword by Edwin C. Bearss.

p.   cm.

Includes bibliographical references and index.

ISBN 0-87338-550-0 (cloth : alk. paper) ∞

1. Phelps, Seth Ledyard, d. 1885.   2. Ship captains—United
States—Biography.   3. United States.   Navy—Biography.   4. United
States—History—Civil War, 1861–1865—Naval operations.   5. Mexican
War, 1846–1848—Naval operations, American.   I. Title.

E467.1.P56S58   1996

973.7'5—dc20   96-12755

British Library Cataloging-in-Publication data are available.

To
Captain Robert J. Slagle,
USN (ret.)

Contents

എ

Foreword

ALIFELONG ROMANCE with the Civil War—its personalities and the rank and file, its heroism, tragedy, and pathos—began in the bitter winter of 1935–36, when I was twelve. I lived with my parents on a cattle ranch at Sarpy, Montana, forty miles from town and three miles from the nearest neighbors. My father, a World War I marine, was a history buff, and on winter evenings he read to my brother and me. Among the books he chose, most of which focused on his war and the Marine Corps, was John W. Thomason's *J. E. B. Stuart*. I was hooked.

Until I attended graduate school at Indiana University in 1953–55, my readings—and beginning in April 1949, when I acquired a car, my visits to battlefields—centered on the war in the East and the titanic struggle between the Armies of the Potomac and Northern Virginia. At Indiana University, I broadened my horizons to include the Western armies and their leaders; the title of my master's thesis is "Patrick R. Cleburne: Stonewall Jackson of the West."

Not until September 1955, when I joined the National Park Service and was stationed at Vicksburg National Military Park, did I begin to delve into what was happening afloat, particularly on the Mississippi and other great rivers of America's heartland. This was necessary if I were to understand and interpret to park visitors the fourteen months of campaigns that led to the surrender of Vicksburg and Port Hudson, permitting President Abraham Lincoln to announce, "The Father of Waters again goes unvexed to the Sea."

During my first months at Vicksburg, I became familiar with volumes 18–27 of *Official Records of the Union and Confederate Navies in the War of the Rebellion,* which addressed the activities of the West Gulf Blockading Squadron and naval forces on western waters. I read Alfred Thayer Mahan's *The Gulf and Inland Waters;* H. Allen Gosnell's *Guns on the Western Waters: The Story of the River Gunboats in the Civil War;* Richard S. West's *Mr. Lincoln's Navy;* Loyall Farragut's *Life and Letters of Admiral Farragut: First Admiral of the U.S. Navy;* and David Dixon Porter's *Incidents and Anecdotes of the Civil War* and *The Naval History of the Civil War.*

These books, along with articles in *Battles and Leaders of the Civil War* focusing on the river war, fired my enthusiasm. I came to understand and appreciate the significance of the partnership between the Union Army and Uncle Sam's webfeet that gave birth to many of the principles of amphibious warfare honed by the United States and Japan in World War II, and that spelled disaster for the Confederacy on the western rivers and the North and South Carolina sounds. Denied this partnership, armies led by Maj. Gen. Ulysses S. Grant, John Pope, and Nathaniel P. Banks—particularly Grant's—confronted by vast distances and mud roads, would, as they thrust deep into the South's heartland, have suffered fates similar to those of Charles XII in Russia in 1708–9, Napoleon Bonaparte in the same country in 1812, and, in our time, Adolf Hitler's *Wehrmacht* in the Soviet Union in the late autumn of 1941 and the winter of 1941–42.

My interest in the riverine war was heightened in the late summer of 1956, when the possibility of locating the hulk of the Eads "City Series" ironclad *Cairo,* sunk by an "infernal machine in the Yazoo River," was discussed with a friend, Warren E. Grabou, a geologist and Civil War buff. Joined by Max Donald Jacks, a riverman, in November we pinpointed and identified the ironclad. *Cairo,* after much hard work and heartache, was salvaged and is now a popular attraction at Vicksburg National Military Park.

What does the foregoing have to do with Lt. Comdr. Seth Ledyard Phelps? So long as my research centered on the 1863 Vicksburg campaign, Phelps was not a major player. But this focus changed in October 1958. With the National Park Service making plans to enhance its interpretive exhibits and programs to meet challenges stimulated by increased visits during the Civil War centennial years, I became research historian for the Southeast Region. My duty station was Vicksburg, but I served the research needs of most of the Civil War parks.

My first projects took me to Stones River and Fort Donelson National Military Parks. At the latter my initial project aimed at supporting restoration of the lower water battery and was titled "Gunboat Operations at Forts Henry and Donelson." It was then that I came to know and appreciate Seth Phelps. One of the first naval officers ordered to the Midwest, he pioneered in building from scratch the mighty Mississippi Squadron that, beginning at Fort Henry in February 1862, teamed with the army to strangle Confederate hopes and dreams on the western waters. As captain of *Conestoga*, he popped up everywhere during these early months of the war. Prowling the lower reaches of the Cumberland and Tennessee rivers, he showed the flag, encouraging pro-Union Kentuckians and overawing secessionists. He was an active participant in the Fort Henry drama. He next led the dash up the Tennessee River by the three timber-clads as far as Muscle Shoals, dismaying Confederates and capturing or destroying all steamboats on the river below Chattanooga.

A tangible result of broadening my horizons was publication in historical journals in the early 1960s of monographs titled "The Fall of Fort Henry" (*West Tennessee Historical Society Publications,* 1963); "A Federal Raid Up the Tennessee River" (*Alabama Review,* 1964); and "The Union Raid Down the Mississippi and Up the Yazoo, August 14–27, 1862" (*Military Affairs,* 1962). In 1963, the Vicksburg Centennial Commission published *Rebel Victory at Vicksburg,* the story of the unsuccessful efforts by the Union Navy to capture the Confederate Gibraltar in the late spring and summer of 1862. Phelps commanded the two raiding flotillas, and had an important role at Fort Henry and at Vicksburg in July 1862; but never, until I had the pleasure of reading his personal correspondence as presented by Jay Slagle, did I know the man or appreciate his significance to the outfitting and early success of the squadron, and the interpersonal relationships that add flesh and substance to the matter-of-fact tone in much of the official correspondence and entries in the ships' logs.

Phelps's Civil War service—first under Flag Officer Andrew Hull Foote and then under Charles Henry Davis—engendered mutual respect and admiration that boded well for his career and contributed to early successes of the squadron. As their number-one subordinate and flag captain under Davis, Phelps expected, with their support, to succeed Davis as commander of the Mississippi Squadron. Despite his lobbying for that choice plum, he did not receive it. He lost out to David Dixon Porter. Equally ambitious, the bombastic, patronizing Porter had more powerful friends in Washington and thus got the job although a stranger to the Mississippi Squadron, along with a promotion to acting rear admiral. Phelps, for his efforts, received a sharply worded letter from navy secretary Gideon Welles condemning his lobbying.

Phelps's career had peaked. During the months following Porter's arrival on the Mississippi, Phelps found his time and energy increasingly absorbed with the ironclad *Eastport,* a jinxed vessel. Captured on her building ways at Cerro Gordo by Phelps on his brilliant raid up the Tennessee River, *Eastport* was rebuilt and outfitted by the navy to be the most powerful ironclad on western waters. She became Phelps's bête noire. He staked his career and reputation on this Jonah, and she failed him. His struggle to save *Eastport,* as told by historian Jay Slagle, is reminiscent of a Greek tragedy. Soon after he destroyed *Eastport,* Phelps, an embattled hero to whom the United States and its navy owe much, resigned his commission and returned to a productive but less challenging and exciting life as a civilian.

Historian Slagle takes the extensive family correspondence of his kinsman Seth Phelps, and with keen insight synthesizes and blends it with information extracted from relevant sources, published and manuscript, into narrative history at its best. Through Phelps and his experiences we gain an insight of what it was like to be a naval officer in the years between 1841—when, as a seventeen-year-old he was a midshipman assigned to the razee *Independence*—and October 1864, when he resigned. Phelps's experiences on foreign and domestic stations, on a small gunboat during the Mexican War, and his candid views of the navy, his brother officers, and its seniority system, will entertain and enlighten. Phelps, as his letters reveal, was no prude. In the years before his marriage, he was akin to many marine and naval officers with whom I served in World War II.

Seth Ledyard Phelps's twenty-three years in the navy will appeal to readers who cherish stories of people and their activities and interactions as they master repeated challenges, and is more vital and exciting than fiction. *Ironclad Captain* is a winner, and I recommend it to all who cherish adventure and who savor what life in the navy was like during the momentous years that Phelps served his country.

Edwin C. Bearss
Emeritus Historian
National Park Service

∾

Preface

THIS STORY is an autobiography even though Seth Ledyard Phelps never sat down to pen his memoirs—which is too bad, for he was a wonderful writer. Fortunately he was a prolific correspondent, and many of his letters have survived. Drawn together from around the country, these letters tell the story not only of his naval career but of the U.S. Navy in the mid–nineteenth century.

Seth Phelps joined the navy for the same reasons young men for centuries have been drawn to the sea. Thoughts of adventure, excitement, and foreign lands motivated the youthful Ohioan to leave the family farm in search of a career. Ambitious, strong-willed, and intelligent, Phelps found the adventure he was looking for. Unfortunately, he also found that a naval career depended upon political influence and seniority. Accomplishments and ability mattered little.

In this period of sail and steam, ambition, honor, and glory motivated Phelps into conflicts not only with the enemy but also with his fellow naval officers. Wherever possible, I have attempted to use the very words written by Phelps and the men with whom he served to describe their actions, thoughts, and feelings—no one can tell their story better than they can. The few lapses in Phelps's correspondence are used to focus briefly on the men and events that influenced his life and career. Unfortunately, Phelps's letters stopped abruptly with the end of his naval service. Many of his correspondents—his father, Elisha Whittlesey, and Andrew Foote—by then were dead. No subsequent letters to his wife have survived.

Seth Phelps's career gives a remarkable portrait of naval life in a period that saw great technological change. The advent of steam propulsion, armor plating, and rifled cannon demanded vision and daring, just as the submarine and the aircraft carrier did a century later. Seth Phelps was one of the younger generation of naval officers who not only embraced the new technology but did so in an alien environment for a sailor—the western rivers of the United States. It was here, during the Civil War, that Phelps found his element and contributed to the defining event in American history.

I would like to thank John Hubbell at The Kent State University Press for his patience and support. I am particularly grateful to Edwin C. Bearss, who took the time to review the manuscript and provide constructive criticism and guidance.

Ironclad Captain

℣

Destroying a Fleet

E STABLISHING new ferries across the Potomac River in early 1861 was hard, cold work. The arrival of spring was welcomed by the Army Engineers, and rumors of war and rebellion that were sweeping Washington City seemed remote in the warm April sun.

For thirty-seven-year-old Seth Ledyard Phelps, a navy lieutenant, temporary duty with the Army Engineers was in stark contrast to the heat and boredom of the Central American coast from which he had just returned. The work was challenging and certainly better than duty at the chaotic Navy Department, now under the direction of a former Connecticut postmaster.

Fort Sumter had surrendered, and the Gosport Navy Yard at Norfolk, Virginia, was in danger of falling into secessionist hands. The navy's senior line officer, Capt. Hiram Paulding, ordered to Norfolk to assess the situation, had reported a rapidly deteriorating condition.

On April 19, Phelps received orders to report to the Washington Navy Yard immediately. Arriving later the same day, he found the screw sloop *Pawnee,* mounting 15 guns, bustling with activity. Her crew was loading a strange assortment of supplies, including 40 barrels of powder, 11 tanks of turpentine, 12 bales of cotton waste, and 181 portfires.[1] Her captain, Stephen Rowan, had orders to be prepared to sail without delay. Phelps was not the only one ordered to report on board the *Pawnee.* The new secretary of the navy, Gideon Welles, had rounded up every officer and seaman he could lay his hands on. After stripping the Washington Navy Yard of its one hundred marines, the *Pawnee* cast off for Norfolk that evening.

As the *Pawnee* steamed down the Potomac River, Phelps noted a change in Hiram Paulding, whom he called in 1858 "probably the best man on the list of Captains in the Navy."[2] The sixty-four-year-old commodore, now chief of the Bureau of Personnel, was exhausted, both physically and mentally; sometimes he spoke in confusing monosyllables to his assembled officers.[3] Joining Phelps were the noted explorer Capt. Charles Wilkes, Comdr. John Rodgers, and nine other officers of various ranks. Paulding explained that Gosport was in danger of falling to Southern forces gathering outside the yard. His orders were explicit: Use force to defend the yard; if necessary, destroy it.

For weeks the new Lincoln administration had been afraid to make any move at Gosport for fear of provoking Virginia into secession. On April 10, Gosport's commanding officer, Commodore Charles S. McCauley, had been ordered by Gideon Welles to ready shipping and public property to be moved out of danger should it become necessary. At the same time Welles cautioned McCauley "that there should be no steps taken to give needless alarm."[4]

Welles's orders only added to McCauley's inability to grasp the situation. A veteran of the War of 1812, McCauley was greatly influenced by his junior officers, who were, it was becoming clear, loyal to their states and not to the Union. When McCauley was informed by these officers that the steam frigate *Merrimack* would need thirty days to be made ready for sea, the navy's chief engineer, Benjamin F. Isherwood, who had been ordered from Washington, arrived, and had the *Merrimack* ready in three.

On the night of April 16, a band of men from Norfolk seized two lightships and sank them in the channel, in an attempt to block access from the sea. Time appeared to be running out for the navy yard. On April 17 Isherwood requested permission to fire the *Merrimack*'s boilers, but was told by McCauley to wait until "tomorrow." The next day the *Merrimack*'s boilers were brought on line, only to have McCauley order them extinguished. Isherwood was furious at the sixty-eight-year-old McCauley, whom he accused of drunkenness and senility.

That same day McCauley's Southern officers, who had professed their loyalty to the United States, tendered their resignations. The situation appeared critical. Numerous ships, hundreds of heavy guns, thousands of tons of supplies, and the navy's best port were ripe for the picking by Rebel forces gathering outside the yard.

Paulding explained to his officers that he intended to remove the *Merrimack, Germantown, Plymouth, Dolphin,* and anything else that was feasible. Other, older ships, like the *United States, Pennsylvania,* and *Columbus,* would, along with everything else, be torched if necessary. Phelps was assigned to the sloop of war *Germantown* under Comdr. William Walker.

At 2:30 P.M. on April 20, the *Pawnee* rounded to off Fort Monroe, across Hampton Roads from Norfolk. More men were needed to man the ships and secure the yard. Three hundred fifty green troops of the 3rd Massachusetts were mustered and began boarding.

By 6:45 P.M. the sun was setting on a still, clear night. As twilight dissipated, the light from a half moon reflected off the faces of the men who jammed the deck of the *Pawnee.* The soldiers manning the parapets of Fort Monroe gave a hearty cheer as the *Pawnee* slipped her moorings and headed up Hampton Roads to the navy yard.

The obstructions in the channel were easily bypassed, and at 8 P.M., the *Pawnee* eased alongside the navy yard wharf. The sailors of the *Cumberland,* who had beat to quarters at the approach of the unknown vessel, were elated at the arrival of reinforcements, and their cheers carried into the city. The Massachusetts volunteers and marines fanned out to the yard perimeter, to block any attempt by the Southerners to interfere.

It was quickly evident to the officers and men on the *Pawnee* that a bad situation had become measurably worse. Several hours before, McCauley had ordered the scuttling of the *Merrimack, Germantown,*

Plymouth, and *Dolphin.* Captain Wilkes quickly ordered the officers to their assigned ships to see if any could be saved. Phelps, with Commander Walker and Lt. George U. Morris quickly made their way to the *Germantown;* they found her already so low in the water that it would be impossible to salvage her.

Upon returning to the *Pawnee,* they heard the other officers report that, with the exception of the *Dolphin,* their ships were sunk. Paulding now faced a critical decision. He commanded about one thousand men, half of them infantry and marines, and more were expected shortly aboard the steamer *Keystone State,* en route from Philadelphia. With the big guns from the *Cumberland* and *Pawnee,* along with others from ships like the *Pennsylvania,* supporting his troops, Paulding could in all likelihood hold the yard for an extended period. If the Confederates made a concerted effort to storm the yard, the big guns could level the city if necessary. Paulding decided instead to destroy what he could and abandon Norfolk.

Officers and men were detailed to different parts of the yard and the various ships to prepare their destruction. Parties of marines and sailors poured turpentine and other combustibles over piles of cordage, ladders, gratings, hawsers, and anything else that would burn. The piles were shaped like a "V," with the apex at the base of the mainmast, then spreading out along the sides of the main deck. Turpentine was also splashed over the ships' decks and beams that remained above water. Makeshift fuses were made by soaking hawsers in turpentine.

In the meantime, Comdr. John Rodgers and Capt. Horatio G. Wright of the army engineers headed to the massive, granite dry dock no. 1 with a large quantity of powder, to see if they could at least disable it. The powder was laid around the pumping apparatus, to be ignited when the signal was given.

Details were sent out with sledgehammers to try and break the trunnions and to spike as many of the 1,500 heavy guns as possible. The men had only limited success, for the metal was of such hardness, especially on the newer Dahlgren guns, that those which were spiked were later repaired and turned against the Union.[5]

Other detachments were sent to prepare the numerous storehouses, shops, and buildings for destruction. All books and papers that could be collected were brought aboard the *Pawnee*. It was rumored that a large quantity of gold had been sent from the Norfolk customhouse and was in the hold of the *Cumberland*.

The frenzy of preparation continued until the moon set just after midnight. Since work was not yet complete, the barracks near the center of the yard was set on fire to provide light for the remaining work. Large numbers of muskets and pistols, along with quantities of shot and shell, were thrown into the water.

By 1:45 A.M. the preparations were nearing completion, so the soldiers and marines were ordered to begin embarking. While the troops were falling back on the *Pawnee* and *Cumberland,* the youngest son of Commodore McCauley came running up the gangplank of the *Pawnee,* asking to see Captain Paulding. With tears running down his cheeks, the youngster explained that his father refused to leave. Paulding sent Comdr. James Alden to McCauley's quarters to explain that his sacrifice would be in vain. Reluctantly McCauley agreed to return to the *Cumberland* with Alden, to join his son.

With the shore parties safely aboard the ships, two cutters remained. Phelps, Lt. Henry Wise, and their party were to fire the yard and ships at the signal. Captain Wilkes would wait with the second cutter for Rodgers and Wright, who were still at dry dock no. 1.

The *Pawnee* stood out into the harbor, followed shortly afterward by the *Cumberland,* towed by the steam tug *Yankee*. At 4:20 A.M. on April 21, Paulding gave the signal, and a rocket was launched from the deck of the *Pawnee*.

Ashore, sailors began applying torches to the various buildings in the yard. They then ran down the wharf, torching each vessel in turn. As Phelps looked at the *Columbus,* a seventy-four-gun ship of the line, he must have mourned her end. The ship was now decaying, but she had been a great ship. As a seventeen-year-old midshipman, Phelps had first seen foreign lands from her decks. The torch was applied, and she soon became an inferno.

"It is a sad alternative to destroy a fine ship but . . . when I touched the brand to the *Merrimack*," Phelps wrote, "I had contempt for the act."[6] It would not be the last of the *Merrimack*.

Rodgers and Wright lit the fuse to the two thousand pounds of powder around the pump house at the dry dock and headed for their cutter. Soon flames were leaping hundreds of feet in the air, and the heat was so intense that they had to abandon any attempt to reach the wharf. Instead they found a small boat and Rodgers and Wright tried to make their way out into the harbor to reach the *Pawnee*. The conflagration had aroused a sleeping Norfolk, and soon they were spotted by local militia and fired on. Rodgers saw a large number of soldiers ahead within easy musket range, so he decided to land on the Norfolk bank and surrender to Maj. Gen. William B. Taliaferro, commanding the Virginia forces.

Back at the wharf, Captain Wilkes moved his cutter ahead of the *Germantown* to be closer to the dry dock. Soon the flames were climbing the masts and rigging of the ships, and buildings were sheets of flame and dense smoke. Realizing that Rodgers and Wright had no hope of making their way back to the rendezvous, Wilkes reluctantly gave the order to shove off.

Phelps and Wise, having started the inferno, departed the landing with large flakes of fire falling all about them. They rendezvoused with Wilkes, who said their boat "appeared as if passing through the flames."[7] The sailors manning the oars put their backs into their work until they had passed the burning *Pennsylvania* and reached relative safety. The two cutters, with the officers and exhausted sailors, finally reached the *Cumberland* and *Pawnee* off nearby Craney Island.

The people of Norfolk and Portsmouth woke to an incredible spectacle. Flames leaping from mizzenmasts and buildings alike were hypnotic in their beauty and horror. The countryside for miles around was illuminated by the conflagration. The *Pennsylvania* was enveloped in fire and became the centerpiece of a nautical volcano. A number of her guns were loaded, and as the flames reached each one, the roar added to her spectacular end. For more than five hours the ship burned, until finally her mainmast wavered and crashed into her hull, sending a torrent of sparks skyward. Her death was complete when "the iron had entered into her soul."[8]

The *Pawnee* and *Cumberland* eased their way north toward Hampton Roads, pausing before the sunken lightships. Around 6 A.M. it was discovered that new obstructions had been placed since their arrival. The *Cumberland* anchored, and the *Pawnee* carefully worked her way through until she was clear. The *Pawnee* proceeded back to Fort Monroe, where the steamer *Keystone State* had arrived. While the *Pawnee* debarked the 3d Massachusetts, the *Keystone State* proceeded with a pilot to guide the *Cumberland* through the channel obstructions.

In Norfolk, Rodgers and Wright were received by General Taliaferro, who granted their parole. Early Sunday morning, the two officers were put up in the Atlantic Hotel, where they stayed until Monday afternoon. With a Confederate officer as an escort, they were taken to Richmond, where they were greeted by Gov. John Letcher and his family. After remaining as guests of the governor until Wednesday, Rodgers and Wright were released and escorted to the train station by the governor, who personally assured their safety.

Phelps and the other officers and marines remained on board the *Pawnee* as she steamed back up the Potomac River. Tuesday morning, all hands were mustered for a salute as the *Pawnee* passed Mount Vernon. Shortly thereafter the *Keystone State* appeared with the warning that the Confederates had placed a battery at Alexandria. The *Pawnee* beat to quarters but found no guns. Instead, she ran aground and had to send for a tugboat to tow her back to the Washington Navy Yard.

The destruction of the Gosport Navy Yard, which would be recaptured the following year, was largely a failure. The buildings destroyed included the immense shiphouses, marine barracks, and riggers', sail, and ordnance lofts. Most mechanics' shops, timber sheds, foundries, sawmills, and officers' quarters were spared. Dry dock no. 1 was quickly repaired, and the Confederates raised the *Merrimack.* Converted into a powerful ironclad and renamed *Virginia,* she threatened the Union blockade until her historic confrontation with the *Monitor.* More important, the Confederacy took possession of more than a thousand heavy guns. This sudden shift of military strength was unprecedented, and for the next three and a half years Seth Phelps would face these guns at such places as Fort Henry, Island No. 10, and Vicksburg.

CHAPTER TWO

 C/D

"Reefers"

SETH PHELPS was born on June 13, 1824, in Parkman, Ohio. The eldest of five children, he was named after his grandfather, a veteran of the Revolutionary War who was commissioned as a second lieutenant in the 20th Continental Infantry in 1776. Lieutenant Phelps was wounded at the Battle of Princeton in early January 1777 and later wintered with George Washington at Valley Forge. He was promoted to captain in May 1778 and served as an aide to General Washington at the Battle of Monmouth Courthouse (New Jersey) on June 28, 1778. Later, the young officer joined the American Light Infantry, the Continental army's first elite unit, under Maj. Gen. "Mad" Anthony Wayne. Phelps was with Wayne when he carried the British stonghold at Stony Point on the Hudson River. Just after midnight on July 16, 1779, Wayne's corps, with unloaded muskets, made a bayonet assault. After a twenty-minute fight, the surprised British garrison surrendered. Captain Phelps was severely wounded in the arm but continued on active service until he was transferred to the Invalid Regiment in October 1780.

Following the Revolution, grandfather Phelps and his wife, the former Lucy Ledyard of Groton, Connecticut, joined the growing westward migration and settled for a time in Aurora, New York. Following the birth of their son Alfred in 1792, the family continued its westward move and settled in Connecticut's Western Reserve, which became part of the new state of Ohio in 1803.

The family's tradition of military service continued in the War of 1812; Alfred was commissioned a lieutenant of infantry in the regular army and assigned to the Niagara frontier. He was with Lt. Col. Winfield Scott during the unsuccessful assault on the British at Queenston, Ontario. While crossing the river on that expedition, Phelps's boat was driven by the current below the landing point and stranded at a place where the bank was very precipitous. Exposed to a hail of musket fire from above, he formed his men and, with fixed bayonets, stormed the heights. During the assault, a musket ball grazed his forehead, carrying away his left brow. With blood flowing down his face, Phelps led half a dozen of his men to the summit, where, after a hand-to-hand struggle, they were overpowered and taken prisoner.

Because of his wound, Alfred Phelps was paroled into American custody at Albany, New York, waiting for a prisoner exchange. Because the United States had no British officers to exchange at the time, President James Madison and his war council decided that paroled officers in their custody could do garrison duty. With orders to rejoin the troops stationed at the forts, Phelps had a choice. He could break his parole of honor or resign his commission. Supported by his father, he regretfully resigned.

After returning home, Alfred Phelps began a law practice and married Ann B. Towsley on July 1, 1820. Shortly after Seth was born, the family bought a farm and moved to Chardon, just east of Cleveland and not far from Lake Erie.

Growing up near one of the Great Lakes, Seth dreamed of the sea while listening to the tales of his father's younger brother, Edwin. He had gone to sea as a youngster and, like sailors everywhere, had stories, often embellished with time and ale, that enthralled the Phelps children during his visits. Seth, with his younger brothers Alfred and Edwin and sisters Mary and Eliza, grew up hearing tales of Oliver Perry's victory over the British on Lake Erie, of tall ships and strong men: "Why, man, she sailed as well in the wind's eye as in her tail! Better—for she was so fast before the wind she'd outrun it, have to round to and lose time waitin' for it to catch up."[1]

Seeking an appointment as a midshipman, the seventeen-year-old Phelps wrote to a longtime friend of the family, Elisha Whittlesey, in Washington. A post office auditor during the Harrison administration, Whittlesey had served eight terms as a congressman and was well positioned to continue to support his constituents. Stating, "From my infancy I have had strong predilections for the sea," Phelps asked both Whittlesey's help and his silence, lest his parents, especially his mother, get wind of his request.

Midshipmen were appointed by the president and the secretary of the navy from candidates recommended by congressmen and influential citizens. With applications far outstripping the navy's requirements, political influence was paramount. Whittlesey's recommendation was successful, and young Seth's appointment finally arrived on October 24, 1841.

Having bade farewell to his apprehensive mother and proud father, Phelps set off for New York. "Remember," said Uncle Edwin, "the big traders and the fighting ships alike—they're all helpless hulks without smart men to sail 'em."

Arriving in New York in January 1842, Phelps was greeted by a sight never seen on Lake Erie. Scores of tall ships, clipper ships and warships, with towering masts and furled sails dominated the horizon. His new ship was the square-rigged *Independence* (known as a 74). On first sight, the massive ship was indeed impressive. Launched in 1814, she was the first in a class of 74-gun ships of the line. She was 190 feet long, had a 50-foot beam, and displaced some 2,200 tons. Three towering masts and a maze of rigging overlooked a long row of cannon on each side of the spotless upper deck. The *Independence* was now a sixty-gun frigate, having been modified in the 1830s in an effort to increase her speed and efficiency.

Phelps's new home was the midshipmen's "steerage." Cramped, often damp, and offering no privacy at all, these quarters often resembled a raucous college dormitory. Phelps discovered immediately that a midshipman "has no thoughts of his own. No right to think, eat, drink or sleep but by the leave of his superior officer."[2] Under the watchful eye of a ship's lieutenant, the new midshipmen began their apprenticeships by learning the art and science of sailing a man-of-war. They must be able to name and place twenty-six different sails without seeing them spread. The different yards, braces, halyards, and a thousand other details must be mastered.

There were also classes in history, geography, mathematics, and English. A professor of mathematics handled the math, and the ship's chaplain taught the other classes. In this way the chaplain could keep a close watch on these young men and guide their spiritual development. Since the sailors' morals, thirsts, and language offered competing values, the midshipmen learned from both worlds.

One thing the seventeen-year-old Phelps found to his liking in New York was the ladies. He wrote to his friend (and his father's law partner) A. G. Riddle back in Chardon:

The Battery is every clear day crowded with the fashionable beauties of New York. God bless their little souls and bodies. As for the boys they are just as gallant, polite, condescending, bashful etc. etc. as ever. Well poor souls they are but fools in the mysteries of loving and being loved.

Burn it as soon as you read. About 2 months ago I went ashore with the carpenter after deserters. Well about ten o'clock at night the thought struck me that I had a spare half eagle in my jacket. Now think says I, carpenter do you know where there are some pretty girls? Aye Aye says he. Away we went to one of the most popular houses in New York. As good luck would have it I there found a girl that was very handsome and withall young in her business. I coasced her up away we went to bed. Well I shan't say what we did but suffice it to say I go ashore about once a week sometimes for all night, sometimes only for the day. Well I never fail to go and see my dear & for that part I am sure to get good lodgings & it cost me but damned little. I paid her some 15 or 20 dollars on the start, and now I pay her nothing and am just as welcome. I don't know what is better than a handsome girl for a bedfellow.[3]

The new midshipmen were anxious to go to sea, but months passed as the ship remained in port. "The Home Squadron is truly a home squadron in every sense of the word,"[4] Phelps wrote. At last, at 8 A.M. on May 14, 1842, the *Independence,* her royals set in a light wind, cast off, and headed for Boston.

The first day at sea was exhilarating. The billowing, snowy canvas caught a moderate breeze that powered the *Independence* through rolling swells. The clear horizon, with blue seas and their contrasting whitecaps, was, unknown to the acting midshipmen, all that was keeping them from their first soul-searching regrets. Queasy stomachs were relieved by keeping an eye on the horizon, but sunset ended all hope of well-being. First the ship seemed to stand on her stern, then on her stem, with a drunken roll thrown in for good measure. Phelps decided there was only one way to survive: he "stumps the deck to keep going, to keep my head up" for thirty-six hours and, unlike his shipmates, avoided the "mistake of getting too near food."

The port visit to Boston marked the end of the probationary period for the acting midshipmen. The captain would now decide on their fitness to continue. On the day of the longed-for nod from the captain, there was also the news that the sister ship, USS *Columbus,* needed midshipmen for her Mediterranean cruise. To qualify for the examination and warrant to the rank of passed midshipman, Phelps needed six months of sea duty—so far he had three days.

The Mediterranean Squadron was considered the choicest foreign duty. Compared with the squadrons that patrolled off Brazil, the West Indies, the East Indies, and in the Pacific, the Mediterranean offered the best place to make career-enhancing connections as well as to visit exciting ports of call. To get a transfer, Phelps utilized the first lesson that all new midshipmen learned—the necessity of having friends in Washington.

Phelps wrote to Elisha Whittlesey and asked for his help in getting a transfer. He noted that the *Independence's* first lieutenant and other officers advised him that all the midshipmen, with one exception, who obtained transfers did so through political influence.

Orders finally arrived, and Phelps, along with about thirty fellow "reefers," ranging in age from fourteen to eighteen, joined the USS

Columbus. Authorized during the War of 1812, the *Columbus* was originally considered the best of the early 74s. She was 193'3" between perpendiculars, and had a 52' molded beam and 21'10" depth of hold.
She mounted long 32-pounders on her main and lower gun decks,
and 32-pounder carronades on her spar deck. She also carried four
eight-inch Paixhans shell guns on the main deck amidships and four
on the lower deck.

Used as a receiving ship in Boston for a number of years, the *Columbus* was in a rundown condition when Phelps reported aboard. All
of the ropes were in poor condition. The breechings on the upper
deck guns were rotten, and several had parted in the neck of the
cinch during daily drills. Most of the rigging, to which men entrusted
with their lives when aloft, was old and unsafe. Before departing
Boston, Phelps and the other crewmen replaced the rigging with new
rope from the ship's stores. An entire set of sails was reported to be
twenty years old. The furniture in the captain's cabin showed the results of years of abuse by the children of the families who had lived
aboard. The galley, a hand-me-down from the USS *Ohio,* was in filthy
condition.

The *Columbus* was regarded as an unlucky ship with poor sailing
qualities. With her false keel, she was said to be difficult to tack, veer,
or hold on course. It was also rumored that she was haunted by the
ghosts of a woman and child who had been murdered on board
years before. Men often declared that they could hear the cries of a
baby emanating from the orlop deck, a dark, gloomy space below the
waterline. An eerie place at night, it was difficult to get a marine to
walk that lonesome post, especially because a "ghost" was frequently
reported descending the ladder of the fore hatch. So bad was the
ship's reputation, in fact, that the captain ordered a boat to be rowed
around her at night to prevent desertions.

On August 24, 1842, the *Columbus* finally set sail with her new
complement of midshipmen. A great spread of square sails—four
tiers high on each mast, rounded off with beautiful jibs and a tailing
spanker—filled with wind that pushed the *Columbus* eastward.

Even though the young men were full-fledged midshipmen in the
Navy of the United States, their schooling continued. An area on the

USS *Columbus*—Rumored to be a poor sailer as well as haunted, this ship of the line proved otherwise during her deployment to the Mediterranean and Brazil squadrons in 1842–44. (U.S. Naval Historical Center)

starboard side of the gun deck forward of the captain's cabin was enclosed with canvas curtains and served as the schoolroom. Now that they were at sea, however, shipboard routine took precedence over classes. During the middle of a lecture, for example, there might be a blast of a whistle and the cry "On deck the starboard watch, reef topsails." The class instantly dissolved, leaving the school-master facing an empty cubicle.[5]

Passed midshipmen were supposed to act as big brothers to their younger counterparts, helping them in the transition from landsmen to sailors. Most were helpful but one, never identified but nick-named Lord Nelson by Phelps's good friend Hal Brown, seemed to take perverse satisfaction in badgering and discouraging them.

Phelps wrote to his father:

> You get the feeling that this fellow is out to make us think we
> landed in hell (excuse me) when we landed in the Navy! It
> seems born to him to make it tough for you, to discourage you,
> so you get to doubt yourself around him. As a passed middie
> he's suppose [*sic*] to help you along. He's no help . . . but I
> think I've got him figured out. He's been nagging and picking
> on [illegible] and [Oscar] Badger lately more than any of the
> others. Stupid as he is, he can see they're showing up as two of
> the best men in the class. So it's plain as your nose he's got it in
> for them, is trying hardest to break them, and because he's
> afraid of them! He lords it over us with his sneers and belit-
> tling. The poor chump knows himself he's not worth his beans!
> As a "big brother" he's a joke—when you can take him that way.

Phelps maintained a low profile until one day during one of
Lt. Augustus Kilty's knot-tying classes. More than fifty different knots,
splices, and hitches had to be mastered, and on this day Kilty decided on a sporting match, to be timed to the second. Several of the
passed midshipmen joined in the competition, and on one of the
particularly tricky knots Phelps was clearly the winner. This earned
him a hearty, friendly slap on the back from Kilty, a twenty-one-year
veteran from Maryland. "Ever since," Phelps wrote, "Lord Nelson has
been gunning for me. If you can believe it, that's what started it. That
back-slap really put me at the head of the class! How did such a pin-
head ever get to wear the uniform?"

The acting midshipmen were not the only youngsters aboard the
Columbus. She also carried a complement of fifty-nine apprentice
boys, ranging in age from thirteen to eighteen. In an effort to alleviate the chronic shortage of seamen, Congress in 1837 established an
apprentice system from which it was hoped that warrant and petty officers might be drawn.[6] Thirty of the boys were from Buffalo and had
never before seen saltwater. Recruited with the promise that they
would become officers after their probationary period, they were bitterly disappointed when they found they had been misled. Their

morale slowly improved, however, with the prospects of going to sea and eventually becoming petty officers. Strong, hardy, active, and intelligent, the boys were assigned duties commensurate with their size and strength. The smaller boys were rotated weekly from messenger duty to the mizzen tops, where they gained experience working aloft with the smaller sails. As they grew and became stronger, they were shifted to the lower mainsail tops and the forecastle to handle the heavier sails. Like Phelps and the other acting midshipmen, the boys attended school for five hours a day, whether in port or at sea, and several proved more learned than the passed midshipman who was their teacher. As with the acting midshipmen, the ship's chaplain devoted much of his energy to keeping the boys from learning too much from the crew.

After a smooth passage the *Columbus* made her first call at Gibraltar. After a short visit she put to sea and shortly afterward spotted a Spanish Guarda Costa vessel chasing a large smuggler's boat rowed by twenty hearty-looking men wearing bright red caps. The smugglers ran under the *Columbus*'s lee, and the Guarda Costa stood off and sailed in company. The smugglers put their backs to their oars to match the *Columbus*'s four knots until nightfall, when they slipped away.

Heading for Port Mahon, the *Columbus* fell in with the frigate *Congress*. The two ships made several sailing trials together. The first afternoon they were struck by a heavy squall, and the *Columbus* performed beautifully. "This ship has very agreeably disappointed her officers," wrote Capt. Charles Morgan, commander of the Mediterranean Squadron, "she sails fast and works and steers handsomely. . . . The *Columbus* was thought a match for the *Congress,* if not her superior, especially in light winds, and it is believed that when the *Columbus* is in trim, she will be the faster sailing ship of the two."[7]

Arriving at Port Mahon, the *Columbus* joined the rest of the Mediterranean Squadron: the *Congress* and the sloops *Fairfield* and *Preble*. Port Mahon, on the island of Minorca, was one of the best harbors in the Mediterranean. It had been the wintering station of the squadron and was known for its great abundance of cheap clothing and friendly women. Phelps quickly availed himself of both commodities. Unlike the letter to A. G. Riddle, which his parents never learned of, a letter to his mother's brother-in-law, Capt. Edward Paine, describing his adventures in Port Mahon, was shown to his father, who was deeply distressed. His father wrote to Phelps:

Your letter from Gibraltar gave us such pleasure and satisfaction; it discovered observation and reflection beyond that to be expected from your years. It left us with such sanguine hopes of your rapid advancement to usefulness, honor and distinction in your profession. . . . Now comes this letter today to your Uncle Paine from Mahon. Must we, from this letter, now think of all our fondest hopes for you as false, built on shifting sand? Now, my son, I have been young, and I know something of the lure of the different shade or blood to be that sort of specially tempting, testing woman for the young man. She may be around the corner, for I've never traveled far. But she is sister of every woman—deserves the same respect as the woman nearest you, whether or not she knows it and asks it. In giving that respect, the man respects himself. That is the sternest discipline life requires of you.

Chiefly I am alarmed, and deeply so, by this admission in your letter to your Uncle Paine of "the impossibility of saying No!" I hope you use exaggerative language. But let me say to you, my son, that whether such fleshy things as women and wine, such foolish things as gambling, or in matters of larger principle—if there is not in your character to say No and to mean it, it will surely hound you to failure and ruin. You will be prey of every evil in the shape of woman or man, victim of every scamp, flatterer, coxcomb, that crosses your path. And I must say to you that most of all I fear this yielding disposition, this pliancy of your character. Combined with your too keen relish of pleasure and social amusement, it will be a pitfall unless you resolve now to stiffen will and purpose against it. That I know you can and will do; the fiber for it somewhere is in you, as it was in your forefathers.

There was a large garrison of Spanish troops in Port Mahon at the time, and inevitably clashes occurred. On Friday evening, October 28,

1842, Passed Midshipman John Smith Patterson was descending the hill to the boat landing, on his way to the *Congress*, when he was attacked. Stabbed three times in the heart, Patterson cried out, "The villain has murdered me!"[8]

The murderer, thought to be one of the Spanish soldiers, was never caught. Captain Morgan decided that because of the murder, "much is to be apprehended. I shall leave this port with the first wind and go to Spezia."[9] After the burial, the squadron headed east, but instead of Spezia, Morgan decided to winter at Genoa, where he moored his squadron.

At the birthplace of Christopher Columbus, the *Columbus* drew particular attention from the local population and was visited frequently. Phelps and his fellow midshipmen were kept under taut discipline while aboard ship, spending their mornings under the chaplain and professor of mathematics, and the rest of the time on watch. Phelps was luckier than most of his younger messmates, for his excellence at his lessons and duties rated extra shore leave. After the Port Mahon letter fiasco, he tried to reassure his father, noting that he had been invited to a ball at the Governor's Palace:

> It was by far the best thing of the kind I have seen. Of course none but the first class people are invited. Perhaps I can give you some image of myself as I enter the Gates of the Court to attend the affair. The dress of our Naval Officers is plain when seen in company with the Genoese Officers. But I am in well-brushed boots, plain navy blue pants that fit my boots so snugly they nearly hide them from the middle of the strap; a vest of buff jersey weave (not seen) under my blue dress coat ornamented only with a tasteful arrangement of some three dozen buttons and a pair of Gold Anchors. The coat, fitting a thick set, powerful frame is buttoned close to the neck. Above the coat collar shows the upper half of a satin stock (with a clean collar above that). My hair is brushed back (fashion) with the ends turning up from coming in contact with the collar. A cocked hat and sword concludes the image.
>
> So there is your midshipman son as he enters the gates, touching his hat to return the salute of the two sentries, which

he does several times while passing through the many halls before reaching the grand receiving room. In groups beyond the receiving Governor and his lady, the many gay, laughing ladies and gentlemen seem to sparkle as much in their lively manner as in their fine evening dress. You don't have to understand what they're saying when you see their faces under the light of great branched candlesticks from the ceiling and every side of the room. It makes you feel a little scared and out of place at first. But the Governor, and his lady too, have a way of helping a fellow get over that pretty quick. He shakes your hand and looks at you—well, like you might be his middle son right off one of the Italian ships in here! So you're soon feeling pretty sure of yourself, not so countrified! And you need to by the time you're introduced to My Lord and Lady so-and-so. There are a number of English guests present, but even a Yankee "reefer" is considered lordly enough to entertain the Lord and Lady.

Even those who speak no more English than I do Italian are determined to give you as good a time as they are having. With these people, father, you really can't help having one! Besides fine music and the dance, there are other amusements to make sure of that. Every one enters in with such spirit—and not with too much wine either! That's just the way people are over here, including the girls. I must say I wish the girls in our country could impart a little more liveliness to our small affairs there, could act as if they enjoyed life, raise the flush of lively amusement as they do here! Please don't misunderstand, father—and don't let the sisters—if I say our girls are too cold and inanimate. I mean only in comparison with the gay spirit of the girls over here, proper girls, who just share that with their elders.

Best of all at giving you a good time, making a fellow feel so much at home, is the Governor himself. His English is good enough with the spirit he puts in it! Since that big soiree he has provided other amusements for us, and we middies have become his particular chickens, as they would term it aboard ship. He shows us more attention than any other rank of officers on the *Columbus,* which makes the others, the lieutenants particularly, very annoyed and gives us a fine chance to plague them!

Phelps found hard work along with hard play could pay off, for before the winter was over, he was given a new assignment.

I am now master-mate of the Main Gun Deck, in which duty I have performed to the entire satisfaction of the officers, and particularly to my own. I like the charge of the deck very much, except that I think there is too much responsibility for so young an officer as myself. The duty is much harder than watch-duty. It properly belongs to a passed midshipman. The First Lieutenant seemed at some pains to explain my getting it in a way that wouldn't swell my head too much!

I haven't let it do that, and I don't want to sound like it in what I'm going to write now. It's about the feeling of some of the midshipmen in this company on the *Columbus* toward the fellows who have made a better record, shown more responsibility, on this cruise and so gained a better standing with the officers. Those in bad standing have only their own laziness or undisciplined behavior to thank for it. But because they are forever in difficulty with their superiors, their one idea seems to be to make trouble for the fellows whose better record makes them favored in assignments, in more shore leave, and in other ways.

Frankly, I am constantly liable to the scheming of several of these sour, cantankerous fellows, but their efforts to get me into trouble so far have failed. One of them now is trying to provoke me into a duel. They are quite common among the younger officers, but I from principle abhor the custom. I'm not putting my life on an equality with any man's, letting him endanger my life because he chooses to insult me. If I can knock him down, I will—at least, if he goes too far I'll find out! But it would be no satisfaction to me to call a man out to be a target for his gun as well as his insults. (And I'm no slow wing shot!) All well know that having anything to do with dueling, either as principal or second, if found out, is cause for dismissal from the service. I have heard the older officers disapprove of it strongly—after

an affair a short while ago between two midshipmen, by which
one has a stiff leg for life.

This particular duel differed somewhat from the standard affair
in that the principals and seconds all went out in the same carriage.
Not able to find their way out of Genoa, the seconds posted their
men in the street and fought the duel before a bewildered Genoese
audience. The duel resulted in a midshipman with a bullet in his
knee, after which they all returned to the boat landing in the same
carriage.

Phelps continued to reassure his father:

No, the threatening duelist is not his Lordship—who by-the-by
is a little less lordly and pestiferous these days, although a little
drunker most of the time! Now that I've come to the high rank
of midshipman, and seem pretty sure of hanging on, he seems
to have lost some heart for a way to hang me. It may revive at
any time—he's hard to predict. But the failure of his mulish
ways to balk as back there on the *Independence* may be what's
driving him a little harder to the bottle. Only a sacred cow, for
sure, could lay on it like he does now and still stay in uniform.
But you get used to something scandalous when you're around
it every day. You get used to a little piece of it like this fellow—
and you'd miss one of Hal Brown's best butts and something
to mimic!

Speaking of Hal, I hope we can ship together right through
our midshipman days. He's any proof you need that a fellow
with a good head can rate as well with the officers as he does
with his fellow middies when it comes to having a good time!
It's the same with the other good fellows aboard. They know
how to enjoy themselves all right! But they do their jobs with it.
They've got the stuff to make fine officers, and better fellows
you wouldn't ask to serve with. Almost every time, its the fellow
a little short on brains that makes as much of a mess of handling himself ashore as he does on ship. Wise Hal passed on
this kind the other day when, speaking of the fellow who wants
to take a shot at me, of his antics ashore and afloat, asked me

"How d'you expect a monkey to read a compass for the right steer on sea or land?" Hal's adjectives added a little color!

Phelps's closest friend was Hezekiah G. D. [Hal] Brown, from Mississippi. The soft-spoken Southern gentleman was the class wit, often coming up with just the right remark at the right time. Phelps noted:

There's more to him than just that soft, drawlin' humor of his. He has a way of knowing things about people, the inside of them. He'd make a good leader, if he wanted to be one, because he understands the other fellow. But you don't get much feeling that he wants to be one, that he wants that much responsibility. Except maybe for that, with his good head he'd be a fine credit to the Navy. But you wonder sometimes if he'll stick. You get more of a feeling he just sort of dreamed his way into the Navy and hasn't put his heart in it much. The service doesn't seem to mean any more to him than maybe the change, the romance, of living on a ship! And so he might quit for any other dream or idea, or maybe just to go home.

His heart still seems right much (as he'd say) down on that Mississippi plantation he was raised on and likes better than anything else to talk about. To hear him you'd think he missed the blacks his place owns as much as he does his own folks. I can't quite make out his feelings about the blacks who work for his folks, whether they want to or not, for board and lodgings! And I've got a picture of the lodgings from hearing him talk. But it seems all natural to him. The blacks are human enough for him to like enough to miss having them around! He doesn't miss his horses that way! But Hal is so easy going and likable— maybe so likable to his own blacks they wouldn't want you to start an argument with him anymore than you feel like doing it yourself. He's easy mannered, polite even to the men—but you'd know better than take it for something too soft in him. I guess you'd call him a gentleman. And you wouldn't give too much credit for that to his coming out of the same Dixie as bred that ornery cross of mare and jackass Hal understands better than any of us! Naming no names.

In the spring of 1843, the *Columbus* sailed for Port Mahon, which, after the refined social life of Genoa, Phelps now found a "most miserable place, borne to the dust almost by Spanish tyranny. The inhabitants are poor and remarkably ignorant, improvements of every kind are a hundred years behind the age."[10]

At Port Mahon the ship took on large amounts of provisions and stores, for orders had arrived detailing the *Columbus* to the Brazil Squadron. A few days after the arrival of her relief, the USS *Delaware,* the entire squadron put to sea in company. "We parted from the squadron the same day," Phelps wrote, "but not until we had a fair trial in sailing. The *Columbus* nobly regained her lost reputation by beating them all, the *Delaware, Congress* and two sloops of war. She has until this cruise been considered a disgrace to our Navy from her poor sailing qualities."[11]

The *Columbus* made port calls at Toulon, Gibraltar, and Madeira before heading for the coast of South America. En route, Phelps was able for the first time to fire the guns in his division. The gunnery drills were always very slow and deliberate. For example, after the guns were aimed, the command would ring out, "Handle your match and lockstring"—"Cock your lock"—"Blow your match"— "Stand by"—"Fire." Finally allowed to see the ammunition for the first time—it was kept locked up—Phelps and the other young gunnery officers were at first unsure whether the fuse or the sabot went in first, or whether the fuse should be ignited before putting the shell in the gun. Once the practical problems were ironed out, the exciting noise and smoke from a roaring broadside was an exciting experience. Accuracy, for now, did not matter; it would come with practice. "We were great too, in 'boarding' and 'repelling boarders,'" wrote fellow midshipman William Parker. "To see the *Columbus'* officers and crew engaged in this business was a sight to behold."[12]

The *Columbus* arrived off Rio de Janeiro in July 1843. While at Rio, Capt. Charles Morgan left the *Columbus* and was replaced by Commodore Daniel Turner, who had commanded the schooner *Caledonia* at the Battle of Lake Erie during the War of 1812. William Parker found him an irascible old fellow who suffered from the gout but whose bark was worse than his bite.[13]

The *Columbus* sailed for Montevideo, the capital of the Republic of Montevideo (Uruguay) on October 5, 1843. After being twice driven off the coast by severe gales and once dangerously situated on a lee shore, the *Columbus* finally arrived on October 21. With the shallow water and her deep draft, the *Columbus* had to anchor five and a half miles from the shore.

War had once again erupted between Montevideo and Buenos Aires, so the *Columbus* was there to protect American interests and show the flag. Occasionally Phelps made a port call to the besieged city of Montevideo.

> Our principle [*sic*] amusement is to go to the outposts and watch the armies fight. For civilized armies, their mode of warfare, especially their treatment of prisoners, is cruel and ferocious. The only other saving grace of this tour are the thick steaks that are so cheaply had in this cattle country. Beef can be bought shipside for six dollars a head, before the fighting the price was a dollar.[14]

Other commodities were not so cheap. A bushel of potatoes cost the ship twelve dollars, and ostrich eggs also were outrageously priced.

While in Rio de Janeiro, Phelps observed slavery for the first time in his life.

> The inhabitants of such a country should be happy and noble people, but from my opportunities to observe they seem lazy and indifferent. Most of the business of Brazil is in the hands of foreigners, and all the work is performed by slaves. The slaves have the right, if able, to buy their freedom; many of them do so by extra labor, they may then rise to places of considerable trust in the community. As freemen they are no longer looked down upon.

In the summer of 1844, the *Columbus* cut loose from the Brazil Squadron and headed for home. The ship made good time, having fine weather for the entire trip. After catching the northeast trade winds, the *Columbus* averaged ten miles an hour for seven consecutive days. After arriving in New York, she anchored inside the harbor opening at Sandy Hook; there the crew was paid off and discharged, and the officers were granted leave.

Nearly three years after leaving home, Phelps returned to Chardon, where his proud mother and father gazed upon a man. His younger brothers, Alfred and Edwin, enviously eyed the uniform with its gold buttons and braid. After three months at home, Phelps was ordered to report to Portsmouth, Virginia, and a brand new ship. Once there, he wrote to his family:

> While I write this in my comfortable boarding house at Portsmouth, our beautiful new ship, the Sloop-of-War *Jamestown*, lies alongside the Navy yard, still under the hands of carpenters. A more perfect ship I never saw. She is something decidedly new in design, with a clear, flush, light spar deck, all the battery being on the main deck. She is one of six new sloops being built from a model chosen in a competition among the country's best shipbuilders. The Navy wanted the best design for the future—a fast, smart sailor, with plenty of gunpower. I think they've got it. I've been on board, and for living, too, she looks like a dream! You can see, as the Navy says, that no expense or pains have been spared.

The USS *Jamestown* was 157'6" between perpendiculars and had a 35' molded beam and a 16'2" depth of hold. She mounted twenty-two guns, and was heavier and more ornate than her sister ships *Portsmouth* and *Plymouth*. After careful trimming with ballast, her sailing characteristics were considered excellent.

When the United States outlawed the importing of slaves in 1808, the U.S. Navy joined with the British navy in patrolling the West African coast to enforce the prohibition. Southern political pressure soon ended American patrols, however. Slavers quickly realized that with the U.S. navy gone, they could operate with impunity by flying the American flag. The U.S. government would, under no circumstances, allow the British to board American vessels. British pleas that the United States either allow the boarding of its vessels or send a squadron to do the job resulted in the Webster–Ashburton Treaty in

1842. The treaty called for each nation to maintain a squadron of eighty guns on the West African coast.

With the *Jamestown* completed, her mission to patrol the West African coast waited on the presidential election in the fall of 1844. A treaty to annex the Republic of Texas had been signed the previous April, but the Senate had refused to ratify it. The question of annexation was now a key campaign issue because Mexico had threatened war should Texas become part of the United States. The narrow election of James Polk, who supported annexation, kept the situation tense, so the *Jamestown*'s crew remained on alert. Phelps wrote to his family:

> Everywhere we hear praise of the beautiful style in which our ship stood down the harbor. She is the admiration of all who can judge such craft. Last week we had the Secretary of the Navy [John Mason] aboard and he was much pleased with our ship. I was honored with an introduction. We are one of eleven vessels of war, some of the finest, now lying in harbor here, and they make a very imposing appearance. But in design and beauty ours stands out among them.
>
> I wouldn't boast it outside of the family, father, but its pretty generally accepted that the best reputed officers in the service have been ordered to the *Jamestown* and her new sisterships. Good crews also have been chosen for ships that rate them. While the ladies of Norfolk may not be too expert in judging ships, it is customary to respect their opinion of men—of men in naval uniform in particular! For his lines, his grace, his all-around cut for speed, they do have an eye! And some of the most charming of these do say that never have they seen such a dashing set of officers as the *Jamestown* musters! To belong to her—and maybe her name helps—is an honor among them and a passport to their favor, of which the fellow with any sense, you'll agree, should make the proper most as I do. What a lot of fair favor; he must store up against those months ahead of such dark complections—and so much of the darkness showing!

While awaiting sailing orders, Phelps found that the social life in Norfolk was expensive. There were "positive orders for every officer to be prepared in every particular with full dress."

Consequently, my tailor's bill is very heavy, besides new cocked hat and sword . . . the king of all the black tribes of Liberia, Hal says, should be properly impressed! At least, there'll be nothing money can buy on that barbarous coast, so it won't hurt too much to leave half my future pay behind on assignment to my tailor! I simply can't pay him now, for besides I've had to pay a confounded board bill of many days, at least nine shillings a day, and now for the ship a fitting out mess bill of fifty dollars in addition to the monthly mess bill. But we do have a delightful mess!

As the flagship of the African Squadron, the *Jamestown* carried the broad pennant of Commodore Charles W. Skinner, a devout Presbyterian:

We're hoping for the best! The Captain [R. B. Cunningham] at any rate, appears to be a liberal and understanding fellow. He promises us every privilege and comfort. Our First Lieutenant is almost idolized by the middies, and the other lieutenants are bearing out their reputation of being good and pleasant officers. No one likes the prospects of that wretched African station, but I might as well take my turn there now as at some future time. And this is certainly the ship to help you through it.

The *Jamestown* finally headed for Africa on January 25, 1845. Sailing in company with the *Portsmouth*, the *Jamestown* ran with a strong northwest wind into heavy, irregular seas. By January 28, the weather was creating serious problems with the new rigging. It was stretching at an alarming rate, and the crew was constantly adjusting the dead-eyes and braces. Eventually the lower rigging had stretched as much as five feet.

After getting the rigging problems under control, the two ships carried out sailing trials. On February 5, they put on as much sail as

USS *Jamestown*—Flagship of the African Squadron in 1845; Phelps was disappointed that she was not used more aggressively in pursuing slavers. (U.S. Naval Historical Center)

they could carry. With a good breeze, both averaged a respectable eleven knots over the course of the day. That night the *Jamestown* shortened sail in a moderate wind so the *Portsmouth* could close, but the *Portsmouth*'s captain held back, claiming the *Jamestown*'s light was bad. Commodore Skinner had an additional lamp placed in the mizzen top and signaled the *Portsmouth* to steer southeast by east. The next morning the *Portsmouth* was nowhere to be seen.

Not withstanding her earlier shakedown difficulties, the *Jamestown* had run 2,037 miles in eleven days. Her length and long deck made her handle well into the swells. Off the wind she proved fast and weatherly. Phelps found her a dry, comfortable ship that steered and sailed remarkably well under all the conditions they had met so far.

After arriving off the west coast of Africa, the duty quickly settled down to one of routine and boredom. The oppressive heat made even the closest crew testy. Dueling among officers was still frequent enough in the short-handed squadron to prompt Skinner to warn of serious consequences for both principals and seconds.

Discipline for the crew was still handled the old-fashioned way, as illustrated on February 27, 1845, when all hands were called to witness Seaman J. Butler receive twelve lashes for drunkenness. Even the boys were subject to the lash or "colting," but the introduction of a "blacklist" or additional duties made the need rare. Discipline for the midshipmen usually involved restriction to the ship while in port. If sterner measures were called for, "mastheading" might be prescribed. The midshipman would be ordered to the top of the foremast for whatever length of time the captain deemed appropriate. In good weather the punishment was easy enough to endure, but in cold, rainy weather, it was a cruel ordeal. It was rare for midshipmen to be flogged, for they were considered officers. Should the captain decide it was called for, the young man would be punished away from the crew.

Provisions for the *Jamestown* were bland at best. The hope on all such cruises was to supplement the normal fare with whatever meats, fruits, and vegetables could be obtained at the squadron depot at Porta Praya in the Cape Verde Islands. Fortunately, oranges were abundant and the natives raised turkeys in great numbers. Small pens for turkeys, chickens, sheep, and pigs, along with the fresh fruits and vegetables, were kept near the brig, where the marine sentry could keep a watchful eye on the valuable cargo, lest it disappear.

Below is a typical day's consumption as entered in the log.[15]

	Expended	*On Hand*
Water	250 gal.	25,700 gal.
Bread	154 lbs.	32,465 lbs.
Pickles	44 lbs.	1,830 lbs.
Vinegar	11 gal.	312 gal.
Whiskey	5 gal.	732 gal.
Beans	11 gal.	60 bu.
Pork	1 bbl.	120 bbl.
Beef	1 bbl.	159 bbl.
Flour	88 lbs.	18 bbl.

These large quantities of baked bread had to be passed through the ship's oven to dry it and kill the insects. Throwing out large quantities of unfit food was not uncommon. On July 29, 1845, 5,040 pounds of rotten bread were taken into Porta Praya and auctioned to the highest bidder.

The salted beef was prepared on shore before the cruise, cut into ten-pound slabs, heavily salted, and stored in white oak casks. The beef shrank over time and became hard as rock. Before cooking, it had to be soaked for twenty-four hours to remove the salt crystals.

The crew was divided into groups of eight to ten men, with one of them selected each week as "mess cook." He spread a black canvas cloth on the deck, laid out the tableware, and fetched the food from the galley. Afterward he washed the dishes, folded up the cloth, and cleaned the area where they ate.[16]

The *Jamestown* spent a good deal of time off the coast of Liberia. For some twenty years the Methodist Church had been conducting a noble experiment with the National Colonization Society of America. The resettlement of American slaves in Africa was having, as Phelps would find out, mixed results.

Phelps described his first trip ashore, in early March 1845, to his parents in a long letter:

> As we got near the breakers they seemed high enough to smash the cutter under us. We slowed down to decide whether to risk it, and about this time at least a hundred naked blacks, who had been watching our approach, swarmed out of the bush onto the beach and some into the water. They motioned us to come on. We decided it was a friendly gesture of help or rescue! From their nakedness they plainly weren't colonists, but they were so near the colony's influence they probably didn't mean to make soup of us! So we kept on in. As we neared the surf some of the blacks launched their canoes smartly through the breakers. They came alongside to offer drier rides ashore, which several of the fellows took. That lighted the cutter for the run through the surf. As we hit it some husky blacks were waiting in the water to grab hold of the boat and shoot us in at just the right

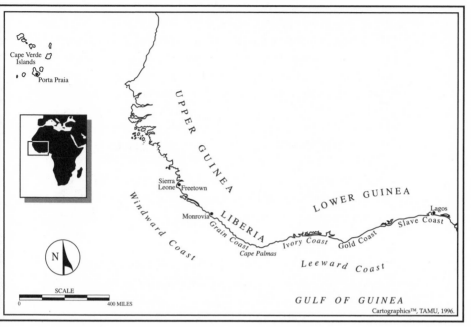

West Coast of Africa, 1845–1846

moment to save us from being stove in! We landed pretty wet
but the cutter was in one piece.

These natives had friendly intentions, but they had intentions, too, on our twopence and fourpence, we soon learned,
for the services they scrambled to perform. (We didn't notice
that much enterprise later on among the colonists!) First our
horde of naked welcomers, showing us the way to Monrovia,
led us through their Kroo village not far from where we landed.
Scattered about were many of their huts, about six feet square,
high enough to stand in, walls of woven split reeds, palm-
thatched roofs. Even those idlers whose curiosity about us
couldn't tempt them to rise from a full stretch on the ground,
or from their peculiar squat, insisted each on an exchange of
salutations. Theirs was always the same sound to my ears. The

scene brought to mind all I'd read of Africa and her sons, little thinking I'd ever be among them.

Leaving the village by the path they showed us, we wondered why so many of the black scamps were following us. We soon saw why when we came to a deep creek and they began to scramble for a chance to earn fourpence to carrying us across. Our white pants suffered in this piggyback ride on their sweating hides but it was better than wading though waist-deep. They showed us along a path through a tropical tangle till we finally came out on a clearing that looked down on Monrovia.

Here was the capital of our noble dream! No American has escaped the noise of abolitionists, philanthropists, and the church have made about it all in their money raising and spending.

In the last twenty years, Monrovia had grown into a small town with a sprinkling of a few stone and frame houses along with native huts of thatch and palm. A stone church of some size stood out among them. There were about seven hundred colonists in the town with several thousand more settled as far as twenty miles from the coast. Phelps noted that Monrovia's streets were those paths where the brush was cut a little shorter.

Phelps's party asked a colonist for directions to the home of a Major Hicks, the man they wanted to meet. They had been told by the commodore that this ex-slave was a more respected power in the community than the black governor. They located the major's modest but comfortable frame house and were greeted by him with a casual ease. Phelps observed that there was not a taint of white in the skin "of this confident fellow, who has pulled himself up by less than his bootstraps—he was born without any!"

The major's wife was gracious and affable, and did most of the talking at this first meeting. Major Hicks impressed Phelps more with his fierce eye and ready scowl than his scant conversation. After a short visit, the midshipmen took their leave to make another call. Mrs. Hicks informed them that if they would return in an hour or so, she would be glad to serve dinner.

The major served as an escort to the home of Reverend Wilson, head of the Church of the Colony of Liberia. Reverend Wilson and his wife had been slaves for a family in Norfolk who had requested the ship's officers call on them. While there, Phelps met the editor of the colony's paper and found him to be an intelligent fellow and clever "propagandist." Phelps had read his paper; its glowing reports were in stark contrast to what he had found.

After Phelps and the other men left the parsonage, they were too hungry, and the sun was too broiling, for them to be in any mood to see more of Monrovia. They followed along, however, as the major led them on a few detours back to his house. Phelps was not impressed with the hodgepodge of little houses, many constructed of native thatch and palm. He also noted that the morale of the colonists appeared poor, judging by their sullen faces and slouching figures. This made polite conversation with the major difficult, but the major did not beg any man's praise. He appeared satisfied that the colony would get along, would justify itself.

Back at the major's house, Phelps found that Mrs. Hicks, with some help who came out of American plantation kitchens, had made the most of their absence. There was a savory promise in the smells emanating from a table set with pretty china and silver. The major and his wife graced each end of the table and managed the honors with aplomb. Mrs. Hicks, not quite a pure black, informed her guests that she was born free in the States, and her conversational grace spoke of some education. As the dinner of fowl, fish, yams, and much else progressed, talk touched lightly at first on affairs of the colony. After some good claret had warmed the acquaintance a little more, Mrs. Hicks turned the talk to some serious fundamentals in the colony. For this she was obviously warmed by more than the wine— by pride in her husband, in his rise from slavery to what she thoroughly convinced Phelps was the most important job in the colony. She attempted to show her guests that he was the man for that job, giving him full credit, even if she had to be pretty hard on many of the colonists in doing it. Soon Mrs. Hicks, somewhat to the major's discomfort, touched on the topic of why the colony was having trouble prospering.

You see, my dear sirs, so many of our people come here filled not only with the idea of being free, of being citizens, but expecting right away more than just tillers of the soil—to be doctors, lawyers, merchants, etc. That of course cannot be. So they become discontented, and instead of diligently working their ground, making nice homes for themselves, they become needy and that makes more discontent. That is our problem with many, the problem Major Hicks understands so well in their nature and handles with such good results, as patiently as he can. We must all be patient in teaching our people that ambition is a good thing but that God requires work of all—the work each one of us is able to do. We must be patient in teaching them many things to make them good citizens of a free land that one day will need no help.

Phelps noted that the major was not a man given to ready conversation, and that Mrs. Hicks was not to be stopped once she had launched on his praise. After Mrs. Hicks finished, Phelps and his fellow sailors turned to the major, who said:

It seems human to expect too much, to think we deserve plenty without sweating for it. We must remember the example of it my people have seen. Some have brought the dream of it here with them. They must be taught, instead, that living by the sweat of the brow is the biblical law. But that the difference, the privilege, the dignity for them here is that they sweat on their own soil. Some are slow to appreciate that after their first disappointment. But with understanding, sometimes a little discipline, all will be taught.

This speech convinced Phelps that the major had been taught a good deal by his privileged wife and promoter. "This ex-slave would be no man to cross swords with on the issues of slavery," Phelps noted.

After the dinner party finished, Phelps and Hal Brown took their leave of Major Hicks and his wife. On their way back to the ship, they agreed on their impressions of the major and the colony. Phelps observed:

If such idealistic words as we've heard do not persuade any fellow black of the privilege and dignity of sweating on his own soil, there seems enough iron in him to use other means. The eye, the jaw, the brow he can bend on you, linger in memory. If they aren't enough to drive home the ideal, they more than hint the man could use the lash to teach the old biblical law! Well, the Major may be a hopeful sign for survival of the community, but the darky, as Hal says, has just traded a white master for a black one, and you don't see any gain for him in the Major![17]

After the *Jamestown* finished her visit to Monrovia in early April, she worked her way down the coast to Cape Palmas, where Phelps, Hal Brown, and the ship's first lieutenant visited one of the colony's isolated farms. To reach it, they had to pass through tribal lands and villages containing some three thousand warriors who held varying sentiments toward whites. The risk was somewhat lessened by the natives' respect for the uniform; they had been taught some bitter lessons, the last of which was Commodore Oliver Hazard Perry's burning of the native settlement of Berbery after a fierce fight.

In these villages Phelps noted many more women than men around each cluster of huts. Each warrior could have as many wives as he could afford, needing only to pay the father the going rate for his choice. The number of wives was a sign of wealth. There was, however, constant warring among the tribes; the men were killed at such a rate that the women had to organize groups to share what men were left.

Many of the coastal tribes actively supported the slave trade. In return for being exempt from the slavers' nets, the coastal tribes captured their inland enemies, thus eliminating foes and profiting at the same time.

Nearing one colonial farm, the party met a smiling old woman on the trail. Phelps wrote to his father:

Her smile spread as wide as her shiny face when a second lieutenant with us told her his native town was Savannah. He hadn't known her but he knew her white family there, and he was sure he did know some younger ones from their town who were somewhere in the colony.

There was no mistaking in their broad, quick smiles the friendly memories the sight of a familiar white face brought back to them. Their experience in their country, you think, might have increased what must have been a pretty friendly feeling for their white folks in the States when they left them. How had they been persuaded against that feeling to come here? Is it something just in the word freedom for any human, whatever his stage? Even in these people, a sort of yeast the Colonization Society can start working with its cheerful promise and reports—let them think what they like till they get here! Whatever brings them back to their land of freedom, they have got to like once they're here. There's no turning back for them. But many, like the old woman with her warm feeling for "white folks," her complaint of the "animules," leave you in little doubt they'd jump at the chance to return to their white families in the States if they had it. You don't ask them that because Navy people are in a sort of diplomatic position, strictly non-political, around the colony. And the colonists know it wouldn't help them with their black masters if they were known to be so disloyal to the colony. But these simple people aren't very good at hiding their feelings. And none we met around here seems to harbor any memory of the cruel tyrant the abolitionist press pictures for you to damn all decent owners! If any had been that unlucky, you wonder if they still wouldn't have been better off staying where they were than in this place!

The lieutenant's old Savannah friends certainly gave every sign they had decent and considerate white families to remember. The several men of these were among about two hundred able-bodied males we estimated in this area of the colony. But the women work right along with the men—maybe harder than some males who feel the tribal example so far from the Major!—as the families sweat a living out of little cultivated patches they call farms. With a little help such as seed and tools from Monrovia, these people are farther from its protection than most of the colonists. Their homes are huts inferior in size and construction, we noticed, to the tribal huts we had passed on the way. They couldn't have less over their heads in the States, though in the perpetual hot summer here they don't need much. Too bad the grown-ups had to bring pants and skirts back with them to this heat! They don't even enjoy, as far as we saw, the naked comfort of their savage brothers! Can these improvements of civilization hold out against the temptation to forget them on some extra hot day?

It was hard after that day ashore at Cape Palmas, father, not to think that any human taken out of this African hell of heat and savagery, even by the slave-trade, doesn't have a chance of something better ahead of him. And that he's just going to lose that chance by coming back here. At least in the States, as Hal says, the negro does have the white man's civilization around him, its better things to see, many to share, all to dream of for himself if he feels that way. Without that here, I agree, he'll soon just slide back to the native level. By their faces and manner, the blacks in the colony strike Hal as a much less happy lot than southern plantation darkies. Maybe just being closer to civilization than to their savage brothers here—with equal sweat in the sun—instinctively makes the difference. Hal may be a bit prejudiced about it all, but I've done my own looking and thinking here before I came to pretty close agreement with him. I've been cured of a lot of nonsense the reformers stuff your head with at home! . . . I hope these thoughts don't shock the family too much.

Traveling among the natives, Phelps discovered one reason that the colonists were so friendly toward the U.S. Navy: the stern lessons taught the natives made potent threats a useful tool in controlling the tribes, even though there was no flag commitment to protect the colony. They also used it, unfortunately, Phelps wrote, "to back themselves up in forcing labor from them, taking their cleared land and other abuses."

While trying to stop the warring between two tribes in the Cape Palmas region, King Freeman, a native autocrat, visited the *Jamestown* unexpectedly during Sunday services. Phelps wrote to his parents:

The King and Governor came on board . . . when the Commodore was substituting for the Chaplain in conducting services. The King's dress was extremely simple—a few rings and a string of beads decorated his person. The only honest thing you felt about the old rascal was his nakedness! I had seen an idol in his hut, and I was amused to see him, waiting near me, politely bow his head in prayer just as we did. It was a casual bow, with no contrition of a naked soul before the Almighty! What could be more dull for him, I thought, than our solemn and restrained ritual after all that goes on in the Voodoo rites and practice of his realm!

The *Jamestown* sailed farther down the coast to the warring region, where the commodore went ashore with King Freeman and the governor, not forgetting to bring along a respectable bodyguard of marines. Since it was an affair for the landing forces, rather than for midshipmen, Phelps remained aboard ship. The commodore asked the tribal chiefs to stop fighting and let him arbitrate whatever it was they were fighting about, but had little success. The meeting served the next best purpose, however. The commodore informed the chiefs that if either side in the fighting harmed a hair on a missionary's head, he would kill their warriors and burn their villages.

Phelps's jaundiced view of Liberia paled in comparison with his view of the British colony of Sierra Leone. A visit to the "training center" at Freetown later in 1845 showed a rank hypocrisy by the British.

The British navy had maintained a patrol against the slave trade for decades. The few slave ships captured by the U.S. Navy had their cargo off-loaded at Monrovia, where the natives were "apprenticed" to the colonists for a number of years, with at least a chance of escaping back into the interior. When the British captured a slaver, however, those slaves not enlisted in the West Indies regiments were taken to Sierra Leone until enough had been collected to send to West Indian planters. This served the British in two ways. It cut the flow of slaves to tropical commodity rivals in Brazil and Cuba, and in turn increased Britain's own "apprentice" labor force.

Phelps wrote indignantly:

Under the name of philanthropy and the disguise of an apprentice system they carry on a trade revolting to humanity. With this prize money for human flesh, England has excited the zeal and avarice of her naval officers beyond all conscience. As the captain of a victimized slaver said to me at Freetown, "these Britishers are the worst slavers on the coast, for they combine piracy with it! They seize a man's ship, and the cargo he's risked life and fortune to collect, to turn both to their profit, in the name of prohibition of the trade!"

There's too much truth even in this Captain's prejudice! In his misfortune incidently [sic], he had lost command of the most beautiful sailing craft I've ever seen. This Brazilian–American brig, a sort of Anglo–Portuguese mixture, probably can outsail anything on the seas. She made eight successful cargo crossings, been chased numberless times by both steam vessels and brigs, before a steamer finally caught her in a calm. And Baltimore probably gets credit for her construction! There are very few slavers on the coast that weren't built there! As with every cargo the British capture, some of the sturdiest black males of this one doubtless were chosen for military training at Freetown, to be impressed into the service of the Crown. Thus at least some sons of Erin are spared service in regions where white men wilt! . . . A black man, educated in England, presides as Governor over the fate of this free Negro colony, which was established about fifty years ago as a British protectorate for negroes repatriated from England. Many probably would have done better to stay there!

The travails of the African station were many. Searing heat alternated with severe thunderstorms bringing torrents of rain. The *Jamestown* was lucky in that she had relatively few men affected by disease. At Porto Grande the *Jamestown* found the *Preble*, whose crew was recovering from a fever outbreak after patrolling up a river. The fever claimed the lives of two officers and sixteen men, and from then on, ships were directed to keep out of the rivers.

At least the boredom, Phelps felt, would be lessened if the commodore were more aggressive in applying the Christian spirit to giving chase to slavers. After all, the *Jamestown* was the fastest ship in the squadron.

Far from annoying the honest slaver, it begins to look like we're his friend, even his accomplice. We don't bother him, but we do scare off the pirate that might prey on his cargo—all except the British Navy pirates! Apparently the government behind the Commodore is as indifferent as he is when it comes to acting on tips and evidence vigorously enough for our ships to give chase. A real good race with a slaver, maybe even a little gunplay, would give us some adventure and excitement! Besides, a few shillings prize money to me for a smart craft would help my debts . . . maybe the Commodore aims to fulfill scripture, beat my sword into a grubhook!

But with pro-slavery [James K.] Polk in the White House, our soft little man pretty well suits his command. He's a little too dried up with age to have much enterprise for a job now, if he ever had. You feel more piety than iron in his soul! But be it said for him, better officers have come to not only slack but cautious, too, about hauling in a slaver as a prize. . . . And then the commander who seized her is apt to get sued for false detention. Loaded slavers are a sight harder to catch, moving away by the black of night and only under a fair breeze. So with the White House looking the other way, why go to much bother on the seas? Anyway why go to the worse bother, and risk, of probing up some of these stinking rivers of death for evidence to anticipate a cargo round-up and sailing? Avoiding that kind of thing is just common sense—under the Polk Administration.

As the months wore on and thoughts turned more and more to home, the midshipmen began to hear about the new Naval School at Annapolis. Phelps hoped to pursue mathematics as far as his naval career would allow. He wrote home:

I might have had a better opportunity for it at West Point, one of the few institutions in the States that teaches pure mathematics in the higher field at all. Most of our colleges, as our professor says, just skim through math, neglecting it as our country does scientific education generally, with not one institution for it. I hope our new Naval School will have as fine a mathematics course as West Point's. I believe it will have and I'm looking forward to the better chance of study there soon.

We've heard out here that the new school is ready and that already many of our date have been ordered to classes there. They're getting that advantage of us and so I'm really buckling down to study now to be a match for them when we join the classes. We've certainly served our time on Africa's benighted coast. Hal and I are trying to get school orders, figuring we can get back to the states some way, maybe in a prize, even if the *Jamestown* is held over here longer. Other ships in the Squadron do haul in a prize now and then. A couple of middies from our ship got the idea ahead of us of going home in a slaver taken by the *Yorktown*. Maybe her enterprising Yankee skipper will haul in another for us—we hope a better tub than the other two middies and a lieutenant started home in several weeks ago. We hope they're still afloat and will get there! Some of these slavers don't look too sound or seaworthy—but we'd take a chance!

The schooner *Robert Wilson* was looking for a crew when she stopped at Key West in late October 1845. After signing on the men needed, she headed for Havana in mid-November. While in Havana, new crewman James Griffen was engaged in taking on a cargo of pipes filled with water. After a quantity of rum in half-pipes was stored over the pipes of water, Griffen became suspicious. He observed other cargo consisting of 4,800 sticks of firewood and several boxes. One box contained a boiler, and the other contained about a thousand wooden spoons. With the pipes and boxes stored in the hold, three thousand feet of planking was brought aboard and used to construct a false deck over the stores. Over this new deck was placed the remaining cargo.

Nine Spanish passengers reported aboard but acted like crewmen. Griffen was told by a Spaniard that one of the two men living with the captain was in fact the Spanish captain and the other was the mate. Griffen watched with interest as the Spanish "captain" frequently took sightings for the chronometer. The Sunday before the schooner was scheduled to sail, Griffen went to the American consulate and stated that he believed the schooner was in fact a slave ship, and he wanted to be discharged. Since it was Sunday morning, Griffen was told to come back at 3 P.M.

On his way back to the consulate, Griffen was met by a shipmate who offered him a doubloon, if he would return to the ship. When Griffen went on board and asked for his doubloon, he was seized by three men, tied hand and foot, and thrown into a cabin. The schooner was then towed out of the harbor by a steam tug, and headed east.

The *Jamestown* returned to the harbor at Porto Praya in late January 1846. The *Robert Wilson* lay at anchor nearby, so Commodore Skinner decided to send a boat to check her out. When Skinner was told that she carried ten Spanish passengers, he immediately suspected that he had a slaver. He sent a party to search the ship, where they were joined by Portuguese customs officials. Discovering the nature of the vessel, both the Americans and the Portuguese claimed the vessel. After a tense standoff, it was agreed to let the Portuguese governor-general decide the ship's fate. The governor agreed to release the ship to the Americans after expense money was paid for removing the cargo.

Phelps volunteered to help sail the schooner home, but had some misgivings when he discovered what a scow she was. After a week of work by the *Jamestown*'s carpenters and caulkers, the *Robert Wilson*'s hull was patched and the boatswain had managed to repair the ship's rigging sufficiently for the voyage home.

At 1 P.M. February 1, 1846, the *Robert Wilson*, under command of Lt. H. L. Chipman, with Acting Midshipman Phelps, a skeleton crew from the *Jamestown*, and the *Robert Wilson*'s crew (under arrest), headed west. The *Jamestown* sailed in company for a short while, then at 3:10 P.M. her crew gave the *Robert Wilson* three cheers and veered off to regain her station.

ℰℐ

Bonita

T HE *Robert Wilson* was to sail to Portsmouth, Virginia, but it soon became evident that just reaching the United States would be a struggle. Chipman and Phelps had only an octant, a Bowditch, and an old Spanish chart to navigate by. The 202-ton schooner's hull continued to leak, and the six seamen and two marines had their hands full with the poor rigging and sails. Adding to their problems, heavy seas caused the bowsprit to become sprung in two places, which made setting her jibs properly all but impossible.

The most serious problem was the discovery, shortly after getting under way, that the supply of fresh water was only forty gallons. Several of the water casks had leaked, and the water originally intended for the cargo of slaves proved unfit for consumption.

For the extremely short-handed crew, Lieutenant Chipman was proving to be of little help. "I was virtually commander," Phelps wrote. "True I had a captain on board, but I did everything but tell him he was no longer such. . . . For the last half of the passage scarce saw him out of his bunk & much less on duty."[1]

With the serious water situation and the ship obviously west of course, Chipman and Phelps decided to head for Charleston, South Carolina. There the schooner was turned over to the Admiralty Court for disposition, and her Spanish captain and mate were put on trial for engaging in the slave trade. Found guilty by the court, the *Robert Wilson*'s captain was sentenced to three years' imprisonment and a one thousand dollar fine. James Griffen was jailed for a time, but after providing testimony in the case, he was released and paid $73.96 from proceeds of the sale of the schooner at auction.[2]

Phelps remained in Charleston to testify, then proceeded to Washington in charge of the two marines, the seamen having been paid off and discharged.

At the Navy Department, Phelps received his long-awaited orders to the Naval School and traveled to Annapolis. Orders to the Naval School did not have quite the same importance as they did on the African station, however, for war with Mexico made the expectation of new orders a strong possibility. "I am in a feverish state about orders," he wrote to his mother, "they are threatened & yet do not come. Perhaps, if this 'war' ends now, as some suppose it will, I shall remain here; but if it goes on, would you have me remain quietly here, while my country is at war in which I might be of aid, and perhaps have an opportunity of distinguishing (or extinguishing) myself? I think not—though your womanly fears would prompt you to express such a wish."

Phelps's first weeks at Annapolis were anything but auspicious. He landed in the middle of a dispute over a sugar dish at the mess table that ended with one midshipman calling another a liar. This serious breach of etiquette required that Phelps put in writing his statement about what happened; it then had to go to Secretary of the Navy George Bancroft for disposition. To top it off, he had fifty dollars stolen from his room. "I had my servant seized," he continued, "taken before a Magistrate. All his things were searched, as also the 'Lady of Color' whom he is about to marry, and her things, but have found no clue to my money. That together with my late heavy expenses will make it impossible for me to visit home."[3]

Phelps and Hal Brown, who had recently arrived at the Naval School after sailing the prize ship *Panther* to the States, were hopeful that with the arrival of orders, they could visit Chardon, then travel to Mississippi to see Brown's parents on the way to Pensacola or New Orleans for transportation to the Gulf of Mexico.

In early June 1846, orders arrived for Phelps and Brown to proceed immediately to New York. Phelps was to report aboard the converted river schooner USS *Bonita,* and Brown, the USS *Petrel.* While Phelps was thrilled to be assigned to "as pretty a little craft as ever floated," he had some misgivings about not visiting home. He wrote to his father:

> I feel at times as if I were doing wrong, or rather as if I had done wrong while at Annapolis in not devoting a few days to visiting home. It sometimes seems to me as if we are forewarned of impending misfortunes; if it is so, surely some dangers threaten me—for I cannot shake off the feeling that ere long I shall have cause to regret not having visited you when the chance offered itself—it is not because I am homesick for I am not; neither is it that I am not pleased with my orders for I was never so well pleased in my life, with the prospects of a cruise as the one now opened to me. Brown and myself are both pleased very much and we have long since concluded that we would not swap our orders for others to any vessel afloat.[4]

By the summer of 1846, the war with Mexico was under way, with Maj. Gen. Zachary Taylor on the march in northern Mexico and the Home Squadron, under Commodore David Conner, on blockade duty along the East Coast. The port of Matamoros, just south of the Rio Grande, had already fallen, and the port of Carmen, on the Yucatan Peninsula, was, for the time being, neutralized by a rebellion, leaving six other ports to watch. Five of those six ports lay up shallow rivers with tricky bars at their mouth. It was precisely these conditions that prompted Secretary Bancroft to seize three river schooners, fifty-nine feet long, built in New York by Brown and Bell specifically for the Mexican navy.

Phelps wrote to his father:

> Our schooners are of the smallest description of armed craft, being of only 74 or so tons burthen and carrying but 21 men—

Gulf of Mexico, 1846–1848

officers and all making the round number of 25; their draft is about 6 feet being built with flat floors but very sharp forward and aft—intended especially for running up those Gulf Rivers. We all mess, that is the Lt. Commanding, 2 Passed Midn., and myself in the cabin which is a fine one considering the size of the vessel. Our gun is a Paixhans 32 pounder. It is a heavy piece for so small a craft and I much fear it will give us trouble, both in heavy seas and in heavy firing for I apprehend it will try the strength of her timbers. She cannot fail to be a fast sailor and will be a very efficient vessel in such warfare as is now going on in the Gulf. Our little draft of water will enable us to act with the Army along the shore and up the rivers. My duties will be those of a Lt.

These vessels are so much alike that one is perplexed to tell "tother from which." Their names are very pretty I think. *Bonita, Petrel, & Reefer.* They are "fore and afters" and owing to that heavy gun will be a dangerous craft at sea—particularly as Navy Officers see little of such sailing. I was obliged to know & learn in that Prize [*Robert Wilson*] though. We now only wait for men of which there is a want just now. It will be a lesson to our wise congressmen and show them that the much talked of rush of sailors in time of war to naval rendezvous is not so probable as they would have made us believe.[5]

The *Bonita* was under the command of Lt. Timothy Benham, a veteran of thirty-two years' service from New Haven, Connecticut. Crewmen arrived slowly, and one by one the little schooners headed for the Gulf of Mexico. The *Bonita* was the last to reach the navy's main anchorage at Anton Lizardo, about twelve miles south of Veracruz.

The crews of the three gunboats took pride in their little craft and were looked upon with some envy by the rest of the squadron. Midshipman William Parker went alongside the first schooner to arrive, the *Reefer*, in a barge that was nearly as long, and, not knowing any better, stepped over her port quarter. "The first lieutenant immediately informed me in no very gentle tone," Parker wrote, "that there was a gangway to that vessel!"

Parker noted that the three schooners looked very cozy and comfortable—at least in good weather—but at sea the swells made them look as if they were mostly underwater. "Oh! there was a good deal of style kept up in these schooners, if they were little. They were gotten underway with the longest of speaking trumpets and the hoarsest of voices."[6]

Commodore Conner had made an attempt to attack the Mexican warships in the Alvarado River, twenty miles southeast of Anton

Lizardo, in late July, but was forced to abandon the plan when the *Cumberland* ran aground on a reef. With good weather and his three new gunboats, Conner decided to try again.

On the evening of August 6, 1846, Phelps wrote:

All of us were anticipating an action which would be desperate for our little schooners. From their light draft they could enter the river, where it was expected of us to seize, take & destroy vessels of a vastly greater force.

Every preparation was made and on the morning of the 7th, the squadron got underway and stood down for the devoted town some 26 miles distant. An extremely light breeze was blowing; the frigates were taken in tow by the steamers. These little craft worked their way down as best they might arriving, however, soon after the others. The best part of the day was gone. Our charts of this part of the coast, which is very dangerous, are imperfect & considerable more time was taken up in sounding for the larger ships.[7]

The larger ships, unable to pass the bar, had taken up a fan-shaped formation off the mouth of the river. When the time came to begin the attack,

Our Captain, nothing daunted at the diminutive size of his craft, stood boldly in and had got within range of the Fort & the vessels of war lying near by it for our long Tom. When the wind failed and became too light to stem the current the river made, we anchored in a very good position being ½ mile nearer than the other vessels though not as near as was desirable. So there we laid hoping and praying that the Mexicans would fire upon us as the Commodore had refused permission to fire; but if they had opened the dance we would not have waited for orders. The flag ship's getting on shore had made the Commodore over cautious. The two steamers were at last where they thought to reach the fort with their 10 inch guns. Signal was then made for us to run down and speak to the Commodore. He gave orders to take a position in shore, where

we could take the fort in the rear. The sun was about one hour
& a half high. We [the three schooners] ran down and took a
position and anchorage at least ¾ of a mile nearer than the
other vessels—our own schooner being the inside vessel. After
all which we opened fire as also the steamers but their shots fell
short—ours told—shot and shell. One Paixhans shell burst directly over the fort and it was amusing to see the fellows run out
& take to the chaparrals. One of our round shot—after passing
through a house—of which there are but two or three on the
point, the town being farther up river—plunged onto the deck
of a sister schooner of ours built at the same time. Finding that
the shots of the other vessels were falling short, the Commodore made signal to cease firing—having as we understood determined to run in farther the next morning—and to find the
soundings etc. in the meantime.

A short time after we had ceased firing all us officers were
standing together aft when a perfect shower of musket balls
whizzed about our heads and directly followed the report.
A party had secreted themselves in the chaparrals along the
beach & on the hill side which is of considerable height. Our
schooner being the nearest in & we standing aft they rightly
judged us to be officers—and put their whole strength in our
destruction. But from their elevation & long range (not less
than from 80 to 100 yards) they made too great allowance &
overshot though many of them gave our caputs but a narrow
escape. A brisk fire was kept upon us and the *Reefer* which was
returned with shells, grape, canister & round shot & musketry.
In about one half hour we had silenced them. It was about dark
when they commenced & it was only by the flashes of their
guns and a small field piece which they had that we knew
where to aim. They fired with very heavy charges and continued in their mistake about elevation. A few of the shot which
passed over us struck the other schooners but without effect.
For my part I fired an old "blunderbuss" which I filled up with
powder and ounce balls until she blew up *everything*, whereupon I took a musket and had some good shots which I flatter
myself took effect. Soon after we had silenced the firing the

Commodore ordered us to run out of range of the shot. We all turned in full anticipation of the morrows work and to dream of glory & the bright eyes of the fair maids of Alvarado. The *Bonita* and *Reefer* had opened the ball and we hoped to end it on the morrow.

Even you, my mother, would not have known me for the 3 previous days I had enjoyed a comfort in the way of a tooth-ache and my face was much swollen as it is now. On my way down it had been almost insufferable, but I soon forgot it and all else but thrashing the bloody Mexicans. But after I got to sleep it resumed its sway and I dreamed all sorts of pains— though it failed to wake me, for I was too tired. Early in the morning our little craft was underway and we stood down for the Commodore. Judge of our surprise and chagrin when he made signal to us to make the best of our way here [Anton Li-zardo] and one to the rest of the squadron to form the pre-scribed order & to bear up for the same place. The weather looked threatening & he apprehended a Norther which would have been a bad customer to be caught in such a place with, but the attack had been commenced & should have been car-ried out, wind or no wind. The humbuging policy of our gov-ernment in regard to its Navy has made timid men of our Captains—afraid of consequences save a few such as the hero of Monterey (C. A. Jones). The fear that a ship might be lost if a gale should come on & the consequences which would follow it scared him off—and we had the pleasing satisfaction of seeing ourselves apparently running from the enemy and giving up the attempt as beyond our strength. No gale has blown yet.

Alvarado might now have been ours & the vessels of war with it which are nearly all the Mexicans have. No doubt in a few days the attack will be followed up but it will be against an enemy twice as strong for we showed them their weak spot.

Phelps had been on blockade duty in the gulf for less than two weeks, but he had already formed strong opinions as to how the war was being conducted.

I am almost sick of such war as this. Coasters & alongshore traders carry on trade as they did before the blockade. A far more profitable one for they trade in the very articles which they are in want of and which we would not permit a regular merchantman to approach the coast with. I have always thought leniency in war to be the meanest of principles in itself and in the effect which is the reverse of that anticipated. Here are our men getting the scurvy for want of fresh provisions and there are thousands of cattle within our reach which are at our mercy but remain untouched unless their owners will commit treason for the money & furnish us though we pretend to seize them. I go in for doing the enemy all possible injury.[8]

For the next several weeks the squadron did little but cruise back and forth or anchor off the rivers to maintain the blockade. Morale and discipline problems that accompanied the heat and boredom of blockading duty on the larger warships were almost nonexistent on the little schooners, for they were kept busy as messenger boats.

Often times we have dodged about these reefs at night in a wonderful manner, having been several times within range of the "barkers" of San Juan de Ulloa without injury. These frequent trips seldom took us without a safe distance of these at once dangerous and friendly reefs. Sometimes, true, we found it uncomfortable but it was excitement. To understand a situation as dangerous as ours, it will be important that you take it as decided that our vessel is not one intended for the sea, but built for these rivers and reefs and with a draft of six feet only which gives little hold on the water.[9]

On the morning of September 17, 1846, a prearranged signal flag was hoisted on the flagship, the *St. Mary's*. On board the *Bonita*, Phelps and the other officers and men mustered on the small deck and turned their eyes toward the flagship. Throughout the anchorage the scene was the same on all ships of the squadron. Commodore Conner had been worried about the discipline of his squadron and chose this moment to make an example. Seaman Samuel Jackson of the *St. Mary's* had been found guilty in a court-martial of several offenses, including using abusive language and striking an officer. With all eyes of the squadron upon the flagship, Jackson, attended to at his own request by the officer he had assaulted, was hanged from the yardarm.[10]

Weather was a constant worry for Conner and the squadron. The Mexican coast was noted for "the vomito" (yellow fever) during the wet summer months and "northers" during the dry winter season. Northers, very strong northerly gales, sprang up suddenly and without warning.

On the morning of September 24, the *Bonita* got under way from the anchorage at Anton Lizardo, to carry messages to the ships blockading the port of Veracruz. The morning breeze soon lessened, and the *Bonita* was forced to come to and wait for the wind to freshen. Later that afternoon the breeze picked up, and the little schooner continued toward Sacrificios Island off the coast from Veracruz. As darkness fell, the "weather came on boisterous," and not seeing any ships, Lieutenant Benham decided to anchor for the night. The next morning at daylight the schooner got under way again with a moderate southwest wind, and went looking for the *St. Mary's* and *Somers,* which had moved well off the coast, fearing a norther, the night before. The *Bonita* sailed as far as Point Piedras but saw nothing until 5 P.M., when a sail was discovered on the weather quarter. By 8 P.M. the *Bonita* maneuvered alongside the *John Adams,* which did not know where the other ships were but took advantage of the meeting to send along her dispatches.

The *Bonita* continued on a northerly course and encountered several squalls as the evening wore on. Benham adjusted the sails accordingly before turning in and leaving Phelps with the watch.

Night came on finely, and everything promised well. I had the mid-watch and until one half hour of its termination the weather was fine but then my suspicions were aroused and I shortened sail at which the Capt. came on deck and expressed a wish to be sure and not drift by the current. Seeing his anxiety & thinking I might be mistaken I again made sail—but had scarce set it before we were struck by a violent "Norther" and the way sail came off our little craft was curious—and soon she was spinning off under a jib at a great rate.[11]

Benham immediately had the foresail brailed and the mainsail lowered. The *Bonita* then came about but could not keep her bow into the sea. In a long letter to his father, Phelps wrote:

> Finding the sea was getting up very fast & the wind increasing nere to a hurricane and that our vessel could live but a short time, balanced reefs were taken and everything prepared for the last eternity. Seas ran as they say "Mountain High" and the leomers began to find their way to our keel & soon like to trip her. . . . For 24 hours we frequently stared death in the face and as I may say shook hands with the Grim Fellow. Several times we looked at one another as much to say good bye, God bless you, but not a lip quivered.

As daylight brought into focus the towering seas that crashed over the tiny vessel every time she fell off into a trough, Benham yelled for his men to bring on deck spars with which to make a drag (sea anchor). After the crew had brought several on deck, he had them lashed together and a span of ropes attached to each end. A hawser was then made fast to the center of the span and passed around the spars at their center, leaving from six to eight fathoms from the drag to the end of the hawser, to which a kedge was made fast and suspended from the drag. As soon as the drag was finished, it was thrown over the windward side, where it veered to a distance of fifty fathoms.

This somewhat relieved the schooner, but the huge seas continued to break over her sides. Benham then lowered the foresail and raised the balance-reefed mainsail and let go the larboard anchor with fifty fathoms of chain. For the first time in hours the little craft kept her head into the seas, but the gale continued to increase in intensity. Toward evening the raging storm once again was threatening to overwhelm the *Bonita,* so Benham had another drag constructed and thrown overboard.

Phelps continued:

The larboard anchor with its 50 fathoms of chain, notwithstanding its weight, was held out as straight and stiff as a harp-
string. Such was the violence of the wind and sea. A tremendous one would come down on to us hissing and snapping as if
it would bury us from masthead down without an effort, strike
her & throw her off into the trough of the sea when this chain
& the drags & hawsers would bring her up & bring her head
back again to meet the next sea. A sea would strike her & fly 10
times her length, leaving the heavier columns of water to find
their way off her decks. In the greatest uncertainty and doubt
we passed the remainder of the day & following night, but you
would little have judged of the secret thoughts of all of us by
the outward show. No lips expressed a doubt of safety. I have
frequently been placed in situations of danger, in launch &
boat duty to say nothing of that Prize craft—but have never
myself felt so indifferent as then.

The Paixhans 32-pounder was well secured and, instead of
making her more dangerous, Benham credited it with making the
vessel more stable.[12]

All through the night of September 27, the *Bonita* and her crew
were blown helplessly toward the southeast. At daylight, according to
Phelps:

We saw the greatest danger. We were driving at rail road speed
when the gale broke and were within from 8 to 10 miles of an
iron bound shore. A short time more & the *Bonita*'s bones would
have been piled on it.

Having drifted some 100 miles with drags and all, and had
the wind not moderated some, we must have gone on shore.

With the gale somewhat abated, Benham had the drags and
anchor retrieved, and raised reefed sails. Their problems were not
over yet, however, for the wind and seas continued to push them
toward shore. Phelps continued:

For the following 8 days, we were beating about the coast of Tobasco & Yucatan where the fresh breezes and strong currents
had driven us under all the short sail which she could carry.

Three days of good weather followed, and we are now standing in for the anchorage to surprise the squadron with our res-
urrection. . . . The whole squadron you may well believe hailed
us with great pleasure. She is the favorite vessel of the squadron. Often we hear it said "I would exchange for the *Bonita* but
none other."

Having cheated death, the crew of the *Bonita* became closer than
ever. The relieved Phelps wrote:

Thanks to the skill of our noble mess mate & commander we
are safe. We love him as his merits deserve. Had it been either
of the other schooners they must have gone down. . . . Our
Captain though a plain & rough looking old fellow more resembling a hardy countryman than an officer. He is loved and
esteemed by all who know him. We who meet him in the
double character of mess mate & Captain feel for him. . . . I did
not believe it possible for a commanding officer to inspire his
inferiors. No wrangling appears among us, no complaints, no
petty trifles mar our peace. The *Bonita* is marked as the happy
vessel of the squadron—and moreover as the one to carry out
whatever duty may be assigned her if bravery or skill may perform them but the best and stoutest of us must succumb in the
war of the elements.

Upon arriving at the fleet anchorage, the crew heard the news
that the schooner *Flint* had sailed for the States, carrying the news
that the *Bonita* had been lost at sea with all hands. Phelps quickly
wrote a note to his parents that was sent aboard a fast steamer, in the
hope that it would reach them before the news was published in the
newspapers. "Have no anxiety in the future for our little vessel on the
score of wind," he told his father. "Though a miniature man-of-war—
flat & heavily loaded with metal, she has proved herself a pretty good
sea boat."[13]

Ten days later the *Bonita* joined the squadron in another attempt to take Alvarado. The squadron departed Anton Lizardo on the morning of October 15, 1846, with the steamer *Vixen* towing the *Bonita* and *Reefer*. Just after sunrise the attack commenced and immediately ran into trouble. The steamer *Mississippi*, with her big guns, could not get within range, and the surf was too high and the winds too low for the small steamers to tow the gunboats into position. Conner postponed the attack until that afternoon, when the normal sea breeze would aid the vessels. At noon he called a council of war with his captains and decided to cross the bar in two columns. The first would consist of the *Vixen* towing the *Bonita* and *Reefer* under Conner's personal command; the second, of the steamer *McLane* towing the *Nonata, Petrel,* and *Forward* under the command of Capt. French Forrest of the *Cumberland*.

The *Vixen*'s column approached the bar about 1:45 P.M. and, after difficulty in working against the current, managed to cross it. The three vessels then opened fire as they passed in front of the fort. The second column ran into trouble at the bar when the *McLane*'s tow rope became fouled and she grounded. Watching the *McLane*'s trouble, Conner turned to Capt. Joshua Sands of the *Vixen* and said; "Well, Sands, what is to be done now?" Sands replied, "Go ahead and fight like hell."[14]

Conner did not feel that his little three-ship flotilla was nearly strong enough to go after the Mexican vessels, so he ordered his ships to come about and recross the bar. The three vessels once again engaged in a running battle with the fort as they made their way back. The fort concentrated on the *Vixen,* which was hit twice; the *Reefer* was struck near her rudder head. Once again the *Bonita*'s luck held as she escaped unscathed.

Even though the *McLane* was not damaged by her grounding, Conner felt she would be of little use, so once again he withdrew from Alvarado. The younger officers were upset with his lack of aggressiveness but hoped to see a change soon. Word was "that [Matthew] Perry is our fighting Commander," according to Phelps. Actually Phelps was premature. Perry, captain of the *Mississippi,* would not assume command of the Home Squadron for another five months.

Eager for some kind of success, Captain Perry urged Connor to seize the weakly defended town of Tabasco. Conner agreed, and gave Perry command of the vessels that had tried to take Alvarado. Perry's vessels, after riding out a storm that separated the *Reefer,* arrived off the mouth of the Rio Tabasco and the port of Frontera on October 21. Two days later Perry took the *Vixen,* with the *Bonita* and *Forward* in tow, and crossed the bar. The *McLane,* with the *Nonata* and surfboats in tow, once again grounded on the bar but this time cast loose her charges, which continued without her.

Perry's column proceeded to Frontera de Tabasco, where they captured all the Mexican vessels except the *Amado,* which escaped upriver. Perry ordered Benham to go after her while he remained to secure Frontera. The chase was on. With all the sail she could carry, the *Bonita* pushed ahead against the current. Phelps and the crew had their blood up as they readied their cutlasses and small arms for boarding. The *Bonita* was designed for these rivers and slowly gained on the *Amado.* By early the next morning, the *Bonita* had captured her prey, and triumphantly returned to the flotilla with the *Amado* in tow.

The expedition then proceeded seventy-two miles upriver to the town of Tabasco, arriving the following morning. At first there was no resistance from the town, but the next morning the Mexicans began shooting at the fleet. Perry shelled the town until a white flag appeared. Foreign merchants had raised the flag, hoping to stop the shelling and avoid damage to their property. Perry agreed to stop if his vessels were not fired on. Later, his prizes were fired on, and the boat sent to their aid was peppered with musket fire that mortally wounded an officer. In return, Perry opened fire on the town, directing his gunners to avoid the foreigners' property. A short time later Perry abandoned the town and withdrew downriver, taking his prizes with him.

Perry had not intended to hold Tabasco, but to seize as much shipping as possible. After the two failures at Alvarado, the success at Tabasco was just the morale booster the squadron needed.

Some 210 miles north of Veracruz lay the port of Tampico, the fleet's next objective. The capture of Mexico's second most important port was considered vital, for it would assist Zachary Taylor's army, help neutralize the state of Tamaulipas, and serve as an advanced base of operations.

When word of the pending American assault reached Gen. Antonio Lopez de Santa Anna, who had been allowed to return from his Cuban exile, he ordered Tampico abandoned. The news of the evacuation was forwarded to Conner by Mrs. Anna Chase, the English wife of the former American consul. Her report confirmed the story received from the blockading ships and prompted Conner to mount an expedition.

On the morning of November 12, Conner's flagship, the *Princeton,* followed by the *Mississippi,* the *Vixen,* and the recently arrived river steamer *Spitfire,* got under way for Tampico with the *Bonita, Petrel, Reefer,* and *Nonata* in tow. The fleet arrived early on the morning of November 14 and formed into two divisions. The *Bonita* was assigned to the second division, under Perry, along with the *Vixen, Nonata,* and the surfboats that carried the assault troops.

At 10:45 A.M. Conner, with the *Spitfire* as his flagship, led the assault force past the shallow bar at the mouth of the Rio Panuco. Meeting no resistance, the boats pushed on until just after noon, when they saw the American flag flying over the city. The flag had been personally raised by Mrs. Chase. Unlike Tabasco, Tampico was to remain occupied by the Americans. Although the seizure of the city was not as strategically important as first thought, a number of valuable Mexican gunboats were seized.[15]

Phelps and the *Bonita* stayed at Tampico for a couple of weeks and then were towed by the *Mississippi* back to Anton Lizardo, along with the *Vixen* and *Petrel.*

In December, Conner decided to go after the coastal trade that had continued unmolested along the Yucatan coast. On December 20, Perry arrived off the town of Carmen with the *Mississippi, Vixen, Petrel,* and *Bonita.* Phelps expected "an attack upon the seaports of Yucatan, which province is now treated as part & portion of the enemy." He was proud "that still more active duties [are] forced upon these little craft while the larger vessels remain in status quo at Anton Lizardo, useless except to keep up a respectable force."

Phelps wrote to his father:

It has been a matter of wonder to me for sometime, that the U. States should permit such trifling, as in the case of the two provinces of Merida and Campeche, forming the government of Yucatan. It has been known for a long time that the sea towns along the coast alone held out neutrality; not because of friendly feelings, but because they had advantages of trade, and in that trade could furnish Mexico by overland transportation with necessities of life of which our blockade deprived them. No less than six different declarations have appeared pro & con—finally it appears that Merida has declared for Santa Anna & Campeche also except the Capitol & Laguna (Carmen). But at the last moment, when they found that the vengeance of America was no longer to be withheld, they have gotten up a new pronouncement and have transmitted it through a flag of truce on board a small vessel of war to Commodore Conner with the hope of delaying his action until their documents should reach Washington & an answer received. But in their hopes they have, at least for the present, been disappointed, for our descent up the Laguna passage & the town of Carmen was about a week after their declaration had left.

Tragedy suddenly struck the *Bonita* as she stood in toward the town. The boat's purser, on the masthead as a lookout, slipped and fell to the deck. He managed only to say good-bye to his messmates before he died in their arms.

Phelps continued in his letter to his father:

Our attack was on the 20th, inst. I say attack for we went there full of fight & expecting plenty of it as it was known they had good fortifications but as in other cases they anticipated us by a day or so & got most of their means of defence out of the way & surrendered on our appearance without parlez. We found some guns & equipment & some muskets with a small quantity of powder etc. Vented our spite as usual upon them in the way of destruction—hoisted the American flag in the forts. Warned some merchantmen, instituted a blockade & the town was fairly in our possession—being Americano.

Phelps was able to spend some time in the town, which he found untouched by the ravages of war. Even the social scene, such as it was, remained intact. Lieutenant Benham, Passed Midshipman Egbert Thompson, and Phelps, along with officers from the other ships, were invited to dine with the British consul.

We had a delightful dinner, and by the chance of war a pleasant party. What a difference, interest makes in a man's idea of things! There was rejoicing among them that we came, in other places there has been far other feelings. The town, containing about 2000 inhabitants is the most pleasant place I have seen— is famous for its green turtle—and affords a very good market of flesh, fowl, fish, vegetables & fruit & that is all I know about it.

Leaving Comdr. Joshua Sands as the military governor of Carmen, Perry boarded the *Bonita* on December 22, 1846, and re-crossed the bar to his flagship. The next morning

We were underway bright and early & standing out of the harbor leaving behind us to maintain the blockade & posses-sion the *Vixen* & *Petrel*. In a short time we had received tow lines from the *Mississippi* & were walking off at a great rate for this place [Frontera de Tabasco]. By the next morning we were an-chored in this river. Our stay here is like to be between 2 & 3 months. Our captain has the *McLane* and this vessel to keep up the blockade of Tabasco.

Phelps noted that Frontera had changed since he was there a few months before:

Some 8 days since the Governor of the Province sent a kind message to the citizens of this place in the most affectionate manner. He proposed to cut their throats & burn their town unless they deserted it at once which the fools accordingly did, building huts in the woods around about for temporary use. It is astonishing what absolute power a cut throat fellow may exercise over these people if he has a few ruffian soldiers at his back, thousands are ruled by them. They say here, we have no fear whilst the place is held by the American forces but as soon as you go they will carry out their threats, so we must obey, yet the man who has exercised such powers cannot bring one man against ten of them if they could defend themselves. Scarce ten persons can now be found in the place which was full of life when we were here before.

Phelps hoped wistfully to "go up to Tobasco before long & catch that Governor & hang him as an act of humanity to these people & rid the world of an infernal scoundrel."[16] Phelps did not get the chance.

Instead, the crew of the *Bonita* was forced for the first time to endure the same routine as the larger blockading ships. At least the *Bonita* was able to use the shelter of the river to avoid the worst of the northers that sprang up.

For the sailors on the larger ships, the coming of a norther was an excuse to take it easy. On board the USS *Potomac*, Midshipman William Parker looked forward to one because all shipboard routines were suspended. With the exception of watch duty, he could sleep as late as he liked, leave his hammock suspended, and spend time riding an upside-down table to and fro on the mess deck as the ship pitched and rolled.

The *Bonita* did not have to remain at Tabasco quite as long as Phelps feared, for early in February 1847, the *Porpoise* arrived and informed the crew that they were being recalled to Anton Lizardo. Returning to the fleet anchorage, the crew of the *Bonita* found preparations under way for an attack on Mexico's principal port, Veracruz.

Maj. Gen. Winfield Scott proposed to make Veracruz the staging point for an advance against Mexico City. Veracruz was a heavily defended, walled city with strong forts to the north and south. Half a mile off the city lay the Castle of San Juan de Ulloa, a well-constructed fort mounting more than one hundred guns that commanded the approaches. The crew of the *Bonita* had taken great delight the previous fall in darting about the reefs surrounding the fort but had never drawn a response.

Scott's army finally appeared, and plans were completed to launch an amphibious assault on the beach opposite Sacrificios Island. The *Bonita* and other light draft gunboats were to sail toward the beach and form a line as close inshore as possible to provide gunfire support for the disembarking troops.

The landings were postponed a day when it looked like another norther might be brewing. On March 9, 1847, "the sun dawned propitiously on the expedition," according to General Scott. At 10 A.M. the fleet got under way from Anton Lizardo and headed north. The larger warships each had in tow ten to twenty surfboats that would be used for the landings. The surfboats were well suited for their amphibious role. Sharp at both ends, with flat floors drawing very little water, each could carry one hundred soldiers; they were manned by one officer and eight to ten sailors.[17]

The combined fleet was an impressive sight. One participant described it thus:

> The tall ships of war sailing leisurely along under their topsails, their decks thronged in every part with dense masses of troops whose bright muskets and bayonets were flashing in the sunbeams; the jingle of spurs and sabres; the bands of music playing; the hum of the multitude rising up like the murmurs of the distant ocean; the small steamers plying about, their decks crowded with anxious spectators; the long line of surfboats towing astern of the ships.[18]

The gunboats arrived off Sacrificios Island at 12:45 P.M. and found the surf to be optimum for the landings. Taking up position less than one hundred yards from the beach, Phelps and the crews of the gunboats watched and waited.

While the soldiers clambered down the sides of their ships into the waiting surfboats, Mexican cavalry could occasionally be seen behind the dunes. As the operation continued, many of the loaded surfboats had a hard time maintaining their position in the surf while waiting for the other boats. Instead of trying to sort the boats out at sea, Maj. Gen. William Worth, commander of the assault, signaled the boats to row for the boat flying their regimental flag when they headed for the beach.

At 5:30 P.M. the signal was given for the surfboats to head for the beach. Everything was strangely quiet as the men of the *Bonita* alternately watched the surfboats and the sand dunes. Soon the gig of General Worth, followed by the main landing force, ran aground just off the beach. Jumping into chest-deep water, the troops, holding their weapons and cartridge boxes over their heads, waded ashore.

Fortunately the Mexicans had fled, and the landing was unopposed. As the troops of the first wave secured a perimeter, the surfboats returned to the ships for more troops and began ferrying thousands of men to the beach. By 10 P.M. all of Scott's troops were safely ashore in a remarkable amphibious operation.

The troops moved toward Veracruz early the next morning and began a siege that was to last for several weeks. The *Bonita* and other gunboats spent much of that time in various supporting duties and riding out a norther that hit on March 21.

During the siege, Matthew Perry relieved Commodore Conner and took command of the Home Squadron. After a dismal start, Conner had regained much of the respect of his men, and after his brilliant success in landing Scott's army at Veracruz, they were disappointed that he could not share in the glory of its capture.

Ashore, Winfield Scott faced a dilemma. He did not want to suffer the heavy casualties that would result from storming the city, but he also did not want to wait for the onset of the "vomito" season, which was rapidly approaching. It was decided that the navy would send ashore a number of heavy siege guns with their crews, and together with the army artillery and naval gunfire from offshore, they would pound the city into submission.

After the Mexicans had been offered one last chance to surrender, which was declined, the bombardment commenced on March 22. Perry sent Comdr. Josiah Tattnall in the *Spitfire*, along with the *Bonita* and other gunboats, to a point about one mile from the city, where they joined in. For eighty minutes the vessels poured shot and shell into the city and drew return fire from San Juan de Ulloa. Finally the gunboats ran low on ammunition and had to withdraw.

The next morning, with a fresh supply of ammunition, Commodore Perry ordered the gunboats in again. When Tattnall asked Perry where he should position his boats, Perry replied, "Where you can do the most execution, sir."[19] Tattnall had the *Spitfire* take in tow the *Petrel* and *Tampico,* and the *Vixen* tow the *Bonita* and *Reefer.* Leaving the *Falcon* as a decoy, the two columns headed toward Sacrificios Island. Once past the shoals off Punta Hornos, Tattnall had the columns come about and head straight for San Juan de Ulloa. They continued until they were within six hundred yards of Ulloa and grapeshot range of Fort Santiago, at the southern end of the city. Everything remained quiet until the gunboats opened fire on the city; then every Mexican gun that could be brought to bear erupted.

Shot and shell whizzed over the boats and churned up geysers all around the little schooners. On board the *Bonita* her gun crew quickly went about working their 32-pounder. They swabbed the barrel of burning residue after each round, then rammed home powder and shell. The gun then was quickly aimed at the fort and fired.

The battle raged for more than an hour; then Perry finally had enough. He signaled Tattnall to withdraw, but the signal either was not seen or was ignored. The little fleet finally got the message and withdrew, to the cheers of the troops ashore and the sailors on the ships offshore. The *Spitfire* had her gig smashed, and several pieces of shrapnel were imbedded in the hull of the *Petrel*'s starboard quarter. Once again the *Bonita*'s luck held, for she came through without a scratch.

The bombardment of Veracruz continued until March 25, when the Mexicans asked for terms of surrender. The end of the siege was marked by a particularly severe norther that struck the fleet that night and caused considerable damage, especially to the surfboats.

Early on the morning of March 29, a twenty-one-gun salute was fired from the Castle of San Juan de Ulloa and the Mexican flag was lowered. That was the signal for the *Bonita* and other vessels of the squadron to enter the harbor, where they were greeted by another twenty-one-gun salute from the city and the lowering of its flag.

With Veracruz in American hands, Alvarado was in a precarious position. Since the two failed attempts the year before to take the port, numerous fortifications had been constructed. Unfortunately for the Mexicans, they had anticipated another assault from the sea and had not made preparations to protect the land approach to the town. As soon as Veracruz had fallen, General Scott took advantage of the oversight and sent a force overland to seize the town.

The small steamer *Scourge* had been sent to keep an eye on Alvarado as the army made its way down the coast. The morning after the *Scourge*'s arrival, Lt. Charles Hunter, her captain, spotted a white flag flying from a nearby fort. Hunter was soon informed that the Mexicans had abandoned the town the night before, so he immediately crossed the bar and took possession, leaving a six-man garrison.

The next morning Commodore Perry arrived with his squadron and, unaware that the town was already in American hands, made ready to begin his assault. Transferring his flag to the *Vixen*, Perry headed toward the bar with the *Bonita* and *Petrel* in tow. Finding the town already occupied, he left a detachment of marines to relieve the six-man garrison and proceeded upriver with his gunboats in search of the Mexican troops who had fled. Not finding any troops, Perry returned to Alvarado that night.

While the men of the squadron admired Hunter for his initiative and the press at home loved it, "Alvarado" Hunter was court-martialed by Perry for exceeding his orders. The reprimand, read on the quarterdeck of every vessel in the squadron, said in effect: "Who told you to capture Alvarado? You were sent to watch Alvarado, and not to take it."[20]

The last major port still in Mexican hands was Tuxpan, located about six miles up the Rio Tuxpan, 180 miles north of Veracruz. Besides being the last major objective along the coast, Perry considered retaking several of the fort's 32-pounders a matter of honor, for the Mexicans had salvaged them from the wreck of the *Truxtun* the previous August.

To mount a coordinated attack from both sea and land, Perry formed a landing force of 1,500 men from his squadron to attack the river defenses from the rear. The gunboats and small steamers would provide close-in gunfire support.

Once again a norther interrupted operations, but the scattered squadron assembled off the mouth of the Rio Tuxpan on the morning of April 17. Early the next morning, the landing party boarded the gunboats and thirty barges that then stood in across the bar. The landing force quickly overran several of the forts, and Perry's fleet continued upriver; after some sharp skirmishing, the town of Tuxpan fell. After destroying everything of military value, Perry and his small fleet returned to Anton Lizardo.

In mid-April, a rumor circulated that Santa Anna was trying to flee to Cuba on board the Mexican schooner *Yucateca*. Perry spread out his squadron to try and intercept him; on April 30, the *Bonita* spotted the vessel and shortly came alongside. The boarding party found no evidence that Santa Anna had ever been there.

The Mexicans had been fortifying the town of Tabasco since the American expedition there the preceding October. The town was deemed to have little importance and was left alone until June 1847, when Perry decided to mount an operation to seize the town for a second time.

The *Bonita,* along with the *Etna,* had maintained the blockade off Frontera de Tabasco since May, and in mid-June they were joined by the rest of the squadron. On the afternoon of June 14, the *Bonita* and *Stromboli* picked up tow lines from the steamer *Spitfire* and followed the first column of gunboats upriver. Just behind them came steamers towing forty boats carrying 1,200 men. The fleet cautiously worked its way upriver but halted when it received word that the Mexicans had set up an ambush.

The next morning the fleet continued on, and soon ran into the first of several ambushes. The boats progressed slowly until dark approached; then they anchored once again. The men on the *Bonita* and other ships who could not find room to sleep below deck formed makeshift barricades with hammocks and slept on deck with their muskets.

The Mexicans had placed obstructions in the river, so the next morning Perry decided to land his force and proceed on foot. The *Bonita, Spitfire* and *Scourge* moved ahead, sweeping the landing area with grapeshot, canisters, and shells. Perry then landed and soon hoisted the flag on a nearby bluff, causing a loud cheer to ring out.

By the end of the morning, the entire landing force was ashore and had begun to move out under a searing sun.

While the landing force made its way through the heavy brush and chaparral, the boats removed the obstacles in the river. After they had done so, the steamers *Scorpion* and *Spitfire* proceeded, and soon engaged the forts along the river. Lt. David Porter of the *Spitfire* landed with sixty-eight of his men and stormed Fort Iturbide.

After the forts had fallen, the town quickly surrendered. The men of the naval landing force were disappointed at not being in on the surrender, especially after their grueling march, but were gratified to see the American flag flying over the town. Perry left a garrison at Tabasco until the ravages of yellow fever forced the town to be evacuated in July.[21]

For Phelps and the men of the *Bonita*, their capture in late June of the Mexican schooner *Montezuma* off Frontera marked their last real excitement. After Benham had been relieved by Lt. J. M. Berrien, Phelps was the only officer left of the original four, and the constant exposure to storms and the diseases endemic on the coast had finally taken their toll. He was sick and exhausted. After the war effectively ended in mid-September 1847, with General Scott's capture and occupation of Mexico City, the ill midshipman returned home for the second time in six years.

❧

CHAPTER FOUR

Between Wars

PHELPS WAS so eager to return to the Naval School that, although not fully recovered from what had been diagnosed as an enlarged liver, he reported to Annapolis in January 1848. It proved to be a mistake. He had been at the school only a few weeks when his health deteriorated to the point that the surgeon recommended he return home for a three-month convalescence. By April he was still so sick that he had to request an extension. He finally returned to the school on October 10, 1848.

The Naval School had been established at Fort Severn, Maryland, the year before Phelps's brief stay in May 1846. Previous to that, it had been held at the Naval Asylum in Philadelphia. The War Department had transferred the fort, built in 1808 and overlooking the Severn River, to the navy on March 15, 1845.

All the classrooms and quarters were converted from the original buildings; there was not a new building on the grounds. The large barracks were used as recitation rooms and quarters. Two small gun houses, called "Brandywine Cottage" and "Abbey," also were converted to quarters. The long barracks were called "Apollo Row" and "Rowdy Hall." The only new construction was a platform by the river, which resembled a ship's gun deck and mounted six 32-pounder guns for gunnery drills.

Phelps was among the last of those midshipmen who joined the navy in 1841 to report to the school. The 183 midshipmen had reported in groups over the past year, which proved to be a blessing. Had they all reported together, "their combined power and relish for mischief would have rendered the maintenance of discipline simply impossible."[1]

"We had all been to sea for six years," wrote William Parker. "I fear we gave our good superintendent much trouble."[2] Comdr. George P. Upshur, the school superintendent, was respected for his gentle manner and pure character. His approach to discipline was so lax, however, that he told the midshipmen, "I cannot govern you, young gentlemen; so if you will only govern yourselves I should be delighted."[3]

The midshipmen took the advice to heart. Not only did they constantly bedevil their instructors with pranks, but their drunken brawls and dueling shocked the citizens of Annapolis. Two duels had been fought in the past year, one on school grounds and one in Bladensburg, thirty miles to the west.

In an effort to keep the midshipmen out of local taverns, Upshur allowed the formation of social clubs. On Saturday nights "reform banquets" were held at which they "regaled with whiskey and cigars, and crackers and cheese, swapped yarns and sang songs until nearly midnight." Samuel R. Franklin described the aftermath of one gathering: "Empty bottles were lying about the floor, half-smoked cigars were scattered in all directions, chairs were turned upside-down, and everything in the room indicated it had been the scene of rollicking dissipation."[4]

The lack of discipline culminated on March 21, 1848, when the midshipmen, protesting Professor Henry Lockwood's efforts to introduce infantry and artillery drill, hanged him in effigy from the school's flagstaff. The three ringleaders were court-martialed and dismissed from the navy.

Phelps arrived after things had quieted down, which was just as well, for he had never shown an interest in such shenanigans. He wanted to study mathematics, and found the ideal instructor in Professor William Chauvenet. Chauvenet had been appointed a professor in the navy in 1841, and after a short tour aboard the USS *Mississippi*, was put in charge of the school at the Naval Asylum. Considered by many to be one of the finest mathematicians in the country and perhaps the finest teacher of mathematics, Chauvenet also taught astronomy and navigation. Under his tutelage, Phelps developed an interest in the stars and planets.

The remaining curriculum included steam engineering, natural philosophy, chemistry, English, French, and infantry tactics. Chauvenet's classes were considered excellent by the midshipmen. Professor Henry Lockwood's natural philosophy, gunnery, and steam engineering classes were rated fair, as was Professor Arsene Girault's French class. Chemistry classes, under Dr. John Lockwood, received little attention. The Saturday English classes with the chaplain and Henry Lockwood's classes in infantry tactics were a farce.

Occasionally guest lecturers were invited to keep the midshipmen up to date on the latest advances in steam engineering. For a time Lt. John Dahlgren drilled the midshipmen at the 32-pounders and tried to provide some practical instruction in filling shells, driving fuses, and so on. Dahlgren soon quit, however. Trying to teach gunnery to men who were already experienced gunners was a waste of time.[5]

In August 1849, Phelps passed his examinations and became a passed midshipman, entitled to wear a star next to the anchor on his collar. This happy occasion was marred by a disappointment, however. Hal Brown had failed his examination, failed a second time, and was forced to resign. After the Mexican War, Brown had married Mary Taliaferro, back home in Copiah County, and his heart was on his Mississippi plantation.

Professor Chauvenet had been an inspiration to Phelps. Desiring to put his knowledge of the stars to work, Phelps applied to the secretary of the navy for assignment to the astronomical expedition to Chile.

He was instead assigned to the Treasury Department for duty with the Coast Survey. Before leaving on extended duty to a faraway corner of the world, Phelps was introduced to the Washington social scene by Elisha Whittlesey. Among the people he met was Capt. William Maynadier of the army's Ordnance Department and his seventeen-year-old daughter, Lizzie.

Shortly after the expedition to Chile had begun operations, one of the assistants, Passed Midshipman Hunter, was injured when thrown from a horse. The expedition leader, Lt. James M. Gilliss, had already found Hunter "wholly unfitted by education habits or disposition to render the least service to us,"[6] so he took the opportunity to send him home. Phelps quickly found himself with new orders to Chile.

Before leaving, Phelps used his political influence to try to obtain an appointment to the next higher rank of master. A student of Navy Department politics, he had determined that there had, on occasion, been appointments to master without regard to regulations. He noted that the department had done just that in the case of instructors at the Naval School. Phelps pointed out that both Gilliss and Archibald McRae, the other members of the expedition, were both lieutenants, and that he would be sharing the same duties. Since passed midshipmen often performed the duties of masters under acting appointments, he hoped the department would do the same in his case. It took several months, but Phelps was finally appointed acting master.

Under the direction of Gilliss, the primary objective of the expedition was to provide simultaneous observations, from a vastly different latitude, with those of observatories in the Northern Hemisphere. With these observations it was hoped, according to Phelps, "to obtain the parallax of the inferior planets (Mars and Venus) and thence a new measurement of distances for heavenly bodies."[7]

With the help of the leading scientific societies in the United States, the Navy Department and the Smithsonian Institution, which authorized the purchase of an equatorial telescope of six and a half inches' aperture, work was begun on the observatory at Santiago, Chile, on December 6, 1849.

Phelps traveled to Chile in the late summer of 1850, making the passage in thirty-eight days. He brought with him a barometer for the expedition that had been calibrated at the observatory in

Washington. So delicate was the instrument that Phelps was to allow no one else to touch it. While crossing the Isthmus of Panama, he carried it mounted vertically in his backpack.

On arrival at Santiago, Phelps found that he had exceeded his $350 traveling allowance by $149, and asked the department to reimburse him. He was especially concerned about his finances when informed that boardinghouses were unheard of; the expedition members lived at the local hotel. "I find that my pay at present," he wrote, "is barely sufficient to pay the expenses of living, without including clothing etc."[8]

Phelps quickly acclimated himself and found his new home agreeable. He noted that Santiago's one-story "doly" exterior houses were not very grand or striking, and were constructed to withstand the numerous earthquakes that periodically shook the city. The city, with a population of approximately one hundred thousand, was built on both sides of a rapid mountain torrent, fed by the melting snows of the Andes Mountains. In the main part of the city an abrupt pile of trap rock rose to a height of 175 feet; upon its crest, the United States built its observatory. Far to the south and north extended the plains of Santiago, more than three hundred miles in length, and as rich and fertile as the prairies of the United States. With a high and pure atmosphere, the view from the observatory was truly grand, commanding a varied scene with the quiet city beneath and the broad plain framed by the mountains.

Phelps felt that the population was largely shut off from the world and thought little of such things as science and industry. "French tastes and French fashions they understand," he noted.

The expedition made a large amount of observations. This was due to the clearness of the atmosphere and the city being rainless for eight to nine months of the year. The expedition cataloged the stars of the tenth magnitude from the South Pole to 50° north, an immense labor. They also made meteorological observations and recorded the force, direction, extent, and duration of earthquakes. In their spare time they collected animal, vegetable, and mineral specimens.

Phelps was delighted with the quality of the instruments and, despite the fact that he was once again far from home, he was quite pleased to use his intellect in such a scientific endeavor.[9] A new experience for Phelps was the frequent earthquakes. One in particular shook the city to its foundations, doing considerable damage. It was the strongest known in fifteen years. The expedition was thought by the people to foresee such things, and it so happened that a rumor circulated just before the earthquake that they had foretold its coming. Afterward their servant was pestered about future earthquakes, so that the people might be outside their houses.[10]

The twenty-seven-year-old Phelps also took an interest in the social life of Santiago.

The women of Chile are a fine race, of splendid forms & good qualities, in fact, far superior to the men in those respects as in intellect. We find a gradual improvement going on by the mixing of blood, notwithstanding the obstacles thrown in the way by the established church, which admits of no toleration. The women display a decided preference for foreigners . . . hence there is little love for them on the part of the men of the country.

The Bishop of Santiago is more powerful in reality than the President of the Republic. Churches, convents, nunneries, priests, friars, nuns etc. abound and the whole country is bound by as great a bigotry as any under the sun.[11]

In April 1851 another great earthquake caused considerable damage in the port city of Valparaiso. In addition, a revolution had begun but soon ended, after the death of its leader.

The election that followed the rebellion "was quite a farce," according to Phelps. Votes were regularly bid for. The price offered reflected the prospects of the political party at each particular table, and varied from $1 to $4.25. Regular banks were established in rooms adjacent to the one in which the polls were located. At the polls were men to see that those who had cards showing that they had sold their votes, voted the right way, and they were countersigned. After voting, the voter stepped into the bank room, showed his card, and drew his money. Of the fifteen thousand voters of Santiago, only some six thousand voted. The opposition declared that the government located the polls so that it was quite impossible for all to vote. Regardless of however much the opposition outnumbered the government party, it stood no chance against their power.[12]

The cold month of July was somewhat lonely because McRae had taken sick and Gilliss was on a short trip north, making magnetic observations and visiting the mines of Copiapó and Coquimbo. Phelps was left to make the observations until Gilliss returned. To make matters worse, another bloody civil war had broken out, which made life uneasy. Fortunately, Gilliss returned, McRae recovered, and the expedition was left alone to continue its work.

Once peace returned and the summer arrived, Phelps did some traveling. In his first trip into the countryside, he spent several days on one of the large haciendas and was able to observe a little of the mode of crop cultivation. He felt that with a small capital of five thousand dollars he could make a fortune in less than ten years. The idea intrigued him, for he had come to feel that the navy afforded a gloomy future. Promotion was excessively slow, and he could not hope to be a lieutenant in less than five years.[13]

The expedition completed its work on September 13, 1852, and returned to the United States. It did not fulfill its primary objective, but its results were of great value in determining the orbits of Venus and Mars. Other accomplishments included 7,000 meridian observations of 2,000 stars, observations of the moon and moon-culminating stars, 33,000 observations of about 23,000 stars within 24° of the South Pole, and the recording of 124 earthquakes. The equipment and telescope were purchased by the Chilean government for its national observatory.

Phelps reached the United States in November and traveled to Chardon for leave. Following six weeks at home, he returned to the Naval Observatory in Washington to help Gilliss reduce and collate the observations in preparation for their publication.

An opportunity soon presented itself that Phelps felt was too good to pass up. He wrote to Elisha Whittlesey:

Messr. Howard & Co. of New York have built a magnificent steamer [*Golden Age*] of 3000 tons burthen, to be the first in the formation of a line to Australia and to be commanded by Lieut. [David D.] Porter U.S.N. They offer me the 1st Officer

Ship with a pay which will be worth from $1500 to $2000 (clear of expenses) a year and a very fair prospect of command soon with a salary far better than that of a Commodore in the Navy.

Phelps did not want to resign his commission, so he asked Whittlesey, now first comptroller of the Treasury Department, to use his political influence to obtain a furlough:

You will perceive how excellent the prospect is for me in comparison with my present expectations. I have been nearly four years on service without leave of absence and on that score am entitled to consideration. My services in the Mexican War were of the most severe description and as you are aware have left me maimed for life. I do not wish to conceal from you that the acceptance of this place may eventually lead to resignation from the Navy, but let a Naval war arise, and I have no doubt that I can easily find my way back in the enormous increase of the service that must take place.[14]

Phelps's request for a furlough was denied. The work involved in preparing the expedition's report was such that Matthew Fontaine Maury, superintendent of the Naval Observatory, determined that Phelps could not be spared.

The rejection was actually a blessing in disguise, for Phelps proposed to Lizzie Maynadier.

I am to take that step from which there is no retreat, which may be for happiness, or misery, though I trust that I have no cause to fear the latter. I know and feel the responsibility of the new position I am to assume & trust that I shall know how to meet it.[15]

The importance of the expedition's report meant there would be no sea duty for several years, so the new Phelps household settled down to a domestic routine. A little over a year later, a daughter named Sally was born.

It was an exciting time to be at the Naval Observatory, for the winds of reform were blowing through the nearby Navy Department. Congress was finally listening to the secretary of the navy and others, who stated that something had to be done to breathe new life into the navy.

Not since the Peace Establishment Act of 1801 had retired two-thirds of the active duty officers had Congress addressed the stagnating seniority system that swelled the officer ranks. Half a century earlier, young men found the way clear to advance on merit, and during the War of 1812 bold and daring captains took on the supposedly invincible British navy. Oliver Hazard Perry was twenty-six when he won the Battle of Lake Erie; Thomas McDonough, twenty-seven, commanded a fleet that defeated the British on Lake Champlain; David Porter was captain of the *Essex* at thirty-two; and Stephan Decatur, who was promoted to captain at the age of twenty-four, captured HMS *Macedonian* at thirty-three.[16]

Without an established retirement system, the only way to remove an officer was by court-martial, of which there had been many. From 1840 to 1854, 114 officers were court-martialed on charges ranging from drunkenness to scandalous conduct. One-tenth of the post captains, one-tenth of the commanders, and one-sixth of all lieutenants were put on trial; only eighteen were acquitted. Those convicted often turned to their political friends to have their sentences remitted or greatly mitigated.

The courts-martial removed the corrupt officers but could not remove the inefficient and disabled. When Congress looked into the problem, it found that secretaries of the navy had, for decades, refused to send to sea those officers that were incapacitated by age, disease, injury, or incompetence. They were given nominal duties or no duty at all. Congress found that only one-fifth of the officers were actually employed. There were commanders who were sixty years old, lieutenants in their fifties, and midshipmen in their forties. There were captains who had not seen service for more than thirty years still on the register, blocking promotions. Commodore Charles Stewart was almost eighty, having been commissioned in 1798 and promoted to captain in 1806. He had captained the USS *Constitution* in some of her greatest victories during the War of 1812, and was held up as a man whom the country should retire with its thanks.

The British navy was cited as having a mechanism by which senior officers would be periodically retired to make room for younger officers. Queen Victoria, upon recommendation of the Board of Admiralty, simply decreed that certain officers be placed on the retired list.

On February 28, 1855, Congress passed "An act to promote the efficiency of the Navy." The secretary of the navy was empowered to appoint a board of officers who would carefully examine line officers and report to the secretary those who were "incapable of performing promptly and efficiently all their duties both ashore and afloat." The board was to recommend those officers to be discharged, furloughed, or retired.

The younger officers were elated at this turn of events. With inefficient officers being culled, the way to promotion appeared brighter. Fifteen distinguished officers—five captains, five commanders, and five lieutenants, including Matthew Perry, Samuel DuPont, William Shubrick, Louis Goldsborough, and Andrew Foote—were appointed, and reviewed the records of 712 officers. Every officer was deemed efficient unless a suggestion to the contrary was made by an officer of the same rank or higher; no officer could pass on another of a grade superior to his own. More than five hundred officers were immediately deemed efficient by unanimous consent. Of the rest, 150 were unanimously ruled inefficient, thirty-three were pronounced by a two-thirds majority, and eighteen were decided by a simple majority. When the board had completed its work, forty-nine officers were dropped as incompetent, seventy-one were placed on the "reserved" [retired] list with leave-of-absence pay, and eighty-one were on the "reserved" list with furlough pay, which was half of leave-of-absence pay.[17]

Phelps was ecstatic.

The "Reserved" list has appeared at last. No wonder there was so much delay in approving; for it sweeps 2 in 7 of the entire number of officers! A list far outreaching my wildest anticipations though I am classed among the radicals. It is a great good to the service—to the interest of the country—to the well being of those who go to sea. Men of character see now that they are reaping the benefit of their energy & attention to the duties assigned them. Now will be revived that zeal which had nearly disappeared in the general downward tendency of this chief arm of defense and now "going to sea" will again become tolerable.

Phelps immediately requested an interview with the secretary of the navy and informed him of his desire to return to sea, preferably as a member of an arctic expedition, as soon as the Chilean expedition's report was published. In the meantime, he was in an awkward situation.

Our Chief [Gilliss], who has been put on the Furlough list, has not yet been notified, and I am forced to be full of deceit in the possession of the knowledge, having intercourse with him, and aware the while that the Dept. may be contemplating his removal from all service, and requiring me to report the condition of the work, but this I do not expect and most assuredly do not desire.[18]

The angry reaction from those removed from the active list was immediate.

I find as a rule that Senators side very much as they happen to be affected in their family connections. The outsiders are moving heaven and earth and the city fairly swarms with them. Among those who are loudest in complaints about their treatment at the hands of the "Board" are those to be found the hardest cases, and in general these are the men most lauded by Senators. There has been more trash and twaddle talked in the Senate in regard to this matter than upon all others combined.[19]

In late 1855 the results of the Chilean expedition were published in six volumes, and shortly thereafter Phelps left the political infighting behind when he received orders to the 3,824–ton, side-wheel steam frigate USS *Susquehanna*. Early in the spring of 1856 he left his wife and daughter for Philadelphia and his new ship.

Three years of idyllic married life in Washington had softened Lizzie's perception of naval life to the point that Seth's departure was a shock. No sooner had he begun helping put the *Susquehanna* in order than Lizzie's sad, almost mournful letters arrived. In response, Phelps wrote:

> I do not pretend that it is not a very painful effort to leave a young, loving and charming wife, and our child, but I try to regard it as something not alterable, and already alone turn my thoughts to the future—your grief adds to my own proper share as what distresses you naturally affects me. I have great faith that your natural flow of spirit will soon return to you & that your fears will take flight. Away with your foolish repinings, foolish self torture. Remember whose daughter & whose wife you are and be brave.[20]

For the first time in ten years, Phelps settled into life aboard a man-of-war. Normal watch duty, along with all the details of assembling a new crew, kept him busy. Gunnery was greatly simplified, for he had only one gun in his division. The giant pivot gun, capable of ranging in all directions, was located aft of the mizzenmast and took all that portion of the quarterdeck. Weighing five tons without mountings and carriage, it was capable of throwing a shell more than three miles, "more than twice the distance from father's house to his farm!"[21]

Living arrangements for the officers were considered excellent. The messroom was very fine for a man-of-war, and the ten officers' staterooms opened into it. Phelps's was the most aft on the starboard side. Entering it, upon the right, was a walnut secretary bureau, and over it an oval mirror eighteen inches in diameter. In front of the bed, or berth, was a neat cornice with a decidedly neat pair of curtains made of worked muslin that reached to the deck. Over and about the berth were shelves for books and other items. Upon the left was a washstand with a large white china pitcher. A fine foot tub was set in the same stand. Near this was Phelps's old trunk, entirely hidden by a fine cushion of green, and across the foot of the berth was a flounce of the same material. The little room, approximately six and a half by nine feet, was not to be entered except at Phelps's invitation. Though one of the smallest, it was quite comfortable. Phelps selected it in preference to a larger room because of the skylight, which threw light directly upon the secretary. One drawback was that the pantry door opened directly opposite his door, but that was of little consequence.[22]

During a dinner party given for the *Susquehanna*'s officers by Commodore R. F. Stockton at the Philadelphia Navy Yard, Phelps was scheduled for the watch.

About 3 o'clock, Mr. [Isaac N.] Brown, the 1st Lieut. came on board and offered to keep my day's duty . . . as Lt. Brown had duties requiring his presence on board & could attend to mine at the same time. I hurried ashore mounting the "full undress tog" and was at the Commodore's by 4 O'C, the given hour. Mrs. Howell [daughter of the Commodore], wife of Lt. [John C.] Howell of our ship, and three other unmarried daughters of the Commodore, and about a dozen Navy officers made up the party. The eldest of the single daughters fell to my share (let me add the prettiest) and I really enjoyed what in general I dread, a ceremonious dinner party.[23]

In the same letter, Phelps wrote of his new shipmates:

We are getting together a fine crew, and as we have a clever set of officers, we are likely to have little trouble. Our Captain [Joshua Sands] is a queer little fellow—little but old—and is somewhat shaky in certain particulars but upon the whole, a very clever, good natured, tolerably easily managed individual. He has killed his man upon more than one occasion, and is somewhat affected as MacBeth's wife was when she charged the Dr. to cure her of "that perilous stuff that weighs upon the brain." He dreams and comes on deck at untimely hours at night like a restless spirit, as if his bed were badly made & served him poorly.

Our mess has twelve members, Howell the 2nd Lt. being caterer. He graces one end of the long mess table, the 1st Lt. being always, by prescriptive right, at the other. Upon the right

USS *Susquehanna*—After a decade of shore duty, Phelps returned to sea aboard this side-wheeler man-of-war in 1857. Attached to the Mediterranean Squadron, the *Susquehanna* supported the first attempt at laying the transatlantic cable and helped suppress William Walker's filibusters in Nicaragua. (U.S. Naval Historical Center)

of the 1st Lt. I sit & upon the left [Paul] Shirley, the remainder of the mess being promiscuously seated about the table.

Of the 1st Lt. [Isaac Newton Brown] I can say little. He is, perhaps too much like myself in certain items for me to readily understand him. Cold, cautious, quick to see an advantage, and not slow to avail himself of it. Of fine talents and good attainments, & withall honorable & conscientious. Voila the man whom I already like and believe to have under all a warm current that will not fail in the hour of need. On the outside there is a clammy coldness that serves to cover a true man. Let me see if this proves true.

Howell is the fancy man of the mess—bold, generous, social & popular, in short, an excellent messmate and leading spirit. His wife has ample fortune & he is able to have things in better style than the rest of us; but withall has no disposition to run the mess into excess. He is sensible & intelligent and well enough looking for common purposes. We were shipmates long years since in the *Columbus* 74 and have many old memories to rake up which from time to time make themselves heard & draw us more together than is the case with myself & others.

For an idler, such as the surgeon, purser or Marine officer, a cruise in the Mediterranean Sea in this ship is scarce more than a yachting trip; but for the regular officers of the ship it is something more; for they have the ship to manage, discipline to maintain & keep the idlers themselves straight.

Just out of Havana on their shakedown cruise, before heading to the Mediterranean, the wardroom officers invited Captain Sands to dinner in their mess, and the stories soon turned to adventures during the Mexican War. Phelps wrote to Lizzie:

The Captain commanded one of the gunboat steamers in the famous musquito fleet, and it would astonish you to have heard related by my messmate, Dr. Ninian Pinkney (the same one who aspired to the Senate from Maryland) and who viewed it at a distance, the pitch we had at the Castle of San Juan de Ulloa one morning. In truth, I make no question that devil may care feat of ours will cling to us all as long as we live for certainly no one who saw us run into the very jaws, as I may say, of that great stronghold ever expected to see one of us come away to tell the tale and we confess to few anticipations of again sipping julips in Yankee land.

The leisurely trip to Havana was just what Phelps needed to help him regain his sea legs. "Water spouts, lunar rainbows, vivid and incessant electrical phenomenon [*sic*] are daily & mighty treats with us," he wrote. "Yet would I give half these for one glass of ice-water. We miss it so much in this unaccustomed heat."

Now a lieutenant but not having been to sea for a decade, Phelps found himself expected to:

> perform duties I never before attempted, and after that long absence from the sea, no wonder. I find myself at a loss, frequently, utterly out, but there is a way of looking wise or indifferent, as the case may be, seeming to direct yet in fact following, trusting to force of routine upon the seamen & divine Providence to be helped out. Either I have the best of fortune or have enacted my part to a fraction, for thus far things have gone on all right and I have sometimes been in tight places. I am more convinced than ever of the necessity there is to keep sea going men from becoming rusty.

An accident marred their first days at sea: a seaman, ill with a fever, fell out of his hammock and struck his head, causing an inflammation of the brain from which he never recovered. Using Phelps's prayer book, "Brown read the service in a very impressive manner and the body was committed to the deep; one plunge and all of life was shrouded forever from those of earth."[24]

Phelps had considered the possibility of Lizzie and their daughter, Sally, following the ship to the Mediterranean, but he was not sure it would be practical. Apparently none of the other officers intended their families to join them, and being alone in a strange land, unable to speak the language, would make living difficult at best.

> Howell thinks his wife will be more comfortable at home. Brown's wife carries on his farm or plantation during his absence. Shirley seems to be doubtful, non-committal. The other two Lieuts. are not married. The purser is a bachelor, two of the Drs. do—about Dr. Pinkney I know nothing.[25]

{ 83 }

While Phelps and the other officers and men were getting the *Susquehanna* ready for their Mediterranean cruise, events to the south would quickly change their plans. William Walker, from Tennessee, had landed in Nicaragua in 1855 with a small band of followers, known as filibusters, to aid the "democratic" party in another of its numerous civil wars. Walker had already made an attempt to "colonize" Baja California and Sonora, with an eye on their gold and silver deposits. His expeditions eventually failed, and he next turned his attention to Nicaragua. With tremendous economic potential but no political stability, the country was a natural for filibusters. Walker, with backing from Cornelius Vanderbilt, landed in Nicaragua in May 1855 with a fifty-seven-man army, and joined the rebels. Successful in overthrowing the government, Walker became commander-in-chief of the army and de facto head of the government.[26]

Following recognition of the new Nicaraguan government by the Pierce administration, some two thousand Americans came in search of land grants, many with the hope of introducing slavery, which had been abolished thirty years earlier. Reviled in the Northern press, Walker soon found himself with more serious problems. The other Central American countries had united, supported by a now alienated Vanderbilt, and were moving against him. The deteriorating situation prompted the Pierce administration to increase its naval presence off Nicaragua, and the *Susquehanna* received orders to proceed to Greytown, on Nicaragua's east coast.

Phelps, greatly disappointed, began to think seriously about his family and career. "I find it hard to go off and leave my young wife & child," he wrote. My poor wife has borne it bravely, but her letters are very sad. The Navy is no profession for a married man."

Phelps was not alone in his feelings. "Her officers and men," he wrote of the *Susquehanna,* "being as discontented men as could be found; for this was a poor exchange for the straits and most of them believed it would detain the ship here permanently."[27]

Their fears were soon realized.

The harbor of San Juan de Nicaragua, or Greytown, is one of the most miserable of all the wretched towns I have visited

upon the Gulf of Mexico. A few frame houses of little preten-
tion and a number of huts suffice to house its 30 or 40 foreigners and some 250 natives. The sight [*sic*] is nearly level with the
waters of the river, and is surrounded by swamps and a dense,
impenetrable tropical vegetation. How wretched it must appear
to the deluded recruits who come out to join the standard of
Walker under the belief that the country is a kind of Eden,
where nature proclaims "here man labors not, but gathers of
the abundance of my spontaneous offerings" and that they
have but to seize upon the wealth everywhere abounding! To
meet with such squalid, miserable poverty must be disheartening indeed . . . it is very unhealthy for the stranger. Walker's
men die in great numbers.

So far as I can judge . . . it is entirely false that Walker has any
partisans, so to speak, in Central America. It is a clear case of
forcing himself upon a people distracted by civil broils, ener-
vated of race and climate by the force of desperate followers,
only too willing to do violence. Nominally he is the head of the
democratic party—in reality he has no party save those who are
obliged to act as such through fear. He has probably about
1500 men, ill fed and still more illy paid, desperate fellows who
are known among us as "shoulder hitters," "strikers," "bounc-
ers," "killers," & the like, ready to commit outrage & pillage
upon friend or foe except when Walker's restraining power is
at hand. Americans living in the interior told me they went well
armed, not on account of the natives but to save themselves
from their countrymen and that these were committing constantly the most atrocious outrages.

He is now at Leon and awaits the onset of San Salvador,
Honduras, Guatemala & Costa Rica. These last had overthrown him it is thought, but for the terrible epidemic that
broke up their army & destroyed two thirds of it. Walker's force
is now greatly increased and he has abundance of arms, powder,
cannon etc. and I hardly think they will be able to overthrow
him. Recruits reach him in numbers sufficient to fill the
vacancies from death & 1500 effective & desperate men will

constantly be at his command. I am persuaded that all Nicaragua would rise as one man to shake off the yoke, if they had hope of success. It is shameful that our country should have recognized a government upon the footing of Walker's.[28]

Walker had raised men and equipment by enlisting the support of Southern sympathizers. On September 22, 1856, he legalized slavery and held out the promise of Nicaragua as a Southern satellite. Just as the situation was becoming more chaotic, the *Susquehanna* was released with orders to proceed to the Mediterranean.

Walker lasted another six months. By late April 1857, he was besieged in the town of Rivas, with total destruction only a matter of time. Rather than stay and be butchered, Walker surrendered to Capt. Charles H. Davis of the USS *St. Mary's* and was transported back to New Orleans, where he was greeted by wild celebrations. With a tremendous outpouring of support, Walker plotted his return.

The *Susquehanna's* crew was delighted finally to be heading for the Mediterranean, but their trip was a rough one. After spending a few days in the Azores, the *Susquehanna* headed to Gibraltar for coal, but found the supply short due to the large number of British transports returning troops from the Crimea. Captain Sands decided instead to run down the coast to Málaga for coal. While there, Phelps had a chance to travel to Granada and spend three days exploring the Alhambra, the world's most beautiful example of Moorish architecture and where "Columbus went to sue for the aid that was to give Castile and Arragon [*sic*] a new world." The roads leading to the interior of Spain were considered dangerous due to "highwaymen," but instead "we were well nigh killed with dust," wrote Phelps. "All the world knows that Spanish dust out dusts all others."[29]

After several port visits, Phelps decided to send for Lizzie and Sally to join him in Genoa, where the *Susquehanna* would spend the winter. Lizzie booked passage on a steamer and joined him in Naples. For her the crossing had been an adventure and the sights of Mount Vesuvius, a wonder. She was full of enthusiasm and interest during a trip to the volcano's rim. With the assistance of a guide, who gave her a strap from his shoulder to hold for stability, Lizzie hiked to the top. Phelps followed close behind and was impressed with his wife's physical ability, especially because the snow was very slippery, the lava flows were very bad, and the volcanic ash and sand were very deep. Phelps noted that it was no little effort for a woman, and that many men had to be pulled or carried up.[30]

Lizzie rented an apartment in Genoa and established herself and Sally for the winter. Considering the initial fears of a long separation, Phelps's decision to send for his family proved to be the right one. "What between ship board duties and running ashore to look after the little family the time flies apace."

In the spring the *Susquehanna* moved to Spezia; Lizzie and Sally followed. Life was idyllic as the ship lay quietly at anchor. Only the arrival of the weekly mail from home created any excitement. Phelps planned to have Lizzie and Sally spend six to eight months in Spezia and located his family in a nice apartment. Their quarters were three floors up, but the rooms were cozy and neat, and the view from every window and the little balcony was very pleasing. Lizzie had met a number of English-speaking people and looked forward to passing a pleasant summer. Sally quickly met the local children and quickly became almost fluent in Italian.

His status as a family man was brought home to Phelps when he came across a newspaper advertisement. "A notice that the Vice Roy of Egypt wanted some English officers, accustomed to manage boats and to making astronomical observations, to join an expedition to explore the sources of the Nile quite aroused my spirit for that sort of thing," he wrote. "Were [*sic*] I alone nothing could have offered more to my fancy."

Still, Phelps was not disappointed. He was particularly amazed and delighted in watching Sally grow. "Sally will soon know more of Italian than English and will return home quite an adventuress," he noted with pride.[31]

On board ship, the crew took some delight in a directive from the Navy Department that forbade officers to have their families live aboard ship. On the *Susquehanna* it affected only Captain Sands and his new, young wife. Sands was quite upset that he had to move her into the city.

The first attempt to lay a transatlantic cable brought orders for the *Susquehanna* to proceed to England to assist the joint Anglo-American operation. The ship got under way from Spezia in May 1857, and after stops at Lisbon and the Isle of Wight, arrived at Gravesend, twenty miles down the Thames from London. There she rendezvoused with the USS *Niagara,* which would carry half of the cable.[32]

The great undertaking was already encountering difficulties, and upon their arrival the crew of the *Susquehanna* were greeted by accusations of whose fault it was.

The object for which we have come are [*sic*] likely to be frustrated, as it is believed the wire will not be ready in time to lay it down this summer. An attempt has been made to saddle the blame upon the *Niagara* as not being calculated to carry her portion of the cable. The captain of her, however, has destroyed this pretence by showing that he is ready to give them the space they require and in the manner of form required. This has taken the Directors rather aback, and they are now evidently hard pressed to find some other means of shirking responsibility, which they had hoped to force upon us. Capt. [William] Hudson has proposed to the company *to cut his ship* so as to meet their requirements . . . the impression is that the cable will not be laid this year. The stock has fallen from 50 per ct. premium to 20 or 30 below par. This shows how much faith has been lost.[33]

A mile south of Greenwich, British workers at the factory of Glass & Elliot were trying to finish construction on their half of the cable. The conducting wire consisted of seven no. 22 copper wires twisted into one strand about 1/16 inch thick, which was coated with gutta-percha to a thickness of 3/8 inch. The wire was then fed into a "serving" machine that wrapped the wire with threads soaked in a mixture of pitch, tar, oil, and tallow. Eighteen strands of no. 22 wire were then twisted around the finished cable. To allow for the tremendous strain on the cable at the midway point, the wire for that part was constructed with steel.

The cable would be laid across 1,690 miles of ocean from Valentia Bay, on the southwest coast of Ireland, to Trinity Bay in Newfoundland, in water up to two and a half miles deep. The screw frigate *Niagara*, the longest and largest vessel of her class, would carry the cable constructed by Newall's works at Birkenhead, and the Greenwich wire would be carried on the British steamer HMS *Agamemnon*. The *Niagara*, with the help of the *Susquehanna*, HMS *Leopard*, and HMS *Cyclops*, would lay the cable until it reached the mid-Atlantic, where the two cables would be joined and the fleet would then continue until it reached Newfoundland. With good weather and good luck, it was hoped to be able to lay the cable in ten days.

The HMS *Agamemnon* was specially modified to carry the Atlantic telegraph cable. Her guns were removed, she received a lighter mast, and her engines were moved aft so the heavy cable could be carried amidship. The twelve-foot-high, forty-five-foot diameter coil was so heavy it increased the *Agamemnon*'s draft from nineteen to twenty-five feet. A special iron guard was constructed around her propeller to keep the cable from fouling.

The *Niagara* was not as well suited as the *Agamemnon* for carrying cable, but Captain Hudson nevertheless made good on his promise to do what was necessary, removing a number of stanchions and cutting up the ship's wardroom to receive the cable.

At the end of July, the Telegraph Squadron assembled in the Cove of Cork, where experiments were carried out with the cable. The squadron then sailed for Valentia Bay. On August 4, the end of the cable was landed by sailors from the American ships on the shores of Valentia Bay and presented to the lord lieutenant of Ireland. Signals were then sent underwater from a temporary station to the terminus of the 1,250 miles of wire on board the *Niagara*, to make sure continuity was maintained.

Following the connection of the cable, an elegant "dejeuner" was held in a storehouse tastefully fitted up for the occasion: adorned with flags, wreaths of evergreens, and flowers. The *Susquehanna*'s officers, led by Captain Sands and Lieutenant Brown, participated in the endless toasts and then listened to a long-winded speech by the lord lieutenant. Following a humorous and graceful toast to "the

Ladies," a ball was held in the storeroom. "The blooming & fair Irish girls," Phelps wrote, "manifested their satisfaction by a hearty display of dancing and much as the song ran 'we danced all night 'till broad daylight and went home with the gals in the morning.'"[34]

In a letter to Lizzie, Phelps described events of the next day:

At daylight the *Niagara* broke the cable that had payed out but a few miles. The shore end is very heavy and difficult to manage having been made to resist the actions of the currents and undertow upon rocky bottom. This portion extends only for a few miles in the Bay to a depth of some 30 or 40 fathoms water. Two days were employed in recovering the cable, renewing the splice, connection etc. At length we made a fair start and slowly worked our way seaward. This was on the night of the 7th.

What a pleasant sight, five men of war of two great nations starting out together to perform an undertaking [that] should become the bearer of thoughts over the boundless waste of waters, telling its tale from shore to shore in one quarter of a second.[35]

Attempting such a new, Herculean task entailed a great deal of uncertainty.

Many conjectures are made and frequently fears magnify each slight change of course or speed. Two or three times we have been greatly excited at seeing the *Niagara* suddenly reverse her engines and stop, showing that all does not work smoothly.

The soundings from the coast of Ireland westward gradually deepen for a distance of 200 miles till the depth is about 400 fathoms when suddenly it becomes 1700 and 2000 fathoms. Those who did not feel faith in the complicated machinery that had been placed on board the *Niagara* and *Agamemnon* for paying out purposes felt that the trial would come at this great bank and the result proved the correctness of these views. The wire was payed out without difficulty till the 1700 fathom depth was reached, when the two miles of cable suspended from the

stern of the ship brought a heavy strain upon the machinery
and showed its imperfections. On the morning of the 11th the
machinery stopped revolving and the cable broke. Three hundred and thirty five miles were lost. The ships had actually run
275 miles.

We are apt to think that the English engineers manage
things better than others but this is proof how unjust such an
idea is. The cable was lost through bad engineering and they
even blundered between geographical and statute miles and in
this way were left with too little cable to make the trial again
after the loss of 335 miles. The affairs of the Company altogether were badly managed.[36]

The Telegraph Squadron remained for a short while to conduct experiments in splicing cables in midocean. After three unsuccessful
attempts, the *Leopard* and *Cyclops* headed for Cork, and the *Niagara,
Agamemnon,* and *Susquehanna* set their course for Plymouth. The
voyage was exciting, for the three ships engaged "in a little ship
racing," according to Phelps. "The *Niagara* we all know was built to
out go the world. The *Agamemnon* is one of the crack ships of the English Navy. We beat her easily. The *Niagara* can beat us in a breeze, but
without it she cannot. In short the *Susquehanna* sustains her credit."[37]

The *Susquehanna* remained at Plymouth while the directors of the
company determined their next course of action. They were in favor
of another attempt in October, but the ship captains, led by the captain of the *Agamemnon,* were adamantly opposed. While the company
debated the options, Phelps managed to see some of the city.

Mr. Brown and I went on shore one day, landing away from all
towns, and walked a circuit of several miles around to the rear
of Plymouth, and found many pretty walks. It is a great Naval
and Military station and partakes of the characters of such
towns. One of its features being the great preponderance in the
number of women. Devonshire women are famous throughout,
I believe, for personal advantages, though not for other excel-
lencies of more importance. I was certainly struck with the

number of women, and of the pretty ones among them, whom we met in the streets.[38]

Weeks dragged on, and the *Susquehanna* remained at Plymouth even though Captain Sands had orders to return to the Mediterranean. Phelps and the other officers were fuming.

Captain Sands persists in his course of obstinate disobedience of orders. What the secret working is that he has devised that renders him so brave when in general he is a very timid man in the face of orders, we do not know. He is very much changed in his conduct on board ship. Even now he and Mr. Brown are no longer on terms and all on board are deep in their denunciations of the poor old man whose cunning and duplicity have been brought so prominently into view.[39]

With all the captains opposed to an attempt in October, and the possibility of using the cable in the shallower Mediterranean to improve communications with India, where a bloody insurrection had broken out, the transatlantic attempt was postponed until the following summer.

In June 1858 the *Niagara* rendezvoused with the *Agamemnon* in the North Atlantic, where the cable was spliced together. The two ships then turned their bows east and west, respectively, and proceeded to their destinations. After several breaks, the cable was successfully landed, and on August 16, 1858, Queen Victoria sent President James Buchanan the first transatlantic cable message. The cable lasted just long enough for both nations to celebrate the achievement before it went silent. The loss of such a large investment and the coming political instability in the United States would preclude another attempt for years.

The *Susquehanna* returned to Spezia only to find orders awaiting her to proceed immediately to Central America. Once again William Walker had returned to Nicaragua. On October 25, 1857, Lizzie and Sally said good-bye and sailed home from Genoa; one hour later the *Susquehanna* departed for Central America. "I watched your little steamer," Phelps wrote to Lizzie, "till night closed her in with wonderful interest."[40]

The *Susquehanna*'s deployment back to Central America and its subsequent effect on his family life greatly irritated Phelps.

There appears to have been about the usual amount of geographical knowledge displayed, and as much care evinced for economy of service in the issue of order changing our station & as is the case, it was the result of pleasing political friends. Our Navy is sadly in want of some head in the Department, having entire disposition of detail, that is conversant with naval matters. A Secretary just begins to learn something of the affairs of the service when his four years have expired and he retires to give place to another wholly ignorant and thus the best interests of the Navy languish, and great inconvenience and expenditures arise.

The *Susquehanna* made good time as she started across the Atlantic. Upon reaching the trade winds, she unshipped the buckets from her side wheels and relied on her sails. Once she reached the windward passage, steam power was again used. Passing to the north of Cuba, the ship sailed through the Old Bahama Channel. Phelps acted as pilot through the channel and made wonderful time, avoiding the longer detour south of Cuba.

The prospects of getting home appeared grim for the crew, and morale left much to be desired. Phelps felt that government timidity and incompetence were making a bad situation worse.

So long as Walker's desperados are allowed to leave the United States for Nicaragua, we shall likely be kept in Central America as a police upon these dainty pirates, who if they must meet with reverse we must succour to receive with all possible care instead of stringing them up as pirates are usually treated. These marauders are it appears in degree different . . . these rascals are too great villains to be punished for offenses but are on the contrary, outlaws as they are, watched over and conveyed about even in public ships. If left to his fate, Walker had long since perished and the Gov't has only itself to thank for the new difficulties he is causing. If they would allow us to exterminate the pirates we would be better satisfied.[41]

Walker managed to land some of his men and supplies on Nicaragua's Atlantic coast under the watchful eye of the USS *Saratoga*, but was unable to proceed inland because the *Saratoga*'s captain would not allow him to steal the boats he needed. On December 8, 1857, Capt. Hiram Paulding arrived with the steam frigate *Wabash* and put ashore for a short meeting with Walker. With the broadside guns of the *Saratoga* trained on Walker's camp and a landing force of 100 marines and 250 sailors, Paulding ordered Walker to surrender or be "cut to pieces." After the meeting, Walker announced that he had agreed to surrender and be transported back to the United States once again.

The *Susquehanna* arrived at Greytown on December 13, and was assigned the task of capturing Col. Frank Anderson, the last of Walker's filibusters. Anderson and his band had made their way eighty-five miles upriver before Paulding arrived, and had seized the fortified post of Castillo. With Walker captured and pressed by Costa Rican troops, Anderson blew up the post and headed for the coast. "Our crazy captain," as Phelps sometimes referred to Sands, organized a landing party and dispatched it into the interior to effect Anderson's surrender. The task proved easy, for they had traveled only nine miles upriver when they encountered the fleeing Anderson and his army of forty-five men.[42]

Phelps was pleased with the way Paulding and Sands had handled the situation. Despite "exceeding" their vague instructions from the Navy Department, for which they, along with Capt. Charles Davis, were vilified by Southern sympathizers, the captains had served their country well.

I am only delighted that these fellows have been baffled in their marauding attempt, and don't think it of much account what were the means adapted. There is a large party in our

country favoring such attempts and of this administration is un-
doubtedly afraid. . . . Walker must have been very badly off as
he could not pay some $200 for boats to go up the river and as
the *Saratoga* would not let him seize boats as had been his practice, he was detained till the Commodore came in the *Wabash*
and seized him.[43]

Phelps admired Paulding, whom he described as "a plain,
common sense, straight forward man, who performs what his good
sense tell [*sic*] him is his duty to his country." Speculating wishfully,
Phelps added, "Had he [Walker] been allowed to ascend the river
not a soul of his party would now have been alive to have left a peg
for 'sympathizers' to have hung their hats upon. A good riddance to
society would have been effected and no one could have talked."[44]

One year later Walker tried again, but this time his ship hit a reef
and sank sixty miles off the coast of Nicaragua. Rescued by the British
and returned to the United States, he tried a fourth time in 1860, this
time using Honduras as a staging area. Hard pressed again, Walker
surrendered to the British navy, expecting his usual treatment. This
time, however, he was turned over to Honduran authorities and sum-
marily shot in the public square of the little town of Truxillo.

The *Susquehanna* remained at Greytown, which was, according to
Phelps:

A horrid agglomeration of negro huts and white men's grog
shops. On board ship there are merely the "everyday duties" to
help time on; the weather is hot, and the mosquitos at night are
pungent. As there is no scenery other than a wilderness of rank
vegetation growing upon a flat marshy country, men must feel
the time drag heavily around. So it is for nearly everyone on
board; but for me the country presents another phase. I am a
born child of the tropical earth, loving the rays of the sun and
dreading the blast that comes from the kingdom of Wabasso.
I thrive in this land and feel the life current run strong. The
harbor presents a beautiful place for boat sailing. The country
offers tolerable shooting, wild hogs, curacoa bird etc.[45]

While hunting provided Phelps with an outlet and the officers' mess with fresh meat, the other officers were miserable.

For many of the mess, Howell for example—no—Shirley is a better representative, this is indeed a sorry place. How heavy life hangs upon their hands! Poor Shirley fails as plainly and certainly as ever poor fellow did. The purser has become a regular crusty growler. For him the East was the one thing desired; he had all his life striven to get there and just as he thought himself on the way, he must come to this horrid place. He has been changed from a man of pleasant mood and graceful humor to a degree of bitterness quite foreign to the man.

Brown is more of a caged hyena than ever. Restless, uneasy, with very few enjoyments that the other men relish and with no social qualifications. This is the last of all places for him.

In this tropical climate a sick list of about fifteen men was normal aboard a ship the size of the *Susquehanna*. On March 17, 1858, Ninian Pinkney, the ship's surgeon, reported to Captain Sands that one of the crew was ill with fever and vomiting. He soon returned and reported a second, then a third. The next day several more cases developed; then suddenly, within twenty-four hours, two men and a boy were dead, one having died in convulsions from "black vomit." Pinkney was not sure of the nature of the disease, but recommended to Sands that the ship leave the anchorage and cruise outside the harbor to be ventilated.

The *Susquehanna* got under way, and for five days cruised off the coast. The cases of fever moderated, and it was felt that the disease had run its course. Sands returned to Greytown but remained outside the harbor just in case. For three days everything was routine; then, on April 1, the fever returned, this time with a vengeance. Sands decided to head for Aspinwall, where he hoped to meet the *Jamestown*, which was en route to relieve the *Susquehanna*. On the way down the coast, Isaac Brown, Howell, Lt. Henry Queen of the Marine Corps, several engineers, and about forty men came down with the fever, and many others were complaining of symptoms.

Surgeon Pinkney determined that he was faced with a yellow fever epidemic and requested that the ship proceed at once to Pensacola, the nearest naval hospital in the United States. Sands agreed, and turned the ship north. After only a few hours, Dr. Pinkney reported that the disease was spreading at such a rapid rate that many of the sick would not survive the trip to Pensacola. He recommended that the ship head for Jamaica. Sands had been conserving coal, having barely enough to reach Pensacola, but now used every ounce of steam to reach Jamaica as quickly as possible, for his crew was succumbing at the rate of one an hour.

On April 4, 1858, Marine Corps lieutenant Henry Queen, a veteran of the Mexican War, died from the "black vomit." With the ship's company assembled and the flag lowered to half mast, his body was committed to the deep.

Phelps had so far been lucky, considering how sick he had been ten years before. With the exception of the surgeon and his aide, Phelps and the remaining healthy crewmen remained on deck as much as possible.

The *Susquehanna* arrived at Port Royal, Jamaica, at 8 P.M. on the night of April 5, with 103 men down with the fever. In the harbor was the HMS *Indus*, bearing the flag of Sir Houston Stewart. On board the *Indus*, a festive ball was in progress when the officer of the deck approached Stewart and informed him that the *Susquehanna* had entered the harbor, signaling her distressed condition. Houston immediately assembled his officers and ordered that all possible aid be given the *Susquehanna*.

The naval hospital on shore was at once made ready to receive the sick. The boats from the *Indus*, HMS *Imaum*, and HMS *Devastation* were fitted up with cots and brought alongside the *Susquehanna;* the sick were gently lowered aboard. All night the boats shuttled back and forth, and by 6 A.M., sixty-three of the most serious cases, including Howell, were in the hospital. Brown elected to remain with the ship and return to the states.

The next morning all the clothing and bedding of the sick were removed from the ship and taken to a cay, where they were burned. The *Susquehanna* then proceeded to Kingston to take on coal, water, and provisions. With half his coal heavers and firemen down,

Captain Sands hired about thirty blacks to take their place. New cases of fever continued, and twenty-two more extremely ill men were transferred to the hospital before the ship left.

The only known course of action was to take the ship to a northern climate, so as soon as she had enough coal, the *Susquehanna* headed north. Before it departed Dr. Fredrick Rose, assistant surgeon on the HMS *Indus,* volunteered to accompany the *Susquehanna* to the United States and tend to the sick.

Pouring on all the steam she could muster, and all the sail she could carry, the *Susquehanna* steamed toward New York. The climate turned colder as the ship proceeded north, and life on deck for Phelps and the other two wardroom officers became more difficult. Sharing all the watches among themselves, they were determined to get their shipmates to safety. New cases diminished rapidly as soon as the ship reached cooler waters, and only two more died.

Flying the quarantine flag, the ship reached New York harbor on the evening of April 15, 1858, after a passage of five days. Isaac Newton Brown, five other officers, and fifty-seven men were landed and taken to the quarantine hospital. Those unaffected by the fever were removed to the quarantine grounds, where, by law, they could be held for thirty days. It was expected that the healthy seamen would have to remain for only a few days, but the mayor of New York City was sufficiently concerned that he arranged for extra policemen to be placed around the grounds to make sure no one left.

Before the yellow fever epidemic had run its course, half of the *Susquehanna*'s crew—155 men—had contracted the disease. Sixteen men died, the last in the quarantine hospital.[46] Newspaper accounts of the epidemic were flashed across the telegraph wires to all parts of the country, and when Lizzie saw the headlines the following day in Washington, she was frantic. Her father immediately wired friends in New York City, who telegraphed back that Phelps was not on the sick list.

After receiving a letter from her husband, Lizzie went to the nearby home of Henry Queen to comfort his wife. "I am feeling very sad after such a distressing interview," she wrote, "and realize more fully than before, if possible, how mercifully I have been spared such affliction."[47]

After being released from the quarantine grounds, Phelps noted that "there were none who entirely escaped the effects of the poisoned atmosphere in which we lived and even now I feel aches that are evident of its presence, but in general my health is good."

Phelps escorted Dr. Fredrick Rose to Washington after they were released. Following a tearful reunion with Lizzie and Sally, Phelps

> felt it my duty to devote to him all the time that Lizzie would spare me. The Senate invited him in upon their floor, an attention the more complimentary, since it was wholly spontaneous. There were no preparative notices of the Dr.'s visit or paper puff. It had been simply stated in the accounts published of our misfortune, that Dr. Rose had come a volunteer. It accidently [sic] became known to Senators that he was in the capitol, and as if by common consent, he was invited into the Senate chamber and received by the Vice President.
>
> I was called upon by the Chairman of the Committee on Foreign Relations for a statement of the circumstances attending our visit at Jamaica. But for the aid given us by the English there the ship could not have been got home, and many poor fellows owe their lives to their kind care. Congress will make some suitable acknowledgement.[48]

Congress passed a joint resolution that authorized the president to make a "suitable acknowledgment" to Sir Houston Stewart and the British naval and medical authorities in Jamaica. The resolution also authorized a special gold medal, with appropriate devices, to be struck and presented to Dr. Rose for his heroic service.

Back in New York harbor, the *Susquehanna* was towed to the Navy Yard. Long before it was discovered that mosquitos transmitted yellow fever, the only known way to decontaminate a ship exposed to the fever was to lower its temperature, so tons of ice and salt were mixed together and lowered into her hold. The ship was then sealed, and pumps were attached to draw out the "contaminated" air.

Phelps was greeted on his return to Washington by the same political firestorm over the retirement board that he had left two years earlier. Many of the 201 officers who found themselves released from active duty had been stunned. There were few public explanations or reasons given as to why they had been singled out. These men appealed to their political friends that a great injustice had been committed, and asked that the Navy allow them a hearing.

Unfortunately for the board, when Congress began to look into the accusations, it was found that the board had kept no record of deliberations. It was agreed by everyone that members of the board were outstanding naval officers, and therein lay the problem. As Congressman Warren Winslow put it:

> Of all the men in the world, the officers of the Navy are the least qualified to discharge judicial functions. There is no position in the world that so contracts the mind. With them, contempt of law and lawyers is proverbial. They scorn and condemn anything like the technicalities and formalities of law, the safeguard of the citizen, and set up their own weak, erring judgement as an infallible guide.[49]

The board had met in private and had often made their decisions based on ex parte evidence and their own personal knowledge. To make matters worse, some members were promoted as a direct result of the men above them being removed. So strong was the reaction to the board that it was often referred to as a star chamber or inquisition. Matthew Fontaine Maury, who was furloughed, was especially virulent in denouncing the board. He enlisted Senator Sam Houston of Texas, who launched a three-hour tirade on the Senate floor against the board and particularly Samuel DuPont's "criminal" influence on its decisions.

With no written record of deliberations, the findings of the board were portrayed by its critics as vague and bereft of logic. One passed midshipman claimed he was removed because the board found him physically unfit even though a surgeon had restored him to duty. In another case an officer claimed he did not "meet certain charges with the dignity and spirit of an officer and gentleman."[50] In other words, he was deemed unfit because he had refused to fight a duel. The board was reported to have gone so far as to inquire into one officer's marital problems.

On January 16, 1857, Congress passed an act that established a review system through which officers could request an inquiry into their dismissal and, if found fit, be restored to duty. A total of 108 officers went before the special court of inquiry, and 67 were restored to duty.

For Phelps and other junior officers, the restorations meant the chance of promotion had gone from slow to all but nonexistent. For example, the number of captains allowed by law was sixty-eight. The Register of 1857 showed only thirty employed, of whom thirteen were at sea. The captains restored to duty increased the number to seventy-five. By law there could be no promotion to captain until the list fell below sixty-eight, which would take years.

Phelps was determined to find a good job in the civilian sector and resign from the navy.

> I do not dislike my profession. It is a hopeless one, and the action of the courts of inquiry, of the Dept. and of Congress, have convinced me that it is a waste of life for me to remain longer in it. I may be obliged to, but will not if it can be avoided.[51]

Phelps hoped to get a well-paying job in industry, but railroads and large ironworks were the only ones that were prospering, and openings were rare. If nothing developed, he had heard that there was a mining company interested in opening a mine in Central America if current internal strife could be settled.

Phelps had no luck finding a suitable position, so he, Lizzie and Sally were off for duty at Sackets Harbor, New York, on Lake Ontario. They had no sooner settled into their quarters than he received new orders to proceed to Panama for duty aboard the corvette *St. Mary's*.

Departing New York on November 20, 1858, Phelps, along with twelve officers and seventy-five seamen, headed for Panama. Reaching the isthmus and crossing to the Pacific, the relief crew for the *St. Mary's* found that she was not expected to arrive there until February.

> So long as I felt that duty called me I made the best of it and came cheerfully. Now that I know that no public service required us to be here; that the Dept. should have known the

chances were greatly against the ship being here, I feel out-raged and hurt. It is precisely such miserable administration of Naval affairs that makes our profession become so irksome, so much disliked. Torn from our home by needless and cruel haste, ordered about (by Department clerks) without regard to life or expense; sent with the utmost indifference to our fami-lies when the necessities of the service force long and frequent separations. "Esprit du Corps" belongs wholly to the past. I find myself here, performing no service, absent from home without an object, exposed to a hot and sickly climate in the very midst of fever and expending most of my pay. My philosophy has left me.[52]

When February 1859 came and there was still no sign of the *St. Mary's*, the crew boarded the frigate *Saranac* and went looking for her. They found her at Acapulco and immediately returned on her to Panama, where they finally relieved her crew. Phelps threw himself into "breaking in a new crew and putting a ship to rights—from her trucks to kilson [keelson]. We have a fine ship of her class, and we flatter ourselves that she is in excellent order."

Restored officers who were returning to duty brought turmoil to the Home Squadron at Panama.

I have always been satisfied that the action of the Board for Re-tiring Officers would in due time be vindicated. It is already being brought to pass. We have two commanders in this squad-ron who have been restored and who have already given satisfac-tory proof of the justice of the original 15 [the board]. Congress has made a pretty mess of the matter and no one can see the end of the evil it has brought about.[53]

In a letter to Lizzie, Phelps noted an example.

A few days since I dined on board that magnificent ship the *Golden Age,* the one I came near going to Australia in some years since. She is one of the most splendid ships I ever saw, and to think that I might have been Captain of her, making about $1000 per month. Our poor skipper [Comdr. Robert Thorburn] at the dinner disgraced himself, offended the ladies by his rudeness, general and individual, and disgusted the guests, particularly Admiral [William] McClunney. Conversing with a young lady, the skipper asked "if she was acquainted with the sounding in Panama Bay?" Being told that she was not, he exclaimed "I had no idea you were so lamentably ignorant." "Mrs. Corwine," the captain added, "you don't eat, but you are fat enough now."

That Commander Thorburn was one of the "restored" officers only reinforced Phelps's belief in the just decisions of the board:

Heaven have pity on the men who could in sober state find conscience to reverse the dictums of the immortal 15! We have had two specimens here, ours and the skipper of the *Cyane*. The last crazy as a march hare, the other just what he says the Board retired him for, being "a damned fool." He seems perfectly aware of the charge the 15 had against him and in talking about it gives irrefutable proof of the truth of the finding.[54]

The days aboard the *St. Mary's* dragged on as she remained in Panama, and relations between Thorburn and his officers deteriorated. "Our skipper is beginning to come out and has quarrelled with almost all the mess except myself. We have not come in conflict as I have confined myself to my legitimate duties. He is weak and petulant—even foolish, but we will either keep him straight or *break him*."[55]

The vindication of the retirement board came all too swiftly. On April 8, 1859, the *St. Mary's* first lieutenant, James Moore, brought formal charges against Commander Thorburn. The *St. Mary's* officers testified at his court-martial that, in addition to his behavior on the *Golden Age*, there were numerous instances of intoxicated oaths spoken against the commodore and others. Phelps related one incident. When he was returning to the ship with Thorburn, their gig missed the gangway. Thorburn yelled at the men: "God-dam you— you sons of bitches—you God damned high binders."

Thorburn, in his defense, denied exhibiting scandalous conduct aboard the *Golden Age*. He admitted, however, the other charges, stating that often "I was in so highly nervous a state, as not to know the import of what I was saying." As to the incident with Phelps, he replied: "For it surely cannot have come to this in the Navy that a Comd'g Officer cannot speak in a loud tone of voice to a lubberly boat's crew . . . lest some of his junior officers should find fault with him therefore."[56]

Thorburn was convicted.

We have been forced by circumstances to deprive our Captain of his command. I cannot but feel sympathy, though I am satisfied of the justice that sends him forth. He was on the retired "leave list." Himself and friends do not seem to have known when he was well off, for there he had $1800 a year and no call to leave his family and home. With all the others, he helped on the howl of persecution and baseness in the part of the "board" . . . that sprung up over our land and brought Congress to meddle and do so much harm. This man was restored to the active list and sent out to command this ship. Before he had been two months in this position we preferred charges against him of varied character but all telling one tale—unfitness to command. He is given a "court of inquiry" which sends him home with our report proven and we await another Commander. His restored career is short. His case goes forth among many that will vindicate that much reviled board of fifteen. But alas our poor Navy will be long in recovering from the effects of the restorations and the foolish and unwise laws of Congress. See even how much our poor skipper has suffered by a mistaken tenderness of that body.[57]

Phelps was not feeling well, having problems with a swollen liver, when another restored officer, Comdr. William Porter, arrived to assume command. Son of the famous commodore and David's older brother, William came to be known by the nickname "Dirty Bill." He and Phelps got along surprisingly well, going hunting and enjoying trips ashore that aided Phelps in returning to good health.

At the end of July, the *St. Mary's* sailed from Panama for San Salvador. There, to his regret, Phelps was ordered to the USS *Cyane* as the ship's second lieutenant. He appealed his orders but received no reply, so he unhappily watched the *St. Mary's* sail for the Gulf of California. "I did not like the change," Phelps noted. "The *St.M.* is a happy ship, this is the reverse. Capt. [Samuel] Lockwood is one of the 'restored' and the officers of the ship had only too much cause to know how just was the decision of the original 'board.'"[58]

Duty aboard the *Cyane*, which had sailed down the coast to Nicaragua, was arranged so that in port, two lieutenants kept all the watches for two days and then had two days off. Phelps took the time off to range far and wide into the interior, and became enamored with the idea that, were it not for incessant civil war and incursions by filibusters, a small investment would quickly grow into a fortune.

In December 1859 the mail brought a reply from the Navy Department granting Phelps's appeal not to be detached from the *St. Mary's,* so he quickly left the *Cyane*. While waiting for a steamer bound for Panama, Phelps decided to do some exploring and ascend the volcano El Viejo. After staying the night at a small hacienda, he was up at 4 A.M. and in the saddle. He started on horseback entirely alone and traveled as far as the path led or the horse could go. Phelps turned his horse to graze and, armed with a gun and heavy knife, began the ascent on foot. The undergrowth toward the top was very dense, and he was forced to cut his way through. Wild animals ranged freely, and Phelps noted their trails going in all directions.

Phelps reached the summit about 2 or 3 P.M. The view was spectacular. All of Nicaragua and parts of Honduras and El Salvador were before him. At his feet upon one side lay the great plains of Leon like a beautiful painting. Upon the other side lay another great plain bounded by the distant and beautiful mountains of Segovia and Honduras. He also could see the great Lake Nicaragua and the Gulf of Fonseca, each studded with lofty volcanic island cones. Cone after cone rose from the line of the volcanic ridge of which El Viejo was part. Phelps could see into four craters. The wind blew strong and cool, and he soon found himself using the high grass as a screen. The breeze moaned among the scattered pines, reminding Phelps of the blasts that blew across Lake Erie.

Phelps enjoyed the time at the summit and regretted not having made arrangements to stay overnight. He could not change his plans now, however, for his horse would have been food for "tigers," and he had had nothing to eat since that morning. Regretfully, he began his descent, following his own trail. Reaching his horse, Phelps found that the wild cattle of Don Pedro's estate had managed to reach a pair of saddle bags, which he had hung in a tree, that contained food for dinner. He had ridden many miles, had been nine hours on foot, and was exhausted. Making the best of it, he found a place to bathe in a stream. The water was colder than anything Phelps had ever experienced in these lands—it nearly froze him—but the effect was magical, and he sprang lightly into the saddle. On his way back to the ranch, he shot four turkeys. Phelps arrived at the ranch at dark, his trip having lasted fourteen hours.

Phelps returned to Panama and found himself attached to the steam frigate *Saranac* until the return of the *St. Mary's*. He was praying for her prompt arrival, for "court martials are to convene as soon as the *Cyane* can be got down to this port, and I shall find myself in the midst of the troubles, myself a troublesome witness, which I had hoped to evade by this journey."[59]

Things worked out well, for when Phelps found the *St. Mary's* was still not expected for several months, he decided to write Lizzie and ask her and Sally to visit him in Aspinwall. They arrived in early 1860, and remained for five weeks.

In early April, Phelps wrote to Whittlesey:

The *Cyane*, which I left in December last, has been here and for two months court martials were constantly sitting on board trying the Captain and officers. The former is a "restored" commander and has been reputed crazy for some years. All these troubles grew directly out of his want of sense and his dishonesty—another instance of the justice done the original "board" and the injustice to the service of the subsequent action of Congress and the President.[60]

Lizzie and Sally's departure made the days pass slowly and the prospects appear grim. "So much of our cruise has been passed in this place and its sameness," Phelps wrote, "with the always dull monotony of men of war life are enough in themselves to leave one exhausted."

One thing that aggravatingly brought his life and future into focus were the numerous people returning to the East via Panama, having made their fortunes in the California goldfields. "I saw the arrival here of two young men who six months since had not a dollar, now having each $40,000 cash in hand, having sold half of a silver vein they discovered for $80,000 & are now gone to the U.S. to see their friends."

Congress, meanwhile, had voted a substantial pay raise for the navy, but Phelps felt they were missing the point. It was not the pay, but the prospects for a career, that mattered most:

I question if it has added one iota to the zeal or efficiency of the Navy. Some officers with large families will no doubt re-member with satisfaction the increase in pay—the great ma-jority scarcely think of it today. As for myself, I would have vastly preferred to have had my old pay reduced to the lowest "living point" and have seen the service placed upon a proper footing. It would be a simple problem for any one to solve to find how, with the present expenditure of money, a satisfactory reserved list could be established and maintained; a healthy activity in promotion created; officers at a proper time of life, considering the character of sea life, brought to fill the places of command, requiring physical activity quite as much as judgement, and in their old age be left to enjoy peace and quiet on shore; how zeal and proficiency would, or could, be made then to count on the long road of promotion, doing away with the present life killing system whereby it is barely necessary for an officer to perform after almost any manner the duty assigned him to insure promotion at equal pace with the best officer in the Navy.

We see Captains of ships return from cruises whose vessels have been unsparingly condemned by examining boards for their state of inefficiency, given in turn—perchance even before their turn comes around—new commands and often the finest ships in the Navy. Lieutenants who are known to the service as worthless . . . are assigned often the most desirable situations. But the great evil is that there is nothing to strive for after examination that passes one from a midshipman's berth. It makes me sad to witness the dull chink the increase of gold had upon the Naval ear and no other proof is required of the nature of the disease we suffer from.[61]

Panama was constantly in a state of revolution, with different factions fighting for an independent isthmus, so the situation for travelers crossing to the Pacific was uneasy. When the steamship *J. L. Stevens* became disabled on her return trip from San Francisco, the passengers en route to California had to be put up at company expense. Anxious to see the passengers on their way, Capt. Allan McLane of the Pacific Mail Steamship Company asked Phelps to take command of its spare steamship *Washington* and sail her to San Francisco. Phelps and McLane had known each other since their days at the Naval School, and their friendship would prove fortuitous.

The *Washington* had recently had her hull repaired after running aground on a reef, and "was in appearance and almost in reality a hulk." After receiving permission to help get the passengers out of Panama, Phelps took command on a Friday, and on the following Monday afternoon received on board about four hundred passengers who could not be kept on shore because of the insurrection. The next day they proceeded to sea.

Never, perhaps, had a captain gone to sea with a greater complication of troubles. According to Phelps, the crew was a rascally set of worthless vagabonds picked up from the isthmus, or natives equally worthless through total ignorance of shipboard routine. Phelps turned the natives into firemen, coalers, servants, and deckhands. The officers were, with a few exceptions, unreliable and inefficient.

The ship herself was almost a wreck. The daily leak amounted to nine feet in the hold, and not a pump in the ship independent of the machinery could be made to work. The engines were completely out of repair, the rigging was gone, spars were rotten, and the decks leaked. The galley stoves would not burn fuel properly, the oven would not bake, and the cooks and bakers knew how to cook only native food.

For days Phelps had trouble providing for the nearly five hundred persons on board, and an even harder time keeping them in a good mood. Slowly he began to improve the situation by getting cooks and bakers from among steerage passengers, and asking other passengers to replace crewmen down with the fever.

The leaking boilers would not make enough steam, and the men wilted before them. Phelps had to exert tact to keep the passengers quiet and to present a stout front to give them confidence, "for many thought they were upon their last voyage in this world." Eight hundred miles below San Francisco, a little above Cabo San Lucas, Baja California, the first assistant engineer, Mr. Cox, burned the starboard boiler so that its supporting arches collapsed, and there was imminent danger that it would give out, scald to death those at work before it, and leave the *Washington* to drift until she could fall in with another steamer. The weather was heavy, and the wind was obstinate—a very disheartening situation. Phelps treated the boiler with great care and made it last until they reached San Francisco.

The next night, fire broke out beneath the aft galley. The heat of the stove, badly placed upon the deck, had been so great as to char the deck through; when air reached it, flames burst forth. Fortunately, the blaze was quickly contained, for fire aboard a wooden ship was often catastrophic. Phelps managed the situation by cutting away the burned areas and securing the stove with fresh timbers. He also posted a continuous fire watch.

The passengers were pretty much kept in ignorance of both mishaps. In a good-humored way they settled down to such amusements as could be provided, hopeful of arriving safely. After a twenty-one-day passage, the *Washington* finally arrived at San Francisco on October 10, 1860.

After taking a few days to visit the Napa Valley and White Sulphur Springs, Phelps returned to Panama. A short time later, "the only officer in the whole Navy who will have made a complete cruise confined to this coast of Central America" was finally relieved, and sailed for home.[62]

Phelps returned to Washington, where he found his daughter recovering from the whooping cough and a country becoming critically ill. Abraham Lincoln was now president-elect, and efforts to heal the deep divisions between North and South had all but ceased.

> Our poor country is in such a sad condition, that I have not the heart to plan anything that has not for its end to wait and hope for some change that may offer a little brightness where all is now so dark. It does appear to me as if the Republicans are determined to split our country to atoms, to force us to civil war. I am troubled to know how to act. I feel that the border slave states are right in the course they have adopted and in their demands. I recognize the right of revolution under wrong unredressed and I consider the policy of the Northern party as aggressive. Shall I permit myself to be drawn then into civil war where my sense of justice and sympathies are against me? My allegiance is to the U.S. and by no means to Ohio. I know no state. But what am I to think of an intolerant Administration representing even a minority of the people of the north and no one of the southern half? An Administration which as a party, in my view, is as much with secession in its action as are the seceders themselves. I believe many of the leading spirits in the Republican party in Congress desire as much to divide our country as does the most rabid man in South Carolina. I am soon to be under the orders of that party which I do not and cannot believe does represent the will of the people of my country. I see little hope of compromise. Shall I lend myself an instrument to sustain a party Govt against those who, I think, justly demand rights that will be denied?[63]

The reality of approaching war became clear when Lizzie's father received a letter from his longtime friend Jefferson Davis, offering him a commission in the Confederate army. Lieutenant Colonel Maynadier, who was from Maryland and whose relatives sided with the South, declined the offer shortly before Fort Sumter was fired upon. For Phelps the reality came with the simple words "Report for special duty . . . ."

CHAPTER FIVE

ℰℐℴ

Mongrel Service

W ITH THE MASS resignations of officers loyal to the Southern
states, an unprecedented opportunity for advancement awaited
Phelps and his fellow junior officers. New assignments awaited as
ships of the line arrived back in the United States following their
recall from faraway duty stations. The United States had announced a
blockade of the South's coastline on April 19, 1861; and these ships,
soon to be joined by many more, would need experienced officers.
Phelps, however, found himself ordered to Cincinnati, Ohio, to help
the army with riverboats.

The importance of the rivers to states west of the Appalachian
Mountains, both North and South, was clear even before the Civil
War began. While railroads were increasing in importance, especially
north of the Ohio River, it was the broad rivers and their tributaries
that provided the lifeblood of the Western states. If the North could
control the rivers, it would tighten the coastal blockade and starve
the South of food and resources.

The West's rivers were also natural invasion routes into the heart of the Confederacy. The Cumberland River led directly to Nashville, and the Tennessee River cut south into Alabama and Mississippi. The Mississippi River was the grandest prize of all, for victory in the West would belong to whomever possessed it.

Confederate strategy was primarily defensive and centered on a series of fortifications to blockade the rivers. The Union army, on the other hand, never seriously considered building forts along the Ohio River, deciding instead to create a riverine navy to carry the war to the South.

To help the army get started, the secretary of the navy sent Comdr. John Rodgers to Cincinnati in late May 1861. Rodgers, whose father had been a commodore in the War of 1812, had joined the navy on April 18, 1828. He had had a varied naval career, including some ten years on the North Pacific Hydrographic Survey. Like all deepwater sailors, Rodgers knew next to nothing about riverboats. Assigned to the command of Maj. Gen. George B. McClellan, he was to advise the army about ordnance and crew.

River warfare was a new concept, and the first to recognize its potential value were businessmen who saw a quick profit. McClellan was besieged by those eager to get government contracts. McClellan stalled. "I have driven some men away in great disgust with my slowness merely because I was not willing to authorize them to go to work until I could ascertain what they intended to do. I feared the loss of time that would be caused by a failure far more than the loss of money."[1]

Rodgers's arrival gave McClellan what he needed: a naval expert who, along with riverboat owner Capt. William Kountz, would provide some guidance in forming a river navy. On May 19, McClellan sent Rodgers to find boats that he thought could be adapted to river warfare. McClellan's letter to Rodgers stated:

> If you find them adapted to the purpose, please close the purchase on such terms as you think the interests of the Government require. I would be glad to have you purchase proper tenders, if the Wrecking Company's boats have not the requisite

John Rodgers—Sent west to aid the army in creating an armed presence on the western rivers, Rodgers formed the nucleus of the Western Flotilla before being relieved of command. (U.S. Naval Historical Center)

speed. Should these boats not answer, I would be pleased to have you find others that will meet the purpose, and let me know, at once, the terms on which they can be had.[2]

Commander Rodgers went to St. Louis to look over the snag boat *Submarine No. 7*. This particular vessel had been recommended by James B. Eads, of the Missouri Wrecking Company, who had suggested that cotton bales be arranged on her deck to protect the battery and crew. Rodgers doubted its feasibility and returned to Cincinnati.

Believing he had approval from General McClellan to do what was necessary, Rodgers claimed jurisdiction over all Western shipping, and in the process, shifted the focus of business interests from McClellan to himself. With lucrative contracts now uncertain, the protests of business agents soon burned the telegraph wires to Washington.

Rodgers knew that river steamers were particularly unsuited for warfare. Their high-pressure boilers were on deck, all steam connections were entirely exposed, and the three-story, white pine superstructures were easy targets.

However, gunboats were urgently needed, so Rodgers, along with Samuel M. Pook, selected three steamers at Cincinnati on June 8. Pook, a naval constructor at the Washington Navy Yard, had been sent by Gideon Welles to help. The *Lexington, Tyler,* and *Conestoga* were deemed to be sound, above-average in strength and were purchased for $62,000.

Pook drew up plans that called for the thin pine deckhouses to be cut down and solid bulwarks constructed of five-inch oak planks. Through experimenting, Rodgers had found that five-inch oak would provide sufficient protection for the crew against the anticipated small arms fire from the river banks. The decks would be reinforced with timbers and beams to bear the big guns. The boilers would be dropped into the hold, and all steam pipes lowered as far as possible. "The boilers and engines," Rodgers wrote, "can not be defended against cannon shot. We must take our chances."[3]

Rodgers anticipated spending an additional $41,000 to complete the conversions. The contract with the Marine Railway and Dry Dock

Company of Cincinnati called for the work to be completed within nineteen days; there would be a loss of 10 percent of the contract for every day's delay after that time until delivery.

The Navy Department was soon deluged with complaints from Congress about the navy interfering with army authority. Gideon Welles, unaware of McClellan's instructions, hurriedly wrote to Rodgers that "the Department can not recognize or sanction any contracts for boats." Trying to impart some of the political pressure he was under, Welles continued: "There has been and is a great sensitiveness among the boatmen and others on the western rivers in relation to the water craft that might be required for the Army, and it was an especial object of the Department in framing your instructions to so restrict them as avoid jealousy."[4]

Rodgers immediately went to McClellan and got written approval for the purchase of the three boats and tersely telegramed Welles: "The written approval of a superior officer makes an act of purchase his own."[5]

Finding his position limited by the Navy Department, Rodgers received the specific authority he needed from McClellan on June 26, 1861. McClellan's orders stated: "You will . . . use your own judgement in carrying out the ends of Government. Spare no effort to accomplish the object in view with the least possible delay."[6]

Just as this crisis was settled, another appeared: low water, the bane of all rivermen. The Ohio River had begun to fall very rapidly. Rodgers ordered the unfinished boats to Cairo, Illinois, but he was too late. With what hands he could muster locally and with a number of carpenters still on board, the unfinished gunboats made it as far as Louisville, Kentucky, before being halted.

Phelps headed west from Washington in late June. He made a quick stop at Chardon to see his parents, arriving at midnight and leaving at ten the next morning. He reached Cincinnati on June 29, along with Lt. Rodger Stembel and Master Joshua Bishop. Stembel, an Ohioan who had joined the navy in 1832, did not expect to stay long in this backwater assignment; a promotion to commander and command of a ship on blockade duty were expected any day. Rodgers used Stembel and Bishop to begin recruiting crews for the gunboats. Phelps was immediately sent to Louisville to try and get the boats through to Cairo.

Phelps took the first train to Louisville, and on arriving, went to the riverfront and hired a small boat to take him the three miles below the city to the Portland bar. There he found the *Lexington* just above the entrance to a canal, and the *Tyler* and *Conestoga* about half a mile away. He boarded the *Conestoga* through a gun port because there was no gangplank. He was received by Capt. S. W. Shirley, president of the Louisville & Cincinnati Mail Boat Line.

Phelps's first impression was anything but favorable. The boats were, he wrote to Whittlesey, "but sorry looking craft; their huge wheel houses disproportioned to the squatty hull and the tall chimneys rather looking as if they would capsize the whole concern. Machinery, under high steam pressure, lies strewn about the deck inviting the attention of every shot that may come along."[7]

After consulting with Shirley, Phelps decided to dredge the bar to clear a path for the boats. This had never been attempted before but was deemed worth trying. Phelps examined the Portland bar and determined it needed to be deepened some two feet for a distance of three hundred yards. This would be difficult, for the current was very fast and full of sand from the island above. Just how unpredictable the river could be was demonstrated that night when a boat grounded on the bar, forcing the sand-laden current to open a new channel and fill in the old one.

Phelps hired three dredge boats, employed in the nearby canal extension, for seventy dollars a day each. Around noon on June 30, the boats began dredging, and after several hours Phelps found the channel deepened six inches, "by natural operation of currents."

While Phelps was still sounding, the grounded boat was freed and started up the river. After a short distance it became unmanageable in the current, drifted down across one of the dredge boats, and stuck fast. In half an hour a new bank was raised below the two boats. This ruined the day's work, and Phelps found by soundings that no one could guess where a channel would be found in the morning.

Phelps was quickly losing faith in the idea of using dredges to get the gunboats across the Portland bar and the many bars below. He wrote to Rodgers:

> I shall be able to judge of the prospect of getting out from the experience on this one, and by tomorrow evening, will feel able to give a decided opinion as to the propriety of attempting it if dredges fail here. I find it is no use talking to river men for opinions. Every man is on his own hook in this respect.[8]

After a second day of futile dredging and word from below of even lower water, Phelps abandoned the scheme. Another idea involved the use of barges as "camels"—attaching barges to each side of a gunboat to lessen her draft. Phelps discarded this plan as too expensive (each barge cost five thousand dollars) and not practicable.

So far there had been little public excitement about the gunboats. Small articles about them in the Cincinnati and Louisville papers were usually buried in the shipping news. Since the gunboats did not yet have their batteries or even small arms, Rodgers suggested that Phelps buy what guns he could in Louisville. Since Kentucky was still officially neutral, Phelps felt that trying to purchase arms would only draw the attention of the secessionists in the city, "who are reckless devils," and requested that arms be shipped from Cincinnati. In the meantime, the *Lexington* and *Tyler* would pull in their gangplanks at night, and all three boats would batten down the gun ports and stay anchored in the middle of the river.

Of the three timber-clad gunboats, the *Conestoga,* which would be Phelps's on arrival at Cairo, was the smallest. Each of her side wheels was driven by a single-cylinder, high-pressure reciprocating steam engine. The single-expansion, narrow-cylinder engines used horizontal fire tube boilers that returned the hot combustion gases from the rear, where they had been delivered by the furnace, through the boiler water to the front of the boiler. Very high pressure, exceeding one hundred pounds per square inch, combined with the large quantities of water at steaming temperatures, made the gunboats extremely vulnerable should a cannon ball rupture a boiler. With their towering chimneys to aid the draft of the boiler fires, they could make more than ten knots on a good day.

Their hurried conversions not yet complete, the *Conestoga, Tyler,* and *Lexington* were in dismal condition. "The more I examine the work on the '*Conestoga,*'" Phelps wrote to Rodgers, "the more disgraceful patching it appears to be. The *Lexington* is fairly done—the *Tyler* next best. The joinerwork is more like the work of Irish laborers than of mechanics."[9] The hulls would not take repeated groundings, Phelps reported to Rodgers, because the thwartship bars, replacing the beams removed when the boilers were lowered, had yet to be installed. In the *Tyler,* one could not get from aft forward without walking over the boilers.

The *Tyler* and *Lexington* had fine decks forward of the boilers that afforded ample space for berthing their crews, but there was no such space on the *Conestoga;* her boilers were close to the bow, and the machinery covered the midship deck to the officers' quarters. Phelps suggested building bulwarks on both sides of the top (or spar) deck, forward of the wheelhouse to the pilothouse. Another light deck or canvas awning could be thrown across to enable the crew to sling their hammocks.

The *Conestoga* had eight "staterooms" for the officers, each six feet square and containing two berths. There were two messrooms, each eight by ten feet. The aft cabin also served as a gunroom. There were no closets or pantries. The toilet facilities for the captain's "roundhouse" consisted of a narrow, inclined seat connected to a 45-degree, eight-inch zinc pipe that led to the outside.

The middle carline and two shorter ones in the *Conestoga* were held up by temporary posts, which would have to come down because they were in the way of the guns. Redesigned supports were needed, for if the posts were knocked out, the pilothouse, bell, and all would come crashing down.

With no immediate prospect of the gunboats passing the Portland bar, Phelps went to Cincinnati to consult with Rodgers. He also made arrangements for Lizzie to join him in Louisville, where he was staying at the Galt House. "I am afraid I am not very well calculated for bachelor life now," he wrote to her. "I have not cared to waste my sweets on woman kind here for so short a period."[10]

Upon returning to Louisville, Phelps found no change in the river. The situation was an uneasy one.

Kentucky is in a bad way. The reckless rebel portion of her people are determined to mix her up on the secession side. An extensive organization of her people exist here sworn to effect this and large numbers are organized in Tennessee ostensibly as Confederate troops, but really, it is said, for the purpose of invading their own state and put down Union men and Union sentiment. Home guards of Union men are being formed everywhere and are preparing for the struggle that is to come. I think the gov't should enlist men here to organize, just over the river if it suits best, to be prepared for the worst and to protect Union people here, many of whom are strong in their support of gov't & its measures as men can be. Great numbers of needy men are enlisting for the Southern Army from shear [sic] necessity. Active agents, having money got by private contribution, are at work secretly sending off hundreds south, everyone of whom could be retained for government [service] if recruiting officers could pay five dollars and give him cloths as the others do. It don't matter what lies answers [sic] the purpose the secessionists have plenty to stuff the recruits with, and the show of ready money acts as a guarantee that the pay will be forthcoming though in fact, the poor fellows will never see a cent after passing the borders of Secessia.

The steamboat captains who were still in charge of the gunboats wanted to obtain appointments as masters. Capt. John Duble of the *Conestoga* was particularly anxious, because his strong Union sympathy was well known amoung Southern boatmen. Phelps felt that these men did not "have the right abilities to fill the position of 1st Lieut. and fewer still to whom it will do to give latitude in military authority. They understand the business of steamboating & questions of freight, but seem little capable of anything else."[11] Men were, however, urgently needed, and Phelps recommended their appointments.

Weeks had passed with no rise in the Ohio River. During that time the carpenters were able to finish much of the work left incomplete at Cincinnati. Phelps wanted to be rid of them, to make room for the new recruits.

Supplies finally began arriving. Rodgers sent five hundred rations for each boat. Eight hundred pounds of lead paint and forty gallons of oil paint arrived. Phelps made a quick trip to Camp Holt, on the Kentucky shore opposite Cairo, Illinois, and borrowed thirty old muskets and five hundred rounds of ammunition, which he divided among the boats.

The recruitment of crews was still a problem. Phelps opened a small office on the nearby canal locks and began competing with the Confederates for recruits. One of the first to be recruited was his younger brother Alfred, whom he appointed paymaster on the *Conestoga*. There were a number of men, including soldiers, who applied, but the ship's doctor rejected many as unfit. Fortunately, Phelps was able to enlist a full complement of firemen and coal heavers. The coal heavers were shipped as "roust-abouts . . . which means all work I am told," said Phelps. For the most part he was not happy with the rivermen who tried to enlist. And, he wrote to Rodgers, "the army is not fit for shipboard and won't do at all. We ought to have some few old men-of-war men."[12]

The recruitment of pilots for the gunboats began a rocky relationship with the navy. In many respects the very heart of any riverboat, the pilots were indispensable if the gunboats were to succeed. The Pilots Association was determined to have its way, asking the going rate of $250 a month for its members. Some members, unfortunately, damaged the credibility of the association. Phelps caught a Mr. Hiner, an association pilot, deliberately falsifying soundings on the Portland bar. Because steamboat business was down dramatically since the start of the war, Rodgers was able to enlist several association pilots for only $150 a month, which aggravated the problem.

The delay in getting the gunboats downriver attracted all kinds of people who had schemes to get the boats through. "They're not interested in the gunboats, they're after a government contract," Phelps wrote to Rodgers. "Get the contract, make a show of carrying it out, even with no chance of success, then go straight to Congress and get two or three times the outlay."[13]

Finally, in early August, the water began to rise. Phelps got the three gunboats over the Portland bar, then became stranded at New Albany, Indiana. While awaiting a further rise in the river, the boats finally received their batteries. The *Lexington* and *Tyler* each got 32-pounders and eight-inch guns. The *Conestoga* got four 32-pounders. The hot August sun made loading the 4,300-pound guns grueling work for the crew, but at least they did not have to wrestle the 6,300-pound eight-inch guns.

Unfortunately, the guns did not come complete. Rodgers's requisition, made in early July, for one thousand boxes of shot, grape, and canister did not leave Baltimore until August 6. In the meantime, small amounts of powder and lead were purchased locally. Gun tackles were improvised from tackles bought in a local general store. A hawser was made from grass and then cut up to make breechings.

Word reached the gunboats that the Confederates in Paducah, Kentucky, would try to capture them if they passed unarmed. Phelps was confident, however, that the imposing barrels of nineteen guns would be enough to scare off any attackers.

On the morning of August 7, with the river only one foot shallower than the deeper-draft *Tyler,* Phelps decided to wait no longer. He ordered the *Lexington* and *Conestoga* to throw hawsers to the *Tyler.* Down in the fire room, the coal heavers and engineers got the word to bring the boilers up to full pressure. The *Lexington* and *Conestoga* then moved into position ahead of the *Tyler.* When Phelps gave the word, churning white water cascaded from underneath the three boats. With smoke and steam pouring from six tall chimneys, the combined power of the three boats slowly dragged the *Tyler* across the bar.

Working their way steadily downriver, the gunboats passed Paducah without incident and reached Cairo, Illinois, on the afternoon of August 12. All three boats were in urgent need of repairs and finishing work. Phelps turned over the *Lexington* and *Tyler* to Rodgers and proceeded back up the Ohio River to Mound City, Illinois, with the *Conestoga.*

The *Conestoga* was turned over to Hambleton Collier & Company, and put on the ways. Phelps oversaw the work this time and had modifications made. He added an extra skylight, pantries, and a gangway. For fifteen dollars he had a proper water tank and fittings installed in his roundhouse. After he had approved a $2,226.84 bill, the *Conestoga* returned to Cairo, ready for service.

Cairo, located at the southern tip of Illinois, at the confluence of the Ohio and Mississippi rivers, would be the gunboats' home port for the next four years. Since it was also the southern terminus of the Illinois Central Railroad, Cairo had become the center of Western river commerce. Broad levees, fourteen feet above the level of the city, extended some three miles from the point where the two great rivers met. Another levee connected the two, forming a delta. The Ohio levee was Cairo's principal street and business district. High-volume steam pumps controlled seepage, but enough water remained that mud was always a chronic problem. Having the consistency and adhesion of mortar, it could not be scraped or wiped off completely. Since only experienced bootblacks knew the secret, and charged upwards of a quarter, bootblacking quickly became a growth industry.

The St. Charles was Cairo's only first-class hotel. With two to four beds in each room, it offered limited comfort. One correspondent noted: "It is a formidable looking structure and very roomy; a condition in which your pockets are likely to sympathize when you come to leave it, the charges being $2.50 per day, with such extras as they think from your looks you are able to stand, and the accommodations in exactly inverse ratio."[14]

The long-awaited arrival of the three gunboats at Cairo was marked by great curiosity but little enthusiasm. The soldiers and civilians who looked upon the strange craft predicted they would be shaken to pieces from the recoil of their own guns, or certainly be sunk by Rebel shore batteries.

The gunboats quickly demonstrated their value as they began their patrols. A reported one thousand Confederate troops had taken Commerce, Missouri, and erected a battery overlooking the river. When Rodgers arrived with the *Tyler* on August 20, the Southerners fled with some forty-five wagons filled with corn. Around 6 P.M. the next day, a Confederate force opened up on the *Tyler* with small arms. A couple of well-placed shells by the inexperienced gunners sent the infantry running. The "wooden band boxes" had given notice that they should not be taken lightly.[15]

Just as the gunboat fleet began to bear fruit, Rodgers was removed from command. The businessmen he had alienated found an ally in Maj. Gen. John C. Frémont, commander of the Department of the Missouri. The famous "Pathfinder of the West" asked that Lincoln have Rodgers removed, hypocritically adding, "Who now serves the country quickly serves her twice."[16] The command was to be turned over to Capt. Andrew H. Foote. Having spent more than three months frantically working to create a navy, Rodgers was stunned and deeply hurt. With seven ironclad gunboats under construction and scheduled to be launched in mid-October, the Western Flotilla would be an important command, and now it belonged to another. Knowing the work that had gone into creating this fleet, Phelps, a cousin of Rodgers's wife, Anne, could only feel sorry for his friend.

On September 3, the presence of the three gunboats took on added importance when Confederate forces occupied the strategic heights overlooking the Mississippi River at Columbus, Kentucky, ending that state's neutrality. With Cairo now vunerable to attack, Union commander Brig. Gen. Ulysses S. Grant quickly countered the Confederate move by seizing the town of Paducah, Kentucky. Possession of Paducah was vital, for the Tennessee River joined the Ohio there, and the mouth of the Cumberland River was only ten miles away.

On September 9, the *Conestoga* and *Lexington* covered a short army advance down the Missouri side of the Mississippi. Scouting ahead of the troops, Phelps discovered a Confederate force at Lucas Bend. Keeping the *Conestoga*'s bow into the current and using her paddle wheels to offset the flow, he provided a steady platform for his gunners. Using his stern gun almost exclusively, Phelps opened up on the enemy artillery. The sound of the duel soon brought the *Lexington,* now under the command of Rodger Stembel, and the Confederate gunboat *Yankee.*

Among the sixteen Confederate artillery pieces were several long-range rifled guns whose shells were soon falling about the *Conestoga.* Once she closed the range, the *Conestoga*'s 32-pounders caused the Southerners to begin a cat-and-mouse game.

They would dash upstream and push out among the weeds on the bank. The first we knew of them would be the whiz of their shot which went all over and about us, but strange to say I believe not one fairly lodged aboard. As more than a hundred shot—perhaps 150 were fired at us, I can't say how this escaped us. They passed between our chimneys, over our bow & stem, fore and aft, under the counters, etc. but not actually aboard.[17]

Soon the *Lexington* arrived and joined in the running gun battle. About 1 P.M. the two gunboats withdrew upriver, hoping to draw the Confederates to the Union forces. They would then drop downriver and catch them in a cross fire. The Southerners soon caught on, and refused to advance.

Hoping to take a crack at the *Yankee*, Phelps dropped downriver shortly after 2 P.M. Stembel hesitated at first, fearing he might be cut off, but soon followed. Once in range, the *Conestoga* opened fire over a land spit with a shell that appeared to ricochet off the water and land in the *Yankee*'s side. The *Lexington*, with the quoin removed from an eight-gun to increase its elevation, landed a fifteen-second fused shell in the *Yankee*'s wheelhouse. The *Yankee* then limped toward the Confederate batteries at Columbus, Kentucky.

Returning upriver, the *Conestoga* was hit by small arms fire from the vicinity of an outhouse. Phelps ordered canister used, and the outhouse soon had extra ventilation. By 5 P.M. the action was over for the day. Having fired some forty-three rounds from her guns and received hundreds in return, the only casualty on the *Conestoga* was Quartermaster Nelson Castle, who was shot through the arm and forehead. "I can not speak too highly of the spirit and will of the crew," Phelps wrote to Foote, "scarcely one of them whom had been under fire before."[18]

"Their own accounts confess to 68 killed & a large number wounded, while other reports state it much higher," Phelps later wrote of the usually inflated casualty figures. "I have tried several times to get a fight from them again in the same locality but they will not gratify me."[19]

With a strong Confederate force at Columbus, just a short distance downriver from Cairo, the *Tyler* and *Lexington* were kept close

USS *Conestoga*—Phelps's first command, this "wooden band box" roamed the Ohio, Tennessee, and Cumberland rivers, establishing Union domination of them. (U.S. Naval Historical Center)

at hand to defend against any attack. Phelps, in the meantime, was assigned to Paducah. His superior was Brig. Gen. Charles F. Smith, who had a reputation as the best all-around officer in the regular Army. Erect, broad-shouldered, with a long white moustache, Smith was known as a stern disciplinarian and an ogre to volunteers and political officers. He and Phelps quickly became friends. Smith allowed Phelps the freedom of movement that soon made the *Conestoga* a familiar sight along the Ohio, lower Tennessee, and Cumberland rivers.

Suddenly appearing off a small town or farm, the *Conestoga* would anchor and fire a signal gun. Sometimes everything would seem deserted. In other places people would come from all around to see this example of Union power.

Phelps used these stops to great advantage. He gathered intelligence from Union sympathizers and preached the Union cause to secessionists. Bartering for food allowed the crew of the *Conestoga* to enjoy fresh fruits, vegetables, meat, and dairy products. The salted meat, coffee, tea, and flour that constituted the standard ration were easily traded for sweet potatoes, butter, eggs, chickens, cornmeal, pecans, and peanuts. Certain farms could always be counted on to have a fresh apple pie or gooseberry tarts.

The *Conestoga*'s crew soon became accustomed to naval regulations and drill. From the day the *Conestoga* first passed Paducah with Phelps, the only gunner, manning a 32-pounder, gunnery drills dominated the crew's routine. The procedures instituted by Rodgers, Phelps, and Stembel became the standard for the fledgling flotilla. The following description of the gunboats' daily routine is a composite derived from different boats later in the war and the archaeological findings from the USS *Cairo*.

Awakened at 5:30 A.M. by the boatswain's call to "turn to," the sailors dressed, rolled up their hammocks, and placed them in the hammock netting. Breakfast was served at 6 A.M.; forty-five minutes later, the crew turned out to scrub, holystone, and swab the decks. The decks were kept immaculate, any stains being taken out with large stones and fresh sand (if available).

About 9 A.M. the crew was given thirty minutes to wash and tidy up. Each morning the boatswain's mate called for "the sick, lame, and lazy" to appear before the surgeon for examination to determine if any should be excused from duty. The surgeon had at his disposal such medicines as potassium chlorate (used for a variety of ailments), blue mass for syphilis, quinine, rhubarb, ammonia, sulfur, zinc chloride (used as an antiseptic and astringent), ferric chloride (used as an iron tonic), iodine, castor oil, camphor, turpentine, linseed oil, and chloroform (used as an anesthetic).[20]

Muster and inspection followed; each division officer reported to John Duble, who had been appointed first master. Duble then reported to Captain Phelps. If a man was found especially dirty, on the evening of his offense he was made to strip and stand under the boat's pump. Five or six of his fellows, armed with scrub brushes and buckets of sand, then washed him down. This was not often repeated, for "a man once washed so is always very careful to keep himself very clean afterwards."[21] Usually three days a week a laundry call was ordered, to clean clothes.

After inspection, the crew drilled for an hour or two. Gunnery drill involved every man on the boat, including the captain. This drill was the most important and precise, for any slipup could result in a prematurely discharged round or burst barrel, which could cause more damage than a direct enemy hit. All hands acted "lively" in removing the hoods covering the hatch gratings, to avoid injury from the concussion of firing. Every obstruction to the free passage of powder was removed, shot lockers were opened, and fire tubs were set in place with wet swabs near them. Each quartergunner carried a bag around his neck containing, among other things, a flask of priming powder, spare locks, lock strings, priming wires, and rags. The gun crews loaded the powder bags and shells, using the rammer to make sure the round was seated; otherwise the gun would certainly rupture. The gunner laid back the lock, punctured the powder bag with his priming wire, and placed a primer into the vent. Directing the crew to use the breeching block and tackle to run the gun out, the gunner then stepped clear of the recoil, and sighted down the barrel. Elevation was set by using a quoin or elevating screw at the breech. The gun crew was directed to pull on the side tackles to sweep the gun left or right. At the word "ready," the men on the side tackles dropped their ropes and took up the breeching tackle for the recoil. At the word "fire," the gunner pulled a lanyard on the firing mechanism to fire the gun, the recoil pushing the gun back. The barrel was immediately swabbed with a wet sponge to clear it of any hot residue, and the gunner cleared the vent with his priming wire. The gun was then ready for another round.

"General quarters" for repelling boarders meant closing the gun ports and hatches, lighting the battle lanterns, and connecting the boat's pump and boilers with a hose to spray the enemy with live steam. Crewmen armed themselves with swords, revolvers, muskets, and even old-fashioned boarding pikes, although the bayonet was preferred.

With drill complete, the crew was put to work sweeping the decks, washing and retouching the paintwork, and general maintenance of the engine and machinery until noon, when dinner was piped by the boatswain. Before the meal was served, the cook took a sample of the food to the watch officer on the quarterdeck for his approval. If it was found deficient, the executive officer was informed, and a survey was held to condemn any food found spoiled or unfit.

The ship's officers ate in the two small wardrooms aft. Their meals were enlivened with a good variety of whiskey, rum, wine, and champagne. The crew, split into messes of about fifteen men each, went to their mess chest and each man secured his own utensils. They then got their food and ate sitting on the gun carriages or squatting on the deck. The galley was dominated by a large cooking range with iron and copper pots. It also had a large chopping block where the cook wielded a giant two-handed cleaver on the salt beef and pork.

At 1 P.M. the crew turned to for more of the same chores or drills until 5 P.M. (4 P.M. in the winter), when supper was served. From 7 P.M. until 9 P.M., the crew had free time during which they wrote letters, played cards, or told stories. At 9 P.M. they had to be in their hammocks when "dous goes the glim" ("lights out") was announced. Hammocks were slung in such a fashion that the officers knew where to find the men they needed at any time. A correspondent wrote:

> By the dim light of the lamp, I could see the great gun within six feet of me, and shining cutlasses and gleaming muskets. . . . I could see the men in their hammocks asleep like orioles in their hanging nests. The sentinels paced the deck above and all was silent, but the sound of the great wheel of the steamer turning lazily in the stream, and the gurgling of the water around the bow.[22]

The constant movement of the *Conestoga* caused her crew to be shortchanged when it came to equipment. Having only thirty hammocks and a few clothing bags and mattresses, Phelps had requisitioned one hundred of each, only to find, during a quick stop at Cairo, that the crews of the *Lexington* and *Tyler* had taken all but twenty-five. By early October the nights were turning damp and chilly, and the light spardeck where the men slept was not enough to protect them from the cold. The crews on the *Lexington* and *Tyler* not only had hammocks, but their berthing spaces were warmed by the residual heat from the engines. Although Phelps's men did not have their share of equipment, there was little griping, for being actively employed up and down the Ohio River was better than staying around Cairo.

Watches were stood four hours on, four hours off, rotated so that the man who had the first watch one night would stand the second watch the next night, and so on. Usually at noon and at eight in the evening, the quartermaster on watch reported to the captain and said, "Eight bells, sir." If all was normal, the captain would reply, "Make it," and the quartermaster would strike the bell.[23]

The master-at-arms was the boat's policeman; along with his assistant, the ship's corporal, he kept a lookout for violations of discipline. Each day those men found deficient would be brought before Phelps, who decided their fate. Flogging had been outlawed in 1852 but Congress had not provided for a substitute, so Phelps and the other captains were left to create their own method of discipline as long as it did not include corporal punishment. Minor infractions were usually handled by having a man "blacklisted," which meant extra, unpleasant duties. For more serious offenses, such as being drunk, the standard twelve lashes were replaced with having the man put in irons and fed bread and water. Extremely serious offenses required more severe and creative punishment. On board the *Lafayette* later in the war, for example, several men were condemned "to ride on the hog chain for flowering a saucy negro."[24] This entailed straddling an iron bar, which braced the hull timbers, for hours—an extremely painful experience.

Uniforms were anything but standard at the beginning. Some of the crew were lucky enough to have one of the few uniforms sent by the Navy Department. Soldiers still wore their army issue complete with branch insignia. Civilian clothes supplemented what the quartermaster could not supply.

As late October began turning cold, the lack of shoes for the men on the *Conestoga* became one more hardship they had to endure. Government-issued shoes, when they finally arrived, had hobnailed soles attached to the uppers with wooden pegs. Some crewmen had the boat's blacksmith make small horseshoes to serve as heels.

Crewmen carried little sewing kits known as "housewives." Usually they consisted of a small tin can containing needles, linen thread, spare buttons, a thimble, and scissors. The few old salts from the regular navy were considered somewhat "dandyish" by their inland mates because they took pride in tastefully embroidering and trimming their shirts, and could always be counted upon to have a surplus of buttons on their trousers. To identify their clothes and belongings, they made stencils from pine scraps.

Crew members who showed natural ability and leadership were advanced as "petty officers." They included one or more boatswain's mates, a master-at-arms, ship's corporal, quartermaster, quartergunners, ship's cook, and others. All orders were issued through the boatswain's mate on watch. To get the crew's attention, he blew his silver pipe or whistle and bellowed, "All hands!"

The three crews were becoming disciplined teams when Captain Foote directed the gunboats not to leave their anchorages without express orders. Foote's first general order was designed principally to rein in the increasingly freewheeling *Conestoga*. Foote wanted the gunboats exposed only when they were after a worthwhile objective, not just on a routine patrol.

On September 22, Indiana governor Oliver P. Morton frantically telegraphed Washington that secessionists had seized the town of Owensboro, Kentucky. He asked that President Lincoln send the gunboat at Paducah to help take back the town. Lincoln ordered General Frémont, who in turn directed General Grant to dispatch Foote, with the *Lexington* and *Conestoga,* to dislodge the Confederates.

Foote took the *Lexington* from Norfolk, Missouri, and proceeded to Paducah to rendezvous with the *Conestoga*. When he arrived at Paducah, the *Conestoga* was nowhere in sight. General Smith informed Foote that she had gone on service and was probably up the Cumberland River.

Foote was embarrassed and furious. This was his first assignment, ordered by the president, and one-third of his command was nowhere to be found. Foote proceeded with the *Lexington* and sent the steamer *Bee* on a vain search up the Cumberland River. Arriving at Owensboro and finding two Union regiments already there,

USS *Lexington*—A wooden-clad gunboat, her five-inch oak planks protected her crew only from small arms fire. (U.S. Army Military History Institute)

Foote ordered Captain Stembel to remain with the *Lexington* until forced out by the falling water.

Foote took the *Bee* and headed for Evansville, Indiana. A short time later they encountered the *Conestoga,* and Foote hailed her to come to, so he could board her. He wanted an explanation from Phelps. It must have been a good one, for this meeting marked the beginning of a very close personal relationship between the two men.

Foote was beginning to understand the different character of river warfare, and looked with growing respect on those officers who seemed to relish this new service. This was especially true considering the number of older "restored" officers arriving to take command of the new ironclad boats under construction. As a member of the retirement board, Foote was keenly aware of the records of these men.

The new captain of the *Tyler*, Comdr. Henry Walke, for example, had been placed on the Reserved List partly because of an infraction in the late 1840s, and had just been court-martialed for disobeying orders. Walke's ship had been at Pensacola when the Navy Yard was captured by Confederates earlier that year. Instead of taking his ship to Veracruz as ordered, Walke returned the yard's paroled prisoners and their families to New York. The press and public applauded his action, but he was censured by Secretary Welles.

William Porter had been placed on the Reserved List in part because of his court-martial in 1841 for scandalous conduct, neglect of duty, and showing contempt for a superior, for which he received a reprimand.

Comdr. Benjamin Dove, a senior commander who had joined the navy in 1826, had been court-martialed in 1830 for fraud and scandalous conduct unbecoming an officer. Found guilty of the last charge, he was reprimanded and set back in his rank twelve months. In 1841 Dove was court-martialed again, this time for sleeping on watch, disobedience of orders, and showing contempt for a superior officer. He was dismissed from the service but restored to duty by order of President John Tyler. In 1848, Dove underwent a court of inquiry into alleged disobedience of orders, and the facts of the case were entered into his record without opinion.

While Foote attended to the completion of the new iron-plated gunboats and his rapidly growing command, Phelps, with General Smith's blessing, had the *Conestoga* constantly moving about. Sometimes he found himself in the role of a diplomat.

I have had the principal people of towns together, where it has been my duty to look after the safety of Union people, or state arms, and have uniformly cautioned them against neighborhood outbreaks and warfare; that in this they could in no way influence the result of the war and would only destroy their own prosperity, peace and neighborhood security, in a fruitless and cruel bloodshed.

Cannelton and Hawseville, one in Indiana, the other in Ky, opposite towns on the river, were rapidly drifting into a state of war, the latter being strongly secession. The few Union people in the place are of foreign birth, miners, and have been on bad terms with the people on the score of a mining quarrel. Near the end of Sept., while lying at Owensboro, I received a message to the effect that the Union people were threatened and that great excitement prevailed on both sides of the river. I proceeded up to Cannelton and found an excited crowd with here and there a half drunken fellow parading about with a musket upon the levee, and as great crowds upon the opposite side. I found the musket men were from Hawseville & represented themselves as having been driven for their lives across the night before. They had taken care to bring away arms placed there for the protection of Union people by the gov't; thus depriving their friends left behind of the means of defense.

I sifted the matter out and became satisfied the alarm was groundless and the ill feeling springing up entirely uncalled for, and at once crossed to Hawseville, invited the principal people to meet me, went on shore among the crowd where I was an object, as a noted Bull on Fair day is, for the wandering crowd to gaze at. We met in the office of the leading Secessionist of the place. I first required assurances of the safety of 80 old flintlock muskets, belonging to the state, and then, before all, investigated the complaints of the Union people and heard the explanations of the other side—Judge Mason of Va., cousin of the Senator, being one of the secession proclivity order— and succeeded in convincing both parties of the error of their ways and their mutual interests and duty.

I was there on the 7th inst, and had the pleasure of seeing all quiet, people attending to their business and in good neighborly relations. I take pleasure in . . . an affair so entirely peaceful because I believe . . . such endeavors are worthy in a war like this. . . . I have done the same thing in other towns and with like results. This vessel has obtained a notoriety along the Cumberland and Tennessee Rivers, from which I have taken a number of prizes, and have all along kept seccesh—there rampart and largely in the majority and of a marauding type— quiet and respectful to his Union neighbor. Many of them swear to shoot me on sight but none has yet attempted it.[25]

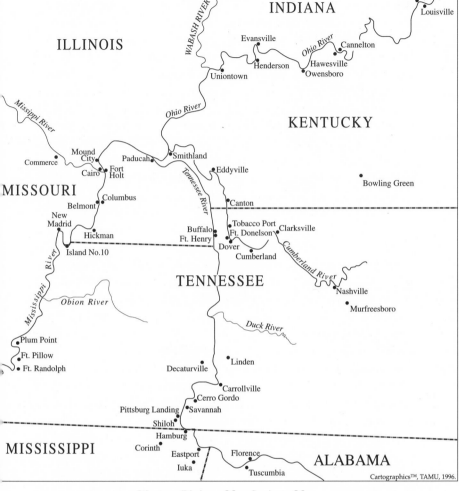

Western Rivers, 1861–Spring 1862

In October the *Conestoga* was active on the rivers above Paducah. At General Smith's request, Phelps began making reconnaissance voyages, water permitting, to Fort Henry on the Tennessee River and Fort Donelson on the Cumberland River. On October 11, the *Conestoga* ascended the Tennessee River, and on her approach to Fort Henry, the crew watched rockets hurtle skyward, warning of their arrival. Phelps anchored in the river for the night.

The next morning Phelps anchored the *Conestoga* below the fort and posted himself in the pilothouse with a spyglass. For hours he studied the fortifications and noted the heavy guns being mounted en barbette. Phelps's shore parties returned with ominous reports of powerful gunboats being converted upriver, including the *Eastman,* reputed to be the finest and fastest steamer in the West.

Having completed his reconnaissance, Phelps left the Tennessee River and ascended the Cumberland River for sixty miles to investigate reports about a fort being constructed above the town of Eddyville. While lying off Eddyville, Phelps learned that Rebel cavalry in the area was harassing Unionists. He warned the townspeople, in strong language, not to threaten the Unionists, or he would be back.

Twelve days later, on October 26, Phelps kept his word. Departing Paducah with three companies of the Ninth Regiment of Illinois Volunteers under Maj. Jesse Phillips, on board the steamer *Lake Erie No. 2,* the *Conestoga* headed up the Ohio River. Aware that the Confederates had a system near Smithland, Kentucky, to warn of gunboats entering the Cumberland River, Phelps devised a plan to make his approach appear to be another routine patrol. Being spotted convoying a transport steamer would raise the alarm upriver. Traveling against the current, it would be impossible to mask the chug-chug-chug of two reciprocating steam engines, so Phelps took the *Lake Erie* in tow with all her lights out, fires screened, and engines stopped. Early the next morning, sentries at Smithland reported another routine passage of the *Conestoga.*

Once safely past the town, the *Conestoga* and *Lake Erie* made all possible speed upriver. At 3 A.M., the two vessels pulled into New Forge Landing, six miles by land and fifteen miles around a bend from Eddyville. Major Phillips quietly disembarked his troops and marched inland. The *Conestoga* and *Lake Erie* chugged upriver to Eddyville, where Phelps left the *Lake Erie* behind a wooded point a short distance from the town. He then moved the *Conestoga* to the end of the main street, where he quietly anchored.

In the meantime, Phillips's three companies covered thirteen circuitous miles along rough, unfrequented roads. Phillips stopped at the homes of several known Southern sympathizers along his route, taking them prisoner lest they sound the alarm. Just before dawn the troops reached a point some six hundred yards from the small village of Saratoga Springs, near Eddyville. A unit of Rebel cavalry camped there was still asleep.

Phillips's skirmishers quietly located the pickets and, one by one, captured them without firing a shot. About 7 A.M. the troops wheeled in column in full view of the Confederate camp, and attacked. Running at the double quick, Phillips's troops got to within three hundred yards before they were spotted. Forming a rough line, the Rebels began firing haphazardly, but too late. At two hundred yards, Phillips charged, and the Southerners broke and ran. At fifty yards the Ninth halted, fired a volley, then charged with fixed bayonets. The Confederate commander, Capt. M. D. Wilcox, stood firing two revolvers while his company deserted him. It took nine minié balls to bring him down.

Some of the Confederates took to their horses and headed for Eddyville. Others hid in houses or behind trees, and kept up a steady firing for about thirty minutes. After taking a number of prisoners, and quantities of supplies, Phillips marched toward Eddyville.

The people of Eddyville were awakened by the sight of the *Conestoga*, her big guns aimed down the main street. A force of marines and sailors had quietly taken up positions around the town to complete the trap. Phillips and the Ninth Illinois reached Eddyville about 10 A.M. Phelps had the captured horses, mules, and wagons put on the *Lake Erie*, and one hundred of Phillips's troops on the *Conestoga*. Hoping a strong lesson had been taught, Phelps told the townspeople: "I will hold secession property in the place and along the river, as well as secessionists themselves, living on the banks, from its mouth to the State of Tennessee, responsible for any violence Union people may be subjected to after our departure." The people stood and watched as some of the troops and sailors waved from the crowded *Conestoga* as she shoved off and headed downriver.[26]

Over the preceding months, Phelps had gotten to know many of the inhabitants along the river, and he began to take a personal interest in their welfare. The internecine conflict was growing increasingly bitter, forcing neighbor against neighbor. Chafing at spending even short periods at Paducah, Phelps suggested that the ironclad *New Era* would be well suited to take the *Conestoga*'s place, allowing him to spend more time protecting the Union people along the river. His suggestion soon became moot, however, for the growing Union garrison at Paducah diminished the need for the *Conestoga*'s guns.

While the *Conestoga* and her sister boats were carrying the fight, the heart of what was to become the Western Flotilla was being hurriedly constructed in Carondelet, Missouri, and Mound City, Illinois. Recognizing that wooden gunboats stood no chance against heavily fortified Confederate strongholds along the rivers, in July the army had asked for bids on ironclad gunboats. James B. Eads won the contract when the bids were opened on August 5, 1861.

Having to build seven gunboats based on a design by Samuel Pook, and deliver them within sixty-five days, Eads sent telegraph messages around the North that contracted the multitude of items necessary in their construction. Timber came on barges from Kentucky, Tennessee, Illinois, Ohio, Indiana, Minnesota, and Missouri. Twenty-one steam engines and thirty-five boilers had to be built. Within two weeks more than four thousand men were employed night and day, seven days a week. With handsome bonuses promised if the work was finished on time, Eads built in weeks what the South could barely construct in four years.

The gunboat *St. Louis* was launched on October 12. The other boats followed in quick succession. They were named after local cities: *Carondelet, Cincinnati, Louisville, Mound City, Cairo,* and *Pittsburg.* Their distinctive profile quickly gained them the nickname "Pook Turtles."

Unfortunately, the rapid construction of the boats was not followed by their swift outfitting and completion. Slowness in requisitions and money from Washington caused repeated delays. James Eads used his own funds, and when they were exhausted, he turned to his friends to stave off default.

The new flotilla commander was Andrew Hull Foote, a man of considerable reputation within the navy. Sporting a patriarchal beard, this devout Presbyterian first made a name for himself while in command of the brig *Perry* off the African coast. At Canton, China, in 1856 he landed a force of sailors and marines to protect American property. As he returned to his ship, the *Portsmouth,* the Chinese barrier forts fired at him. Bringing his ship within seven hundred yards of the forts, Foote returned fire, and after silencing the Chinese guns, he personally led his marines and bluejackets into the forts to force their surrender. Foote lost forty men; the Chinese, four hundred. This show of force made a deep impression on the Chinese that led to subsequent treaties.

While in command of a three-ship squadron off the China coast, Foote was able to convince every officer and man to sign the pledge of temperance and give up their rum ration. At the outbreak of the Civil War, the thirty-nine-year navy veteran was in charge of the Brooklyn Navy Yard. Foote asked his boyhood friend Gideon Welles for a command, but a riverboat navy was not exactly what he had in mind.

Foote found the lack of funds to be one of his biggest headaches. Eads was not the only one close to being destitute. Many of the men had enlisted so they could feed their families, and when the promised wages were not forthcoming, Phelps, Stembel, and Walke found themselves with serious morale problems.

The officers, too, suffered financially. The navy's fourth auditor had determined that under Section 3 of the Act of 1861, service on the rivers was not sea service, and therefore the officers would not receive sea pay, a difference of up to $750 a year. The act was based on English maritime law that had jurisdiction in piracy and mutiny cases; "where the tide made, there was the sea." Phelps wrote to his friend Elisha Whittlesey, comptroller of the Treasury in the Lincoln administration, pointing out:

> I command a vessel intended to be a complete man of war in equipment, armament, and discipline, and to be engaged in every style of warfare, but I shall not, it appears, receive credit for such meritorious service, or be paid as highly, as if I were a

Andrew H. Foote—A devoutly religious man, Foote charged into the guns of Forts Henry and Donelson but became cautious at Island No. 10 and Fort Pillow. (National Archives)

watch Lieutenant in a ship on the coast blockade, with few cares and responsibilities.[27]

Under the influence of Whittlesey and Senator Benjamin Wade of Ohio, it was not long before the auditor changed his mind.

The value of the gunboats was clearly demonstrated in early November when the *Lexington* and *Tyler* provided crucial support during the Battle of Belmont. Acting as a diversion for a Union operation in Missouri, General Grant moved 3,100 troops on transports, in convoy with the two gunboats, to Hunter's Landing on the Missouri side of the Mississippi, across from Columbus, Kentucky. Marching on Belmont, Missouri, Grant's troops succeeded in pushing back the Confederates until his green troops stopped and started plundering the Rebel camp. Phelps wrote to Whittlesey:

That force had been entirely successful, but, like most of our volunteers, without discipline, had become disorganized after the first brush, and the fight was more a rabble contest than a soldierly battle. Belmont captured and the camp destroyed, the force should have instantly retired in good order, as there were 30,000 on the other side of the river who of a certainty would reinforce their defeated comrades, as they did. Several thousand strong following our retiring men and flanking them. They rushed after them to the very bank where the transports lay that had landed our troops. There the gunboats opened a most destructive fire and cut up the enemy in a most terrible manner. Whole regiments were swept away, while our force had the opportunity to embark. On the other opposite side of the river too, above Columbus, the gunboats had fired with destructive effect upon the men in the rebel lines & fortifications. The Federal loss in killed and wounded is about 250. The rebel lost in killed alone over 500. If a due proportion of wounded is added, we have a total rebel loss of some 1500. A majority of this destruction must be laid to the account of the gunboats.

The day for the Union brightens. We shall never have a well disciplined army, nor will the rebels, but in this respect they

USS *Tyler*—This wooden-clad gunboat played an important role in the Union victories at Shiloh and Helena. (Massachusetts Commandery, Military Order of the Loyal Legion, and the U.S. Army Military History Institute)

will out do us. The gov't resources will more than counterbalance this advantage of the rebels and they must go to the wall. Our whole system is rotten even now and I begin to feel afraid that the sad lessons of war will do little to heal it. When I find Captains, Colonels, Generals remembering only that the men under them have votes to cast for officers I feel little confidence in the efficiency of the army in the day of trial, and as little hope for the stability and earnestness of the Gov't supported in such a manner. I do hope that good may come of this war in creating for us more of a government and a more nationalized people, and in bringing us to a humiliating sense of our imperfections. We have boasted till we believed ourselves perfection. I look now for a better management of "this" Military Dept. under the new Gen'l. [Maj. Gen. Henry W. Halleck].

In mid-November, Phelps and the *Conestoga* were requested by Maj. Gen. William T. Sherman, Federal commander in eastern and central Kentucky, to keep an eye on Uniontown. "I came up to this place . . . by telegraphic request of Genl. Sherman, without knowing exactly why I came, or, rather, what for," Phelps wrote. The only Rebel activity was "a swaggering braggart on shore who is shouting for Jeff Davis and brandishing a revolver." As in most cases, Phelps sent an armed party after the man, who then jumped on his horse and took off. Not finding any Confederate activity, Phelps made another reconnaissance voyage up the Cumberland River.

The *Conestoga*'s continuing incursions up the Cumberland and Tennessee rivers emphasized how vulnerable the Confederacy was. Willing to try anything to block the rivers, hundreds of Confederate soldiers worked for two weeks to fill five barges with 1,200 tons of stone and sank them at Ingram's Shoals on the Cumberland River. Five days later, Phelps eased his boat past the obstruction, then took delight in announcing his arrival.

> The Confederates sent down a number of large barges filled with stone and sunk them in shoal places in the river thinking to stop us, but we passed over them the first attempt, and I sent word "from their own territory" that I would not molest them in amusing themselves as much as they pleased in the expensive luxury of sinking barges in the Cumberland.

Sharpshooters were a constant problem, and the *Conestoga* was frequently targeted by butternuts who fired from heavily wooded places where they felt safe. During one routine passage up the Tennessee

River, the *Conestoga* was fired upon near the town of Tobacco Port. As a warning to the citizens of the town who permitted such attempts, Phelps fired a shell that exploded near an old barn on the side of a hill. Suddenly a number of soldiers fled in all directions; the *Conestoga* had, to Phelps's surprise, fired into a Confederate camp.

To emphasize that the sharpshooting was to stop, Phelps sent a messenger to Tobacco Port, and decreed that if this irregular warfare did not cease, he would burn the town. Anyone found sniping who was not in the Confederate army would be shot as a murderer. Coincidentally, Confederate authorities had been circulating rumors that the gunboats were manned by released felons given free rein to burn, pillage, and loot. This had the desired effect, for on their next passage the *Conestoga* did not take a shot.

While Phelps was patrolling upriver, Lizzie and Sally had moved to Paducah shortly after its occupation by Union troops.

> They are living very snugly in a private boarding house with a pleasant family. I would remove them farther from the scene of war but for my profession which has kept me so much separated from them, and will continue to do so in after years. The war over, I have nothing to expect but a cruise of two or three years to follow upon this service. I must, therefore, see as much of the wife and child as due performance of duty will admit of.[28]

Although the *Conestoga* was rarely at Paducah for more than one day at a time, Lizzie and Sally took every opportunity to visit. "Sally has been so much on board ship," Lizzie wrote to Whittlesey, "that she is never more at home anywhere & is perfectly delighted & a great *pet* here on her Papa's ship, as she calls it."[29]

Lizzie was anxious to go on a patrol up the Ohio, but Phelps would not permit it. He would, however, take his family with him when the *Conestoga* made the run between Paducah and Cairo. Phelps noted, "Lizzie has come on the cruise with me for the fun of the thing and would like to see a 'brush,' she thinks."[30] For Lizzie, however, it was the "brilliant autumn tints of the foliage on the banks & in this lovely weather" that she enjoyed. "I almost lose the realization that the purpose of all by which I am surrounded is the sad one of man."[31]

On November 19, Phelps headed to Canton, Kentucky, where reports indicated a cache of Confederate supplies was located. It was a trap. Confederate cavalry, under Nathan Bedford Forrest, lay in wait, hoping that the *Conestoga*'s crew could be lured ashore. As the *Conestoga* docked, Phelps sensed something was wrong. Soon a lone German man approached the *Conestoga* and told them that a force of three hundred Confederate cavalry with a 12-pounder cannon was two miles downriver, waiting to attack. Phelps had the drummer beat to quarters and his 32-pounders loaded with canister. The *Conestoga* shoved off and headed downriver. Before they had traveled half a mile, while passing within fifty yards of the wooded point at the edge of town, Forrest's men opened up. From behind every log and tree, muskets roared, their balls raining like hail against the oaken bulwarks. The *Conestoga*'s starboard guns erupted like giant shotguns. Phelps had the *Conestoga* rounded to, and used his stern gun as it was brought to bear. The recoil of the Confederate cannon rolled it backward into a gully, forcing the gunners to withdraw it about half a mile, after which they fired one more shot. Besides a large quantity of lead imbedded in her side, the only damage to the *Conestoga* consisted of a broken guy wire, numerous holes in her chimneys, and a flesh wound to Phelps's dog, Sancho.

After the fight, Phelps noted: "We had three valiant Kentuckians on board when the rebels, near Canton Ky. brought a gun to bear on us at 50 yards dist. and I found the three after the action was over in my bed room sprawled out on the floor! Lizzie is worth a hundred such."[32]

On her return down the Cumberland, the *Conestoga* came upon the steamer *Pink Marble* with a large barge in tow, heading for Confederate territory. Ordering her to come about, Phelps boarded her and asked her captain to produce his papers. With the approval of Secretary of the Treasury Salmon P. Chase, and the Collector of Customs at Louisville, Evansville, and Smithland, Phelps could allow only the cargo of machinery for the McMinnville cotton factory to pass. Knowing full well that the trade would benefit the South, the crew of the *Conestoga* had their first example of the profiteering that helped to prolong the war. Ironically, the safe arrival of the *Pink Marble* at Nashville once again pointed out the folly of the sunken barges while at the same time demonstrating that a simple signature could defeat what cannons and barricades could not.[33]

By late autumn the exploits of the *Conestoga* were becoming well known to those involved in the Western campaign. The professional reputation that Phelps worked hard to build was showing results. The recognition that was forthcoming would not, however, overcome what he saw as a serious roadblock—lack of seniority.

Phelps saw more and more senior officers arrive for duty. Especially galling was the fact that most of these were "restored" officers. The command of a new ironclad boat was quickly becoming less certain. In late November, Phelps laid out his desire for command to Foote. The *Conestoga*, which he had come to love, was still a "second rate craft that could not approach batteries when the southern movement takes place."

To his longtime patron Elisha Whittlesey, Phelps wrote:

The new gun boats being constructed are likely to prove very formidable craft. I am to be disappointed no doubt in a command of one of them, which has been promised me from the beginning, the Department having ordered out a large number of old commanders, some of whom entered the service before I was born, and there are more of these than there are vessels being constructed. I came out when the service was in bad repute and esteemed more hazardous than any other. These very commanders scoffed at the idea of such a mongrel service. Most of them are totally unfit for it. I suppose I must content myself with the command of this vessel or make a struggle for one of the new sea going gunboats. Captain Foote, however, assures me that if within his power I shall have one of the new ones here and so matters stand.

Our Government is very heedless in such matters, and cannot get over the idea of seniority. Having once ordered a junior officer upon a service of this kind at the beginning, with

the care of nursing it into life thrust upon him in no considerable share, it should be careful not, with utter indifference,
to rob him of the fruits by a simple application of an aimless
seniority rule.[34]

The army engineers, with whom he had worked in the spring, in-
advertently provided Phelps with some leverage. They had unoffi-
cially asked if he would consider returning to duty with them. Phelps
told Foote that he would rather do that than command a supporting
vessel.

Foote asked Phelps not to be hasty. "I have been wanting a personal interview for some time that we might talk over your case and
see what could be done to ignore seniority. . . . You certainly deserve
not only the command of an iron plated steamer but promotion for
your services in the flotilla." Unable to grant a command, Foote tried
to soothe Phelps's ego by adding, "General Halleck . . . remarked
that [you] had really performed important service which was very
creditable to you."[35]

On December 8, 1861, a rainy, misty day, the *Conestoga* eased her
way up the Cumberland River. Sent by General Smith to evacuate
Union refugees, she anchored at Linton, Kentucky. Sixty cold and
wet people, traveling from the backcountry in small parties, managed to reach the *Conestoga*. From the refugees Phelps learned that
the Confederate government was intensifying efforts to fortify the
Cumberland River below the town of Dover, at Fort Donelson. The
Rebels feared an attack on Nashville, and were frantically rushing to
prevent an ascent by Union gunboats. The secessionists were calling
up Kentucky troops and impressing Union people into service. They
were also seizing slaves of Union and Confederate owners alike. Not
wanting their property misused, even Confederate owners were telling their slaves to flee. One slave taken on board the *Conestoga* had
been so instructed by the sons of his owner, even though they were
avowed Secessionists.

More ominous to Phelps, however, were the continuing reports of
powerful ironclad steamers being constructed up the Cumberland
and Tennessee rivers. The *Eastport* now emerged as the boat to be

feared. She was reported to be 280 feet in length and one of the fastest boats on the Mississippi. Efforts to iron-plate her were said to have failed, and cotton bales would now protect her. Phelps, trying to find out more, hired a spy. His man evidently met the same fate as the spy sent by General Smith, for neither returned.

Christmas 1861 was the first opportunity for Phelps and his family to be together for the holiday since Genoa in 1857. On December 23, Foote sent a message to Paducah requesting that the *Conestoga* come to Cairo. Lizzie wrote to Whittlesey:

> As it was so near Christmas, I was afraid to lose sight of my husband so I gained my petition that Sally & I might go down with them in the *Conestoga*. Christmas eve we spent off Cairo where there is now quite a formidable fleet of gun & mortar boats assembled. Sally & I did not go ashore but the Flag Officer [Foote] came off to see me. It is the first time I have met him . . . all my prepossession in his favor was more than confirmed on meeting so kind & pleasant a gentleman. . . . Sally was quite disturbed for fear St. Nicholas would not come on the gunboat to fill her stocking, but her father provided as well as the Cairo toy shop would admit to play St. Nicholas for her. So Christmas morning she wakened up early to find as she supposed, that St. Nicholas really had been here & left a well filled stocking.[36]

Early in January 1862, the *Conestoga* once again steamed up the Tennessee and Cumberland rivers to obtain information about the two forts. After reconnoitering Fort Henry, Phelps proceeded up the Cumberland River, where he learned that the Confederates were reported to have blocked the river with trees chained together, sharpened points facing downriver. Upon arriving just below Fort Donelson, which, unlike Fort Henry, sat on high ground approximately one mile from a narrow bend in the river, Phelps used the trees along the bend for cover. He eased the *Conestoga* to a point where one more boat length would expose the craft. The crew then nervously watched as several shells landed just off the bow. Phelps had been told by his informants that the guns were mounted en barbette, and it was obvious that the Rebel gunners knew their business.

Phelps informed Foote that a successful assault by the gunboats would be greatly aided by mortars. The angle at which their cannon would fire would require the shells to burst at the exact moment they passed over the Confederate positions; otherwise, they would pass harmlessly to the rear, possibly hitting Union troops. Mortar shells falling among the Confederate gun crews, Phelps suggested, would make manning the guns very hazardous while the gunboats aimed to dismount the guns.[37]

The time was rapidly approaching when the Western Flotilla would begin its advance south. The commissioning of the gunboats *St. Louis* and *Essex* ("Dirty Bill" Porter renamed the *New Era* in honor of his father's ship) would be followed shortly by the other "city boats" and the powerful *Benton*.

Comdr. Henry Walke was ordered to take command of the *Carondelet*, and on January 15, 1862, Phelps received orders to take command of the ironclad gunboat *Cairo*. "She is of light draft of water," Foote wrote, "and promises to be the fastest of the boats."[38] Phelps had his ironclad.

On January 20, having made arrangements to hand over command of the *Conestoga* to Lt. James M. Prichett, Phelps received a shattering note from Foote informing him that the *Cairo* would not be his after all. Lt. Nathaniel Bryant, senior to all the lieutenants in the flotilla, had unexpectedly reported for duty along with Lt. Egbert Thompson. Foote vainly tried to ease Phelps's disappointment with praise:

> From your past efficient services as commander of the *Conestoga*, which has made her the terror of the rebels bordering on the Ohio, Tennessee, and Cumberland rivers, I am exceedingly anxious to place you in command of a boat carrying a more powerful battery and capable of enduring a heavier fire than the gunboats built without iron casemates at Cincinnati.[39]

For six months the Ohio, Tennessee, and Cumberland rivers had been his. Soon they would belong to the ironclads. Seeing no prospect of advancement or glory, Phelps applied to Foote to be detached from the flotilla.

Foote found himself in a predicament. He could not ignore seniority, but he dared not lose one of his most experienced captains. He appealed to Phelps:

> I fully appreciate your views and feelings. Yes I must consider your knowledge of the rivers. Your name here being a dashing officer of the best judgement, and in view of further service you may perform, I do hope that you will permit me to return you your letter. Let me as a friend also suggest that hard as I consider your case to be after your great services, that your application, in this time of war, will not be well received by the Department.[40]

A meeting soon afterward between Foote and Phelps produced the prospect of command of the USS *Benton*. Not yet in commission, the most powerful Union gunboat on the western rivers was a command worth waiting for. In the meantime, Foote had another job for Phelps. As soon as Fort Henry fell, he would take the *Conestoga*, along with the *Tyler* and *Lexington*, and make a dash up the Tennessee River to destroy the Rebel ironclads known to be under construction.

℘

CHAPTER SIX

Fort Henry & the Tennessee River Raid

T ENNESSEE was central to several strategies that were considered in the fall of 1861. The Union Army was still unprepared, however, and the gunboats were not finished. On November 4, 1861, General Frémont, whose tenure was notable mostly for his unauthorized antislavery edicts, was replaced by Maj. Gen. Henry W. Halleck in a reorganized Western department. Halleck found his new command in a shambles. Needing to stabilize his base in St. Louis, he was not prepared for any offensive operations. Neither was Brig. Gen. Don Carlos Buell, who had replaced William T. Sherman in Kentucky.

Lincoln had hoped to launch an offensive to seize the vital Cumberland Gap and secure East Tennessee, but Buell was not ready to commit his army to a movement toward Knoxville or Nashville without Halleck's support. Senator Andrew Johnson and Congressman John Maynard were demanding that Lincoln do something. Their loyal constituents in East Tennessee were under a harsh Confederate occupation.

Buell had little enthusiasm for a move into the desolate mountains of East Tennessee. Instead, he looked toward the center of the Confederate defensive line that connected Bowling Green and Columbus, Kentucky. Buell was not the only one looking in that direction. Generals Grant and C. F. Smith were focusing their attention on Fort Henry, on the Tennessee River. General Smith had surveyed Fort Henry with Phelps in the *Conestoga*, in mid-January, and on his return, he recommended to Grant that the fort be taken. Although increasing in strength daily, Fort Henry, at river level, was poorly sited. It was vunerable to flooding, and its guns lacked a height advantage. This would enhance the effectiveness of the Union gunboats' iron plating. Also, since the gunboats would be attacking from downstream, any disabled craft would be carried out of danger by the current. After coordinating his plans with Flag Officer Foote, Grant traveled to St. Louis and presented his case to Halleck, who rejected the plan.

Halleck had also been thinking about Middle Tennessee, but it was not until reports reached him that Confederate General P. G. T. Beauregard was headed west with fifteen regiments that Halleck decided to act. In late January, Grant and Foote were ordered to go ahead.

Foote intended to take the ironclad gunboats *Cincinnati* (the flagship), *Carondelet, St. Louis,* and *Essex.* The three wooden gunboats would form a second division under Phelps. The mortar scows under construction were not yet ready. The gunboat *Mound City,* under Comdr. Augustus Kilty, would remain at Cairo to guard against any movement from Columbus, and the gunboat *Cairo* would be sent to Fort Holt to watch over the Mississippi River.

The wooden gunboats would take up position astern of the ironclads and shell Fort Henry from long range. After the fort surrendered, and on signal from the flagship, Phelps was to lead his division up the Tennessee River and destroy the Memphis & Ohio Railroad bridge. He would then proceed as far upriver as the water allowed.

It was an open secret that Union forces would soon move against Fort Henry. At Cairo preparations were under way; coal was shipped and provisions stored. The *Conestoga* was given the job of one last reconnaissance of the fort. Before leaving Paducah, Phelps called at the headquarters of Brig. Gen. Lew Wallace and, after explaining his mission, invited the general to go with him. Wallace later wrote:

> The courtesy was one to be instantly accepted. The experience would be novel. I could see somewhat of sailor life under unusual conditions. Besides being an officer of ability and dash, Phelps was a gentleman refined, well-read, and a delightful companion.
>
> Being a landsman of the ultra-lubber variety, I shall not try to describe the *Conestoga*. Indeed, I remember not more of her than that she was flat-bottomed, very broad, and black all over; that her upper deck was in the style of a sea-goer, with bulwarks up to my shoulder; that there was a great gun at her bow, and that the pilot-house and commander's quarters were on the upper deck. I remember, also, the exceeding whiteness of the planking of that deck, the stealthy silence of the ships going, and the cheerfulness with which everybody on board went about his duty.
>
> So too at meal-times, the table-cloths and napkins did much honor to the laundry, and the table-ware was so above suspicion, and the courses brought on were of such wholesome variety and masterly preparation that I could not help rating my host for the advantages of his service compared with ours of the land.

The *Conestoga* anchored in the middle of the river that evening (January 30, 1862) to avoid the possibility of running aground or hitting a snag.

> Next morning the vessel was under way early. We breakfasted as usual, after which I accompanied Phelps in his rounds of the quarters. There was no excitement and but few words; yet even I could see the readiness for action. The inspection ended by our bringing up at the bow. The big gun there stood out uncovered, looking for all the world like a long, black, lathe-turned log. At hand lay a red flannel bag which I recognized at once as

the regulation charge of powder, and by it a shell suggestive of a nail keg standing on end. The men serving the monster fell into position and saluted. Two sailors I observed leaning over the bulwark, one on either side of the bow, gazing into the water. They did not look up.

"We are going slow," I said to my host.

"Yes," he replied, "we are in the torpedo zone as reported."

I looked at the two sailors at the bow, and understood why they were fishing with their eyes so intently in the water. I, also, mentally approved of going slow.

After some one called out, "Yonder—who are they?"

"Where?"

"On the left bank, pretty well up."

Phelps whipped out a long binocular hanging strapped to his shoulder, and, making it ready, followed the shore slowly.

"Soldiers, mounted and going full speed," he said. "If the enemy is not already notified of our coming, he will be."

"Vedettes," I suggested.

"Very likely."

"What island is that ahead?"

"Panther Island."

He went to the man at the wheel, and presently we were entering the western channel of the island. I could not help admiring the good sense of the manoeuvre. Upon rounding the insular obstruction, the *Conestoga* would be in sight and in easy range from the fort; instead, then of offering the vessel broadside on the multiplied chances of a hit, should force be opened upon her, our bow, built strong for fighting, would be the target; at the same time we would be in position to reply immediately.

Phelps then rejoined me. The moment, I freely admit, was warm with interest.

"If they open on you," I asked, "will you fight?"

"No, my business is to look, and if I should shroud the ship in smoke my occupation would be gone."

We cleared the channel and moved boldly into the main steam. Nobody spoke; everybody strained his eyes seeing what he could of the stronghold at the end of at least two miles of unbroken waterway.

The boat slowed, then came to a stand-still. The view was fair. Heaven's best light was in our favor. While we were looking, a man, evidently an officer [Wallace later recognized him as Brig. Gen. Lloyd Tilghman], stepped out on the parapet by the big gun of the lower bastion of the fort, and entertained himself returning our bravado like for like.

"I am satisfied," Phelps at length said. "There is one large gun newly mounted—the third one from the water-battery."

Putting up his glass, he turned to the wheel-house and waved his hand, and the boat began dropping back—back— and almost before I knew it we were behind the screen of Panther Island. And so ended the last observation of Fort Henry before the grand expedition assembled and moved against it.

Wallace later referred to his trip on the *Conestoga* as "an experience so altogether novel and full of excitement that in my best thought I class it as one of my choicest memories."[1]

Upon his return, Phelps reported that everywhere along the river, the people he talked to anticipated an attack and that the Confederates were prepared to defend the fort at all costs. He also confirmed another ominous threat. In the right channel, near the foot of Panther Island, were numerous buoys, evidently marking the location of submerged infernal machines or torpedoes. Since the channel had been clear only a few days before, Phelps was certain there must be more obstacles above the head of the island, where the attack would take place.

Early on Sunday morning, February 2, the gunboats *Cincinnati, Carondelet, Essex, St. Louis, Lexington,* and *Tyler* departed Cairo with the troop transports and headed up the Ohio River for Paducah.

Soon after arriving, General Grant and his staff held a conference with Brig. Gens. C. F. Smith and John A. McClernand. Because of the shortage of transports, Grant decided to move McClernand's division that night to a position below Fort Henry, then return the transports to Paducah for Smith's division.

USS *Baron de Kalb, Cincinnati,* and *Mound City* anchored off Cairo, Illinois, in 1863. The USS *St. Louis* was renamed *Baron De Kalb* when it was pointed out that the navy already had a ship named *St. Louis.* (U.S. Naval Historical Center)

By Monday afternoon everything was ready, and the boats began moving upriver in intervals, led by the *St. Louis* and *Essex.* The weather began turning ugly. The pleasantly warm weather brought low clouds and strong southerly winds. Soon the rain began, and built to a torrent as heavy thunderstorms lashed the steamers.

Some thirty miles upriver, the *Essex* and *St. Louis* stopped and made fast to one another, then proceeded ahead of the others. The transports and remaining gunboats remained far behind, and did not come within hailing distance of the duo until late Monday night.

Early Tuesday morning, February 4, all the steamers had anchored in the vicinity of Itris Landing, some seven or eight miles below Fort Henry. General Grant's steamer, the *W.H. Brown,* was the first to put her nose on the east riverbank. Soon McClernand's division began disembarking from the transports. Grant, in the meantime, went aboard the *Essex* and proceeded farther upriver with two other gunboats, to take a firsthand look at the fort.

At 4:30 A.M., as the three ironclads crept passed Bailey's Landing, three miles below the fort, a rocket hurtled skyward, announcing their arrival. It was immediately answered by a rocket fired from the fort. The Confederate gunners immediately set about loading the eleven guns bearing downriver. When they were within two miles of the fort on a fast-moving, rapidly rising river, the gunboats opened up and were greeted with return fire from the fort's rifled 24-pounder and ten-inch columbiad. Their shells fell some three-quarters of a mile short. Soon a nine-inch shell from the *Essex* exploded directly over the fort, followed by another. The defenders also began to find the range. One shell struck the *Essex* just back of the wheelhouse; it tore through Captain Porter's cabin, passed between his clock and bureau, then underneath his table, and exited out the back and into the river. It caused no other damage except cutting the feet from a pair of Porter's stockings. "Good shooting that," Porter remarked as he surveyed his cabin. "Now we will show them ours."[2] After throwing a few more shells toward the fort for good measure, the gunboats dropped back downriver and anchored a mile below the foot of Panther Island.

Grant decided that the area known as Bailey's Ferry would be a better location for landing his troops, and ordered the transports to reembark those already on shore. About 3 P.M. the transports had arrived opposite the town of Buffalo, Kentucky, and once again began landing McClernand's division. By Tuesday night the unloading had been accomplished, and in the steamer *New Uncle Sam*, Grant returned with the transports to Paducah for General Smith's division.

Grant's scouts were reconnoitering the area when they came upon a farmhouse where nearly thirty women had gathered for safety. During questioning, one of the women mentioned that her husband was a captain in the Confederate army at the fort. "By tomorrow night, madam," remarked one of the scouts, "there will be no Fort Henry. Our gunboats will dispose of it." "Not a bit of it," was the reply, "they will be blown up before they get past the island."[3] This remark was made with such conviction that the scouts interrogated her further. The terrified woman finally described the torpedoes and their location as best she could, wailing at the realization of her betrayal.

The scouts quickly sent this confirmation of the torpedoes back to the flotilla, and Flag Officer Foote dispatched Phelps's division to try and sweep them up. The *Conestoga* and *Tyler* proceeded to the channel between Panther Island and the west bank of the river. Here the island shielded the gunboats from the fort while Phelps commenced dragging the river. With the river now twenty-five feet above low water, thanks to the torrential rains, Phelps used his cutters to bring the torpedoes to the surface with ropes and grappling hooks at a safe distance. The division succeeded in retrieving six, all soaked and harmless.

All day Wednesday, February 5, transports plowed their way upriver with men, horses, wagons, and artillery. A number of troops were landed on the west bank of the river to move against the Confederates at Fort Heiman, opposite Fort Henry.

The Confederate steamers *Dunbar* and *Lynn Boyd* were observed running to Fort Henry from upriver, bringing reinforcements from the 48th and 51st Tennessee. The *Conestoga* and *Tyler* ran up between Panther Island and the west bank, and threw a couple of shells at the fort and the steamers. After the shelling, Phelps decided to sound the channel, reconnoiter the woods on either side for hidden batteries, and search for more torpedoes. Finding two more, he had them hauled out and towed to shore.

That night a line of heavy thunderstorms moved through the area, causing another rise in the river. On board the *Conestoga*, the crew worked feverishly to keep her from being dragged downstream by the heavy driftwood, lumber, fences, and trees that the swollen Tennessee River was carrying. Coal heavers kept the pressure up all night so that the giant paddle wheels could help keep the boat anchored in the river. In the officers' wardroom, Phelps reviewed plans for the next day with telegraphers who would have a special job in the next few days.

Thursday morning, February 6, dawned cloudy, but the clouds soon gave way to sunshine. The day was cool and crisp. Water was standing everywhere, and the roads were quagmires. Fifteen thousand troops formed up on both sides of the river and moved off in columns. Just before 10 A.M., the gunboat captains arrived on board the *Cincinnati*. Flag Officer Foote, who had "agonized in prayer for victory"[4] the night before, gave them words of encouragement, shook hands with each, and asked God to look after them. The captains returned to their vessels, and the fleet soon came to life. The four ironclads formed a line abreast, with the *Essex* on the right and the *Cincinnati* on the left. The *Conestoga, Lexington,* and *Tyler* ranged themselves abreast and followed about half a mile behind.

The gunboats moved slowly toward the west channel, intending for Panther Island to shield them as long as possible. Entering the narrow chute, the gunboats crowded together, almost close enough for a person to walk across them. As the four ironclads emerged from the shelter of Panther Island, they expanded their battle line. In the distance lay the fort with the Stars and Bars waving defiantly. A strange silence persisted. All ears strained to hear the *Cincinnati*'s guns commence firing.

Half a mile to the rear, the three timberclads maintained their interval. The gunners, lanyards in hand, kept adjusting their pieces as the range slowly closed. Phelps, along with Lt. William Gwin on the *Tyler* and Lt. James W. Shirk on the *Lexington,* kept one eye on the fort and the other on the flagship.

About 1,700 yards from the fort, Foote gave the word to Comdr. Rodger Stembel to open fire. The *Cincinnati*'s three bow guns erupted, followed immediately by the bow guns of the *Carondelet, St. Louis,* and *Essex*. The three timberclads, having moved toward the left bank to avoid firing over the ironclads, joined in by lobbing shells into the fort.

As the Confederates returned fire, the roar was deafening. General Smith's men, on the west bank, let out such a cheer at the beginning of the bombardment that it was heard half a mile away on the other bank. Although the muddy roads and flooded lowlands were making the attempt to cut the Confederate line of retreat all but impossible, the Union troops pressed ahead, often in mud up to their knees. "We had to make a wide detour to avoid backwater from the river and then did not altogether," wrote Lt. Ira Merchant of the 28th Illinois. "About a half mile out we struck a slough [Panther

Creek] and there being no time for bridging, the men plunged in cheering and yelling like tigers. They had to hold their cartridge boxes up to keep the powder dry."[5]

Earlier that morning, Confederate commander Brig. Gen. Lloyd Tilghman had decided that his position was untenable. With part of Fort Henry underwater and the Dover road the only avenue of escape, he had already sent most of his command to Fort Donelson. Tilghman selected fifty men from Company B, 1st Tennessee Heavy Artillery, to man the guns and stay behind to engage the gunboats.

Taking up position at the center gun, Tilghman and his staff waited for the gunboats to open fire before firing his ten-inch columbiad and rifled 24-pounder. As the gunboats' range closed, the fort's remaining 32- and 42-pounders joined in.

Soon a thick veil of smoke enveloped the gunboats, with quick flashes of flame seeming to lift the smoke just enough for the gunners to see their targets. Men threw off their coats and shirts in order to work faster. Blackened with grime and powder, they worked with spike, rope, and rammer. With each telling shot there was a wild cheer.

The *Cincinnati* received the most attention from Tilghman, for she flew the pennant of the flag officer. One shell struck the pilothouse and knocked the wind out of Foote for several seconds. It was the *Essex*, however, that suffered the worst damage. After it had been hit numerous times, a shell pierced the casemate above the larboard porthole, decapitated Acting Master's Mate S. B. Brittan, and penetrated the middle boiler. Capt. William Porter had just gone below to the gun deck when the shell hit. Standing in front of the boilers—which, in contrast with the other boats, were above the waterline—Porter ran for a starboard gun port and threw himself out, expecting to go in the water. Seaman John Walker caught Porter around the waist and, supporting him with one hand, clung to the vessel with the other until help arrived.

The *Essex* drifted slowly downriver until the tug "*B*," which had been watching the fight and blowing her whistle at every telling shot, hustled up to throw her a line and tow her to safety.

Inexplicably, the *Carondelet* suddenly dropped out of line. Given the command by Commander Henry Walke to go ahead, Daniel

Weaver, the pilot, rang the wrong bell. Realizing that the bell lines to the engine room were somehow reversed, Weaver pulled the reverse bell, and the *Carondelet* once again moved forward.

The second division of wooden gunboats kept up a steady fire. The *Conestoga* fired seventy-five 32-pound shells, with ten- and fifteen-second fuses, taking pains to avoid firing over the ironclads. Since the Confederates concentrated on the ironclads, the only shells encountered by the timberclads were ricochet, none of which hit.

The *St. Louis* was hit seven times with no casualties. She fired 107 shots during the action. The *Carondelet* was hit some thirty times and also suffered no casualties. The *Cincinnati* received thirty-two hits; her chimneys, after cabin, and all of her boats were wrecked. Two of her guns were disabled, and one shot passed through the casemate shield, killing one man and wounding several others.

The Confederates put up a valiant but futile fight. Their ten-inch columbiad fired only a few rounds; then its tremendous recoil broke a clamp attaching the carriage to the chassis. Next it was spiked when the priming wire jammed and broke off in the vent. The 24-pounder rifled gun burst and killed those manning it. The fort's earthworks, six feet high and eight to ten feet thick, backed by woven hickory, were chewed up by the Union guns. Large areas facing the river were plowed up as, one by one, Tilghman's guns dropped out of the fight.

With his gunners exhausted and most of his command now safely on the road to Fort Donelson, Tilghman decided to surrender. A white flag was raised but was not seen due to the thick smoke. Tilghman then ordered the Confederate flag lowered, but it was not taken out of sight of the gunboats, so Flag Officer Foote, fearing a trick, held his fire and waited. Soon a small white boat, containing two officers, put out from the fort. On approaching the *Cincinnati,* they stated that they wanted a conference with the flag officer, which was granted.

The crewmen on the *Cincinnati* let out a loud cheer. "I had to run among them & knock them on the head to restore order," Foote wrote. "The surgeon hollered and howled & I told him that he ought to be ashamed of himself."[6]

With the lowering of the Confederate flag, the timberclads slowly approached the ironclads. Because the *Cincinnati*'s cutters were all out of service, Foote ordered Phelps to proceed to the fort with

Commander Stembel in one of the *Conestoga*'s cutters. At the shore by the fort, Stembel and Phelps were met by General Tilghman, who announced he was surrendering the fort and the surrounding camps with about sixty prisoners. Upon entering the fort, Stembel and Phelps went directly to the flagstaff and raised the American flag. Stembel returned to the *Conestoga*'s cutter, then escorted General Tilghman and several members of his staff to the flagship. Phelps remained behind with the Confederates to ensure naval custody of the fort until it could be formally turned over to the army.

Advance elements of Grant's cavalry, seeing the Stars and Stripes flying over the fort, approached warily. On entering the fort, they found Phelps with the prisoners, waiting for someone to take them off his hands. About an hour later Grant arrived and took formal possession of the fort, after which Phelps returned to the *Conestoga* and headed upriver with his division.

A mile away, the Confederate steamer *Dunbar* lay anchored as her crew witnessed the fight. Following the surrender, they waited to see what would happen. They did not wait long. Soon clouds of smoke were heading their way. Capt. Gus Fowler ordered the *Dunbar* to head for the drawbridge of the Memphis, Louisville & Clarksville Railroad at Danville.

Arriving at the bridge about 4 P.M., those on the *Dunbar* gave the alarm to the citizens of Danville. Fowler had opened a lead on the Union boats when Phelps discovered the camp of the 48th and 51st Tennessee regiments, and decided to stop and destroy it.

Meanwhile, there was great confusion in Danville. Hurried plans were made to remove the hospital, commissary stores, and other government and private property. The Confederate transport steamers *Time, Samuel Orr, Appleton Belle,* and *Lynn Boyd* had arrived at the bridge, and began taking what they could. As soon as they were loaded, the transports quickly headed upstream. The *Dunbar* was a government steamer, and Captain Fowler resolved to stay behind. Sentries were placed on the bridge, and a train was held at the Danville station.

About eight that evening the three Union timberclads arrived at the bridge. Seeing the fleeing Rebel transports in the distance and the *Dunbar* by the shore, just on the other side of the drawbridge, Phelps announced their arrival by firing one of his 32-pounders at the *Dunbar.*

The few Confederate sentries fired at the gunboats and fled aboard the train. Fowler needed no further inducement to stay, so he hastily headed upriver. Stalled by the closed drawbridge, the *Conestoga* fired eight more shells that landed all around the *Dunbar;* none struck her. A fast steamer, the *Dunbar* "flew like a deer before a pack of hounds, giving warning to all boats and all points along the river."[7] As the gunboats approached the bridge, the train pulled out with the telegrapher, his equipment, and those who did not wish to stay behind.

Phelps nosed the *Conestoga* to the bank next to the 1,200-foot bridge and sent a party to open the draw. Finding the draw works disabled, the crew set about repairing it. For an hour—"a season of cussin' those goddamn Rebels who won't give up"[8]—the *Conestoga*'s engineers toiled. Finally the draw opened, and the *Conestoga* and *Lexington* were off.

Phelps left Captain Gwin and the *Tyler,* the slowest of the three gunboats, behind to destroy what they could. Gwin sent a shore party under Second Master Jason Goudy to tear up the track and cut the telegraph lines that connected Albert Sidney Johnston's defensive line between Columbus and Bowling Green. After confiscating the equipment the Southerners had left behind, Gwin headed upriver after the other boats.

The bridge was not destroyed, as directed by Foote, but only damaged. Perhaps the scent the navy men had for the chase and for prizes propelled the pursuit—besides, the bridge would be there on their return.

After five hours the faster *Conestoga* had left the *Lexington* behind and had closed on the fleeing transports enough to make the captain of the *Sam Orr* decide to destroy his boat rather than see it fall into Union hands. With a cargo of submarine batteries on board, the boat was fired in hopes that the Yankees might get too close. Explosions soon ripped the *Sam Orr,* but the *Conestoga* remained a safe distance away.

William Gwin—One of the younger gunboat commanders, Gwin succeeded Phelps as captain of the *Benton*. (Massachusetts Commandery, Military Order of the Loyal Legion, and the U.S. Army Military History
Institute)

Farther upriver, the captains of the *Appleton Belle* and *Lynn Boyd* soon saw the *Conestoga* closing fast and realized their fate was sealed. Spotting the home of Judge Creavatt, a noted Union sympathizer, the two captains landed their steamers in front of his house. The torch was applied, and soon both steamers were ablaze.

Seeing the burning steamers, Phelps ordered the *Conestoga* halted about one thousand yards away. No sooner had the *Conestoga* stopped than a tremendous explosion racked the *Appleton Belle,* loaded with cannon, shot, grape, and three thousand pounds of powder. The explosion was so violent that the *Conestoga*'s skylights were shattered, her light upper deck was raised bodily, doors were jarred open, and locks and fasteners were broken.

The *Lynn Boyd,* lying next to the *Appleton Belle,* was shattered, as was the home of Judge Creavatt. "The whole river for a half a mile around was completely beat up by the falling fragments and the shower of shot, grape, balls etc.," Phelps wrote.[9]

Phelps decided to wait for the *Lexington,* which had no pilot on board, and the *Tyler* to catch up. After stopping to cut down a Confederate flag at Hawesport, the three gunboats continued until they arrived opposite Perry's Landing at just after 11 A.M., on February 7. Here they discovered the first signs of strong Union sentiment. People who had gathered on the banks waved hats and handkerchiefs, and an occasional American flag.

The three-boat flotilla, with the *Conestoga* in the lead, pressed on. Dubbing the *Conestoga* "the flagship," the men of the three "wooden bandboxes" began to see their raid deep into the Confederacy as unique. Carrying the flag to an oppressed people was immensely satisfying.

By 7 P.M. the three timberclads approached the landing at Cerro Gordo, eight miles downriver from Savannah, Tennessee. The *Conestoga* was fired on by small arms; five-second shells from her and the *Tyler* were launched in return. The three gunboats hove to and began to lower their cutters. The cutters headed for the riverbank, where their crews discovered the Confederate gunboat *Eastport* partially scuttled, her suction pipes broken. As they ran through the half-complete gunboat "like a pack of hounds in a rabbit's nest,"[10] the armed men found evidence of a hasty departure.

Upon searching the boat, the men discovered papers belonging to an old *Susquehanna* shipmate of Phelps, Isaac Newton Brown, now signing himself "Lieutenant, CSN." The letters revealed Confederate attempts to build a fleet to counter the growing Union threat. Brown had been sent by Confederate secretary of the navy Stephen R. Mallory to buy river steamers for conversion to gunboats, much as John Rodgers had been sent by Secretary of the Navy Gideon Welles the previous summer.

Some of the letters dealt with paying for the steamers. Mallory directed Lieutenant Brown to get the owners to accept half the purchase price in Confederate bonds. Brown quickly replied that "the parties wish to sell for cash only." Obtaining the *Eastport* was a stroke of luck, however. She was owned by Northerners, and her captain was only too happy to turn her over to Brown for service in the Confederate navy. In another letter Brown asked to be relieved because he had been refused command of one of the ironclads under construction at Memphis. She had been assigned to Lieutenant Carter, CSA, his junior. The "denying of which to me," Brown wrote, "at this juncture, is an implied disgrace, so far as such an act of denial from a soldier can reflect upon one of my profession. Exigent as the times are, there can be no right in any one to decree the dishonor of another."[11]

Three letters were from another old colleague, Matthew Fontaine Maury. The fifty-four-year-old "Pathfinder of the Seas" had been the superintendent of the U.S. Naval Observatory at Washington during Phelps's tour with the astronomical survey in Chile. The stocky, balding scientist, who had written *Physical Geography of the Sea,* was in fact the inventor of the torpedoes found at Fort Henry. Maury had prematurely declared the torpedoes a failure, however. There was a lack of the necessary wire in the South for galvanic batteries used in detonation, and Maury felt that driftwood would make contact torpedoes useless.

Confederate Maj. Gen. Leonidas Polk had "bought" the 260-foot *Eastport* on November 28, 1861, and began converting her into an ironclad gunboat. Phelps found the steamer dismantled to the deck with a partially erected inclined wooden frame that would support her iron plate. The chimneys were still intact, but her wheelhouse had been removed, leaving the wheels exposed without their buckets or arms.

The crews of the gunboats stopped the leaks aboard the *Eastport* and commenced pumping the water out of her. A quick examination revealed a large quantity of nails, machinery, and other items necessary for her completion. Some 250,000 board feet of lumber were neatly stacked on the riverbank, along with the iron plating that would have made the *Eastport* a formidable foe.

Once again leaving Lieutenant Gwin behind with the *Tyler* to guard the prize, the *Conestoga* and *Lexington* headed upstream after the remaining steamers. Soon after daylight on February 8, the two gunboats passed Eastport, Mississippi, and farther upriver overtook the *Sally Wood* and *Muscle* at Waterloo Landing. The *Sally Wood* was loaded with iron destined for Richmond and the Tredegar Iron Works, then the South's only plant capable of manufacturing heavy ordnance. A prize crew from the *Conestoga*, under Second Master Charles Noble, boarded the *Muscle* and towed the *Sally Wood* downriver, arriving at Cerro Gordo at 2 A.M. the next morning.

The *Dunbar* had arrived at Florence, Alabama, at 8 P.M. on Friday, February 7. Warned of the approaching Union gunboats, several companies of Alabama volunteers loaded military stores on a train and ran it to Tuscumbia. During the night the *Sam Kirkman* and *Time* arrived at Florence, having so far eluded the Yankees.

The news of Phelps's raid spread across the South. Reports of large Union troop movements toward Tuscumbia, Alabama, alternated with reports of troops capturing Eastport and Iuka, Mississippi. At one time or another every bridge over the Tennessee River was reported both destroyed and intact.

The call to arms spread throughout the region. War was now at the doorstep of those who had previously been willing to let others do the fighting. Alabama Governor John G. Shorter called out the militia; volunteer companies formed quickly and moved toward Tuscumbia.

General Polk, Confederate commander in West Tennessee, feared the Federals would land at Eastport and head for the vital Memphis

& Charleston Railroad bridge over Big Bear Creek. He ordered six companies of Col. Robert F. Looney's 38th Tennessee and James Deshler's Arkansas Battery to proceed to Iuka, Mississippi, to defend the bridge.

Jefferson Davis urged the units gathering at Huntsville, Alabama, to destroy the Union raiders. "The number of men who can have been transported by four [sic] gunboats," he wrote, "should never be allowed to tread upon our soil and return. I hope you may also capture the gunboats."[12] The people of Huntsville had only one 6-pounder, along with the two 6-pounder Parrott guns belonging to the Memphis & Charleston Railroad, to meet the invaders.

At 8:30 Saturday morning, February 8, a telegram sent by General Johnston was received in Florence. It ordered that the railroad span crossing the river be cut in order to allow the Confederate steamers trapped there to pass Muscle Shoals and escape. By this time the steamers *Dunbar, Julius Smith, Time,* and *Sam Kirkman* had their backs against a wall. The people of Florence were not happy at this turn of events. The fifteen-pier bridge connected the city with the railroad on the south bank of the river. It had been built and paid for by the citizens, and consequently they took great pride in it.

A meeting was held by boatmen and the stockholders in the bridge to decide what to do. The argument that the steamers were more valuable than the bridge was countered with the logic that if the steamers could get above the shoals, so could the gunboats. It was decided to wait and see if the gunboats were coming before doing anything. A short time later the *Conestoga* and *Lexington* were spotted only fifteen miles downriver, heading for Florence. By this time it was too late to destroy the bridge, for the gunboats would arrive in less than two hours. The *Dunbar* and *Alfred Robb* set off to find a stream in which to hide. At 2:30 P.M. the two Union gunboats came in sight of the city.

The three remaining Confederate steamers were set on fire. The *Julius Smith* was cut loose with her paddle wheels turning in reverse, in the hope that she would destroy the Federal invaders just as the English had destroyed part of the Spanish Armada with fire ships. As she drifted downriver, the two gunboats easily moved out of her way.

The *Sam Kirkman* and *Time* were set afire at the landing. Phelps nosed the *Conestoga* in to the landing, and his crew immediately set about securing cargo from the burning steamers. After removing what they could, the two boats were cut adrift to clear the landing.

A delegation of twenty citizens now approached the gunboats with a flag of truce. After asking whether it was Phelps's intention to occupy or destroy the city, they pleaded that their wives and daughters be allowed to leave unmolested. They also asked that their prized and profitable bridge not be destroyed.

Phelps "told them we were neither ruffians nor savages, and that we were there to protect them from violence and to enforce the law."[13] With regard to their bridge, Phelps said that since Muscle Shoals prevented him from proceeding further and the bridge had little military value, he would leave it intact. Immediately upon landing, the telegraphers Phelps had brought went with an armed party to the telegraph office. Anticipating that the operators had taken their instruments with them, the telegraphers brought their own. Soon they were in operation, listening to all the traffic that passed through Florence. Eventually news reached nearby Tuscumbia as to what the Federals were up to, and the operator there cut them off. The word spread quickly throughout the South to send all telegrams by way of Montgomery, not Florence.

The sailors searched the warehouses of Florence for contraband goods. Supplies marked for Fort Henry were loaded aboard the gunboats because no flats nor barges could be found. Iron plating for the *Eastport* also was confiscated.

As the rapid loading continued, a number of local businessmen scrambled to provide Phelps with proof of private ownership. Once proof had been established, Phelps directed his men to leave certain goods behind. Several hundred barrels of whiskey, forty to fifty bales of cotton, and other articles were left undisturbed. Private property that had already been taken aboard was off-loaded and returned to its owners.

That evening, having accomplished what they could, the *Conestoga* and *Lexington* left Florence. Going with the current, the two gunboats arrived at Cerro Gordo later that night.

While Phelps and Shirk had been busy upstream, William Gwin and the men of the *Tyler* had been feverishly getting the *Eastport* ready for the trip downriver. Since the morning of February 8, when the *Tyler*'s crew began loading materials aboard the *Eastport*, hundreds of men, women, and children had arrived from the surrounding countryside. They told stories of forced conscription into the Confederate army even though the Confederate Congress had not passed the new nation's first conscription law. "We breathe freely again," remarked one, eyeing the Stars and Stripes flying from the stern of the *Tyler*. "Old grey-headed men wept like children and they implored us to stay with them," wrote John Sebastian of the *Tyler*.[14]

After Phelps returned to Cerro Gordo, he consulted with Gwin and Shirk about a proper course of action. Emboldened by their successes so far, they determined to attack the camp of Lt. Col. James M. Crew's Confederate regiment near Savannah. It was reported to be manned mostly by six hundred to seven hundred pressed men, so the odds seemed reasonable for their small force.

With the *Lexington* left behind to guard the *Eastport*, the *Conestoga* and *Tyler* headed upstream to Savannah. With Gwin in command and Shirk as his second, a force of 130 sailors and marines, along with a 12-pounder rifled howitzer, stormed ashore, only to find that the camp had been hastily deserted. Shoes, clothing, and camp utensils that were deemed valuable were hauled aboard the two gunboats. The remaining equipment and the winter log cabins were burned.

Finding Union sympathizers more circumspect in expressing their loyalty, Lieutenant Gwin gave notice that "if any of the rebels interfered with the Union men, he would, on his return, punish them severely."[15] Less than two months later Gwin and Shirk were back, at a nearby place called Pittsburg Landing.

After returning to Cerro Gordo, the three gunboats, stuffed to the gunwales with Confederate supplies, made ready for the return trip. Later that Sunday night, February 9, the *Lexington* and *Tyler* took up position on either side of the *Eastport* and began to tow her downriver. The *Conestoga* took the *Sally Woods* and *Muscle* in tow, the latter under steam. During the voyage the *Muscle* sprang a leak. Despite frantic efforts to keep her afloat, she sank, taking a large quantity of lumber with her.

James Shirk—Shirk commanded the USS *Lexington* during Phelps's raid up the Tennessee River in February 1862. (U.S. Naval Historical Center)

Upon arriving back at the drawbridge on Monday morning, Phelps found Union troops protecting it. Much of the day was spent getting the prizes through the draw; the *Sally Woods* was fairly easy in the fast current, but the 260-foot *Eastport* soon became stuck. Through the efforts of two companies from the 14th Missouri Volunteers who were at Danville, and the crews from the three Union boats, the *Eastport* was squeezed through the draw and the little flotilla was on its way.

The success of the raid was apparent: three steamers seized, six others burned with the loss of tremendous amounts of supplies. Phelps claimed the half-finished *Eastport* as his. Perhaps the biggest prize was the realization that there was a substantial population of Southerners loyal to the Union. Unfortunately, their loyalty had to return underground after he left and the Confederates regained control.

In his zeal to show goodwill to the people of Florence, Phelps erred in not destroying their bridge, for it later helped Johnston's army withdraw from Middle Tennessee.

The propaganda flowing from the raid had begun with the fleeing Confederate steamers spreading the alarm of burning, ravishing, and plundering Yankees. The press on both sides took up the cause. The *New York Times* reported from Cincinnati that "the people of Florence are so delighted at finding the Stars and Stripes once more giving protection to them that they were prepared to give a grand ball to the officers of the gunboats, but they could not remain to accept their courtesies."[16]

Conversely, the *Tuscumbia Constitution* reported that "as yet [we] have heard of only one man, who at Florence went down and showed them where to land and took bacon for his services. Quite a solus turn out of the Lincolnites of North America."[17]

The feeling in the South may well have been summed up by a Confederate clerk:

The mission of the spies to East Tennessee is now apparent. Three of the enemy's gun-boats have ascended the Tennessee River to the very head of navigation, while the women and children on its banks could do nothing more than gaze in mute despair. No batteries, no men were there. The absence of these is what the traitors, running from here [Richmond] to Washington, have been reporting to the enemy. Their boats would no

more have ventured up that river without the previous explora-
tion of spies, than Mr. Lincoln would dare penetrate a cavern
without torch-bearers, in which the rattle of venomous snakes
could be heard. They have ascended to Florence, and may get
footing in Alabama and Mississippi![18]

CHAPTER SEVEN

ϾϿ

Fort Donelson

THE SAILOR in the pre–Civil War navy had two basic career goals. One was promotion, which was a matter of longevity, and the other was receiving official approbation—being "mentioned in dispatches." Medals and decorations, with the exception of the Purple Heart—only three of which had been awarded in the last years of the American Revolution by Gen. George Washington—were deemed European, and therefore unsuitable. Receiving recognition, especially a vote of thanks by Congress, was the ultimate one could strive for. Therefore, with the navy's victory at Fort Henry, each officer's share in the honors that followed was jealously scrutinized.

All the honors that flowed of course centered on Flag Officer Foote as flotilla commander. "'Uncle Abe' was joyful," Henry Wise wrote to Foote, "and said everything of the 'Navy Boys' and spoke of you in his plain sensible appreciation of merit and skill."[1]

Phelps and the wooden gunboats also received praise, too much for many of the ironclad sailors. "We were scarcely mentioned in the Fort Henry affair," wrote a *Carondelet* crewman, "while those western bandboxes, the '*Conestoga*,' '*Lexington*,' and '*Tyler*,' were puffed up by the papers, when they were astern during the whole of the fight." According to Comdr. Henry Walke, the three wooden boats "were present, but not engaged in the battle."[2]

Foote's reports on the actions at Fort Henry illustrated the relationship that had developed between Phelps and himself. In the official list of officers attached to the gunboats at Fort Henry, Phelps and the *Conestoga* were listed second to the flagship.

Phelps's Tennessee River raid had captivated the nation almost as much as the capture of Fort Henry. To a nation starved for good news, the daring raid was icing on the cake. The press loved it: "Too much praise cannot be awarded to Capt. Phelps . . . the Flag Officer, the Navy Department, and the people are free to acknowledge their indebtedness to Capt. Phelps,"[3] wrote the *Cincinnati Commercial*. And the *Cincinnati Gazette* went further:

> The selection of Captain Phelps for this important expedition has proven one of the best that could have been made. In a man who, like him, unites with the loyalty of a patriotic American citizen the coolness and intrepidity of an experienced commander there can be little wanting to make him equal to any emergency that the service of our country in her hour of peril may present.[4]

The *New York Times* wrote, "Never has a more gallant officer trod a plank."[5]

Foote, too, was elated. "I can not too highly commend the conduct of Lieutenant Phelps . . . he has, with consummate skill, courage, and judgement, performed a highly beneficial service to the Government, which no doubt will be appreciated."[6] Phelps's friendship with Foote blossomed after the successful raid. At the same time his relationship with Henry Walke and some of the other senior commanders declined.

As Phelps's timberclads were returning to Cairo with their prizes, they passed Walke and the *Carondelet*. Walke had been ordered by General Grant to wait for the wooden gunboats and then to proceed with them to Fort Donelson. When Walke ordered the timberclad flotilla to come with him, Phelps refused. He had received a message to rendezvous with Foote at Cairo, and he was not going to leave his prizes in the middle of the river for someone else. Commander Walke felt "this conduct on the part of naval officers, to be an act of insubordination," but nothing was said by Foote. "Discipline," Walke noted, "should have been more strictly enforced."[7]

While General Grant prepared to move overland and attack Fort Donelson, Foote insisted on returning to Cairo for repairs and more training for his men. He recognized that a token force with partially flooded magazines had caused considerable damage to his flotilla. "I never again will go out and fight half prepared," he wrote. "Men were not exercised & perfectly green. The rifle shots hissed like snakes. [General] Tilghman, well he would have cut us all to pieces had his best rifle not burst & his 128-pounder been stopped in the vent."[8]

When Grant learned that only the *Carondelet* would support his army, he urged General Halleck to order Foote to send more ironclads at once. Foote at first said he would need more time, but soon relented. By transferring men from the damaged gunboats, he constituted another flotilla.

Early on the morning of Wednesday, February 12, a squadron consisting of the *St. Louis, Pittsburg,* and *Louisville* passed the *Conestoga* and *Lexington* en route to Cairo. Foote hailed both vessels, and ordered the *Conestoga* to turn around and join him. The *Lexington,* which had been damaged in an accident, continued to Cairo for repairs. At Paducah, the flotilla was joined by twelve heavily laden troop transport steamers.

The fleet left Paducah on Wednesday, February 12, at 4:30 P.M. under pleasantly warm skies. The *Conestoga,* towing a barge loaded with coal, followed the ironclads. As the fleet passed Eddyville, it was greeted by men and women lining the east bank and waving small American flags. With the exception of one house that displayed a Confederate flag, which was promptly torn down by the crowd, evidence of the *Conestoga*'s influence for six months was apparent.

The run up the Cumberland to Fort Donelson was routine until they were some thirty-five miles below the fort. There the vessels encountered the tug *Alps,* which had helped tow the *Carondelet* to Fort Donelson.

After being rebuffed by Phelps, Walke had proceeded alone, arriving above Fort Donelson on the morning of February 12. Just after noon, the *Carondelet* approached the fort, and at 12:50 P.M. it opened fire to announce Walke's arrival to General Grant. After firing ten shells into what appeared to be a deserted fort, Walke retired downriver.

On February 13, Walke received a message from Grant stating that he had arrived and asking that the *Carondelet* bombard the fort at 10 A.M. Starting an hour early, the *Carondelet* kept up a steady fire until 11:30, when the Confederate ten-inch columbiad found its mark. The ball struck the corner of the port broadside casemate, spraying splinters over the gun deck, then just missed the steam drum. With a dozen men wounded by splinters, Walke decided to call a halt while he transferred his injured men to the *Alps* and repaired damage. After lunch the *Carondelet* resumed her bombardment until dusk, when most of the ammunition had been expended.

Foote "exhibited great anxiety" upon learning that the *Carondelet* had already begun the fight. He understood that General Grant would wait until the fleet arrived after completing repairs at Cairo. Hurrying to join the fight, Foote ordered the *Alps* to help tow the *St. Louis* and *Pittsburg* up the Cumberland, against the current. The premature start of the fight was not Foote's only problem. The weather, which had been unseasonably warm, was now bitter cold. Heavy rain and sleet turned to snow, reducing visibility; but with several experienced pilots, the squadron pressed on.

In preparation for the coming battle, Foote ordered Phelps to inspect the *Pittsburg* and *Carondelet*. In yet another sign of Phelps's growing influence, Foote appointed him acting fleet captain for a day. In an order in which Foote got his captains confused, he ordered Phelps to

> report on board the steamers *Pittsburg* and *Carondelet,* taking with you Gunner [John] Hall, and report to Commanders Dove and Thompson that you have been directed to make, in my place and for me the inspection of their vessels. You will direct those officers to have a short exercise, when you will see that the men understand pointing and training their guns, and

direct that the best marksmen in their ship fire them in the coming action. You will examine . . . in fact everything pertaining to a vessels readiness for action and direct the officers to exercise well today.[9]

The attack on Fort Donelson would follow the same plan as that at Fort Henry. Grant's army would surround the fort, and the navy would destroy the water batteries. The garrison would then be pounded into submission. It was hoped that the fort could be captured quickly. However, unknown to Grant, it had been reinforced, and he faced a garrison of seventeen thousand troops.

Donelson's water batteries were built on a high bluff overlooking a slight bend in the river. Named after Brig. Gen. Daniel S. Donelson, the fort encompassed about twenty acres and was shielded by a line of rifle pits. It was fronted by deep gullies that provided natural defensive lines against a land attack. To guard the river, twelve heavy guns were mounted in two batteries. The lower water battery was about twenty feet above the river, and the second, about fifty feet above.

The gunboats arrived two miles downriver from the fort at 11 P.M. on February 13, joining the *Carondelet*. By six the next morning, with the temperature at twenty degrees, the transports began landing men and supplies to reinforce Grant.

A 9 A.M. conference was held by Foote and Grant at which it was agreed that the simultaneous assault would commence with a barrage from the gunboats.

Preparations were made on the ironclads to protect their unarmored upperdecks against shot from the enemy heights. Large numbers of bread bags were filled with coal from the barge and laid on the upper decks along with anchor chains, lumber, and coiled hawsers. Capt. Leonard Paulding, son of Adm. Hiram Paulding, had the hammocks on the *St. Louis* stacked like sandbags around the conical pilothouse. The dark tarpaulin used to cover the white hammocks blew away, however, leaving what looked uncomfortably like a perfect bullseye.

At 1:45 P.M. a signal was raised on the *St. Louis* and the gunboats headed upriver for several hundred yards. There a line was formed, from right to left, with the *St. Louis, Louisville, Pittsburg,* and *Caronde-let.* The *Conestoga* and *Tyler* followed about a quarter of a mile behind. Proceeding at three miles an hour against the current, the gunboats passed the wooded bend in the river at 2:35 P.M. and came in sight of the fort.

After the *Louisville* and *Pittsburg* had been signaled to "steam up," the flotilla slowly advanced on the fort. About a mile and a half from the fort, the Confederates fired two shells to get the range. Both fell short. Several more were fired at the gunboats, but all missed. About a mile from the fort, Foote gave the word, and the eight-inch bow gun of the *St. Louis* opened fire. The shell dropped just in front of the lower battery. The firing by both sides was slow at first but gradu-ally increased in intensity.

With the *Conestoga* and *Tyler* some one thousand yards to the rear and firing over the flotilla, Foote pressed ahead, just as he had done at Fort Henry. Instead of remaining out of range of the seven Con-federate 32-pounder cannons and having his gunners concentrate on the 10-inch columbiad and 6.5-inch rifled gun, Foote continued until the flotilla was within four hundred yards of the fort. The firing became incessant.

A 128-pound shell hit the *Carondelet*'s anchor, smashing it, then took off part of a chimney. Another shell hit her boat davits, causing the cutters to drop into the water. Shells tore away armor plate "as lightening tears the bark from a tree,"[10] sending iron and wood splin-ters flying.

For a good deal of the time, Foote observed the fire of the *St. Louis* from the pilothouse, using a speaking tube to urge on his gunners. He commended a well-placed shot, and also got after any gunner who was short of his mark. "A little further, man; you are fall-ing too short."[11] Then a 32-pound shot struck the "bullseye" pilot-house of the *St. Louis,* penetrating the inch-and-a-half iron plate and its fifteen-inch oak backing. Fragments and splinters flew every-where. Three men were wounded, and pilot F. A. Riley, who was standing next to Foote, was killed. Foote, hit in the left ankle, grabbed the wheel and continued the fight. After repeated hits the vessel was not responding well to her helm, so Captain Paulding tried to steer the boat with relieving tackle. It was soon evident that the relieving tackle was not working well enough to keep the boat from turning her more vulnerable broadside to the enemy, so Foote ordered Paulding to let her drift downriver. Foote then went down to the gun deck to have his wound tended to, urge his gunners on, and help supervise the treatment of the wounded crewmen. As he was standing on one side of a gun, a shell struck, knocking down five of the six who were manning it, and wounding Foote in the left arm.

The tiller ropes on the *Louisville* were shot away, rendering it difficult to steer her. When her pilot, Sam McBride, ran to the stern to try and repair the damage, a short shell from one of the wooden gunboats burst overhead, forcing McBride and others to seek shelter under the casemate. Without steering, Capt. Benjamin Dove was compelled to let the *Louisville* fall out of line.

The *Pittsburg* received a number of shots below the waterline; to keep her from sinking, Lieutenant Thompson ordered her downriver. As the *Pittsburg* dropped out of line, she struck the *Carondelet*'s stern, smashing the starboard rudder.

Walke and the *Carondelet* were the last to leave the fight. Having been struck repeatedly by ricochet shots aimed to hit the waterline, the *Carondelet* began to ship water. Her decks were slippery with blood—she had been hit fifty-four times—and the other gunboats were retiring. Walke had had enough.

For thirty minutes the gunboats remained under fire while they drifted downriver. Once safely out of range, they anchored as best they could. The *Pittsburg* was ordered to tie up to the east bank due to the large amount of water she was taking on.

Having surveyed his boats, Foote expressed confidence that after repairs, he could take Fort Donelson. Inwardly, however, he had serious doubts. His flotilla had been shot to pieces: the *St. Louis* hit fifty-nine times, the *Pittsburg* twenty times, and the *Louisville* thirty-six times. The design and construction of the "Pook Turtles" were quickly showing their weaknesses. Had he concentrated on dismounting the Confederates' two long-range guns, Foote could have laid back and disabled their 32-pounders and shelled the fort at will.

Phelps had been right. The fire from the gunboats passed over the Confederate positions, doing little damage. Confederate Capt.

USS *St. Louis*—One of seven gunboats referred to as "Pook Turtles" after their designer Samuel Pook and their distinctive profile. The *St. Louis* served as the Union flagship during the attack on Fort Donelson. (National Archives)

B. G. Bidwell observed that "their fire was more destructive to our works at 2 miles than at two hundred yards. They over fired us from that distance."[12]

The Confederates were jubilant. They had decisively defeated the dreaded gunboats, and were confident they could do the same to the Federal soldiers. Their commanders were not so sure. They were surrounded by Grant's army and threatened from the river by a still deadly flotilla. If they stayed, they would be trapped.

Brig. Gen. John Floyd, the Confederate commander, called a council of war with his division commanders, Gideon Pillow and Simon Bolivar Buckner. He stated that the fort could not be held with fewer than fifty thousand men, and that a breakout should be attempted. Pillow and Buckner agreed, and for the rest of the night, men were shifted from the right to Pillow's sector on the left. Planning to throw three-quarters of his army and Nathan Bedford Forrest's cavalry against McClernand's division on Grant's right, Floyd hoped to open an escape route.

Thirteen thousand Confederate troops began their advance at 5 A.M. on Saturday morning, February 15. The Union soldiers were just waking up and trying to get their freezing bodies in motion when the attack came. The Federals fought well but were steadily pushed back. McClernand called for help from Brig. Gen. Lew Wallace's division. Wallace, holding the Union center, sent Col. Charles Cruft's brigade on his own authority while couriers were sent to find General Grant. Meanwhile, the Confederate onslaught continued until an escape route over a mile wide was opened.

General Grant had just arrived ashore from a meeting with Flag Officer Foote when he was informed of the battle raging to the south. He immediately returned to the battlefield. Surveying the situation, Grant requested that the navy make a show of force. Foote had already departed for Cairo with Phelps on the *Conestoga,* to secure the *Benton* and the mortar boats, so Commander Dove, senior naval officer present, conferred with Walke and Paulding. Paulding volunteered the *St. Louis.* Covered by the *Louisville,* she moved to a position a mile and a half below the water batteries and fired several shells into the fort.

The Confederate plan had worked. Three roads were opened for a withdrawal, but for some reason, Pillow suddenly changed his mind. With increasing casualties, he felt it would be wiser for his troops to return to their trenches. Buckner protested vehemently, but Floyd reluctantly agreed with Pillow. With Grant on the scene and McClernand's men getting a chance to catch their breath during a lull in the Confederate advance, the tide turned. Wallace's and McClernand's reorganized brigades now moved to retake the ground they had lost that morning. Grant, reasoning that the strength of the Confederates' attack meant they had weakened their right, rode to General Smith's headquarters on the Union left and ordered a counterattack. Smith personally led the charge that seized several hundred yards of enemy rifle pits, and with that, the Confederate offensive collapsed.

That night, with thousands of dead and wounded men from both sides lying out in the freezing weather, Floyd decided to surrender. He and Pillow felt that to fight their way out would cause too many casualties. Any large-scale attempt at escape was thwarted by what the frightened generals mistakenly believed to be a Union stranglehold on all roads crossing the Fort Donelson perimeter. Floyd and Pillow decided to flee, leaving Buckner to surrender the Confederate army. One unit that refused to surrender was Nathan Bedford Forrest's cavalry, which, with Buckner's blessing, escaped.

Early on the morning of February 16, Buckner sent word to Grant that he desired terms of surrender. Grant replied, "No terms except unconditional and immediate surrender can be accepted."[13] Buckner felt this "ungenerous and unchivalrous" offer insulting.

As insulting as the offer was, Buckner had no choice. Either by siege or by starvation, surrender was now inevitable. When two white flags appeared from the parapets of the fort, Commander Dove took a tug and proceeded to a landing near the fort. "I was met by a Major," Dove later said, "who handed me his sword, which I declined to receive, thinking it proper to consult with General Grant. I took the Major on board the tug and proceeded up to General Buckner's headquarters, where I found General Wallace. General Grant arrived about half an hour after the fort had surrendered."[14]

For Phelps, the Confederate capitulation meant that the gunboat battle must have been "decisive." He wrote to Whittlesey:

> The Gunboats had demoralized the great rebel force, surrounded by our Army and which rendered the capture of this stronghold by a land force possible. But for the Gunboat fight we here all know that Genl Grant's Army would have been as far today from the possession of the works as they were before leaving Fort Henry to attack.[15]

Accounts of the surrender incensed Phelps.

> Com. Dove, the Senior Naval Officer, went to the shore in a tender to ask what it meant, and the officer commanding the rebels tendered his sword, saying that he surrendered the forts

to the Gunboats and will you believe it, this Com. Dove declined to receive the surrender saying that it must be made to Genl. Grant!!—thus depriving the Gunboats of this bright success. DOVE IS ONE OF THE RESTORED OFFICERS.[16]

Foote, too, was upset at "that old, stupid Dove"[17] for refusing the major's sword. Dove had assumed that the fort had already been surrendered to the army, and left without inquiring further about it.

Notwithstanding the credit he felt the gunboats deserved, Phelps heaped praise on his friend Brig. Gen. C. F. Smith:

> Do you know that our Army was at one time defeated before Fort Donelson & that General Smith—the same regular officer whom radical papers had so much abused as being traitor under the title of Paducah Smith—one of the first soldiers of our country, retrieved the fortunes of the day by leading his brigade to the charge of the chief redoubt, himself the first man in it! The Genl. stuck his cap upon the point of his sword and called upon his men to follow his lead. It is no stretch to say that defeat or victory hung upon his life & heaven guarded him in the terrible fire that for a while forced upon him & his command.[18]

Back in Paducah, Lizzie pitched in as the hospitals and public buildings were prepared to receive the wounded.

> We ladies were called upon to make bed sacks & pillows for them. When Monday morning several boats came in with our wounded & the glorious news of the surrender, some fifteen or twenty ladies, here as I am to be near their husbands, nearly all having their husband's fates yet to hear, were assembled at work for the comfort of these poor wounded men, great was the excitement & pale & anxious the faces. Soon the more slightly wounded were seen passing by & one of the ladies went out & brought him in. He was supplied with hot coffee & something to eat & most eagerly questioned by all in regard to those they were most nearly interested in. He was very young, quite a

boy, had his arm shot and apologized to the ladies for his face being unwashed saying he could not do it well with his left hand. After this we went under the supervision of one of the hospital nurses into one of the churches where those deemed more slightly wounded were but even these seemed *very terrible* to me. Truly this is the sad side of a great victory to see so many poor mangled men. They were generally so patient even cheerful under their suffering.[19]

The surrender was hailed in the North, and a grateful President Lincoln promoted Grant to major general. While the victory was almost entirely an army success, Foote was disappointed that the flotilla was not getting the credit it deserved: "We so demoralized the rebels, that it fell an easy prey to the army the next day as they are afraid to see the black boats arriving into their teeth and belching forth shot and shells."[20]

Foote was shaken by the pounding he had taken at Donelson. His wounded foot and the mangled bodies of his men made a profound impression. He felt he had been forced into battle before he was ready, had fought a much more desperate fight, and was not getting the proper recognition. After arriving at Cairo with Phelps late on February 15, Foote wrote to his wife, assuring her that "we will keep off a good distance from the Rebel forts in future engagements. I won't run into fire again, as a burnt child dreads it."[21]

Unaware of the fort's surrender, Foote planned to return within ten days, with the mortar boats and the *Benton*. Before he could reorganize his fleet, the *Carondelet* returned to Cairo early on February 17 and brought news of the surrender of the fort.

With the Cumberland River now open to Union shipping as far as Cumberland City, Foote sent six newly outfitted mortar boats along with the ironclad *Cairo* to Fort Donelson. Since the rest of his fleet was undergoing repairs, he departed Cairo on the eighteenth with Phelps on the *Conestoga*. Buell's Army of the Ohio was marching on Nashville, and Foote was anxious to have his gunboats in on the capture of the biggest prize yet.

The surrender of Fort Donelson caught General Halleck by surprise and brought confusion, for now Halleck had an open road to

Buell's objective but the two could not agree on how best to exploit it. Another threat added to the necessity of resolving their differences. Confederate troops and gunboats were reported assembling at Columbus, Kentucky, with the objective of attacking Cairo or Paducah. General in Chief McClellan decided to leave Nashville to Buell, which suited Halleck, for with his gunboats either "on the ways" or up the Cumberland River, he had little with which to defend against a Confederate attack on Cairo or Paducah.

Departing Fort Donelson on the morning of February 19, the *Conestoga*, carrying Flag Officer Foote's pennant, and the *Cairo* made their way upriver toward Clarksville, Tennessee. At 10 A.M. they passed the smoldering ruins of the Cumberland Iron Works, which the Confederates had fired on news that the gunboats were coming. By that afternoon the smoke from the gunboats was visible in Clarksville. The slaves who had heard of the gunboats' coming gathered at the waterfront, eagerly awaiting the men in blue.

By 3 P.M., the two gunboats reached Linwood Landing, about two miles below Clarksville. As the boats rounded a point, Fort Severe loomed into view, two hundred feet above the river. With guns at the ready, the two gunboats proceeded cautiously toward the confluence of the Cumberland and Red rivers, where a second fort, Fort Defiance, was situated. Since no flag could be seen flying from Fort Defiance, the *Conestoga* and *Cairo* slowed while one of the officers waved a handkerchief. Finally Phelps had the *Conestoga* blow her whistle. As if on cue, a dirty rag was run up the flagstaff.

As bluejackets were dispatched to occupy both forts, smoke could be seen rising from the unsuccessful attempt to burn the railroad bridges. The two gunboats then proceeded to the town, where the *Cairo* anchored in midstream and ran out her guns to cover the *Conestoga*, which docked at the Clarksville landing at 5 P.M. White flags flew throughout the town, and a number of people came down to the landing to see what fate the Yankees had in store for them. "See there—they have run the black flag up" exclaimed one, sighting the wet, dark-colored flag officer's pennant on the *Conestoga*. On being informed that the flagship was the *Conestoga*, the people said they had heard of the "pirate" before.[22]

Judge Thomas Wisdom, Mayor George Smith, and Cave Johnson, a friend of Foote's father, called on Foote to see what his intentions were. Foote informed them that he had no intention of harming the people or the town. He expected all military stores to be turned over to him and "that no secession flag or manifestation of secession feeling shall be exhibited."[23]

Ignorant of orders not to proceed past Clarksville, Foote returned to Cairo with the *Conestoga* to hurry up the repairs and get his gunboats back into action. The *Conestoga, Cairo,* and eight mortar scows were not enough to go after Nashville. When Foote arrived in Cairo and found that Halleck had no intention of taking Nashville, he decided to disregard the order and cooperate with General Grant's troops in the capture of Nashville. Halleck's chief of staff, Brig. Gen. George W. Cullum, would not release the repaired gunboats, however, so after several appeals to Halleck and the Navy Department, Foote and Grant abandoned the idea.

Phelps was angry:

We were about to proceed to the capture of Nashville, when a positive order came for the Gunboats not to pass Clarksville, but to leave the Cumberland. I immediately believed I knew what this meant, which was this—that Genl. Buell must have his chance to glorify and therefore the gunboats could not be allowed to follow up the victory at Donelson by scouring the Cumberland as we had done in the Tennessee. But we had already done the work for in the words of a Nashville paper— "while we have nothing to fear from the Yankee Army those Gunboats are the devil." The capture of the strongholds on the Tennessee & Cumberland forced the rebels to evacuate Bowling Green, and thus we shook the bush while Gen'l Buell was sent to "gather" the fruit in the capture of Nashville.[24]

If Phelps was angry, Foote was furious. The Cumberland River was open, and the Confederate army was evacuating Nashville in anticipation of Foote's arrival. After the hard fighting of the previous two weeks, to be denied the grandest prize of all was a slap in the face. "I am disgusted that we were kept from going up & taking Nashville," he wrote. "It was jealousy on the part of McClellan & Halleck." As far as the pending move down the Mississippi was concerned, Foote was "determined to wait till I get the gun & mortar boats ready & will not obey any orders except the Secretary's & President. I can well afford to be independent now."[25]

By February 26, Nashville had been evacuated by the Confederates and occupied by Buell. The *Tyler* and *Lexington* were once again ranging down the Tennessee River as far as Florence, Alabama. Halleck and Foote were preparing for the attack on Columbus, Kentucky, and Phelps had his ironclad, the USS *Benton*. "I take Phelps, a glorious officer, as Flag Captain of the *Benton*," Foote wrote to his wife. "[I] will there have an easy time myself. He is bold & cautious."[26]

CHAPTER EIGHT

ๆ

Island No. 10

THE USS *Benton* was the most powerful gunboat in Union service on the western rivers, "probably one of the most powerful naval vessels in the world," wrote Phelps.[1] Although similar in appearance, at one thousand tons she was almost twice as heavy as the "Pook Turtles." The *Benton* was 186 feet in length, and 74 feet in breadth. With a depth of hold of 8.5 feet, she drew about 5 feet of water.

The *Thomas H. Benton*, originally built as a snag boat by the government, was sold to the Western Wrecking Company and known as *Submarine No. 7.* It was the same boat that Comdr. John Rodgers had turned down in June 1861. In November 1861 she was purchased by General Frémont and altered according to plans prepared by James B. Eads. Having learned from the construction of the seven gunboats designed by Samuel Pook, Eads improved on the design by making her a true ironclad.

She was floated onto the Daggett & Morse ways at Carondelet, and two hundred men set about working seven days a week. Her twin hulls were covered with three- and four-inch planking to form one strong hull. Forty watertight compartments divided the interior of the hull, making the likelihood of sinking from hits by one or even several shells remote.

The *Benton*'s armor plate was three inches thick around the bow, two and a half inches at the stern and abreast of the engines, and five-eighths inch on the rest of the sides. The plating was fastened by iron bolts that were riveted on the inside and countersunk on the outside, making it difficult for shot to knock the plating loose. Backing the armor plate and supporting the casemate were oak timbers twenty-four inches thick at the bow and 12 inches thick in the less exposed areas. The casemate angled at 45 degrees to a height of seven feet, four inches, forming a spacious gun deck. Her battery consisted of sixteen heavy guns: six-inch, eight-inch, nine-inch, and rifled seven-inch guns.

Below the gun deck, in separate areas, were the powder magazine and shell rooms. They were made watertight by tongue and grooved boards secured with brass nails, covered with sheets of lead soldered together. Lighting was provided by lamps placed in boxes lined with copper and containing several inches of water. Each box was covered with a dome and fitted with a pipe to carry off the smoke. All metallic fixtures were made of copper. A large faucet allowed rapid flooding in the event of fire.

One large, center-mounted paddle wheel replaced the two independent wheels on the outside of the snag boat. The wheel was located in an opening a little forward of the stern and midway on the breadth of the vessel. The wheelhouse was covered with six-inch timber and covered with boiler iron. The original machinery was retained but would prove inadequate, considering her increased displacement. Four boilers fed steam to two engines with twenty-inch cylinders and seven-foot stroke. A Gwin pump, capable of pumping sixty barrels a minute, would handle any water in the bilges.[2]

The *Benton*'s maiden voyage, in December 1861, was under the direction of Capt. John Winslow, accompanied by Flag Officer Foote and James Eads. Proceeding to Cairo, the *Benton* stuck on a bar, and all attempts to free her only served to make her harder aground.

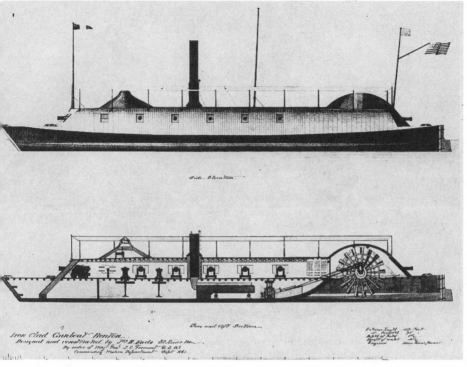

USS *Benton*—Blueprint drawing of James B. Eads's design. (U.S. Naval Historical Center)

Eads, with decades of river experience, offered his help, which Winslow quickly accepted. An eleven-inch hawser was run out to the shore, followed by several others. The *Benton* was equipped with three steam-powered capstans behind the forward casemate, and these were used in an attempt to pull the boat free. One of the hawsers ran through a snatch block chained to the side of the boat. As the capstans slowly turned and the hawsers groaned under the strain, the chain holding the block shattered. One piece dented the armor plate, another was found on the bank more than five hundred feet away, and a third tore through Winslow's arm.[3]

USS *Benton*—Considered one of the most powerful warships in the world, she mounted sixteen heavy guns but was ponderously slow. (National Archives)

Captain Winslow took a leave of absence to recover from his wound. With his departure, the way was clear for Foote to make good on his promise to Phelps.

With the pending descent of the Mississippi, Phelps now had the vessel he had sought. "Flag Officer Foote has been a warm friend," he wrote, "and has managed to reserve for me this splendid command of his Flagship."[4] With the prospect of his prize, the *Eastport*, being an even finer and faster gunboat when construction on her was finished, Phelps had the command he had always dreamed of.

Ambition, however, still drove him. Phelps explained to his mentor Elisha Whittlesey:

I do not know why I should not write to you as I would to my father with a frank admission of what is in my heart, as I have indeed, always done, hardly conscious that you are not as much in the relation of father to me as any one on earth. Before the capture of Fort Henry and Donelson Flag Officer Foote told me that he had already informed the Navy Department that I deserved promotion for my services on the Tennessee, Cumberland & Ohio, and since my expedition on the Tennessee to Alabama, he tells me he regards it as certain. Those officers [Gwin and Shirk] commanding vessels under me in that expedition so regarded & spoke of it, but the Flag Officer thinks this a matter which friends at court should look out for, and adds that he shall leave no exertion he can make in my interest unmade.

Now I confess that a promotion coming as a reward of acknowledged service would be infinitely grateful. We who are taken as boys and trained for the service attach an importance to such an honor no words can express. I feel still that with our government and its fractions, unless there are friends who claim what is due, an officer may be passed by, except where some brilliant exploit makes a quick recognition by promotion only an obedience to the popular will. I am now led to believe by opinion of officers of the Army and Navy about me that a claim can be made without impropriety in my behalf, but it is not within my power to write that such are my thoughts to any one less near to me than you. Now that I command a splendid vessel I look back with pride, which may be weakness, upon the reputation of that crazy craft the "*Conestoga.*" All this is predicated upon the assumption that promotion out of succession by seniority is determined upon by the government for good services rendered.[5]

While Phelps supervised completion of work on the *Benton* at Cairo, the move to open the Mississippi began on February 23, 1862, as Foote led a flotilla consisting of the *Cincinnati, St. Louis, Mound City, Carondelet,* and *Conestoga* downriver. With five transports and two mortar boats accompanying the refurbished fleet, everyone expected an assault to be made on Columbus, Kentucky. At 10 A.M. the fleet rounded the point above Columbus and was saluted by a Confederate shell hitting the water a mile ahead. The transports halted while the gunboats continued ahead. Another shell fell short as the gunboats formed into a line of battle. No sooner had the line been formed than a Confederate steamer appeared, bearing a white flag. The *Cincinnati* and a tug dropped down to see what it meant. From noon until 1:45 P.M. a conference was held at which the Confederates requested that the families of officers captured at Fort Donelson be allowed to pass through Union lines and join them. While this request was being relayed to General Halleck, the gunboats weighed anchor at 2:45 P.M. and returned to Cairo. General Halleck granted the request the next day; in the meantime, the flag of truce had been used to good advantage by the Confederates in preparing the evacuation of Columbus.

Rumors were rampant in Cairo about Columbus. Now that the Tennessee and Cumberland rivers were open, Columbus was vulnerable to a land attack, but no one was sure what the Confederates would do. At one time or another it was reported both evacuated and reinforced. When the *Lexington* returned from up the Tennessee River on Monday morning, March 3, rumors circulated about Cairo that a move up that river was imminent. That afternoon the gunboats, including the *Benton*, were ordered to get upsteam. As each boat raised maneuvering pressure, it eased into the river and anchored. Troops began embarking on the transport steamers early the next morning, and at 4 A.M. Foote ordered the flotilla down the Mississippi toward Columbus.

Making good speed with the current, the formation arrived at Lucas Bend, three miles above Columbus, at 7 A.M. In the distance, on a clear and cold morning, bluffs of American chalk rose to a height of 150 feet. Three rows of batteries mounting a reported 140 guns were thought to command the river. The trees on Belmont Point, across the Mississippi, had been cut down to give the Confederates an unrestricted view upriver.

Foote received reports that the position had been evacuated, but intelligence was notoriously inaccurate and it was difficult to determine the situation with a spyglass.

As the crews were beat to quarters, the gunboats came about and faced upriver to maintain better handling in the current. For the next thirty minutes crews once again began protecting the upper decks from plunging shot with hawsers, spars, coal bags, and chains. Furniture was cleared from the wardroom and rear cabin to facilitate the working of the stern guns.

Union gunners were confident that the lower two rows of batteries could be taken by firing into the cliffs, which would collapse the chalk onto the Rebels below.

Still not certain that the fortifications had been evacuated, a tug carrying Phelps and Brig. Gen. William T. Sherman ran in toward the lower battery. As the tug approached, the two officers could not see any guns. The fortifications looked deserted. The two officers landed and dashed to the summit, carrying a United States flag. As they planted the flag, they were greeted by the wild cheers of Sherman's 2nd Illinois Cavalry, which had occupied the fort the day before.

The Confederate evacuation of the "Gibraltar of the West" had commenced the week before. Twenty thousand men removed stores and ammunition to the Mobile & Ohio Railroad terminus at Columbus. The few guns that could not be removed were tumbled into the river or lay at the foot of the cliffs. A reported eighteen thousand bushels of corn and five thousand tons of hay were burned by Confederate cavalry that pulled out on Sunday.

Following the occupation of Columbus, the gunboats returned to Cairo. Additional repairs were needed (the *Benton*'s pilothouse still was not armor-plated), and men and supplies to fill out each gunboat's complement were taken aboard, in preparation for the next objective: Island No. 10.

The Union movement to control the Mississippi River began when troops under Brig. Gen. John Pope advanced down the Missouri side of the river and arrived at the town of New Madrid on March 1. A few miles above the town lay the Confederate bastion on Island No. 10, so named because it was the tenth island downriver from Cairo. With the flotilla expected to arrive north of Island No. 10 shortly, cooperation between Pope and Foote would be crucial.

Flag Officer Foote was tired and depressed. His wound was not healing properly, and the constant demands placed upon him were taking their toll.

It has added two years to my age constitutionally and is quite enough to break any man down. I would this moment give all I am worth could I have been in the Atlantic, a captain of a good steam frigate, instead of out here under a pressure, which would crush most men, and how I have stood I can only account for that God has been my helper thus far. All is confusion and I am almost crazy and in despair.[6]

Refusing to be rushed by General Halleck, Foote finally issued sailing orders on Tuesday night, March 11. The fleet was to be ready to head downriver by three the next afternoon. That afternoon a series of countermanding orders were issued, the last one for the fleet to stand down. After urging Foote to hurry up, Halleck now ordered him to wait until Pope could establish siege guns below New Madrid to cut off any Confederate retreat.

Finally, early on Friday morning, March 14, the flotilla began its descent. By 5 P.M. it had made its way to Hickman, Kentucky, about twenty-five miles below Columbus, where Foote decided to anchor for the night. As the *Benton* eased her way to the town's landing, several women and children waved, but generally there were only silent stares. A Confederate cavalry detachment, which had been watching them from a nearby bluff, disappeared, presumably to spread the word of their coming.

The 26th Illinois landed their band and, with a detachment carrying the colors, marched through the town to the strains of "Yankee Doodle." This attempt at public relations ended with a shrill whistle and the sharp sounds of muskets being fired. A Confederate train had arrived; as soon as the Federals were spotted, it made a hasty retreat.

The flotilla got under way again just before 6 A.M., on March 15. Just below Island No. 8, the Confederate steamer *Grampus* appeared through the fog. Startled at the sight of the gunboats, the *Grampus* stopped her engines and struck her colors. Having second thoughts, however, her crew quickly turned her about and headed downriver, several shells from the *Benton* falling astern. Crewman Symmes Brown, on board the *Mound City*, noted that the *Grampus* "ran and hollered [whistled] worse than a scared dog with a tin pan after dinner and soon dodged behind a bend."[7]

The Mississippi curled in numerous directions in the vicinity of Island No. 10, crossing the Tennessee–Kentucky border several times. Heavy rains had caused the river to flood its banks. As the island came into view from the *Benton*, Phelps and Foote saw in the distance a chain of batteries, each covering the one above it, extending for four miles along the crescent-shaped Tennessee shore. In the lower corner of the crescent lay Island No. 10. Any boat attempting to pass would be subject to a cross fire from at least fifty heavy guns mounted on the island and the Tennessee shore.

As the *Benton* continued slowly down the segment of the river, between Island No. 8 and Island No. 10, known as Seven-Mile Stretch, Phelps scanned the trees, for masked batteries. Firing shells into likely hiding places but uncovering no cannons, the *Benton* stopped at the point formed by a double bend in the river. Just above the bend were the *Grampus, Falls City, Ohio Belle,* and *Red Rover,* which still bore the inscription "U.S. Mail Packet." Next to the island was a floating battery mounting twelve guns.

When it was determined that the point was clear of Confederates, a tug was dispatched to find a suitable place for the mortar boats to tie up. Just after 1 P.M., the no. 1 and no. 12 mortar boats were secured to several cottonwoods, and one hour later they opened fire. At 3 P.M. the *Benton* threw a shell at the island that exploded just as it reached the top of its arc, thanks to a defective fuse. A second rifled shell, its fuse wet, fell just short of the *Red Rover,* which hurried downriver, followed by the other steamers.

With enemy guns silent, Phelps took a tugboat and headed downriver. Surveying the work of his guns, he had the tugboat dart back and forth within range of Confederate batteries, hoping to draw their fire and thus learn their strength. When no gun took the bait, Phelps returned upriver to the *Benton*.

With Foote constantly moving about the upper deck on his crutches, the rest of the afternoon was spent throwing some fifty-five shells at the fort and receiving several in return, all of which fell short. The *Benton,* being a heavy craft, absorbed the shock of the firing much better than the other gunboats. The curious spectators who went to witness the firing of the stern guns, however, were in for a rude shock; the top of the wheelhouse was not the place to be. The concussion of the firing caused several to complain of severe headaches.

For the sailors on Comdr. Augustus Kilty's *Mound City*, watching the action was almost too much to bear. Not yet having been in battle, "everyone was all excitement to 'pitch in,'" wrote Symmes Brown, "but the Commodore was more considerate than us hot headed greenhorns and kept us back."[8]

After the Union army occupied New Madrid, Pope proceeded twelve miles farther downriver on the Missouri side to Point Pleasant, where he placed his artillery to blockade the river. In order to get at Island No. 10, however, he needed to cross the river. And to do that, he needed gunboat support to suppress Confederate batteries on the Tennessee shore and to keep their gunboats from interfering.

The wound to the flag officer's foot, which was not healing properly, served as a constant reminder that the direct assaults that had carried him to glory would not work here. It would be almost impossible for his gunboats to pass the batteries without exposing their lightly armored sides to Confederate guns. There were at least three times as many guns as he had faced at Henry and Donelson. Any disabled vessel would be carried by the current into the teeth of the enemy guns and certain destruction.

Phelps wrote:

The rebels have an immensely strong position here, and the Gunboats cannot get at them, the slowness of our vessels and the powerful current of the river rendering disaster more than probable unless we proceed with great caution, and have an army to assist. The rebels have selected this place with this knowledge and we cannot get troops to where they are except from below, on account of the overflow of the banks. It is a work of time to effect this; but be assured we are not idle.[9]

Caution was also dictated by the realization that Foote had only twelve gunboats with which to protect hundreds of miles of river. The Union army had expended little effort to build the forts necessary to protect against a Confederate invasion should the gunboat fleet be destroyed. Any large losses would make cities from Cairo to Cincinnati vulnerable. General Halleck realized this when he wrote to Foote not to expose his gunboats unnecessarily: "The reduction of these batteries this week or next, is a matter of very little importance."[10]

Upon arriving above Island No. 10, Foote sent a message to Halleck, informing him that he would wait until all was ready.

> The troops and transports are not here, and I consider it unsafe to move without troops to occupy No. 10 if we capture it, as we can not take prisoners with gunboats. Hence, should we pass No. 10 after its capture, the rebels on the Tennessee side would return and man their batteries and thus shut up the river in our rear, as we should be short of coal and towboats to get back to reattack No. 10 or the opposite shore.[11]

Eight mortar boats were towed into position on Sunday morning, March 16, along the point on the Missouri shore. The mortar boat was a raft sixty feet long and twenty-five feet wide. Six-foot sloping sides, plated with quarter-inch iron, protected the crew from small arms fire. Iron hatches covered openings for entry and exit. Eight small chambers held the powder and shells. With a distance of seventeen inches from the thirteen-inch bore to the outer rim, each mortar weighed 17,200 pounds and was mounted on a 4,500-pound carriage. This tremendous weight made the boat float near the deck level, so the bulwarks were corked and waterproofed to a height of two feet, to allow for the recoil. A canvas covering sheltered the crew from the weather.

That afternoon a tug arrived from Cairo, carrying James B. Eads and U.S. Representative Elihu Washburne. There to discuss construction of new, shallow-draft gunboats, Eads watched as the *Benton* threw shells downriver. Next to Eads, Flag Officer Foote was observing the shelling through his lorgnette when an officer handed him a dozen or more letters that had come on the tug. Eads later wrote:

> While still conversing with me, his eyes glanced over them as he held them in his hand, and he selected one which he pro-

ceeded to open. Before reading probably four lines, he turned to me with great calmness and composure, and said "Mr. Eads, I must ask you to excuse me for a few minutes while I go down to my cabin. This letter brings me the news of the death of my son, about thirteen years old, who I had hoped would live to be the stay and support of his mother."

Without further remark, and without giving the slightest evidence of his feeling to any one, he left me and went to his cabin. . . . he returned after an absence of not more than fifteen minutes, still perfectly composed.[12]

As Foote focused on the work at hand, he requested that Eads return to Cairo, not wishing to lose such a valuable man to a chance shell.

Foote was now compelled to summon all his faith in God. "I am very much exhausted," he wrote to his grieving wife. "My feelings are so much lacerated by the shock of dear William's death that I am unfit for anything but I must stand up to my duty. If it were not for you & the dear children, Oh how I should welcome death at God's earliest pleasure."[13]

On Monday morning, March 17, Foote called his captains together for a council to decide how best to proceed. It was decided to lash the *Benton, St. Louis,* and *Cincinnati* together to form a floating battery able to approach the Confederate batteries head-on. Once again crews set about preparing the boats. Upper decks and boilers received their usual hammocks, hawsers, chains, and spars. Hoses were attached to pumps on the boilers so any boarders could be repelled with live steam. Surgeons prepared their instruments, and fires were extinguished, except for the forges of the boats' engineers, so they could rapidly provide any bracket, brace, or engine part needed. All obstructions to the free passage of shot and powder were removed, fire tubs were filled, and slings were prepared to lower carpenters and their materials over the side for stopping shot holes.

Just after noon the cumbersome three-boat monster, the *Benton* in the center, got under way and started down the east side of the river. The *Carondelet* and *Mound City* were on the west side of the river, and the *Pittsburg* moved to the east side. Foote commanded "Fire!"

With all the gunboats and mortar boats firing, the Confederate guns were initially silent. When they did open fire, their shells fell short.

With the paddle wheels of the three key boats turning slowly in reverse to slow the descent against the current, course was changed slightly to bring the ten bow guns to bear on the lower shore batteries. Confederate gunners now began to find the range of the gunboats—several shells whizzed overhead. One shell landed astern of the *Benton,* throwing up a geyser of water, and another struck between the *Benton* and *St. Louis* at the waterline, soaking everyone on the upper decks.

Suddenly an explosion racked the *St. Louis;* broken glass from her skylights rained down on the *Benton.* One of her rifled guns had exploded, killing two men and wounding eleven. Men, their faces blackened by powder, carried the lifeless body of one of their shipmates to the stern of the boat. This second fatal rupture of a rifled 42-pounder caused a loss of confidence in these weapons. It was feared that the rifling process removed too much metal, thus weakening the gun.

At 3:15 P.M., a Rebel sixty-four-pound shell struck the *Benton* amidship on her starboard side, ripping through five-eighth-inch plate and five-inch timbers before striking the gun deck below, "scattering splinters all about, and, bounding up, struck the beams of the upper deck, & then fell back upon a small desk of the Flag Officer, depositing itself quietly in the drawer."[14]

Ten minutes later another shell struck the ventilator, then penetrated the port chimney, knocking out an iron support. It shattered a skylight and tore up two sections of deck iron before harmlessly rolling against the hammock nettings.

With Flag Officer Foote in the pilothouse and Captain Phelps directing his gunners from the gun deck, the bombardment continued all afternoon, both sides giving as good as they got. A number of the *Benton*'s nine-inch shells exploded as soon as they left the guns, causing their gunners to wet the fuses and fire them as solid shot. Several Confederate shells hit the *Cincinnati,* causing minor damage, and a shell struck the *Benton* on her forward casemate, bouncing off just as it was intended to. By 5 P.M. the three gunboats neared the bend of the river, where they would be subject to a cross fire.

As the sun began to set, the unwieldy gunboats wheeled about and headed upriver. The Confederates in the water battery mounted their parapets and cheered, believing they had carried the day. The bombardment had lasted six hours, and the *Benton* had fired 281 shots. With the exception of the burst gun on the *St. Louis,* the affair settled little. It was fought largely at long range, so neither side gained an advantage, although stalemate favored the Confederates.

Tuesday, March 18, brought only sporadic shelling by the Union mortars and gunboats. Later that night Col. J. W. Bissell, Pope's senior engineer, came on board the *Benton* to confer with Foote. Compelled to find a shortcut from New Madrid, Bissell, along with two soldiers, had taken a skiff through the bayous and swamps.

With yet another request from Pope to send gunboat support, Foote again called a council of war with his captains. "The officers," Foote wrote, "with one exception, were decidedly opposed to running the blockade, believing it would result in almost certain destruction of the boats which should attempt to pass the six forts, with fifty guns bearing upon the vessel."[15]

Colonel Bissell pleaded with Foote:

> I strongly urged that one of the gunboats might be allowed to run the batteries, and by her help General Pope would be able to capture the island in a single day.
>
> Captain Phelps, at the time commanding the *Benton,* strongly seconded my efforts to induce Commodore Foote to send a boat, and requested to be allowed to command it. When Commodore Foote objected on account of the danger to the remaining boats, should the one that started be captured, Captain Phelps feelingly replied that if he were entrusted with a boat it should not fall into enemy hands; he would go through prepared to blow her up, and would destroy her rather than she should be used against us. . . . Had Captain Phelps been allowed to try, as he requested, the island would have been taken nearly four weeks sooner. Fort Pillow at that time had no guns and the opening of the river would have been very easy.[16]

For Foote the problem was obvious. Because the river at Point Pleasant was a mile wide, Pope thought running the batteries would be easy. To get past Island No. 10, however, a gunboat would have to run a gauntlet of heavy guns at a distance of only three hundred yards. If Confederate gunners missed at that distance, Foote wrote, "we would in the Navy consider the gunners totally unfit for employment in the service."[17] The memory of Confederate gunners scoring almost half their rounds at Fort Donelson was fresh, as were the consequences of being rushed by the army.

Although he did not get the answer he had hoped for, Bissell still did not return to General Pope empty-handed. His journey through the flooded swamps satisfied him that there might be a way for transports, if not gunboats, to reach New Madrid while bypassing Island No. 10. Bissell discovered a route and set his engineers to work digging and clearing a channel through the sunken trees and other obstacles. The route cleared through St. John's Bayou was used by a number of small vessels, but it was not the answer to Pope's problem. He needed gunboats, and Foote would not send them.

At 10:30 A.M. on Sunday, March 23, Lieutenant Bishop called "all hands to muster." The *Benton's* sailors, clad in their plain blue uniforms, assembled on the forward port side of the gun deck. Facing them on the starboard side were the marines standing "at ease" with their muskets and fixed bayonets resting on their left shoulders. In the foreground was a capstan covered with the Federal Union Jack. Around it stood Flag Officer Foote, Lieutenant Phelps, Col. Napoleon B. Buford, and other officers. As the flag officer approached, he was saluted by all hands, who stood with uncovered heads. The bright, showy uniforms of the officers were in striking contrast to the plain garb of the sailors and marines. Foote reminded the crew that this was Sunday, the day set aside for rest and worship. This was the first worship service held on the *Benton*. The preceding Sunday had been occupied with the heavy shelling of Island No. 10.

The continuing bombardment became so monotonous that one officer with Pope's army remarked, in response to an inquiry about the navy: "Oh! It is still bombarding the State of Tennessee at long range."[18] Wrote Symmes Brown on the *Mound City:*

One would be led to judge from the unconcerned and quiet-like manner in which we are pursuing this attack, that it was more a trial of gunnery or a 4th of July demonstration than otherwise. We sit about the decks, reading newspapers, magazines, letters &c with as much comparative confidence of our safety as though seated at home.[19]

On March 25, a break in the routine occurred when the men of the flotilla watched the ascent of a balloon to observe the bombardment. Capt. J. H. Steiner of the Aeronautic Corps had been sent by McClellan to aid Halleck. Halleck was not interested, and sent Steiner to Cairo. While waiting for some word from Halleck, Steiner offered his services to Foote as he was preparing to head downriver. Foote accepted, and placed a large flatboat at his disposal. On March 20 the flatboat, with Steiner's balloon, *Eagle,* and its generator, were towed downriver.

The flatboat was anchored about a mile upriver from the *Benton,* and on March 23, twelve thousand cubic feet of hydrogen were pumped into the silk balloon. The ascent had to be postponed for two days after high winds developed.

On March 25, the wind abated, and at 3 P.M. Steiner, Phelps, and Capt. Henry Maynadier, Lizzie's older brother and commander of the mortar division, made the ascent, tethered to the flatboat. Their observations were somewhat limited due to smoke and haze, but they saw seven Confederate steamers at the lower end of the island and no gunboats.

The next day Steiner made the ascent with Colonel Buford and Maynadier. This time they saw the Confederate positions and the mortar shells falling well to the rear of the batteries. The direction was satisfactory but the charges were too large, causing the mortars to overshoot their targets. With this information, Maynadier corrected the firing of his mortars and made them much more effective.

This was the only time that a balloon was used for observation in the West during the Civil War. Steiner returned to Cairo to await word from General Halleck, who was still not interested. Without his approval, nothing else was accomplished.[20]

Foote called another council of war after Colonel Bissell had brought a second letter from Pope urging an attempt to run the batteries. Pope was becoming so frustrated that he was considering asking Halleck's approval to remove the bluejackets and run the batteries with army crews. Against his better judgment, Foote finally decided to risk a boat. He was not, however, going to let Phelps and the *Benton* make the attempt.

Phelps's quiet pleas were rejected. "[The attempt] possessed me," he wrote, "and made me persistent about running the blockade at Island No. 10."[21] Foote would find another captain. The loss of the flagship would be an incalculable morale blow to the navy. Allowing Phelps to command one of the other boats would imply cowardice on the part of her captain. Foote decided to ask for a volunteer.

After consulting privately with each captain in order of seniority, Foote announced that Captain Walke had volunteered the *Carondelet*. He told Walke to wait for a foggy or rainy night; this inspired little confidence on the part of General Pope, for the moon was nearly full and the foggy weather was behind them. Pope began preparations to build his own crude gunboats, for by now he had lost confidence in the navy.

When Walke received his formal orders to run the batteries on March 30, he set about preparing his vessel in the usual way. In addition, a coal barge laden with coal and hay was lashed to the lightly armored port side for added protection. Finding the hay stacked on the outside of the barge, Walke set his crew to moving it to the inboard side, up to the top of the broadside gun ports and along the stern casemate. The guns were run in and the hatches were closed. The engineers routed the escape steam through pipes into the wheelhouse, to muffle the puffing sound it made when blown through the chimneys. One observer noted, "The *Carondelet* at that time resembled a farmer's wagon prepared for market."[22]

Considering the risk involved, Walke asked for volunteers. First Master Richard Wade declined to go and was replaced by William Hoel, first master of the *Cincinnati,* whose 194th trip to New Orleans, it was hoped, would soon be complete.

On the evening of April 4, twenty-three volunteer sharpshooters from the 42nd Illinois boarded the *Carondelet* to assist in repelling

Henry Walke—Something of a martinet, Walke commanded the *Caron-delet* from Fort Henry to her unfortunate encounter with the *Arkansas*. (U.S. Naval Historical Center)

boarders. By 10 P.M., the moon had set and gathering storm clouds provided the near total darkness needed to sneak past the Rebel batteries. Walke passed the word—"All ready"—and lines holding the *Carondelet* to the shore were cast loose. After a little difficulty rounding to, because of the awkward barge, the *Carondelet* headed downriver. Only occasional flashes of lightning pierced the darkness to reveal the shoreline. So quietly did the engines propel the *Carondelet* that one of her officers asked the engineer if he was "going ahead on her."

The passage had gone undetected when a thunderstorm burst over the *Carondelet*. Darkness that had protected the gunboat was now punctuated by lightning flashes: "almost every second, every brace, post, and outline could be seen with startling distinctness, enshrouded by a bluish white glare of light."[23] With discovery possible at any moment, Walke called for flank speed.

When the *Carondelet* was opposite battery no. 2, bright flames leaped from the chimneys. Word was quickly passed to the engineer to open the flue caps, and the flames subsided. With the *Carondelet* looking like a floating roman candle, her crew held their breath. Their luck still held, for nothing but silence followed. Suddenly flames again leaped from the chimneys. "Why in hell were the flue caps not kept open?" demanded Hoel. The soot in the chimneys, which normally was kept wet with the engine steam now vented to the wheelhouse, had become so dry that it caught fire.

The sound of muskets in the distance revealed that the *Carondelet* had been spotted. Flashes of lightning illuminated Confederate gunners as they scrambled to bring their guns to bear. Walke yelled down the speaking tube for the engineer to give her everything he had. The boatswain's mate was sent to the forecastle with lead and line to make soundings. The soundings were relayed to Master's Mate T. S. Gilmore, on the upper deck, who relayed them to William Hoel, standing outside the pilothouse.

With Confederate shells now falling all about her, the *Carondelet* pressed on. Guided by flashes of lightning that illuminated the shore and constant soundings, Hoel calmly relayed commands to the pilot at the wheel. The lightning began to abate, and during a long stretch of darkness, the current moved the gunboat toward the riverbank.

Hoel realized they were headed for certain grounding. "Hard-a-port, hard-a-port," he shouted. The *Carondelet,* the barge still lashed alongside, grudgingly came about. In the darkness, one of the pilots heard a Confederate officer shout, "Elevate your guns!" With barrels depressed to keep out rainwater and no clear target to aim at, the Confederates now raised the elevation too much and fired over the gunboat.

After what seemed like an eternity, the boatswain finally cried, "No bottom." Now there was only one more obstacle. The floating battery had been moved three miles downriver after heavy shelling from the gunboats several days before. Hoping to keep as much distance as possible between the *Carondelet* and the battery, Walke hugged the Missouri shore as the battery fired six or eight shots, one of which lodged in a hay bale on the barge.

Finally the *Carondelet* passed out of range, and the crew breathed a collective sigh of relief. A short time later she arrived at New Madrid. As the crew congratulated themselves, Purser George Nixon asked Walke for permission to "splice the main brace." Walke gave his permission, and soon the shout of "Grog, oh!" resounded through the gunboat. Foote would have been aghast, but that night the *Carondelet* had a merry and relieved crew.

Late on the evening of April 6, Phelps and Egbert Thompson anxiously watched the increasingly cloudy sky from the spar deck of the *Benton.* As the two officers conversed, others speculated about what the night skies would bring.

Not long after midnight, Thompson returned to the *Pittsburg,* which was at the *Benton*'s starboard side, next to the Missouri shore. With Phelps and Foote looking on, the *Pittsburg* cast off and floated away with the current. Word quickly spread that the *Pittsburg* would attempt to run the batteries. About thirty or forty sleepy sailors appeared on deck and watched the boat disappear into the dark night. "There she goes!" "That's the *Pittsburg*!" "Good luck to the craft!" Soon numerous guns were heard in the darkness, and everyone held their breath. Phelps remained on deck in the rain until 4 A.M. At breakfast, word was received that the *Pittsburg* had made it.[24]

Having convoyed Pope's army across the river to the Tennessee side, the *Carondelet* made her presence felt south of the island. The

Confederates had already begun abandoning the island and its supporting batteries when the passage of the *Pittsburg* added urgency to the withdrawal.

Later on April 7, a steamer approached the *Benton* with all her lights showing and blowing her whistle repeatedly. Taking no chances, the *Benton* beat to quarters, but the steamer *De Soto* carried a flag of truce. Confederate Lts. George S. Martin and E. S. McDowell, bearing a message for the flag officer, were escorted aboard. Following a meeting with Foote and Colonel Buford, Phelps accompanied the Confederate officers back to Island No. 10. He returned at 2 A.M. on April 8, to announce its unconditional surrender.

e/Ɔ

Fort Pillow & the Battle
of Plum Point Bend

A FTER SEVERAL DAYS of repairs and resupply, the Union fleet
steamed south toward its next objective. Fifty miles north of
Memphis lay Fort Pillow, the last major Confederate stronghold protecting the city. Constructed on nearly vertical bluffs overlooking
a hairpin turn in the river, the fort mounted some forty guns and
reportedly was manned by six thousand troops. The Confederates
had taken advantage of the sharp ridges, deep gorges, and streams to
enfilade and command any Union land attack. Miles of trenches
and numerous batteries mounting guns up to ten inches made Fort
Pillow every bit as formidable as Island No. 10.

With General Pope and his army operating from the west bank of
the Mississippi, a repeat of the successful tactics that took Island
No. 10 was anticipated. A new element appeared on April 12, however, when a Union transport spotted the Confederate gunboat *General Sterling Price*. The transport was pursued by the *Price* until she
passed the Union fleet at the mouth of the Obion River. Unsure of

the size of the Union fleet due to darkness, the *Price* withdrew to announce the arrival of the Federals.

The *General Sterling Price* was one of sixteen converted river steamers that formed the Confederates' River Defense Fleet. These gunboats were constructed with double pine bulkheads bolted together every eighteen inches and stuffed with compressed cotton. Although they carried one or two guns each, it was their reinforced bow of four-inch oak and one-inch iron, together with their great speed, that provided their offensive power.

Commanded by James E. Montgomery and J. H. Townsend, former riverboat captains, the River Defense Service was made up of civilian steamboat crews. Each captain completed and armed his boat as he saw fit, for as Gen. Albert Sidney Johnston remarked, "Mississippi captains and pilots would never agree upon anything after they had gotten under way." Wishing to remain independent, the rivermen "entered the service with the distinct understanding or condition that they were not to be placed under the orders of naval officers."[1]

Confederate Maj. Gen. Mansfield Lovell, commander of the military district headquartered at New Orleans, found these rivermen also were not suited for command in the army:

> The river pilots who are the head of the fleet are men of limited ideas, no system and no administrative capacity whatever. I very much fear, too, that their power of execution will prove much less than has been anticipated—in short, unless some competent person of education, system and brains is put over each division of the fleet, it will in my judgement, prove an utter failure.[2]

The *Price* rendezvoused with several other rams, and early the next morning they formed in line of battle to meet the Union fleet. As the opposing forces closed to within three miles of each other, the *Benton* opened fire. The Confederate gunboat *Maurepas* replied with her nine-inch Dahlgren gun, both shots falling short. By this time the entire Union fleet had come into view, and Capt. Thomas B. Huger,

Confederate flag officer on board the *McRae*, decided this was not the time or the place for a battle. The Confederate fleet withdrew downriver, leaving the *General Sterling Price* to finish the welcoming. Turning to and waiting until the *Benton* had closed to within two miles, the *Price* opened fire with her stern gun, then dropped downriver, engaging in a running gun battle with the Union boats until 11:30 A.M., when she reached Fort Pillow. There was no damage on either side, except for a Confederate shell that burst over the *Benton,* showering her bow with shrapnel.

That afternoon, General Pope and Assistant Secretary of War Thomas Scott came on board the *Benton* for a conference with Flag Officer Foote. They decided that Pope would cross the river about five miles above Fort Pillow and attempt to work his way behind it. When Pope's army was in position, Foote's gunboats and mortars would open fire in a coordinated assault.

The plan turned out to be impractical because of the high stage of the river, which flooded the swamps behind the fort. It was then proposed to cut a canal across the base of the peninsula on the Arkansas side of the river, and run gunboats and transports through to attack the fort from the south. This plan was abandoned, and the whole situation changed completely when the Tennessee River once again became the center of Union strategy.

After the victories at Forts Henry and Donelson, General Grant had moved his army up the Tennessee River to Savannah, Tennessee, in preparation, along with Buell's army, for a move against the important Confederate rail junction at Corinth, Mississippi. By early April most of his army was massing across the river at Pittsburg Landing, awaiting the arrival of Buell's army, which was marching southwest from Nashville.

Confederate General Albert Sidney Johnston was not, however, going to wait for two Federal armies to descend upon him. Early on the morning of April 6, Johnston threw his hastily reorganized army against Grant at Shiloh Church. After being pushed steadily back, Grant rallied his troops. With the timely arrival of Buell's army, together with gunfire support from the *Lexington* and *Tyler,* the Federals prevailed the following day in the bloodiest battle fought on North American soil to that point.

After the Union victory, General Halleck arrived on the scene and assumed overall command. He decided to reinforce his already formidable army before he moved on Corinth, and ordered Pope to abandon the attempt against Fort Pillow and proceed with his army to Hamburg Landing, just upstream from Pittsburg Landing. Halleck was not giving up on forcing open the Mississippi River, however. With Corinth in Union hands, both Fort Pillow and Memphis would be cut off and ripe for the picking. In the meantime, Foote was left with only fifteen hundred troops to garrison the fort, should the Confederates decide to evacuate.

"The question here presents itself in a somewhat different light," Phelps wrote. Reflecting the confidence and caution that characterized his influence with Foote, he continued:

> Just below the fort lie 13 rebel gunboats of which 7 or 8 are rams, a kind of floating animal of which we possess not one. We have seven gunboats, called ironclad, and the old *Conestoga*. We could run the fire of the batteries, and, attacking the fort from below, no doubt capture it; but we have a much more numerous fleet to fight as well as the heavy guns on shore, and the question involves the control of both the Ohio & Mississippi. If we, in such odds, are disabled, such has been the carelessness of our military people that nothing effective checks the rebel way to Cincinnati. Under these circumstances the Flag Officer deems time of less consequence than the risk. The battle of Corinth will seal the fate of this place.[3]

Tending to his command was becoming increasingly difficult for Flag Officer Foote because his wounded foot, later diagnosed as a broken bone, was not healing, becoming more inflamed and swollen. Moving around the flagship had become such a painful exercise that the *Benton*'s officers and men were increasingly concerned for his health. The warm spring temperatures made the interior of the *Benton* uncomfortable, and with the addition of hordes of swarming gnats and mosquitoes, sleep was often impossible. It was not uncommon to wake in the morning covered with mosquito bites, sometimes so numerous that one's eyelids were swollen shut.

With Phelps increasingly assuming the day-to-day responsibilities of running the flotilla, Foote realized that although he passionately wanted to stay with his men, to do so would not be in the best interests of his command. Several of the captains, "some of whom entered the service before I was born," Phelps wrote, resented his increasing power within the flotilla. Walke derisively referred to Phelps as Foote's "aide" and "executive officer," and as leader of "the previous conspiracy against [me]." Walke later wrote that Phelps was one of "the attaches of the flag-officer, his informants and spokesmen."[4]

On April 15, Foote summoned three surgeons to examine his case and make a recommendation to the Navy Department as to his fitness for command. The three unanimously concluded that his wound "would probably soon totally unfit you for the performance of your important duties as flag-officer; and we would therefore respectfully suggest that for the future interest of the flotilla you be permitted to return home to recover your health."[5]

Foote forwarded the recommendation of the surgeons to Secretary of the Navy Gideon Welles, with his request that Capt. Charles H. Davis succeed him. In the same unofficial letter to Welles, Foote planted a seed that would lie dormant for the next few months. "Although Lieutenant-Commanding Phelps, the flag captain, is qualified to command any squadron, you will see, by his being a young officer, he can not act for me when I am laid up without exciting a feeling among officers ranking him that would prove injurious to the efficiency of the flotilla."[6]

The Navy was still bound by seniority, at which Phelps chafed. Combat service and accomplishments, of which no one on the Western rivers had more, would be his way to promotion and command if a reform bill before Congress passed.

With that in mind, Phelps appealed to his influential friends, urging enactment of the bill. He also passionately objected to the reinstatement of officers who had voluntarily left the navy. These men "who left five, ten, fifteen years since, [would be] placed on the list just as if they had never been out."

Of those nominated three are to be put above me and several below. The first of the three above me left because it suited his purposes & received from his father-in-law a large interest in a furnace or foundry and was thought to be making a fortune. The concern failed, he now wants to get back to the service, and, not willing to enter as a Lieutenant from the date of his recent acting appointment, as any other volunteer Lieutenant from the Merchant Service would, is to be placed in his number on list as Commander, though he resigned as a Lieutenant. The second was forced from fear of a court martial impending over him on account of dissolute habits, to resign. The third in order, after being four or five years at the Naval School as teacher when ordered to sea, as he had married a rich wife and thought the prospects of promotions very gloomy. The government has never promoted an officer in the Navy in this war for gallantry because it recognizes the right of promotion by seniority. By what right then are men, after years of absence to be credited with service for that period and placed on the list just as if the service had been bona fide? By what principle of justice can Mr. [Joseph] Sanford be credited for the past eight years, spent in his foundry, and be returned over the head of [John L.] Worden the gallant defender of Hampton Roads? Let justice be done, and these men be confirmed as Lieutenants from the date of their present acting appointments and take their chances in seniority as we all do, and, if they can get a vote of thanks of Congress, or nomination by the President, for gallantry in action let them be promoted as others would be if the law before Congress passes. We await very slow casualties for promotion, and it will be hard indeed to find men coming back over our heads, to be our superiors & defer our promotions, who have been for years enjoying life on shore, most of them with wealth and idle ease, while we have been away on every disagreeable service.[7]

Gideon Welles appreciated the sentiment of the younger men, but following the resignations of 259 officers at the outbreak of the war, he needed officers. The rapidly increasing number of ships had made acquiring experienced officers a top priority. Although he was sympathetic, the interest of the country came first. Phelps's argument was persuasive, however, for the Senate refused to restore the men as if they had never left the navy.

The man at the top of the list, Joseph Sanford, was a close personal friend of Foote and had visited the flotilla several times. Although he would not be reinstated as a commander, he became the flotilla's ordnance officer and did such a good job that Phelps later had a change of heart and asked several of his influential friends to see if something might be done on his behalf.

The flotilla settled into the routine that characterized the siege at Island No. 10. An attempt to run the batteries was ruled out, however, for numerous deserters were arriving daily, full of contradictory stories about the Confederate fleet anchored just around Plum Point Bend. Since their arrival, the Union flotilla had been expecting some sort of action, but days passed with only routine bombardment to remind the men that a war was on. On April 28, however, eleven deserters found their way to the gunboats in groups of two or three. They all had the same news: that an attack on the Union flotilla had been decided upon for that night. The deserters reported that the attack would have taken place the night before, but Captain Montgomery had decided to await the arrival of a new gunboat from Memphis—perhaps the vaunted *Arkansas!*

Foote ordered preparations for a general night engagement. All watches were doubled, the sick were moved, the transports were ordered to keep up steam, and the gunboats were anchored with their bows facing downriver. Just after dark, Phelps ordered the *Benton* to cast off and steam farther downriver, hoping that the Confederates might pass in the darkness and he could cut them off. With all hands at quarters, the Union fleet awaited an attack that did not come.

At daylight on May 8, after several days of quiet, a Confederate gunboat rounded Craighead Point with two others in her wake. All the Union gunboats beat to quarters and dropped out into the river. The Confederate boats retreated after several shots from the *Benton* and the *Cincinnati* splashed about them.

These forays by Montgomery's ram–gunboats, although inflicting no damage, were having a profound secondary effect. The Union flotilla was becoming complacent. On the afternoon of May 9, the Southerners appeared with a flag of truce, wishing to return two prisoners taken during the Battle of Belmont. While this was obviously a ploy to scout the Union flotilla, the general feeling was expressed by Phelps: "The more they see of us the better. They won't like us any more for what they witness. They are welcome to all they can discover."[8]

Earlier that day, the men of the *Benton* witnessed the departure of their beloved commodore.

The severe illness of the Flag Officer has reduced him so far that he is now confined to his bed and wholly unable to attend to his duties or to write. His wounded foot, which has become no better, has affected his general health and left him prey to the prevalent disease of the locality, diarrhea and fever combined, and he is now very ill of these combination of evils.[9]

All hands were mustered on the crowded deck to hear the flag officer's final words. Newspaper correspondent Junius Brown observed:

As the Flag Officer appeared, supported by Captain Phelps, he was greeted by tremendous huzzahs. Old tars swung their hats, and not a few of their eyes moistened when they looked, as they supposed, upon the brave old Commodore for the last time. The flag officer paused for a few moments, and, removing his cap, gave those near him to understand he would address them.

The Commodore said he had asked to be relieved because he could not fill his office in his existing condition of health. He was willing to sacrifice himself for his country, but he knew he would be injuring the cause by retaining his position any longer.

He had been growing feebler and feebler every day, and his physician had often told him he could not improve while exposed to the excitements of the service and confined to the Flag-ship. He complimented the officers and crew of the *Benton* in the highest manner. He had always found them faithful, brave, and true, and fondly hoped to remain with them until the war was over. That he could not was a cause of great regret; but wherever he went, he would bear with him the memory of the *Benton* and her gallant crew, and, if his life were spared, he would often revert to the scenes he had passed among them with mingled feelings of sorrow and pride. The interview was impressive and affecting, and at the close the Commodore could hardly speak for emotion, and the tears, answered by many who were present, stole down his thin and pallid cheeks.[10]

Foote was then assisted to his cabin, weak and trembling from his emotional farewell. At 3 P.M. the former Confederate steamer *DeSoto* dropped down to the *Benton* to convey the commodore to Cairo. With the crew looking on, Foote was gently half-carried by Captain Davis and Lieutenant Phelps to the transport. After he had been placed on a chair on the upper guards facing the crew, some minutes passed before the *DeSoto* cast off. The correspondent continued:

As he looked at the *Benton,* perhaps for the last time, and saw the many familiar faces that fixed their kind eyes upon him so earnestly, his trembling hand frequently sought his quivering lip, and nervously twitched his whiskers. One could see his efforts to suppress his feeling, but nature prevailed, and the brave officer covered his wan face with a fan he held to dissipate the heat of the afternoon, and wept like a child.

The bell was rung, and the wheels splashed mournfully, and three loud, long and ringing cheers were given by the crew. The Commodore stood up on his crutches as the *DeSoto* moved up the broad Mississippi, and with tremendous voice said: "God bless you all! Heaven knows how hard it is for me to leave you! Better and braver men than you never trod a deck. I would much rather stay with you and die with you than go away. But my duty to my country compels me to yield to stronger, though I hope not more willing hands. God bless you, my brave men, God bless you all!"[11]

There was hardly a dry eye while the flag officer spoke, and for Phelps the parting was especially sad. "Flag Officer Foote," he wrote,

"I am as much attached to as a mess mate as I have ever been as a considerate and wise commander."[12]

The new flag officer, Capt. Charles H. Davis, looked somewhat older than his years. Of medium height and weight, with blue eyes and distinguished gray hair and sideburns, he was a man of noted scientific achievment.[13] His career had been spent largely on survey duty, culminating in the publication of the *American Nautical Almanac.* Having been briefed by Foote and Phelps on the status of the flotilla, Davis passed his first evening in command aboard the *Benton* as a wispy fog settled on the river.

Early the next morning the *Cincinnati* routinely dropped down the river to cover the mortar boats for the day's bombardment. Her crew had just begun to holystone the gundeck when smoke was sighted from the direction of Craighead Point. "Steaming rapidly around the point below us," wrote crewman Eliot Callender, "pouring dense clouds from their funnels, came first one vessel, then two, then more, until six war vessels under full head of steam came surging up the river barely a mile below us."[14] The crew, bare-legged and soaking wet, threw their buckets aside and sprang to their guns.

At 6:25 A.M. the Confederate rams were spotted by the *Benton;* the crew was beat to quarters and the ship cleared for action. The crew of the *Carondelet,* which had suspected something after seeing the smoke above the morning haze, had already cleared her for action when at 6:35 A.M. orders were passed to beat to quarters. Captain Davis ordered the signal to "get under way" hoisted, but the haze made the flags difficult to see. Richard Birch, first pilot on the *Benton,* used a trumpet to hail the other boats, and soon the *Benton, Carondelet,* and *Mound City* had cast loose into the river.

With low steam pressure, it was apparent that the *Benton* would take longer to move her great mass than the lighter Pook Turtles, so Davis ordered Walke and the *Carondelet* to pass her. On the other side of the river, Augustus Kilty and the *Mound City* had not seen the signal from the *Benton,* but had spotted the Confederate fleet and proceeded to the aid of the *Cincinnati.*

Meanwhile, the *Cincinnati* had slipped her lines and stood out in the river to meet the oncoming fleet. Her engineers were frantically throwing oil, rags, coal, and anything else that would burn into her

Charles Davis—Given temporary command of the Western Flotilla, Davis spent his first day on the job fighting the Rebel ram fleet at Plum Point Bend. (National Archives)

fires. With the *General Bragg* in the lead, the Confederate rams bore down at full speed on the *Cincinnati* and *Mortar Boat No. 16*.

At a distance of fifty yards, Captain Stembel opened fire from his starboard battery; four 32-pounders erupted into the bow of the *Bragg*. With splinters and cotton flying, Captain W. H. H. Leonard kept the *General Bragg* steady. With less than fifty feet now between them, Stembel swung his bow so that the fearsome crash was at an angle. A twelve-foot chunk was gouged out of the *Cincinnati*'s starboard quarter, flooding her magazine. The force of the collision temporarily lodged the *Bragg*'s ram in the *Cincinnati*'s hull. As the two boats pivoted together, the *Bragg*'s starboard wheelhouse rode up on the *Cincinnati*'s casemate. With the *Bragg* literally stuck in the *Cincinnati*'s starboard gunports, the *Cincinnati*'s gunners had trouble ramming home powder and shot. As the *Bragg* finally slid off, the *Cincinnati*'s guns were run out and fired. Once more cotton bales tumbled and splinters flew.

Soon after the *Bragg* broke free, the *General Sterling Price* struck the *Cincinnati*'s aft quarter and carried away her rudder sternpost. This pushed the *Cincinnati*'s stern directly in front of the oncoming ram *Sumter*, which struck a crashing blow three feet into the *Cincinnati*'s fantail, destroying the steering apparatus and splitting her hull wide open. With the *Cincinnati* slowly approaching the bank and shallow water, her "watertight" compartments were only slightly slowing the intake of water. In danger of being boarded, Captain Rodger Stembel organized his men on deck with small arms, cutlasses, and boarding pikes. William Hoel spotted a Confederate sharpshooter leveling his rifle at Captain Stembel, and yelled at him to watch out. Stembel turned toward the safety of the pilothouse, but before he could reach it, a minié ball struck him in the back and exited his throat just under the chin. With water now filling the hull of the *Cincinnati* from three directions, the gunboat gently settled on the bottom.

In the meantime, the crew of *Mortar Boat No. 16* had lowered the elevation of their piece and, using reduced charges, was firing at the oncoming rams. Using fuses as short as half an inch, they lobbed eleven "Lincoln Pills" among the cottonclad boats, which, while doing no real damage, showered the Confederates with shrapnel, giving them one more reason to destroy the pesky raft. The enemy directed several of their guns at the mortar boat and struck it twice, but caused no casualties and did not sink her.

The *Mound City* had arrived and was met by the *General Earl Van Dorn*. Wrote Symmes Brown of the *Mound City:*

> The *Van Dorn* having passed across our bow about 500 yards distance was now coming on our starboard side as fast as she could travel. Notwithstanding we were pouring broadside after broadside into her, and ran into us striking us about four feet from the bow. This turned us clear around so that we headed up stream, and she passed close in front of us receiving the contents of our three bow guns and then struck the Arkansas shore which immediately stopped her. Our boat began to go down as soon as the *Van Dorn* struck us, for she opened an awful hole in our bow so we were compelled to run ashore on a bar about two miles above.
>
> After she crossed our bow and ran into the Arkansas shore we would have run into her and held her there had not our boat been so severely injured, and as the *Benton* was then below us we thought she would capture the *Van Dorn* and the Captain [Capt. A. H. Kilty] remarked as we left her, "the *Benton* will finish her up."[15]

Following the *Carondelet*, the *Benton* arrived in the midst of the melee. Flag Officer Davis had gone below and was manning one of the aft guns. As she neared the submerged *Cincinnati*, with her crew on top of the wheelhouse, "perched like so many turkeys on a corn-crib," Phelps had Horace Bigsby, her pilot, turn the *Benton* in a tight circle. "She gave them first her bow battery of nine inch Dahlgren guns," wrote Eliot Callender, "and then, wheeling, her starboard, stern, and port broadsides. By the time her bow guns swung around, her guns were loaded; and repeating her circling again and again, she delivered upon the enemy a withering sheet of death and destruction."[16]

In the hold of the *Benton*, a Rebel spy being held in the brig cheered the rams. Seaman William Van Cleaf noted:

USS *General Bragg*—A Confederate ram, the *General Bragg* was taken into Union service following her capture at Memphis. (U.S. Naval Historical Center)

He stuck his head out of the brig and commenced to talk. The sentry told him to go down to which he made a reply that he would go down when he got ready and some of the men called him a secesh and told him that if he did not go down they would put a cutlass through him.[17]

With the *Pittsburg* and *Cairo* now joining the free-for-all, as well as the other Confederate rams, which were only using their guns, the smoke from repeated broadsides mixed with the morning haze to reduce the visibility to less than a quarter of a mile. With Union gunboats and Confederate rams moving about through the fog of burning powder, the confusion was tremendous. The deck of the *Carondelet* was swept with canister fired by the *Pittsburg*. Both the *Benton* and the *Carondelet* claimed to have hit a steam drum or boiler of one of the Confederate rams, but later reports from Captain Montgomery made no mention of such an explosion.

USS *General Price*—A Confederate ram captured after the battle of Memphis. Note her two nine-inch guns. (U.S. Naval Historical Center)

With all the Union gunboats except the *St. Louis* now engaged at close quarters, Montgomery decided to call it a day. He had achieved a stunning tactical victory; his rams had sunk two Union gunboats, to none of his own. His rams had been considerably cut up, the *General Price* having received a 128-pound shell "between wind and water," but not one was lost. Since cotton and pine were the South's only unlimited resources, the rams were easily repaired. After both sides withdrew to lick their wounds, the *Cincinnati* and *Mound City* were raised and towed to Cairo and Mound City for repairs.[18] Although caught napping, Phelps and the men of the Union flotilla believed they had won a victory, for the Confederates had been the ones to abandon the battle, and deserters were reporting up to 108 dead. "The loss of the Rebels must be very heavy," Phelps wrote to Foote, "their vessels were literally torn to pieces, and some had holes in their sides through which a man could walk. Those that blew up—it makes me shudder to think of them."[19]

After the excitement had died down, Phelps expressed a more re-alistic view of these "floating animals." "Sinking the Rebel craft," he wrote, "which, on account of their being so stuffed with cotton, is a difficult thing to accomplish with shot alone." Having learned their own weaknesses the hard way, Phelps arranged for the flotilla to better protect itself from the Confederate "buts" in the future. Cy-press logs were chained alongside the hulls, and on the *Benton*

> three bars of railroad iron were secured between and along the fantails, so as to prevent cutting there, and also heavy frames in-closing rudders, and ironed. Along the casemate, where the iron is light, I have had ½ inch plate flanged and firmly bolted, to increase the strength of the angle at that vulnerable point. If we have time to secure the bows with ¾ inch plates already here, we will be able to split any boats that hit us there.[20]

Davis's report to Secretary Welles about the battle commended Phelps along with Stembel and Kilty. Walke was only mentioned. Phelps's influence was still apparent.

Strengthening the gunboats against another attack was only one of a host of problems facing Davis in his new command. The pilots and crew from the *Pittsburg* petitioned that they had not been paid for two months, and their families were destitute. Scurvy was appear-ing through lack of foraging due to the flooded river, and soldiers from the Army of the Potomac who had been assigned to the flotilla for three months petitioned to be released to their regiments.

During the quieter moments, Davis was visited by Captains Dove and Kilty, who talked over the "good old times," while Egbert Thompson was "always flying about loaded down with very small weights." Davis, like Foote, relied on Phelps and his experience as flag captain. Phelps had his opinions as to how the flotilla should be run and was not shy in expressing them.

> Captain Dove is here with the *Louisville*. Now we have the *Cairo*, *Pittsburg*, and *Louisville* to "count" among the six vessels of the fleet. I would rather have either one of the other two

[*Cincinnati* and *Mound City*] than all three. Little Thompson is very busy getting his vessel secured so that when the rebels "come around the Point" again he can "pitch into them."[21]

Phelps was unimpressed with a visit from the *Benton*'s former captain.

Captain [John] Winslow came down to the fleet, arriving just in time to witness the fight, and has applied to be sent to Cairo to superintend work on the *Eastport*, or to St. Louis to perform similar duty, and thither he has gone. This looks as if pressure of public opinion in Boston sent him out.[22]

In hearing from Foote that Davis had denied Winslow a command, Phelps wrote back stating flatly, "It is false." He pointed out that a junior lieutenant was temporarily in command of the *St. Louis* and Stembel was seriously wounded. "Capt. W. injured himself greatly by his course," Phelps wrote, "and may by this time be aware of it. Before Commodore Davis gave him his orders to St. Louis, he offered him the command of the *Cincinnati*."[23]

In Winslow's defense, Foote wrote, "With regard to Winslow, he intimated to me when I met him the night I left you that he would prefer a command but coming out as he did he could not ask any thing to the prejudice of others." Foote also had heard from St. Louis "that Winslow felt rather disappointed that he could not have a command. This is all I had to base my conclusions upon. I am not disposed to offer him a command now, although I feel disappointed and regret that Winslow has impressed you and Davis unfavorably. He will do well in supervising the boats at St. Louis."[24]

Winslow soon was given command of the *Cincinnati* in place of the wounded Stembel, and later of the shipyard at Memphis. Foote was prophetic in his prediction that Winslow would do well, however, for as captain of the USS *Kearsarge*, he sank the Confederate raider *Alabama*.

With the gunboats strengthened against being rammed and the flotilla reorganized to meet another Confederate attack, the routine once again settled down to periodic shelling. While Phelps was seeing to the transfer of new guns to the *Benton* from the *DeSoto,* a spar broke and fell fifteen feet, striking him in the head and knocking him down. The blow caused headaches and nausea that, combined with news of Lizzie's imminent departure from Paducah for Chardon, prompted Phelps to exercise a privilege of command.

The tedium of gunboat life for the men of the *Benton* was lifted for a short time by a visit from Lizzie. While some grumbled about officers, others, not having seen a woman for months, were more than willing to make the *Benton* sparkle for a visit by a woman. Because of the fight at Plum Point Bend, "the accident so nearly fatal to me and for other reasons not to be told," Phelps wrote, "I telegraphed her to come."[25]

While Phelps was awaiting Lizzie's arrival, the question of using contraband slaves as crewmen was finally settled. On May 11, three slaves boarded the *Cincinnati,* seeking asylum. Andrew Foote had opposed the use of contrabands, but with the flotilla chronically short of men, the three found immediate employment as firemen. Shortly thereafter their owner, a Mr. B. Embry of Tennessee, heard of their whereabouts and visited the fleet, demanding the return of his property. Phelps informed him that he could not return them unless he had a requisition from Governor Andrew Johnson. Embry traveled to Nashville and obtained not a requisition, but a letter of introduction to Captain Davis, stating that Embry was a loyal Union man and asking that his slaves be returned to him. Davis refused to give up the contrabands, asserting that a law of Congress forbade his doing so.

Free African Americans and emancipated slaves had served in the navy during the Revolution and from the War of 1812 on. For the new inland navy, however, using slaves presented special problems. Besides having to deal with irate owners, there was a real concern about the effect of armed blacks upon the Southerners with whom the gunboats dealt with on a regular basis. By mid-May, Davis was in command, and with an April 30, 1862, directive from Gideon Welles encouraging his commanders to employ contraband slaves, the cork was out of the bottle. With rapidly increasing demands for sailors, slaves who sought asylum aboard the gunboats and were found fit for duty were offered the opportunity to enlist. Many jumped at the

John Winslow—A friend of Andrew Foote, Winslow made a decidedly un-
favorable impression on Phelps and Capt. Charles Davis by requesting
shore duty after witnessing the battle of Plum Point Bend. (U.S. Naval Historical Center)

chance and were mustered in; those who declined were sent off the boats, for the navy would not subsidize civilians.[26]

Newspaper accounts of the transfer of General Pope's army to the Corinth area brought to a head another festering problem. Since the publication of articles stating that the *Benton* would attempt to run the blockade at Island No. 10, Phelps had been upset with the press. Correspondents had had freedom of movement within the flotilla and naturally congregated most often on the flagship; this came to a halt when "Capt. S. L. Phelps of the *Benton* issued peremptory orders forbidding correspondents from going on board the flagship—a rule, however, that extends to no one else." While a number of correspondents were understanding, and upset at their colleagues for printing confidential information, others were howling mad. Junius Brown of the *New York Tribune* wrote:

> Captain Phelps has shown himself a brave and competent officer; but for some reason or no reason is deeply and narrowly prejudiced against the press, always preferring to be rude and discourteous to its representatives to treating them as a gentleman should. Capt. Phelps is very unpopular in the fleet, and, so far as I have seen, deserves his unpopularity as richly as any officer I can now remember. He was prevented, I think, during Commodore Foote's incumbency, from carrying out his antipathy to the Press, but has seized the first moment of the new regime to begin an oppression it is not impossible he may live long enough to regret.[27]

This situation did not last long, for a pass system was developed that allowed controlled access to the *Benton*.

As the days droned on, the news from Foote was encouraging. "I am better again to day," he wrote, "and still hope that I will be in Cairo in two weeks and go down in the *Eastport*." He had already been visited by Phelps's parents and, Foote added, "I had two delightful calls from your dear wife. My wife was charmed with her. My wife wants so much to see you." Foote had also been busy on Phelps's behalf. "In a private letter to Secretary Welles I have urged some few promotions and recapitulated your services and told him that you ought to be nominated as a Commander." Some two weeks later, Foote wrote, "I will work for you with all that tenacity for which I am famous when well but you now stand so high that few men can add anything in your behalf."[28]

An ugly incident occurred during this time when it was discovered that three Confederate prisoners, sent downriver from Cairo by the army, to be exchanged for Union prisoners, had smallpox. Brig. Gen. John B. Villepigue, commander of Fort Pillow, sent a flag of truce and a scathing message accusing the Union of trying to introduce small-pox into his garrison. Since the boat carrying the Confederate prisoners had come directly from Cairo, no one in the flotilla knew anything about this, but it was Davis who had to handle the unfortunate situation. He refused to take back the three infected men, and Villepigue reluctantly kept them, stating that moving them would only expose others.[29]

On May 18 the men of the flotilla watched the arrival of the first of seven rams of their own. Col. Charles Ellet's fleet was in many ways similar to Montgomery's. Having selected swift river steamers, the fifty-seven-year-old civil engineer proceeded to convert them by running three heavy, solid timber bulkheads, from twelve to sixteen inches thick, fore and aft from stem to stern, placing the central one directly over the keel. He then braced the bulkheads against each other, using iron rods and screw bolts. The outer bulkheads were secured against the hull, and all were secured to the deck and floor timbers. The boilers and machinery were not dropped into the hold but braced with iron stays and protected with two feet of oak timbers bolted together. Mounting no guns, Ellet's fleet were strictly rams.

Like Montgomery, Ellet chose riverboat men to crew his vessels; including his brother Alfred, he placed seven other Ellets in his fleet. Although the flotilla and the ram fleet were both under army jurisdiction, Ellet took his orders from the secretary of war, Edwin Stanton, not Captain Davis. This awkward command structure left much to be desired, for Ellet was free to act independently of Captain Davis.[30]

Upon arriving, Alfred Ellet reported to Captain Davis and offered the services of his rams. The only reply he received initially was a request to make a demonstration for the benefit of the Rebels who were carrying General Villepigue's message to Davis. Ellet, eager to get at the enemy, was informed that the flotilla would not make any move against Fort Pillow until Brig. Gen. Isaac Quinby, who had arrived with his troops, was reinforced.

Phelps was somewhat amused by Ellet. He wrote to Foote:

Our Ram Colonel is as crazy as our friend . . . , he has been writing absurd things to the commodore, quoting his instructions from the War Department to prove that he is not under orders of the naval officer commanding; and he proposed running the fire of the fort and attacking the rebel fleet below. In his letters to the War Department, he styles his mode of warfare as "peculiar," and not likely to be approved of by naval officers; and that, therefore, it is not possible that he should be restrained by their authority. The War Department is cautious in replying; but, upon the whole, desires that the naval commander should not interfere, unless the operations of the Ram Colonel would greatly interfere with the regular naval operations, or imperil public interests, or to that effect.

The Ram Colonel wrote that he proposed immediately to proceed against the rebel fleet, passing the fire of Fort Pillow. The commodore replied that while he did not approve of the enterprise, he would offer no opposition, and wished him luck. Two or three days after, sure enough, the Ram Colonel got underway in a rain-squall, and started down around Craighead Point, followed by the junior rams. Head ram had not passed from our view before a fire was opened from the fort, and ram's head came around double quick, and all rams paddled back, followed by a sharp fire from the fort, though we could not in the rain judge of how the shot fell. A few minutes after our rams had come up, two rebel rams appeared round the Point, and, as plainly as rams ever talked, said, "Come on, Yankee rams; we are here on neutral ground ready to butt our difficulties out;" but Yankee rams said not a word. The conclusion is, we shall hear no more from our Ram Colonel about running batteries. It was probably the best way to silence the fellow—to let him hang himself.[31]

The siege of Corinth had been shaping up as a monumental struggle that would decide the fate of the Mississippi Valley and perhaps the Confederacy. But Gen. P. G. T. Beauregard, who had assumed command after the death of General Johnston at Shiloh, decided his 50,000 troops, beset with typhoid and dysentery, were more important than holding Corinth at all costs against Halleck's 120,000-man army. So on May 29, he ordered the city quietly evacuated along with Fort Pillow.

During the afternoon of June 4, dense smoke and explosions came from the direction of Fort Pillow. Just before 7 P.M., Phelps took a tug and proceeded to Craighead Point to see if everyone's suspicions were right. Well after dark he returned to the *Benton* and reported to Davis that, indeed, the Confederates were abandoning the fort. For hours sounds of thunder came from the dull glow on the horizon. The Confederates had overloaded their guns and then set fire to the carriages. When the heat from the fire burst a gun, it also dismounted it from what was left of the carriage. Along with breastworks of cotton bales, buildings, and stores, everything the Confederates couldn't carry off was put to the torch.

At four the next morning—June 5—the signal went up from the *Benton* for all boats to get under way. By dawn the Union fleet was anchored in front of Fort Pillow. If nearby Fort Randolph was abandoned, as expected, then Memphis was wide open.

CHAPTER TEN

❧

Memphis &
the *Mound City* Disaster

AT 1 P.M. on June 5, the fleet got under way for Memphis. With the
Pittsburg remaining at Fort Pillow to back up the Union garrison, and the *Mound City* standing by to escort the army transports,
the hybrid Union fleet cautiously began working its way downriver.
At every bayou and rapid, the boats split up and carefully looked for
the Confederate rams. The river was quiet; willow and poplar trees
grew to the water's edge, and there were magnificent plantations,
many of which appeared deserted. Here and there, slaves came to
the river and waved. Some fields of cotton had been put to the torch,
and numerous bales of cotton were floating in the river.

Just after 2 P.M., Fort Randolph appeared in the distance. "You can
go down," yelled Captain Dryden of the *Monarch*. "The stars and
stripes wave over Fort Randolph. We put 'em up." On the quarterdeck of the *Benton,* Lieutenant Phelps and his executive officer, Lieutenant Bishop, were observing the fort through their spyglasses.
"There's the stars and stripes," remarked Bishop, to which Phelps responded, "There's a wharf boat they have left—see."[1]

Just after 4 P.M., above Island No. 37, the fleet encountered the Confederate steamer *Sovereign*. A warning shot from the *Benton* signaled her to come about; instead, she turned tail downriver. "Fire again, Captain Phelps," ordered Davis, "bring her to." The *Benton* opened up, followed by the *Carondelet* and the *Cairo;* soon the old steamer, with geysers all around her, disappeared around a bend. Intent on capturing the steamer, Davis ordered Lieutenant Bishop to take the fast little tug *Spitfire,* which had a 12-pounder howitzer on her bow, and run the steamer down. The race was on, the nimble *Spitfire* gaining on the *Sovereign* by cutting sharper turns in the winding river. Finally in range, Bishop fired his howitzer and forced the crew of the *Sovereign* to run their boat into the bank. Before they escaped, they attempted to blow up her boilers, but a sixteen-year-old boy, who had been pressed into service, remained behind and removed the weights holding the safety valves closed. He then opened the fire doors and flue caps, and put water on the fires.

The Union fleet, with the transports and mortar boats stretching back ten miles, slowly made its way downriver until, at dusk, they reached a group of islands, just north of Memphis, known as Paddy's Hens and Chickens.

"There's Memphis! Don't you see the lights on the bluff?" exclaimed First Master Thomas Bates, who was on watch on the *Benton*.

"How is the water? Can we anchor here?" asked Phelps.

"Yes, sir," replied pilot Dan Duffy, "there's plenty of water."

"Then round the *Benton* to," said Phelps.[2]

As the *Benton* turned about and dropped anchor, the tugs passed the word for the fleet to anchor in line of battle and to remain within signaling distance. The transports tied up to the Arkansas shore and put out extra pickets. That night men slept by their guns with cutlasses, pistols, and boarding pikes nearby.

James Montgomery's River Defense Fleet had arrived at Memphis just as the Union fleet was departing Fort Pillow. The vessels were low on coal, and word was sent to the community to bring what they could spare. The general understanding among the Confederate crews was that they would not make a stand at Memphis, but would take on coal and return to intercept the Union fleet at Island No. 40. That plan evaporated with the arrival of the Union fleet that night.

To warn of any further movement of the Federals toward the city, Montgomery sent pickets, in the small tug *Gordon Grant*, to watch the Union ironclads. The tug ran aground at the foot of one of the islands less than a quarter-mile from the *Benton*. With all the Union tugs safely anchored upriver, the *Benton*'s quartermaster recommended giving the *Gordon Grant* a shot. "No that won't do," remarked Bates, "as the Commodore don't desire to wake up the enemy before morning."[3] The question became academic when the *Grant*'s captain and his crew applied the torch to the tug and made their way back to Memphis.

As a cloudless dawn broke over the city, large crowds began to form along the bluffs. The smoke from the Union gunboats had become visible in the city the afternoon before, and word spread quickly. The *Memphis Avalanche* published an edition announcing the coming battle. Others became caught up in the excitement of the moment. One woman wrote, "Mamma sat up with a sick lady that night, and as she came home early, and saw the . . . smoke of old Lincoln's gunboats . . . again, just around the point, two miles above the city, and she woke us up in a hurry; and we went on the bluff."[4]

With darkness giving way to daylight, Davis had the *Benton* and *Louisville* weigh anchor and drop downriver, stern first, to take a look.

The men on the Confederate rams, looking at "one solid cloud of black smoke," were not sure what they were going to do. Montgomery, however, soon knew he had only one choice. The crowds along the river were swelling. Knowing they looked on him as their only hope, Montgomery could not run away. He informed his captains that they would stand and fight. Forming in two lines, with the boats mounting 64-pounders on their bows in the lead, the Confederate River Defense Fleet would try to save the city of Memphis.

Having returned to his anchorage, Davis was in no hurry and told his men to finish their breakfast. There would be time enough for battle.

Before long, the eight Confederate rams were spotted picking up speed against the current, and the Union gunboats began drifting stern first to meet them. The "ball was opened" by the Confederate ram *General M. Jeff. Thompson* as her first round passed over the gunboats and landed near the tugs. The next shot plowed into the water next to the *Benton*. With the Confederate rams now coming fast, Davis opened fire even though the city was in the line of fire.

Charles Ellet, unaware of the coming fight, had just tied the *Queen of the West* up to the Arkansas shore when the sound of cannon fire told him the fight was on. He immediately cast off, signaled to the *Monarch* to follow, and hoisted the flag telling the *Lancaster No. 3* and *Switzerland* to prepare for action. The *Queen of the West* and the *Monarch* took off downriver; the pilot on the *Lancaster* became so excited that he accidentally backed the boat into the riverbank, disabling her rudder. The captain of the *Switzerland* followed his order to stay half a mile to the rear of the *Lancaster,* so the two rams remained behind.

As the two fleets closed on each other, the smoke from the boats' chimneys mixed with the sulfurous smoke of cannons to form a huge cloud that slowly drifted from the center of the river. The captain of the *St. Louis,* Lt. Wilson McGunnegle, descended to the gun deck to urge his gunners on. Passing from gun to gun, he cautioned his men to be calm and deliberate. "Slow and well directed firing," he told his men, "will do much more execution than careless shooting. Here is a chance to distinguish yourselves, and sustain the fair reputation of the *St. Louis.*"[5]

After some minutes of firing with the stern guns, Davis gave the signal for the Union gunboats to come about and go for the Confederate rams. Just after the gunboats turned about, the *Queen of the West* appeared out of the smoke and, at full speed, passed between the *Benton,* on the Union left, and the *Carondelet.* With a large plume at her bow and a churning wake, the *Queen,* followed by the *Monarch,* caught everyone by surprise. This "bold and well executed dash," as Phelps put it, had the Union sailors cheering.[6]

Montgomery and his men were stunned. From between the lumbering behemoths came two swift Yankee rams in what must have looked like a perfectly coordinated assault. Heading for the *General Beauregard* and *Colonel Lovell,* Ellet was uncertain which to aim for. Approaching bow on, and closing rapidly, Capt. James Dellaney on the *Lovell* made the first fatal mistake. Trying to veer at the last second, he gave the *Queen* his broadside. Ellet went for the *Lovell* and hit it just forward of the wheelhouse. "The crash was terrific," wrote

Ellet, "everything loose about the *Queen,* some tables, pantryware, and a half-eaten breakfast, were overthrown and broken by the shock. The hull of the rebel steamer was crushed in, and her chimneys surged over as if they were going to fall over on the bow of the *Queen.*"[7]

Before Ellet could free the *Queen* from the *Lovell,* she was struck by the *Sumter* in the port wheelhouse, breaking her tiller ropes and crushing her wheel and a portion of her hull. As Ellet rushed from the pilothouse to check the damage, he was shot in the knee. He continued in command, ordering the *Queen* to the Arkansas shore before she sank.

The spectators on the riverbank cheered wildly. "When our boat ran into her wheelhouse, thousands of shouts of joy went up from the banks of the river," wrote one woman. "I screamed 'Glory, Glory, Glory!' as loud as I could bawl." The cheers quickly quieted as the crowd watched the panic-stricken crewmen on board the *Lovell* run about her deck, unsure about abandoning her. "One poor fellow, with his left arm torn off by a cannon shot, with unspeakable horror in his countenance, was seen, now beckoning to those on shore, and now looking up to heaven to the great Father of us all for help." When the water reached her boilers and filled the boat with steam, "our poor men had to jump out into the river, and so many of them drowned right before my eyes. No human being can imagine my feelings, and all the ladies on the bluff just cried to break their hearts"[8]

The *Benton,* along with several other gunboats, lowered one of her cutters to save as many as possible. Before the boat shoved off, however, so many volunteers had rushed to the cutter that they partially swamped it and nearly drowned two sailors. The *Benton*'s cutter saved a number of men, some badly scalded, but many others, including the *Lovell*'s pilot, William Cable, an old riverman, drowned.

In the meantime the *Beauregard* and *Monarch* headed for each other and "struck head on, but glanced." The *Monarch*'s momentum carried her below the battle, so Alfred Ellet brought her around and aimed for the *Jeff Thompson.* The *General Price,* also heading upriver, angled for the *Monarch* and struck her starboard quarter, causing little damage but rounding her to. Capt. J. Henry Hart had, in the meantime, wheeled the *Beauregard* around and also was bearing down on the *Monarch.* The *Monarch*'s course had been changed just enough, however, that the *Beauregard* missed her and struck the *General Price* instead. The *Beauregard*'s bow tore off the *Price*'s port wheelhouse, crippling her. As the *Beauregard* backed away from the *Price,* one of her gunners fired a forty-two-pound shot at the *Benton.* With Davis in the pilothouse, Phelps had descended to the gun deck, where he manned one of the bow guns. As the *Beauregard* turned away from the *Price,* Phelps sighted down the white stripe painted on top of the gun for aiming in the poor light of the gun deck, and pulled the lanyard on his 50-pounder rifled Dahlgren. The shot crashed into the *Beauregard*'s hull, exploding her boiler. Quickly taking on water, the *Beauregard* began to sink. Captain Hart accepted the *Monarch*'s offer of a tow to the Arkansas shore, where she sank in twenty feet of water.

Meanwhile, the *General Price* limped to the riverbank, where she, too, sank in shallow water. The *Monarch* next went after the *Little Rebel,* which was heading for the Arkansas shore, having been riddled with shot, including a hit in her boiler. Approaching from the rear, Ellet rammed the *Little Rebel* hard enough to drive her to the riverbank.

The *General Bragg* and *General Earl Van Dorn* had "stood off and looked at the fight," according to Captain Hart. When it became clear what the outcome would be, the *Van Dorn* turned to and headed downriver. The *Bragg,* with timbers forward of her wheelhouse and her hull riddled with shot, headed for the Arkansas shore, where her crew escaped.

The battle had raged for more than an hour, and the current had carried both fleets below the city. Riddled with shot from the gunboats, the remaining Confederate rams put in to shore so their crews could escape. The crews of the *Sumter* and *Jeff Thompson* took to their heels, the gunboats lobbing shells after them. The *Jeff Thompson,* run ashore just below the *Little Rebel,* was torched before the crew took off. After burning for an hour, the fire reached her magazine and she blew up, throwing fused shells into the air; they exploded there, providing quite a spectacle. The *General Bragg* was soon boarded by Lieutenant Bishop, Pilot Duffy, and a crew from the *Benton.* Engineer Sam Bostwick found her boilers dry and red hot, but some timely care enabled him to bring them under control. Some of her cotton bulwarks had caught fire, and after frantically cutting away the surrounding bulkheads, Bishop extinguished the blaze and saved the boat.

Captain Maynadier, whose mortar boats were anchored upriver, took a tug first to the *Beauregard* and then to the other boats, claiming them as prizes for the flotilla. Only the *Van Dorn* escaped downriver.

With the battle over and the crowds dwindling, the gunboats returned upriver to the city. Colonel Ellet sent his son, Medical Cadet Charles R. Ellet, Jr., with a message to the mayor stating that he would raise the United States flag over the post office and customhouse. Young Ellet proceeded to the post office, where he was taunted by an angry crowd. Braving some rocks and a few wild shots, he went to the roof and raised the flag.

The *Benton* dropped anchor off the end of Union Street and sent her gig to fetch a well-dressed, middle-aged gentleman waving a white handkerchief. Stepping on board the *Benton,* the man was taken to see Captain Davis, where he introduced himself as Dr. Dickerson. Following a short interview with Davis, the doctor was accompanied back to the city by Lieutenant Phelps and Master's Mate G. W. Reed. Phelps proceeded to city hall with the official request for the city's surrender.

A few in the crowd who followed Phelps cheered for Jeff Davis and called Phelps "a blue-bellied Yankee" and a "son of a bitch," but he ignored them, preferring to look at the women. "I . . . was saluted by a number of ladies," he wrote, "and passed through the immense crowd without molestation or evidence of an exasperated or bitterly hating people, and saw no scowling women."[9]

To the message delivered by Phelps, Mayor John Park replied to Davis: "Your note of this date is received and the contents noted. In reply, I have only to say, that as the city authorities have no means of defense, by the force of circumstances the city is in your hands."[10]

Several shells had landed in the city but had caused little damage or injury. One sixty-four-pound shell passed through a roof, struck a large tree, then hit a chimney, knocking it down and covering a little boy lying in bed. The shell did not explode, and the boy escaped unhurt. Another shot hit the city's ice house, causing minor damage, and another landed on the bluff near the crowd but did not explode. Later, Henry Walke would accuse Phelps and the *Benton* of "an atrocious act," the deliberate shelling of the city. Walke's source was a Memphis newspaper that supposedly quoted one of the *Benton*'s masters as saying he thought shelling the city "would be a good thing."[11]

The formidable ironclad *Arkansas*, which was being built at Memphis, was gone, taken downriver the preceding Sunday. The people of Memphis boasted that she was another *Virginia* and would destroy the entire Yankee fleet. The charred remains of her sister ship *Tennessee* remained at the city's boatyard. In the telegraph office the operator left a note stating: "although you can whip us on the water, if you will come out on land, we'll whip you like hell."[12]

For Phelps and the flotilla the next few weeks involved a change of pace. Instead of the long, boring days that had been their routine for the last three months, now there was real work to be done. "I . . . have had prizes—war vessels and transports—to save, send off, repair, and provide with people," Phelps wrote to Foote, "to say nothing of the thousand wants of the people of Memphis to look after."[13] Never missing an opportunity to keep Foote informed on flotilla gossip, Phelps sarcastically wrote, "Captain Dove flourishes here. Walke is a perfect ship keeper." And, as usual, "the *Eastport* will be ready in 'one month.'"[14]

Phelps wrote with some pride to Elisha Whittlesey:

> The *Benton* attracts great attention here. The people of the south are much addicted to fixing upon some one object in which is centered to their view most of the power of mischief of an entire force. Thus the *Benton* is much the most formidable of our vessels, as they know, and the *Benton* is talked of to the exclusions of the others. It is quite a point, I find here, to be Captain of the vessel. I mean in the estimation of these people . . . I go all about, never think of arms, and never anticipate or realize any kind of manifestation of ill will. . . . There seems to be among all the people of this section a conviction that the rebellion is effectually killed.[15]

The question of prizes had become a sore point between Ellet and Davis. Both men claimed the *Little Rebel,* which was in the custody of the flotilla and had become a "special pet" of Captain Davis. Ellet claimed that the *Monarch* not only ran the *Little Rebel* ashore but accepted her surrender from the three Confederates still aboard. Having left the *Little Rebel* to aid the *Beauregard* in getting to shore, Alfred Ellet was forced to watch the *Little Rebel* towed off by Davis's tugs. In a letter to Davis, Charles R. Ellet said, "I do not ask you to give her to me . . . but merely to restore her to me as she was before she was taken from me. She is mine, commodore, the spoils of my first and, I fear, my last naval engagement."[16]

Charles Ellet's fears proved prophetic. The wound to his leg, at first thought serious but not fatal, began affecting his health. He remained in command of his fleet from bed as long as possible. Soon, however, his only hope became a change of climate, so on June 18, with his wife and daughter, Ellet left Memphis on board the *Switzerland,* bound for Cairo. It was too late. On June 21, as the vessel approached Cairo, the "Ram Colonel" died. The shock to his grieving widow was such that, shortly afterward, she, too, passed away. Col. Charles Ellet was given a state funeral at Independence Hall, Philadelphia.[17]

The news from Cleveland was not good. "I do not improve as I expected," wrote Foote. "I am still in bed . . . the diarrhea has not left me, though becoming less troublesome [and] two physicians told me . . . my liver was greatly enlarged."[18] Some ten days later, Foote wrote, "My dear Phelps, I send you the Doctors certificate which I wish you to show officers, pilots etc. as I want them to know that necessity causes my action." He continued, "Davis, in a letter says, he shall be glad to see me back and inferring that he does not want the command for more than two or three months."[19]

The little seed that Foote planted when he left the flotilla began to sprout. Feeding the ambition of the thirty-eight-year-old Phelps, Foote wrote:

You are prominent in the fleet and with the public as your merits and services justly entitle you to be. There is no one of whom so many enquiries [are] made about as you are. Even strangers to you ask me about you, as you are known as the pioneer in Miss. and Alabama and the active spirit at No. 10 and about Fort Pillow as well as at Memphis. Several persons have said to me that you ought to command the flotilla if I leave it.[20]

With little prospect of his returning to the flotilla for at least four months, Secretary Welles relieved Foote of command and appointed Davis flag officer. Attending to the little details of Foote's retirement from the flotilla, Phelps arranged to send him his napkin ring, gold pencil, letter books, and papers. Also two small mortars, taken at Island No. 10, would be delivered to Farragut's fleet, now working its way up the Mississippi River from New Orleans, for delivery to Foote's family home in Connecticut. Other personal items, such as linens, blankets, furniture, and stores, which Foote calculated cost $800, he offered to Davis for $150. To Phelps he gave an old pea jacket and an India rubber coat.

Now that Foote would not be returning, Phelps wrote to him, stating what he was unable to say in person:

We all, probably, indulge the imagination in pictures of the "porvenir," and mark out a future associated with the friends about us, I have done this in this war with an intensity the greater because of its stern realities and the entire manner in which my sense of duty in it had taken possession of my mind and thoughts. When you induced me to "withdraw" that application, I did it designing to return to my duty in these waters with still greater earnestness of purpose; but the whole future was to be inseparably connected with you. Whatever I might hope the flotilla would accomplish was with you as the leader, the head and front. All we have passed through since you left has not sufficed to turn my thoughts from the plans, hopes, and wishes of the future confidently built upon months since.

I have more reason than all others combined to feel your absence, and I have more acts of benefit and kindness to remember and cherish than they; and I, too, have more reason to feel grateful for the foresight and solicitude that so soon led you to apply for and secure the commodore for your relief. But I have

fallen upon a strange strain; one terribly egotistical; one in
which I shall fail to make myself understood. . . . If I were given
that way, as the commodore is, I should quote you Shake-
speare.[21]

Now that Davis was officially flag officer, he proposed an expedition to cut off the remaining Confederate gunboats thought to be
up the Arkansas and White rivers. This plan was later limited to the
White River after Davis received a telegram from General Halleck
urging him to establish communications with Maj. Gen. Samuel R.
Curtis, who was marching his army through northeast Arkansas
toward the Mississippi.

The men of Augustus Kilty's *Mound City* were justifiably proud
that it was the flagship for the expedition, which included the *St.
Louis, Lexington,* and later the *Conestoga.* At 4 A.M. on June 14, the
Mound City dipped her distinguishing pennant, in a salute to the flag
officer, as she led the expedition past the *Benton.* Early on Monday,
June 16, the *Conestoga* joined up with the transports *New National,
Musselman,* and *White Cloud,* which were crowded with troops and
supplies. The reinforced fleet then proceeded up the White River to
a point about seven miles below the St. Charles battery, where they
anchored for the night.

Tuesday morning, June 17, dawned warm and muggy. Numerous
bales of cotton were floating in the river. Since they were selling for
premium prices in the North, Kilty directed that one of the transports gather up this rich prize while the fleet headed for St. Charles.
The little fleet pressed on until just before 8 A.M., when St. Charles
and its suspected batteries came into sight.

Defended by one hundred men under Capt. A. M. Williams, Confederate Engineers, and a number of crewmen from the Confederate gunboats *Pontchartrain* and *Maurepus,* St. Charles was the first
high ground along the river suitable for defense. Expecting an attack
on the night of June 16, Lt. Joseph Fry placed the *Maurepas* across
the river and waited. When it was obvious that the Federals were not
coming, Fry decided to scuttle his boat and move his guns to shore.
The Confederates had two rifled 32-pounders on the bluff under
Lt. John Dunnington and three smaller guns under Midshipman

Augustus H. Kilty—Kilty was a lieutenant during Phelps's first cruise aboard the USS *Columbus* in 1842. Twenty years later, he commanded the USS *Mound City* during the navy's worst single disaster on the western rivers. (U.S. Naval Historical Center)

Francis M. Robey about four hundred yards below. Below Robey's battery, thirty-five men with Enfield rifle–muskets waited for the expected assault. Those men without muskets were sent to the rear.[22]

As the *Mound City* moved forward, followed by the other gunboats, she fired several shells, but the Confederates stayed quiet, well hidden in the trees and brush. At 8:45 A.M., Colonel Graham Fitch and his 46th Indiana were landed and proceeded up the left bank toward the bluff. Soon his skirmishers encountered Williams's men, and with the first Confederate positions pinpointed, the gunboats opened a heavy fire of grape and canister that forced Williams and his men to fall back. Fry's light guns now joined the fight, and at 10 A.M., Dunnington opened up with his battery. Kilty soon silenced Fry's lower battery and moved the *Mound City* to within two hundred yards of Dunnington's battery. By this time Fitch's men were in position to storm the meager defenses, but Kilty told him not to risk his men; the *Mound City* would silence the guns.

As the *Mound City* passed the lower battery, Kilty ordered his men below to avoid the small arms fire from Confederate sharpshooters. Suddenly "there was a 'crack,' a rushing sound, and an awful crash." Commander Kilty had just opened the trapdoor to the gun deck and was shouting orders when a blast of live steam came rushing into the pilothouse. Kilty was thrown back and the pilot, blinded by the steam, fell through the opening to the steam-filled gun deck. One of Dunnington's shots from the rifled 32-pounder had penetrated the port casemate, tearing through four men; passed through the steam drum and heater; then lodged in the steerage cupboard.

Symmes Browne provided an account:

In an instant, as I stood facing the opposite side of the boat, I saw the steam condensing as it came in contact with the cooler air, and I knew that the boiler must have been entered by the ball. I sprang up the companion-way and ran over the starboard quarter-deck to the stern or fantail, but was not quick enough to escape entirely, for the rush of steam through [an] opening alongside the wheelhouse caught me and slightly scalded my right hand and right side of my neck. As I jumped on the fantail, I passed Dr. [George] Jones and called him to jump in the small boat, whilst I ran to the wardroom port to assist the men whom I saw jammed in the porthole to make their escape. I pulled out two, when I found the third stuck fast and the escaping steam told me it was dangerous to remain there, so I returned to the small boat and jumped in. Just at this moment Second Master W. H. Harte came floating by, and I pushed off the boat to pick up him, and Mr. Kinzie, who was near him in the water. The latter I saved, but Mr. H. went down; and after rowing for some fifteen minutes and picking up five sailors, our boat reached the gunboat *Lexington*.[23]

As steam enveloped the *Mound City*, men frantically tried to escape by jumping overboard. Rebel sharpshooters on the banks began firing at the scalded men desperately trying to save themselves.

The *Mound City*'s plight brought a quick response from Colonel Fitch and the other gunboats. Fitch ordered the gunboats to cease fire, then charged the enemy positions. Lt. George M. Blodgett, in the meantime, brought the *Conestoga* alongside and secured a line to the *Mound City*'s stern, then began to tow her downriver. As Fitch's men overran the Southerners, cutters from the other boats were lowered to rescue as many survivors as possible.

The *Mound City* was towed downriver about a mile and secured to the bank, after which the *Conestoga*'s bluejackets entered the casemate. They were shocked at what they found. The scene was described by the correspondent from the *Cincinnati Commercial:*

Here lay the bodies of some 20 men scalded to death, others with their mangled bodies severed asunder by the fatal shot. The gun deck was literally strewn with from 75 to 80 others, who, being badly scalded and horribly disfigured, were tearing off their clothing, and long strings of bleeding flesh dangling from their finger ends, hands, arms, and lacerated bodies, and with eyes burnt out and closed, crying out for "Help, help—water, give me water, water—save me. Oh God, save me, save me. Oh! kill me, shoot me. Oh! do end my misery. Doctor, will I live? Tell my wife how I died," and numerous pitiful exclamations and pathetic appeals of this character. The features of all were wonderfully distorted. Many could not be recognized by their most intimate friends.[24]

As many as 150 men were killed, wounded, or missing. With only two doctors, men tried their best to tend to the wounded. Dr. George W. Garver of the *Lexington* and Dr. William H. Wilson of the *Conestoga* organized what meager medical resources they had to deal with this catastrophe. They had a boat from the *Lexington* gather up cotton from the river with which to make beds. The *Conestoga* still had a good supply of ice, which became more valuable than gold. With soft beds of cotton for the wounded to lie on, the *Conestoga* and *Musselman* headed for Memphis that night at flank speed.

The *Conestoga* arrived at Memphis about 11 A.M. on Thursday, June 19. As word about the catastrophe spread quickly, Lieutenant Phelps boarded his old boat to see what could be done for the wounded men and for Augustus Kilty, a mentor from his first cruise on the *Columbus* back in 1842. "No imagination can picture to itself the condition of those burned, scalded, and wounded who still live," Phelps wrote. "It is the most piteous spectacle human suffering could present. Poor Kilty was, they said, doing well; but he suffers terribly. His heart is as tender as a woman's. Scarcely any of them are recognizable."[25]

The worst fears of every gunboat sailor were now grimly laid before their eyes. With sorrow and rage Phelps tried to describe what happened:

> She had 160 lbs steam. Think of steam, in such pressure per square inch, being suddenly let loose among men! Of 175 persons on board 25 escaped unhurt. Some who had jumped into the river were shot by the enemy from the banks. Thirty eight poor, scalded, burned & wounded men now lie still alive on our Hospital Boat, the remainder of the gallant crew—113 in number—are buried. A more piteous sight than that presented by the wounded on the Hospital Boat no man ever saw. The one shot doing all this terrible harm, was the only one that injured any of the four vessels. The wonder is that a similar accident has not happened long ago & often. I think that our

Naval Constructor, Mr. Pook—who devised these miserable craft called in the country "Iron Clad" but far from being such in fact, should be hanged for this mischief.[26]

Phelps's anger would have to be brief, for orders soon arrived that would require his undivided attention. The flotilla was headed for Vicksburg.

CHAPTER ELEVEN

ↇ

Vicksburg

Aᴄᴛᴇʀ ᴏɴʟʏ six months the Mississippi River was almost completely under Union control. A strong Union fleet under Flag Officer David Glasgow Farragut had accepted the surrender of New Orleans in late April 1862 and, after taking Baton Rouge and Natchez, was anchored just above the last Confederate stronghold: Vicksburg. Eight ships of Farragut's fleet had passed the city's batteries on the morning of June 28, but with only three thousand troops, taking this city was another matter. Farragut sent a message to General Halleck requesting some of his one hundred thousand troops occupying Corinth, but was informed that the army was in a "scattered and weakened condition," and none could be spared for at least several weeks. Reflecting on this lost opportunity, Gideon Welles later wrote, "Halleck was good for nothing then, nor is he now."[1]

When Flag Officer Davis received a request from Farragut to join him, Davis immediately scraped together what boats he could and departed Memphis early on the morning of June 29. The *St. Louis* remained behind to keep a watchful eye on the city; the *Benton,*

Cairo, Louisville, and six mortar boats headed the four hundred river miles to Vicksburg.

The plantations along the way appeared to be deserted. Fields that once flourished with cotton now grew corn, for with the Union in control of the river, Southern planters had no access to markets.

The irony of slaves apparently left to guard their masters' plantations was not lost on the flotilla's sailors as they watched the passing countryside. At several places along the river, large numbers of slaves gathered to wave and cheer "de Linkum gunboats." The degree of jubilation depended on the proximity of their owners and overseers. At one point about two hundred slaves had gathered on the bank, mostly just watching. With the consequences of "three times thirty-nine" lashes across their backs clearly in mind, half a dozen men dropped down under the bank and vigorously swung their white hats around their knees, not daring to wave them overhead lest they be seen. "The women, seeing the action of their braver brothers, stooped down and waved their cotton aprons so as to be observed only from the river, but all the time faces were turned backward over the shoulder to keep watch over 'Massa' and his spies."[2]

A number of slaves had been told by their owners that the Union army was coming to hang, draw, and quarter them. That story was quickly dismissed when rumors spread among the slaves that the Union army was really an emancipation legion whose mission was to free them from slavery. So desperate were some slaves for freedom that they walked miles to reach the river, then swam to the gunboats and asked to be taken aboard. If they were found fit, the contrabands were recruited, for they helped alleviate the constant manpower shortages. Initially offered jobs as coal heavers and firemen, considered the most menial on a gunboat, the slaves laughed at suggestions by the crew that life in the field was preferable to life around a gunboat's boilers.

The arrival of the flotilla above Vicksburg on Tuesday morning, July 1, was met by cheers from Farragut's fleet. Forgetting for the moment that Vicksburg was being strengthened daily with the arrival of guns sent from Mobile and Pensacola, and thousands of troops under Maj. Gen. Earl Van Dorn, the sailors celebrated the rendezvous of the two fleets. Along with Farragut's flagship the *Hartford,* Phelps wrote, "the lower fleet has vessels of the class of the *Richmond, Iroquois,* and *Winona.*"[3] About a week later he wrote to Whittlesey: "The vessels of this lower fleet are very beautiful as contrasted with our strange looking river craft; yet not one of them would have floated five minutes in the fire concentrated on four of our queer rafts at Donelson."[4]

The attitude of Phelps's former shipmates about the gunboats was somewhat different. When reminded of the combat that the gunboats had endured, the officers of the deepwater fleet would scoff: "Nothing but mud forts, sir." "No naval engagement at all, sir." "Why on board of our ship we laugh at the mere idea of fighting at a mud bank like Donelson and Henry and Island No. 10." An officer on the *Richmond* remarked that "our ship could wipe out the whole of Com. Davis's flotilla in three hours." The reply to this was that the *Benton* alone could demolish both the *Hartford* and the *Richmond* on any river in a short space of time and come out of the engagement uninjured.[5]

As the *Benton* steamed past the lower fleet, the great excitement was evident on all the vessels. Davis wrote:

> [For] the majority of the men and volunteer officers, everything was strange and wonderful. My own people almost lost their senses. Captain Phelps and myself were very much amused at their bewilderment, at the first sight of a fleet of regular men-of-war. Our own gunboats were objects of great curiosity, also, to the men-of-war's men; so were the little tugs. When I passed through the fleets in the [tug] *Jessie Benton* to Flag Officer Farragut's ship, to make [being the junior] the first call, with the red flag indicating my rank and presence, the higher decks and ports of every vessel were crowded. I should not have thought beforehand that so striking and exciting a scene could have been created by the meeting of two squadrons.[6]

The meeting of the squadrons brought old friends together with a great deal of catching up to do. Phelps wrote to Foote:

> this great "New Orleans Fleet" is at sixes and sevens, not at all under control, without system, or head, or plan and great

discent prevails. . . . There is a great deal of gossip among the officers. Captain [Thomas T.] Craven has differed with the flag officer, and, after failing to get by the batteries the other day, has demanded to leave his command, and has actually gone home. There are criminations and recriminations, petty quarrels, etc. I am happy to inform you that our flotilla manifests its better lessons under your hands, and has no outside gossip in return for the abundance offered by the lower fleet. Capt.——— said to Commodore Davis "how the devil did Winslow, Dove, Walke get out here?" as much as "how could such imbeciles get commands?" "They came by rail" was the quiet but effectual damper put upon further inquiries.[7]

One piece of news was particularly distressing to Phelps and the other regular officers of the flotilla. Phelps quickly wrote to Elisha Whittlesey, hoping to stop "an impulsive act of the President likely to do great injury to the service and much injustice."

On the excitement of the news of the capture of New Orleans, he [President Lincoln] nominated every commanding officer in the squadron—some 30—by name for a vote of thanks of Congress, and I believe the nominations have been acted upon in the house. Now many of these were not in the fight, and the voice of the squadron condemns many of those who were. Yet all were voted thanks alike, good, bad, indifferent. These are the only commanders of single ships recommended, except [John L.] Worden & [George U.] Morris, for votes in this war, and most of these have been only in this one fight. Where are the numerous officers in other squadrons who have been in repeated battles, some much severer than at New Orleans? The result of the capture of the city is splendid; but the actual fighting cannot compare with Forts Henry & Donelson. There is so little thought given to the bearing of such acts! Flag Officer Farragut is not consulted. Who would value a vote of thanks of Congress if he found his name associated on the list, that should be wholly of honor, with those who were backward, inefficient, perhaps worse? This vote of thanks has heretofore been a great incentive and highly prized.[8]

A grateful and jubilant Congress might have voted just as Phelps feared had Farragut's report to the Navy Department supported the account of the battle that Capt. Theodorus Bailey delivered to the Senate. Farragut failed to mention that Bailey had led the first division past Forts Jackson and St. Philip or his acceptance of the city's surrender while surrounded by an ugly mob. Within minutes of receiving a vote of thanks, Bailey was told by Senator James W. Grimes of Iowa, a staunch navy supporter, that the vote would have to wait for clarification from Farragut. After several months the Congress voted thanks only to Farragut by name. All the officers and men of the squadron were mentioned only in general. A mortified and crestfallen Bailey would wait until 1869 before the record of his gallantry was set straight.[9]

Once the excitement of the rendezvous of the fleets had subsided, questions needed answers if plans were to be made. Phelps wanted to know, for instance, "For what purpose did the fleet come above the batteries?"[10] Farragut was not sure why he was sent, and felt his hands were tied. To Phelps,

The object proposed in running the fire, losing many lives and many maimed, not to mention the risk of vessels, does not appear and has not been explained by the closest observers. The vessels gained no advantage and we possessed the river above. On the other hand, no attack can be made from above nearly as well as from below, and these eight vessels will have to run by the batteries, get below, about ship, and begin where they were before coming up.[11]

Phelps was not impressed with Farragut. He described him as

an impulsive man, who only thinks that he must be doing something or it will be thought he is doing nothing, who acts without

purpose or a plan well enough based to make it reasonably practicable, may be led for want of a little cool common sense. The
feeling seems to be that vessels and lives are liable to be sacri-
ficed without an object. It is very plainly seen that considerable
damage to Commodore F.'s reputation has resulted from
coming up here.[12]

Farragut had been raised as a foster son by Commodore David
Porter, hero of Tripoli, scourge of the British Navy in the War of 1812
as captain of the USS *Essex,* and father of William and David. The old
commodore, remembering that he had quit the U.S. Navy after a
court-martial for punishing some West Indies authorities for insulting his flag, had taught his sons that the public was very peculiar. "It
blamed an officer if he fought," Farragut said, "and damned him
forever if he did not fight; so, when there was a question between
making or not making an attack, it was better to attack, if for no
other purpose, to save one's reputation as a commander."[13]

The city of Vicksburg was the hub for trade in the entire Yazoo
Valley, one of the most fertile regions in the South. With a population
of five thousand, the beautiful city lay astride a hairpin bend in the
Mississippi River that was overlooked by bluffs rising two to three
hundred feet.[14] This allowed the Confederate batteries to command
not only the river but the riverbank and slopes as well, making a frontal assault suicidal. Work on the defenses at Vicksburg had not begun
in earnest until after Farragut had taken New Orleans, and by early
July only an attack from the rear was feasible. Had Halleck promptly
provided troops, the combined Union forces stood an excellent
chance of success, but the three thousand troops from Maj. Gen.
Benjamin Butler's army, brought by Farragut from New Orleans,
were not enough to take the city.

The troops Farragut brought were instead occupied, along with a
thousand slaves, in a repeat of the largely unsuccessful attempt at
Island No. 10 to dig a ditch across the peninsula formed by the bend
in the river. This time, however, the intent was not just to bypass the
Confederate batteries but to cut off the city. The distance around the
peninsula was twelve miles, but only a mile and a half across the base.
According to Phelps: "This difference of distance gives a level of

David Glasgow Farragut—Phelps considered him rash and impetuous, but Farragut emerged as the navy's greatest hero of the Civil War. (National Archives)

Vicksburg, Summer 1862

3½ ft. between the terminas of the ditch. Now, if the falling river itself will force its way through, forming a new channel, and, deserting the old one, will leave Vicksburg several miles inland there to meditate upon the beauties of secession."[15]

Once again, siege by river became the order of the day. Six of Henry Maynadier's mortar scows were positioned across the peninsula and began the routine bombardment that characterized the action at Island No. 10 and Fort Pillow. The accuracy of the mortars was poor, in large part because the gunners could not see through the tall trees and thick undergrowth on the point. Spotters had to run back and forth across the peninsula to report the effect of the shells.

The mortar boats were beginning to show signs of strain. The heavy weight of the mortars and the recoil from repeated firings had caused the decks to flex downward to such a degree that the caulking was constantly in need of repair. They were complemented, however, by a fleet of mortar schooners anchored below the city. The schooners had accompanied Farragut from New Orleans and were commanded by Comdr. David Dixon Porter.

Life aboard the gunboats once again settled into the dull routine of holystoning the decks, exercising the "great guns," and general shipkeeping. One marked difference from the previous sieges was the intense heat. The trip down from Memphis had afforded a constant breeze throughout the boats, and just after their arrival a weak cold front passed through, providing cloudiness and a light northeast wind. This proved to be only a temporary respite, however, from one of the hottest, driest summers on record. Despite the canvas awnings erected over the gunboats' spar decks to provide shade, the searing sun bore down relentlessly on the iron plate, turning the gunboats into floating ovens.

One advantage not enjoyed by the crews at Island No. 10 and Fort Pillow was the success of their foraging parties. The swollen Mississippi had prevented the crews from reaching solid ground for weeks on end, but here parties ranged far and wide for fresh fruits and vegetables. One commodity not readily available, however, was coal. It had to be brought by barge from Cairo, and with the lower fleet to supply as well, what supplies arrived were stretched thin. To conserve the precious fuel, Farragut had the lower fleet put out their boiler fires, and the flotilla kept their fires low or put them out. The *Benton* kept her fires low, maintaining about thirty pounds of pressure in her boilers.

Disease soon began to spread throughout the fleets. Although none of the illnesses were life-threatening, the toll on each ship's efficiency was apparent. The *Benton* often reeked of vinegar as the men bathed with it to combat an epidemic of prickly heat.[16] Two-thirds of the troops digging the ditch were soon incapacitated. Phelps had so far been lucky. "My health remains unimpaired," he wrote. "Coming out here in the beginning, more than a year since, I have withstood the climate of this region, which has pretty much used up all my first comrades."[17]

The inactivity weighed on everyone. What about the *Arkansas?* She was known to be up the Yazoo River after her escape from Memphis, and Flag Officer Davis wanted to go after her. Davis faced a dilemma, however. Farragut had talked daily since their arrival of running back past the batteries and returning downriver to New Orleans. With the Mississippi River dropping steadily, Davis assumed that Farragut would leave at any moment. His gunboats would be needed to draw the fire of the upper Confederate batteries and to provide covering fire for the lower fleet. As important as the *Arkansas* was, her completion in the backwaters of the Yazoo might take months, and seeing the lower fleet pass the batteries safely was Davis's first priority.

The first real excitement enjoyed by the combined fleets was the Fourth of July fireworks. With all the vessels flying flags from their mastheads, each fired a twenty-one-gun salute at noon; the exception was the *Richmond,* due to the large number of sick on board. During the day Davis invited Farragut to go downriver with him in the *Benton* and get a closer look at the enemy batteries, including their new rifled Whitworth cannon. With Farragut observing the *Benton*'s gunners, Davis gave the word to open fire. Soon the Confederates returned fire, and a general engagement ensued. Suddenly a shell penetrated one of the *Benton*'s bow gun ports and exploded, killing one man and injuring several others. "Damn it, Davis," Farragut shouted, "I must go on deck! I feel as though I were shut up here in an iron pot, and I can't stand it!" With that he climbed a ladder to the upper deck, followed by Davis, who pleaded with him to return to safety. Farragut finally sought shelter in the pilothouse.[18]

As an old saltwater sailor, Farragut had an aversion to these new ironclad contraptions. At least "when a shot passed through [a wooden vessel] the worst has happened," Farragut said, ". . . no one can anticipate the disasters that might result from a shot through the sides or casemate or decks of [an ironclad.]" With the *Mound City* disaster fresh in everyone's mind, Farragut stated that he had a natural dread of scaldings: he "would rather be cut to pieces than touched with hot water."[19]

For Phelps, the frustration in waiting for Farragut to leave was matched by the interminable delays in the completion of the *Eastport*. Since her capture the preceding February, Phelps had looked forward to the day when she would become the flagship. She "will be fleet," he wrote, "so I may know something of the old *Conestoga's* cruising."[20] Being a realist, however, Phelps had to be patient. "The *Eastport* will be ready in time—if enough be given."[21]

One man who didn't have to worry about the *Eastport* anymore was Isaac Newton Brown. After Phelps had so rudely stolen his gunboat, Brown found himself without a command. While in Vicksburg on May 28, 1862, he received a telegram from the Navy Department at Richmond "to proceed to Greenwood, Miss., and assume command of the Confederate gun-boat *Arkansas,* and finish and equip that vessel without regard to expenditure of men or money." This was the first Brown had heard of the *Arkansas's* escape from Memphis ahead of the Union flotilla.

When Brown arrived, he found his new command in a shambles. The vessel had no armor, there were no gun ports cut, her engines were in pieces, and the guns were lying about the deck without carriages. The officer in charge of her completion had lacked a sense of urgency, so Brown had to act quickly and decisively.

Brown had the hulk towed to Yazoo City and was relentless in his efforts to get the *Arkansas* ready. This time no Yankee would waltz in and steal his command out from under him. Those people who stood in his way he had imprisoned; no one was allowed to be idle. Soon two hundred men, many from a nearby army detachment, were put to work. Brown pressed fourteen blacksmith forges from the surrounding plantations into service, setting them up along the riverbank. The necessary iron rails needed to complete the casemate were scrounged from the countryside. Machinery on board the steamer *Capitol* was modified to drill holes for the bolts that would fasten the rails to the casemate. No carriages for the large guns had been built in Mississippi, so Brown contracted with two men from Jackson and received five good carriages from each.

Isaac Brown—Brown served with Phelps aboard the *Susquehanna* before joining the Confederate navy. Their paths would cross again on the western rivers.
(U.S. Naval Historical Center)

For five weeks the workers toiled around the clock. There was no
shelter from the sun during the day. They were not allowed to go
home; rather, they lived on board the *Capitol,* which was anchored

next to the *Arkansas*. The fact that a powerful Union fleet was only five or six hours away added to the urgency in completing the *Arkansas*.[22]

Conflicting reports from Confederate deserters and refugees so greatly disagreed that after two weeks of inactivity, Davis finally decided on a reconnaissance up the Yazoo River to see just what he was up against. Once that was determined, the stage would be set for a repeat of the Tennessee River raid. According to Phelps, "I was to have commanded an expedition up that river to destroy batteries, obstructions, ram, & all."[23]

Mother Nature was calling the shots this time, however, because the drought was causing a rapid drop in both the Yazoo and the Mississippi. With the Mississippi having fallen to about eighteen feet and Farragut's ships drawing sixteen feet, the question of when Farragut would leave was fast becoming academic. Anticipating that Farragut would soon be gone, Davis decided to send the *Carondelet, Tyler,* and *Queen of the West* up the Yazoo on reconnaissance.

Brown, too, was worried about the fall of the Yazoo. It had a deep, narrow channel, but if the river fell too much, the *Arkansas,* which drew almost thirteen feet of water, would be trapped by the Satartia Bar.

Hoping, in vain, for arrival of machinery to bend the railroad iron for the stern quarter, Brown could wait no longer. He quickly had boiler iron tacked over the unprotected casemate and reinforced the pilothouse with a double thickness of one-inch bar iron. Once that was done, Brown sent the mechanics ashore and took on his crew.

The *Arkansas* now appeared as if a small seagoing vessel had been cut down to the water's edge at both ends, leaving a box for guns amidships. The straight sides of the box, a foot in thickness, had over them one layer of railway iron; the ends closed by timbers one foot square, planked across by six-inch strips of oak, were then covered by one course of railway iron laid horizontally at an angle of thirty-five degrees. These ends deflected overhead all missiles striking at short range, but would have been of little security under a plunging fire. This

CSS *Arkansas*—In a feat of incredible bravery, the *Arkansas* fought her way through two Union fleets at Vicksburg in July 1862. (U.S. Naval Historical Center)

shield, flat on top, covered with plank and half-inch iron, was pierced for 10 guns—3 in each broadside and 2 forward and aft. The large smoke stack came through the top of the shield, and the pilothouse was raised about one foot above the shield level. Through the latter lay a small tin tube by which to convey orders to the pilot. The battery was respectable for that period of the war: 2 8-inch 64-pounders at the bows; 2 rifled 32 (old smoothbores banded and rifled) astern; and 2 100-pounder columbiads and a 6-inch naval gun in each broadside,—10 guns in all.[24]

For part of his crew Brown collected about one hundred men left over from the ill-fated River Defense Service. Brown could not get all he needed from Montgomery's fleet, for after being paid off, many had made their way to Memphis and New Orleans to join the Union. Brown supplemented what he had with sixty Missourians who signed on for the trip. On July 12, the *Arkansas* dropped out into the Yazoo and passed below the Satartia Bar. Brown gave his executive officer, Lt. Henry K. Stevens, one day to organize the crew and to get in some gunnery practice; the time had come to go "in harm's way."

As Brown was making final preparations for getting under way, Commodore William F. Lynch arrived from Yazoo City and proposed to go along. He was Brown's superior, so he would have command. Brown's heart must have sunk; all that hard work, and now someone else was stealing his command—again. Brown respectfully said, "Well, Commodore, I will be glad if you go down with us, but as this vessel is too small for two captains, if you go I will take charge of a gun and attend to that." Realizing the implications of his offer, Commodore Lynch replied, "Very well, Captain, you may go; I will stay. May God bless you!"[25]

Early on the morning of Monday, July 14, 1862, the *Arkansas* headed down the Yazoo. She had gone only fifteen miles when it was discovered that all the powder from the forward magazine was wet due to steam from the leaky boilers and engines. Stopping at an old sawmill, Brown had his crew spread the powder on tarpaulins in the hot sun. By constantly shaking and turning the powder, the crew salvaged much of it, which was then stored in the after magazine.

After anchoring near Haynes's Bluff to rest, the crew prepared for the coming fight. All hands were at their stations, guns were loaded and cast loose. The decks were sprinkled with sand, for decks covered with blood were slippery. Drinking water was poured in tubs and placed, along with fire buckets, throughout the boat. Below, in the berthing deck, the surgeons prepared their instruments, stimulants, and lint, and passed out tourniquets to the division officers. Lining the passageways were crewmen stripped to the waist, handkerchiefs tied around their heads, ready to pass powder, shot, and shell from the magazines to the guns. Shortly after the boat was under way, what passed for coffee was distributed to the crew.

At 4 A.M. on the morning of July 15, the gunboats *Carondelet* and *Tyler* and the ram *Queen of the West* departed the sleepy flotilla and headed for the Yazoo, six miles upriver. After a delay in taking on a pilot, the three boats had made about seven miles up the Old River, into which the Yazoo empties, by 7 A.M. Many of the crews were at breakfast when the call "A boat in sight" rang out on the *Tyler*. Lt. William Gwin immediately sprang to the upper deck and, with a spyglass, looked at what appeared to be a small, rust-colored vessel with a single chimney slowly coming at him. Other glasses were brought to bear on the strange craft. Was it the *Arkansas?* Many could not conceive that the Rebel boasting was true, that the Confederates could complete such a vessel in such a backwater place. There was no time for debate, however; all three captains called their crews to quarters.

By sunrise the *Arkansas* had entered the Old River, which was a lake formed by a cutoff from the Mississippi. With the sun rising above the lake on their left, Brown and his crew spotted the three vessels headed their way. Brown called his officers together on the shield and said: "Gentlemen, in seeking the combat as we now do we must win or perish. Should I fall, whoever succeeds to the command will do so with the resolution to go through the enemy's fleet, or go to the bottom. Should they carry us by boarding, the *Arkansas* must be blown up, on no account must she fall into the hands of the enemy. Go to your guns!"[26]

Brown ordered the broadside guns that could be brought to bear to open fire. Not wanting the recoil from his bow guns to diminish his speed, he ordered them to stand by. Brown directed his pilot to head for the *Carondelet*, which he hoped to ram.

On board the *Tyler*, Gwin heard the whiz of a round shot pass over his boat. He ordered the *Tyler*'s engines reversed, and began backing down the river. Realizing that the Confederate gunboat was quickly gaining, he ordered the *Tyler* swung about and the engines full ahead. By this time the *Arkansas*, was almost on her, and fired three rounds in rapid succession. The *Tyler* replied with a broadside of her own, but the shot seemed to bounce off.

Walke ordered his bow guns to open fire as the vessels closed to within a half mile. The shots were wide, and Walke then made a fateful descision. Fearing the *Arkansas*'s ram, he ordered the *Carondelet* to come about. Instead of closing and keeping his heavily armored bow facing the *Arkansas*, Walke now offered Brown his vulnerable stern. The superior speed the *Arkansas* enjoyed as a result of her twin screws was such that even though Brown had to steer first to port, then to starboard, to keep the *Tyler* and *Queen of the West* from gaining a favorable position on her, she still gained on the *Carondelet.*

Instead of trying to organize a coordinated attack, Walke yelled at Gwin to leave as fast as possible, to warn the fleet that the *Arkansas* was coming. Gwin, however, was not going to run away and leave the *Carondelet* to the mercy of this Rebel monster.

Brown now opened up on the *Carondelet* with his bow guns, and each shell seemed to disappear within her stern. Walke's two stern guns were blazing away, but the shot mostly glanced off the *Arkansas*'s railroad iron. Even with his bow guns firing and his vessel occasionally swerving to the left and right, Brown steadily gained on his former shipmate.

As stout as the *Arkansas* was, she was not invulnerable. One of the *Carondelet*'s shells hit with such force that Brown received a severe cut on the head from iron fragments. Another shell, fired from the *Tyler,* penetrated the pilothouse, cut off part of the wheel, mortally wounded Chief Pilot John Hodges, and wounded the Yazoo River pilot. As he was being taken below, the pilot said, "Keep in the middle of the river."[27] Brown still wanted the Union gunboat, so he ordered his Mississippi pilot to "keep the iron-clad ahead."[28]

As Brown closed on the *Carondelet,* the pesky *Tyler* would not go away. With the *Carondelet* slowing noticeably, so did the *Tyler,* which brought her sharpshooters within easy range. Realizing that he was the only man outside the shield, and that Gwin's riflemen were taking their time and firing in volleys, Brown headed for safety. Just as he approached the hatchway, a minié ball grazed his right temple; Brown collapsed down the ladder and landed on the gun deck. Upon regaining consciousness, he found that the *Carondelet* was just ahead. With her steering shot away, the Union gunboat was drifting toward the shallow, reed-covered bar on the inner curve of the Yazoo. Since the *Arkansas* drew thirteen feet to the *Carondelet*'s six, if she continued on her present course, she would certainly run hard aground. Coming alongside the *Carondelet,* Brown ordered "Hard-a-port and depress port guns." Now almost touching, the *Arkansas*'s broadside fire rocked the *Carondelet* so violently that she heeled to port and then rocked to starboard, causing water to ship over her bow.

Realizing that he would not be able to fight it out, Walke ordered "Boarders away!" As his men scrambled to the hatches and gun ports, the blinding smoke from the broadsides was so great that they became disoriented and confused. Finding the *Arkansas* too far away, the boarders quickly shut the hatches. As the *Carondelet* drifted into shallow water, Brown ordered the *Arkansas* to leave her and continue downriver. After the two boats had drifted farther apart, Brown fired one last salvo from his stern guns. As the smoke finally drifted away, Brown gazed upon his now silent prey. All her ports were closed, there was no flag flying, and not a soul was in sight.

Inside the *Carondelet*, Walke and his crew assessed the damage and tended to the wounded. The boat was a mess. More than twenty shots had penetrated her stern. Blood and splinters were everywhere. Steam from severed pipes caused a number of men to jump overboard in panic even though the amount of steam was not fatal. Dozens of beams and timbers were shattered or cut away. Thirty men were dead, wounded, or unaccounted for.

Gwin, in the meantime, had kept the *Tyler* several hundred yards downriver; now that the *Carondelet* was out of action, he had no reason to remain. He took off but found that the *Arkansas* was just as fast as the *Tyler*. With a lead of two to three hundred yards, the bow guns of the *Arkansas* began to rake the stern of the wooden boat. The stern gun on the *Tyler* replied, but its shells just bounced off.

With the *Arkansas* limited to the middle of the river, Gwin shouted at Capt. Joseph Ford on the *Queen of the West*, which was ahead of the *Tyler*, to circle back and ram the *Arkansas*. Ford instead put on all possible speed and ran for the fleet. Gwin, in a towering rage, used his trumpet to scream at Ford in the "wustest kind of language."[29]

The *Tyler* was taking a terrible beating. Wrote Master S. B. Coleman of the *Tyler*:

> Things looked squally. Blood flowing freely on board, and the crash of timbers from time to time as the *Arkansas* riddled us seemed to indicate that some vital part would soon be struck. In fact our steering apparatus was shot away, and we handled the vessel for some time solely with the engine[s] until repairs could be made.

Here is where Gwin showed his high qualities as a commander. He was ablaze with the spirit of battle. All knew that the vessel might go down and all of us be killed, but there would be no surrender. In fact he made that reassuring remark to the first lieutenant in my presence, when that officer suggested such a possibility. We were fighting for our existence and we all knew it.[30]

Downriver, the sounds of distant gunfire were heard. Since it was routine practice to shell places on the banks suspected of concealing hidden batteries, the noise was attributed to that or possibly firing on the numerous partisans who infested the area. "Most of us," wrote Davis, "came to the conclusion that the firing was upon guerrilla parties only. But Captain Phelps was the first to apprehend something serious, and sent to me for permission to raise the steam."[31]

The firing from the *Tyler* had found one vulnerable spot on the *Arkansas*—the breeching that connected the furnace to the chimney. The grape and canister had perforated it so many times that the draw of her fires was seriously affected, letting flames out on the gun deck and causing the temperature to rise to 120 degrees. Brown went below to inspect the engine and fire rooms, and found the heat unbearable. The furnaces were glowing red, and temperatures around them exceeded 130 degrees. Men had to be rotated every fifteen minutes, often carried out by the relief parties. Another problem was the engines themselves. They had a habit of stopping on the center of the crankshaft at the wrong time and place. The automatic stoppers never worked properly together, and steering the boat became a nightmare.

Before long, the running gunbattle carried out into the wide expanse of the Mississippi River. Many in the fleet listened to the sounds that were steadily growing louder. Soon the *Queen of the West* came boiling around the bend. The *Tyler* then appeared, followed by a strange earthen-colored craft. For a few moments, the Union bluejackets stared in disbelief.

"By the time we had 60 lbs steam the Rebel was coming around the point," Phelps wrote.

At first, everyone thought the *Arkansas* would turn around and go back up the Yazoo, her job of dispersing the Federals accomplished. But onward she came. The masts of Farragut's men-of-war loomed into view as the *Tyler* fired one last shot, then ducked behind the *Hartford*. On board the *Benton*, Phelps and Davis waited. "We had 60 pounds, the gauge rose slowly."[32]

As the *Arkansas* neared the Union fleet, Brown saw Farragut's ships in line on the east side of the river. Inside that line were a number of rams and gunboats, and on the west side of the river were more gunboats. Brown said to his pilot, "Brady, shave that line of men-of-war as close as you can, so that the rams will not have room to gather head-way in coming out to strike us."[33]

With steam pressure down to twenty pounds, the *Arkansas* was largely carried by the current as she passed the *Louisville* before coming abeam of the first of Farragut's large ships. With vessels now on both sides, the *Arkansas*'s gunners no longer needed to look for targets; they just fired at whatever ship was in front of their gun after it was reloaded.

Each warship loosed a broadside at the low silhouette of the *Arkansas* as she passed.

> The *Richmond* with her 9 inch shot had riddled the Rebel, but the *Hartford* overshot her. Some of the smaller vessels with heavy guns gave her very damaging shot. The rail road iron flew from her sides, & great holes were made. A gun outside the casemate was knocked over as if it had been a pop gun. A great piece was knocked off her bow & other injuries done her. But the plucky craft still kept on, never stopping to make fight, having the one object in view to run our fire.[34]

Phelps received word from the engine room. "Now we have 100 lbs., enough to turn the wheels."

With most of the Union fleet now behind him and the temperature under the shield around 120 degrees, Brown "sought a cooler atmosphere on the shield, to find, close ahead and across our way, a large iron-clad displaying the square flag of an admiral. Though we had but little headway, his beam was exposed, and I ordered the pilot to strike him amidships."[35]

"The old *Benton* smoked vigorously; still there was not steam to move her huge hulk," wrote Phelps. Then "our cable is slipped, we have 120 lbs steam; we can barely move."[36] But move she did.

"He avoided this by steaming ahead," Brown wrote, "and, passing under his stern, nearly touching, we gave him our starboard broadside, which probably went through him from rudder to prow. This was our last shot and we received none in return."[37]

"A rifled shot from her about this time, cut away a stanchion on board and left its trace on the back of my coat," Phelps wrote. "It was an ugly, whizzing 60 lb fellow and shows there is not much in the 'wind of a shot.'"[38] The *New York Tribune* reported: "A round shot passed so near Capt. [S]. L. Phelps, of the *Benton,* as to take the nap from his coat, without doing him any injury. This is as narrow an escape from propulsion from this planet as usually occurs, and quite as near as any one not enamored of death would desire."[39]

"So much for the favors of my friend Brown," Phelps added later.[40]

The *Arkansas* continued to float with the current, followed by the *Benton,* which now had enough steam to make a futile chase. The *Benton,* trailed by the *Cincinnati,* proceeded downriver until they drew the fire of the upper batteries and began a general engagement. Phelps's and Davis's instincts told them to keep going, to destroy the *Arkansas.*

The question is, shall we pursue the rebel to his den and attempt to destroy him under the fire of all the heavy guns of Vicksburg as well as those of the "ram." A very serious question. [Davis and I] believe we can do it, but 400 miles of river lie between us and Memphis possessed by rebels. The old *"Benton"* can make $2\frac{1}{2}$ miles per hour up stream and alone of all our vessels contend with the rebel ram. Manifestly at $2\frac{1}{2}$ miles the ship could never come back through the fires of so many guns, although to go with the current is an easy matter comparatively. The river from here to Cairo must be kept open. Our boats are many of them disabled. Seven of Pooks' terribly slow &

miserable craft are mostly disabled and never can make up stream more than 3 miles per hour. The *"Benton"* might fail to destroy the rebel & certainly could never pass back above the batteries & would have to remain below. The rebel could then get possession of the river above and drive our army out of Memphis. This would never do. We came up out of range with two wounded men.[41]

Brown had done the impossible. He had run past two fleets carrying more than two hundred heavy guns, had taken their best shots, and had arrived at Vicksburg. Southerners erupted with joy. The war had been going poorly in the West, and they needed a victory. Crowds of soldiers and civilians rushed to the wharf, shouting for joy. Things had been so dismal, and now there was hope. Isaac Brown, with blood still trickling down his cheeks from his head wound, and his blackened, sweat-soaked crew provided a sight on which the South could now fix its pride.

The jubilation was tempered with the cost. Lt. George W. Gift, who suffered a broken arm, summed up that cost:

> Our smoke-stack resembled an immense nutmeg-grater, so often had it been peppered. A shot had broken our cast-iron ram. Another had demolished a hawse-pipe. Our boats were shot away and dragging. But all this was to be expected, and could be repaired. Not so on the inside. A great heap of mangled and ghastly slain lay on the gun-deck, with rivulets of blood running away from them. There was a poor fellow torn asunder, another mashed flat, whilst in the "slaughter-house" brains, hair and blood were all about. Down below fifty or sixty wounded were groaning and complaining, or courageously bearing their ills without a murmur.[42]

Brown had wanted to refit and recruit a new crew to replace the dead, the wounded, and those who had signed on for this one trip and had no intention of pressing their luck. He had hoped to go after the lower fleet later that afternoon, but there was too much to be done and not enough daylight to do it.

With the *Arkansas* safely under Vicksburg's big guns, the officers and men of the Union navy were crestfallen; they had let it happen again. They had been taken by surprise, and this time there was no rationalization that this was somehow a victory. They had been humiliated, and the repercussions were ominous. The *Arkansas,* though gravely damaged, had shown she was every bit as formidable as the *Virginia.* Farragut's wooden ships wouldn't stand a chance if the *Arkansas* could be properly repaired, as the sinking of the *Cumberland* at Hampton Roads had demonstrated. Davis's "Pook turtles" were also no match; only the *Benton* and the *Essex* had the armor and firepower, but they were slow and vulnerable to being rammed. If Brown could get his boat ready, there was only one that might stop her—the *Eastport.* She had the speed and a formidable battery, and drew only six feet of water. The *Eastport* also was now a ram. President Lincoln had approved $56,000 to rebuild her, but she was still not finished.

Meanwhile, Farragut was furious. "Commodore Farragut, who has no large share of judgement, I must say, came on board and desired to see the batteries, some of them new," Phelps wrote. "[Farragut] was full of going down immediately to destroy the rebel with his fleet going off at once; couldn't waste a moment."[43] "We dropped down again and once more opened on the work. A shot took off the head of one of my men, entered the Flag Officer's & my apartments & put things to the right about in a hurry."[44]

According to Phelps, he and Davis had one more reason to be angry, and not at Brown and the *Arkansas.* "It is a singular fact that a deserter reached Commander Farragut at 10 o'clock at night," Phelps wrote to Foote, "telling him that she was coming the next morning. Nothing was said to us; no preparations made." Farragut convened a council of war but, according to the *Hartford*'s surgeon, he did not believe the deserter.

Farragut decided to run his fleet back downriver, and was set on leaving as soon as steam could be raised.

It was very justly urged upon Commander F., that he would do better to wait till near sundown to make his passage down with the fleet, when the sun would be in the enemy's eye, but it was hard to dissuade him from his bent for desperation in destroying the *Arkansas*. It was settled that we, at 6 o'clock, would engage the upper batteries while the lower fleet was passing, which would leave ample daylight for them to see the rebel gunboat, which is painted an earth color, not distinguishable at night. Anchors were suspended from main yards and grapplings from the crossjack yards; in short, most elaborate preparations made for the advantage of the rebel intruder, and none could doubt of its immediate destruction. Our grand ram, the *Sumter*, was loaned for the occasion. At six o'clock we were underway, and while the sun still blazed in its glory were again in hot exchange of compliments with the enemy's battery of six rifled 6-inch guns. No vessels of the other fleet moved yet, and for three-quarters of an hour we were still watching to see them come. At last, as the twilight began, they started, and we even could scarcely tell when the foremost vessel passed the upper battery and saw nothing of the hindmost ones.[45]

On board the *Arkansas,* Brown and his crew spotted the masts of Farragut's ships in the distance. As daylight faded into darkness, a range light was seen on the opposite bank, trying to mark the *Arkansas* for Farragut's gunners. Brown ordered preparations for getting under way and shifted the *Arkansas* several hundred yards downriver. As the guns from the upper water battery were heard in the distance, signaling the approach of the lower fleet, a thunderstorm broke, dumping torrential rain and making the task of Farragut's gunners all but impossible. The *Hartford,* in the lead, opened with a broadside at the spot where the *Arkansas* had been. The *Arkansas*'s bow guns returned fire, marking her new location. Each of Farragut's ships now unleashed a broadside as it passed, most shells missing their mark. One eleven-inch shell did penetrate the *Arkansas*'s hull, cutting two men in half, destroying the dispensary, and disabling the engine. For Lieutenant Gift, the fight was a spectacle. "The great ships with their towering spars came sweeping by," he wrote, "pouring out broadside after broadside, whilst the batteries from the hills, the mortars from above and below, and the iron-clads, kept the air alive with hurtling missiles and the darkness lighted up by burning fuses and bursting shells."[46]

Farragut's fleet was finally below the batteries. Davis's gunboats had accomplished their part by drawing the enemy's fire. The *Benton* was hit nine times, more than all the ships of the lower fleet combined. The *Arkansas,* although wounded again, was as much of a threat as before.

Early the next morning, the combined mortar fleets opened up a bombardment that gave Brown cause for concern. Any one of the thirteen-inch shells could sink the *Arkansas,* because she had no protection from plunging shot. A shell could penetrate through the entire boat, sending her to the bottom. The mortar bombardment caused Brown to move the *Arkansas* frequently, to keep the Union mortarmen guessing. Still, although the exploding shells often came very close, none hit the ram. The psychological effect was another matter, according to Brown:

> I know of no more effective way of curing a man of the weakness of thinking that he is without the feeling of fear than for him, on a dark night, to watch two or three of these double-fused descending shells, all near each other, and seeming as though they would strike him between the eyes.[47]

Brown and his crew spent the next several days getting the *Arkansas* ready to sortie against the Union fleet. With the *Arkansas*'s glory still fresh, Brown initially attracted volunteers from the army to fill his complement. But, when the soldiers reported on board and saw the damage, and experienced the continuing rain of mortar shells, a number suddenly developed ailments.

Farragut had his own problems with his bluejackets as they watched and sweated, because they now not only had to endure temperatures nearing 100 degrees but also had to keep up steam, waiting for the *Arkansas* to move. Disease was so rampant that the sanitary needs of the fleets matched the need for revenge as Farragut's driving motivation.

> We were likely to be soon entirely disabled, as 40 per cent of our people were sick. In my own ship the crew was already reduced from 240, all told, to 200, and of these 50 had the fever

and the new cases were from 10 to 20 daily. 168 of the 200 have now had the disease.[48]

For the next several days, Phelps felt that the hot temperatures were matched by the hot air from Farragut. In a message to Flag Officer Davis, Farragut stated, "I am going up this evening to attack that fellow, and I shall continue to attack him till I have destroyed him or my whole fleet is destroyed." Davis counseled patience: "I have watched eight rams for a month, and now find it no hard task to watch one. I think patience as great a virtue as boldness."[49]

That night Davis's gunboat flotilla watched and waited for the opening guns from the lower fleet, but nothing happened. According to Phelps, "He [Farragut] had apparently only been restrained by our commander and some of his officers, who incessantly watched him, from taking his vessels up under those formidable batteries for the destruction of the one ram."[50]

Finally Farragut crossed the peninsula on the hottest day of the year and held a council of war aboard the *Benton*. It was decided that the *Essex*, along with the rams *Queen of the West* and *Sumter*, would attack the *Arkansas* at first light, with the flotilla engaging the upper batteries and the deepwater fleet engaging the lower batteries. Farragut insisted that his fleet pass the lower batteries and attack the *Arkansas*, but Davis advised against it. Later that night an officer arrived with a note from Farragut asking Davis if he thought it advisable for his fleet to pass the lower batteries and attack the *Arkansas*. An exasperated Davis answered that that was not part of the plan; that the three attacking vessels would destroy the *Arkansas* or drive her to one of the Union fleets.

Early on the morning of July 22, the *Essex* got under way, followed by the *Queen of the West*, as the flotilla commenced firing on the upper batteries.

On board the *Arkansas*, the firing caused Brown to rouse his men from their hammocks to man their guns. The Union attack could not have come at a worse time. His engine was disabled, and only forty-one men answered the roll call on the gun deck. The crew quickly scrambled to man what guns they could, for the *Essex* soon appeared from out of the smoke.

{ 274 }

Instead of using the current to obtain maximum speed, "Dirty Bill" Porter came down abeam of the *Arkansas,* then turned crosscurrent to ram her. This cut his speed substantially. Guessing that the *Essex* would try to ram the *Arkansas* amidships, Brown had the bow hawser cut. This allowed the current to carry the bow out into the river—Brown hoped the *Essex*'s blunt bow would be presented to the *Arkansas*'s sharp ram. The *Arkansas*'s guns had already opened fire as the *Essex* pressed silently ahead. At a distance of fifty yards, the shutters over the *Essex*'s two bow guns were raised and her guns run out. Brown's timing was off, for the *Essex* missed the *Arkansas*'s ram and caught her broadside at an angle; but at least the *Arkansas* was far enough from the bank to avoid being driven aground. As the *Essex* slammed into the *Arkansas,* her bow guns erupted. One of the shells hit forward of the broadside port, shattering the railroad iron and driving massive splinters among the crew. Suddenly, half of Brown's crew was dead or wounded.

The plan had been for the *Essex*'s crew to grapple the *Arkansas* and hold her for the *Queen* to ram. The *Arkansas* was now helpless to stop it. Porter's men, however, were unable to expose themselves because of a murderous fire from small arms and nearby shore batteries. With guns from three batteries, some as close as a hundred feet, pouring their fire into the *Essex,* Porter backed off and allowed the current to carry his vessel downriver. Alfred Ellet had followed at a distance in the *Queen of the West;* to his surprise, when the *Arkansas* came into view, the *Essex* was not alongside but already half a mile below. To add to the confusion that was the hallmark of this operation, Ellet saw Flag Officer Davis waving his hand and shouting "Good luck, good luck." Ellet mistook this for "Go back, go back," and gave the order for the *Queen*'s engines to be reversed.[51] The misunderstanding was quickly corrected, but not before valuable time was lost. Pouring on the steam, Ellet charged ahead and ran into withering fire. He tried to get a better angle on the *Arkansas*'s broadside, but struck her only a glancing blow aft of the third gunport on the port side. With a broadside from the *Arkansas* as her reward, the *Queen* drifted astern. As several of Brown's crew rushed to the gun ports to reload, Ellet and his son emptied their revolvers, allowing the *Queen* a few precious seconds to withdraw upriver.

William Porter—The older brother of David Porter, "Dirty Bill" commanded the USS *Essex* at Fort Henry and Vicksburg. (U.S. Naval Historical Center)

As the *Queen* made her way back upriver, another of several monumental misunderstandings became evident. Davis had assumed that Ellet would not try to run back upriver, against the current, but would follow the *Essex* down to the lower fleet. Once the *Queen* had engaged the *Arkansas,* Davis withdrew his gunboats, leaving the upper batteries to play with the *Queen* as she struggled against the current.

Although the *Arkansas* had been badly damaged she survived. Once again accusations flew as to who was responsible. Ellet accused Davis of abandoning him. Davis claimed he didn't expect to see the *Queen* return upriver. He blamed Farragut: "There was a want of cooperation, most unaccountable, on the part of Commodore Farragut, by which one important vessel was not brought into the action, and by which the support of his squadron was withheld." Later, referring to Farragut, Davis wrote: "This childish impatience I have no sympathy with, and I have as little with that absurd state of mind that refuses to recognize and accept a disappointment or a misfortune. . . . Some natures seem never to rise to the dignity of self-command."[52]

During the engagement the oceangoing fleet had remained silent. Farragut claimed that he was not supposed to engage the lower batteries. "You will perceive from Flag-Officer Davis's letter of the evening before," Farragut wrote, "the lower fleet were to have no share in the affair until the ram was driven down to us."[53]

Phelps's dislike for Farragut now erupted with considerable bitterness.

We did our part, the two boats from above went gallantly to the attack, but the lower fleet moved not, nor did Com. Farragut even advise the Captain of our ram *Sumter,* with his fleet at the time, of his change of purpose so that the Captain could act independently of that fleet and with us when he heard our guns. The attempt was got up at the solicitation of Farragut and he has not and never can explain his failure to cooperate. He should at least have notified Com. Davis of his change of mind. Because the lower fleet failed to act the whole affair failed of its purpose though the attempt was a gallant one.[54]

To Flag Officer Foote, Phelps wrote:

The whole thing was a fizzle. Every day we heard great things threatened only to realize fizzles. I fear that both S. P. Lee and [James S.] Palmer had too much influence with Commander Farragut in the matter of the attacks on the *Arkansas,* but that does not excuse his "great talk and little action." I tell you, my old commander, I would rather have your little finger at the head than he who led the attack at New Orleans. My growl is done.[55]

The *Arkansas* had survived the numerous botched attempts to sink her, and now the Union navy was leaving. The day following the attack, July 23, Farragut received permission to retire downriver. With his captains advising against another attempt on the *Arkansas,* he threw in the towel and planned a retreat.

On July 24, 1862, the heat abated to a pleasant 90 degrees with a fair breeze as Farragut headed downriver. With understandable eagerness the *Brooklyn, Hartford,* and *Richmond,* followed by their gunboats, formed into the starboard column and the six troop transports towing the mortar boats formed the port column. The *Essex* and *Sumter* acted as a rear guard should the *Arkansas* try to follow.

As the transports took the last of the troops on board, the blacks who had spent weeks vainly digging, trying to divert the Mississippi, implored the Union officers to take them along. "I tells you, dis 'ere chile lubs Massa Linkum," said one, hopefully. Scores of slaves who had toiled for the Union, who had withstood the rigors of the swampy climate, beseeched the officers not to be left behind. With tears flowing, they begged—they would work for nothing, do anything to be taken away. They had no place to live, no place to go. Would the "good gemmen," they asked, "for de Lor's sake," take them away?[56]

Most Union soldiers were indifferent to the slaves; they were fighting for the preservation of the Union, their pay, and their friends and unit. In this case, however, every heart was touched by the frantic appeals. The blacks had sweated blood, and the soldiers and sailors knew it. But what could they do? There was no room on the transports.

Now that Farragut was gone, Flag Officer Davis decided to withdraw north to a healthier climate. "If we had remained a week longer at Vicksburg," he wrote, "I should not have had engineers nor firemen enough to bring the vessels up. As it is we have depended very much on the contrabands to do the work in front of the fires."[57]

The underpowered *Benton* needed the *Switzerland* on the port side and the *General Bragg* on the starboard to push her great mass against the current, and then she could move only as fast as the mortar boats were being towed. The tedious voyage ended when the flotilla reached Helena, Arkansas, on the evening of July 31.

On the way to Helena, Phelps provided Davis with a piece of trivia that was not comforting. Capt. Isaac Brown had a plantation some six miles across the river from Helena, so perhaps he would bring the *Arkansas* to that part of the country with which he was familiar. Davis and Phelps didn't have to worry for long; Confederate Maj. Gen. John C. Breckinridge had other plans for the *Arkansas*.

With both Union fleets gone and repairs well under way, Brown asked for a short leave to go to Grenada, Mississippi. As soon as he arrived, he became violently ill. Meanwhile, Lieutenant Stevens received an order from Breckinridge, through General Van Dorn, to proceed to Baton Rouge to support a Confederate land attack on that city. Stevens telegraphed Brown about the orders, and Brown wired back that he should remain at Vicksburg until he arrived. Disregarding his illness, Brown took the first passing train.

Desperately wanting to complete repairs and wait for the arrival of the captain, Stevens appealed to Commodore Lynch in Jackson, Mississippi, to resolve his conflicting orders. Lynch, not knowing anything of the *Arkansas*'s condition, ordered Stevens to obey Van Dorn and ready the *Arkansas* for action. Early on the morning of August 4, the *Arkansas* headed downriver. All that day the trip went smoothly, the *Arkansas* making about fifteen miles an hour with the current. Early the next morning, almost within sight of Baton Rouge, the starboard engine stopped. With the chief engineer, the one man who knew the *Arkansas*'s engines, in the hospital, the other engineers could only guess as to how to repair the engine.

Meanwhile, when Brown reached Jackson and requested a special train to take him to Vicksburg, he was told that the *Arkansas* had already left. He then caught the next train to Pontchatoula, Louisiana, the closest rail station to Baton Rouge.

Repairs on the *Arkansas* were not going well, and it was only a matter of time before she would be discovered. On August 6, the *Essex,* under a full head of steam, was spotted by the *Arkansas* crew. Not able to bring any of his guns to bear, Stevens ordered his crew ashore and set fire to powder trains leading to the magazine before jumping into the river. With her flag flying, the mighty *Arkansas* exploded.

Arriving on the opposite bank shortly after the explosion, Brown gazed upon the remains of one of the South's most formidable fighting vessels. For Isaac Newton Brown, perhaps it was ironic that his ship had met her end after he had once again had her taken from him.

∽

CHAPTER TWELVE

Fair Play & Politics

T HE FAILURE to take Vicksburg ended, for the time being, the Union navy's drive to open the Mississippi River. With no immediate move against Vicksburg forthcoming, the flotilla reverted to patrolling against Confederate guerrilla activity and keeping their part of the river open.

Davis chose Helena, Arkansas, as his forward base of operations after Maj. Gen. Samuel Curtis had occupied the town on July 14 with his Army of the Southwest. Curtis and Davis agreed to combine operations and created an amphibious strike force to keep the Confederates off balance.

Helena, Arkansas, was not much of an improvement over Vicksburg. Built on a dusty plain that reflected and intensified the pounding rays of the sun, Helena offered little relief from the heat. The bluejackets found little shade, and ice sold for the outrageous sum of eight cents a pound. The consumption of cheap Catawba wine, the only alternative to warm Mississippi River water, was put to a halt by the post commander, Brig. Gen. Cadwallader C. Washburn. Reputed to be one of the few temperance men in the army, Washburn issued an order forbidding the landing of all wine, beer, ale, and spirits. The morning after his order was issued, a boat loaded with wine came downriver. The sutlers, fearful of losing this lucrative business, flocked to the general's quarters and pleaded for the ban to be lifted. Washburn refused to relent. His provost marshal, however, made the mistake of allowing the cargo to land and did not place it under guard. By noon all three hundred cases of wine had disappeared into an underground railroad of skiffs, drays, and canoes. When Washburn heard that the contraband had reached the surrounding camps and gunboats, he was outraged. From then on, a guard was placed on all boats carrying spirits until they could be sent back.

With administrative matters needing his attention, Davis returned to Cairo and left Phelps in command as "flag officer–pro tem" of the flotilla at Helena. Quickly flexing his muscles, Phelps, newly promoted to lieutenant commander, departed Helena on August 5, to show the Confederates that although they still held Vicksburg—that was all they held.

As the "Flag" remains on my vessel I in fact command the fleet, thus it is that I am on an expedition in the broad sense of "I." I left Helena night before last with the *Benton, Louisville, Mound City, Bragg,* two of Col. Ellet's Rams & three transports. And twenty miles below was joined by more troops. These last landed at a point where contrabands had reported seven field guns in battery. As the battery was not found those troops returned to their camp while we continued on down to the mouth of White River where the *Louisville* left with the remaining troops to operate in that stream. We continued down to Napoleon. We found no signs of an enemy or of movement along the river. The boats in White River found too little water and were, of course, obliged to come out.[1]

The movements of the Union flotilla were being closely watched from across the river by pickets from the 28th Mississippi Cavalry. These men, together with other observers stationed at intervals along the river, were to warn Vicksburg of any Union move downriver.

While Phelps and the flotilla were back at Helena, taking on coal and provisions in preparation for their next patrol, large Confederate shipments of arms, ammunition, and supplies bound for Little Rock were arriving in Vicksburg from the east. The steamer *Fair Play* was provided to transport the supplies across the Mississippi River to Milliken's Bend, Louisiana. The first load of two thousand Enfield rifle–muskets, two hundred thousand rounds of ammunition, two mountain howitzers, and various other stores and supplies were shipped across the river, then were transferred by wagon to the railhead. Returning to Vicksburg, Capt. James White of the *Fair Play* took on a second load and departed at dusk on August 17. He arrived at Milliken's Bend at 1 A.M. the next morning, and decided to wait until daylight to begin unloading the steamer. Captain White, who lived at Milliken's Bend, went home, and the men on board and in the nearby camp turned in.

Back at Helena, Phelps wasted little time, shoving off at daybreak on the sixteenth. His fleet this time was composed of the *Benton;* the *Mound City,* now under the command of William Gwin; and the *General Bragg,* the Confederate ram now in Union service. The rams *Switzerland, Monarch, Sampson,* and *Lioness,* under Colonel Alfred Ellet, along with the transport steamers *Rocket* and *McDowell* with Col. Charles Woods's Second Brigade (comprising the 58th and 76th Ohio), rounded out the task force.

Phelps made several landings along the river and found things quiet. Instead of anchoring for the night on the seventeenth, however, he pressed on and unknowingly outran the Confederate couriers carrying word about the fleet's approach. Just before 2 A.M. on the eighteenth, as the fleet approached Milliken's Bend, just above the mouth of the Yazoo and only twenty miles from Vicksburg, lookouts on the *Benton* spotted lights on the west bank.

Extinguishing the one dim light that had been visible near the pilothouse of the *Benton,* and passing word for the other boats to do the same, Phelps soon determined that a riverboat was tied up to the bank. Since it could only be an enemy boat, Phelps decided to seize it as a prize.

Word was passed for the boarding parties to stand by. Crouching low along the hammock nettings on the spar deck, sailors waited

Mississippi River, Spring 1862–Spring 1864

quietly with weapons ready. While still some distance away, Phelps ordered the engines stopped. The *Benton* became a huge black shadow as she drifted with the current toward her victim.

A sudden bump and the shout of "Boarders away" sent Phelps and his men scrambling aboard the steamer. On board the *Fair Play*, men awoke to pandemonium as the Federals swarmed over the boat. When Phelps reached the upper deck, he saw a Confederate encampment on the other side of the levee and directed the transports to land. The men of the 31st Louisiana and a Texas regiment emerged from their tents to see numerous boats, and Union troops atop the levee. After firing a volley, the Union troops charged down into the bewildered camp, meeting only by feeble return fire as the Southerners fled. Forty Confederates were taken prisoner.

As his men were securing the *Fair Play*, Phelps received word that some ladies in nightgowns had been seen running toward a nearby cornfield. Phelps dispatched a trusty guard to round up the ladies, and soon Mrs. William Blanton and five frightened Vicksburg ladies were captured. They were induced by Phelps to board the *Fair Play* and get dressed, after which he saw them safely on their way.

Phelps quickly discovered what a prize he had. Twelve hundred new Enfield rifle–muskets and four thousand new muskets, along with accoutrements, as well as a vast amount of small arms and artillery ammunition destined for Maj. Gen. Theophilus Holmes, the new commander of the Confederates' Trans-Mississippi Department, were found on board. The amount of arms and ammunition lent credence to captured documents stating that of the thirty thousand Confederate troops in Arkansas, only about three thousand were armed. The South could ill afford the loss.

The captured crew of the *Fair Play* could not believe what had happened. They had been told that the Yankees were hundreds of miles away, and that there would be plenty of warning should they come near. One Confederate quartermaster, refusing to believe in circumstance, insisted that only treachery by his own men could have brought the Union fleet at just the right moment.

Colonel Woods's bluecoats, in the meantime, pursued the Confederates in the intense heat and suffocating dust for about nine miles. Then they came upon another camp of some three hundred

USS *Fair Play*—Photograph taken after her conversion to a "tinclad." As a Confederate steamer loaded with enough arms and ammunition for a division, her capture by Phelps and the USS *Benton* earned him and his crew a tidy sum. (U.S. Naval Historical Center)

men who had heeded the alarm of the fleeing troops and headed for the nearest town. As the Federals entered the town of Tallulah, they found it almost deserted, the last of the inhabitants having just departed. After confiscating eleven hogsheads of sugar and some ammunition, Woods set fire to the depot and eight railroad cars. He also took the telegraph with him. Not wishing to chase the Southerners further, Woods and his men pressed into service every horse, mule, ox, and wagon they could lay their hands on for the return march to the river, where they arrived shortly before nightfall.

All the boats took what camp equipment they could, but still Phelps had to leave behind some sixty mules and a number of wagons. After everything was loaded, the fleet ventured downriver to within sight of Vicksburg.

The Confederates had been expecting Union boats with thirty-nine hundred prisoners from Camp Morton, Indiana, in the West's first prisoner exchange (the *Eastport* would soon be under way, escorting the prisoners from Cairo). After Phelps had received a flag of truce and informed the Confederates that he had no prisoners, they assumed the worst. Word was sent that the Federals were back, and soon troop trains began arriving as Vicksburg was quickly reinforced. Meanwhile, Phelps determined that the ditch across the peninsula was still dry, and after showing the flag for a day, headed north to the Yazoo.

On the morning of August 20, the expedition entered the Yazoo River, leaving the transports at the mouth. Phelps deemed it too risky to try to take the unarmored boats up the narrow, winding river, so one hundred troops boarded each of Ellet's rams. As the gunboats approached Snyder's Bluff, some seventeen miles upriver, they discovered the Confederates in the process of erecting a battery. A few shells and the sight of the gunboats convinced the Confederates not to remain. Ellet's rams landed the troops, who discovered six pieces of artillery lying on the ground, ready to be mounted in the works when they were completed. Loading the heavy cannons was deemed too difficult in the shoal water, so Phelps ordered them destroyed. Ellet had a brand-new 24-pounder brass howitzer and an antique Mexican brass cannon, inscribed with a Spanish crown and the date 1776, put on board the *Switzerland*. The seven thousand pounds of powder, plus some of the one thousand shells, shot, and grape that could not be taken aboard the boats, were thrown in the river. Phelps said he would not use the powder anyway, "when I can get better."[2] The pieces that were left behind were loaded with powder and shot to the muzzles, which were then inserted into the embankment. Slow fuses were lit, and as the fleet pulled away, the guns exploded into pieces.

The next day the fleet continued up the Yazoo to the mouth of the Sunflower River, which Colonel Ellet's light rams entered, looking for Confederate steamers reported to be above, in Lake George. While Ellet was exploring the Sunflower River, the remainder of the fleet dropped back down to Snyder's Bluff to await his return. After dark, a small enemy force approached the boats anchored in the river and opened fire with small arms. One of the bullets wounded Second Master Thomas Bates before several shells from the *Benton* ended the skirmish.

With the return of Ellet's light rams, the fleet headed for the mouth of the Yazoo, which they reached on the twenty-first. The return was interrupted briefly when several glistening flashes were spotted in the woods just above Greenville, Mississippi. The gunboats let fly with several rounds, and a small force of Confederate troops broke cover and ran. Colonel Woods's soldiers were landed but made no effort to pursue the foe, examining the town instead. The flotilla made a number of landings on the slow return trip and had several minor skirmishes. Just before dawn on August 27, Phelps and his weary command returned to Helena.[3]

The capture of the arms and ammunition aboard the *Fair Play* had, in effect, eliminated a division of Confederate troops without the loss of a single man. After the *Arkansas* debacle, Captain Davis was elated at the success of Phelps's fleet. "This expedition has occasioned a loss to the rebels of certainly $300,000, and perhaps half a million of dollars," Davis wrote to Gideon Welles. "His reports . . . exhibit a fine illustration of his mind and character," Davis continued. "They are simple, concise, and yet full, and they show clearness of view and purpose, energy, and prudence. . . . Lieutenant-Commander Phelps is well known to the Department by his services in the Tennessee. He is, however, a growing and improving character, and the experiences of the passing day add to his power and means of usefulness." Davis stopped short, however, of recommending to Welles that Phelps succeed him. Instead, he added:

If the Department should adopt a suggestion (which I shall have the honor to make at the proper time) of dividing the Mississippi River into sections, and assigning those sections as separate commands, under one commander-in-chief, I should recommend that the command of one of these sections be given to Lieutenant-Commander Phelps. His knowledge of these Western waters makes this the fittest station on which he can be employed.[4]

With Davis leaving soon to head the Bureau of Navigation and no likely successor apparent, the seed that Foote planted burst forth. Phelps wrote to Foote:

> The idea flashed upon me that I might possibly, with the influence of the N.W.[Northwestern states], obtain command of the Flotilla. I have thought over this a good deal. The idea came suddenly and uninvited, but clung to me like one of those I have come to regard as of the character of inspiration. I cannot believe that it is either presumptuous or vain of me to assert the opinion I have arrived at, that the interests of the public service coincide with mine in this matter. . . . Who is there on the rolls of the Navy, eligible to the command . . . fitted by experience and qualification for the post? You know that among the older officers on the station there is no one qualified for the position. . . . I have been longest on the rivers of all in the Flotilla . . . and have advantages in experience possessed by no other officer. General success in the service assigned me and contact with the officers on the station has given me a degree of self-reliance I did not possess. These considerations may account in part for the confidence that enables me to aspire so beyond my seniority and general attainments as well. . . . I had already talked with [William] Gwin and [James] Shirk, as well as Lt. Col. Ellet about this matter and I at once consulted with the Commodore. He furnished me with a copy of a confidential letter which he had sent to the Dept. paving the way for me quite as much as if he had known my thoughts & hopes.[5]

Phelps wrote to Whittlesey:

> The same day that I reached Helena (27 ult.) on the return from the Yazoo Expedition of which I had command, I left for Cairo & home, reaching here [Chardon] the 5th. I found a

little "girl" in the house 10 days old and flourishing, too well cared for and too healthy to indulge in any efforts beyond simply eating & sleeping. Lizzie is doing perfectly well. I was disappointed that it should have been a girl, but feel in this matter as in others that all is for the best.[6]

Phelps threw himself into organizing a full-scale campaign to win command of the flotilla. He had his strategy mapped out. Winslow and Walke were captains, eligible for higher commands, and should shortly be leaving. Nathaniel C. Bryant, captain of the *Cairo*, was sick and had gone home to recuperate; Dove and Thompson had been passed over for promotion. If his junior rank till stood in the way, then he suggested he command under Davis's flag until such time as President Lincoln could appoint him.

Describing his efforts and qualifications for the command to Whittlesey, Phelps wrote:

I went to Jefferson yesterday to see Mr. [Ohio Senator Benjamin F.] Wade, but was disappointed in finding that he was absent. The ride of about 60 miles in a buggy was pretty tiresome. This morning I have a severe headache and otherwise do not feel well. For three or four days, I have been a little troubled.

I went to Burlington, Iowa to see Senator [James W.] Grimes [who encouraged Phelps by telling him "you are the strongest man in America"[7]] and to Columbus to consult with Gov. [David] Tod. Commodore Davis will soon be relieved of the command of the Flotilla, being appointed to the Bureau of Navigation & I am making some effort to obtain the command. The difficulty lies in my being comparatively a junior officer and is one of rank. I believe that the disposition of the Department would favor me, my long experience on the rivers giving me advantages over other officers of more capacity and professional attainments in general, since the service in the west is peculiar.

I am impressed with the idea—and I cannot believe that there is much vanity in the assertion, that my desires & the interests of the public service coincide in this matter. I feel assured, and it is that kind of conviction that would make one ready to stake life and all that is dear upon the issue, that I could greatly increase the efficiency of the Flotilla & its usefulness. I am familiar with every foot of the vast river navigation embraced in the limits of cruising & know what is required & where vessels of each class can be best employed. I am familiar with the character & qualifications of the river men who are employed as officers and possess, from former good fortune, their entire confidence & that of the crews. My physical powers have endured the climate of the Mississippi for 15 months unimpaired and the commander of the Flotilla needs to have energy of decided character & the physique to make it available. The Military & Naval features of the country, the method of operations upon rivers, the conduct of combined land & river movements, can only be understood by study and actual experience. If ever needed this fall will be the time when our flotilla can be most useful & should be most active.

I have thought of the wishes of the North West, as expressed by some of the leading members, would have weight with the President and the Dept.—The Flotilla is a N.W. institution and I am from that section. There is no one senior to me on the rivers who could be considered by the Dept. as qualified in all respects—indeed no one is, but there are certain absolute requisites wanting. Long experience, uniform success, and contact with others has given me a confidence wanting till lately. In my case it can be urged that I am a junior officer; but in reply I would say that my experience in actual warfare exceeds that of any living officer in our Navy. I alone was in every engagement in which our Navy took part in the Gulf during the war with Mexico, and I have served in all the long series of actions and operations on the Western rivers. These considerations should weigh some in the balance of term of service.

I have written with a frankness that I conceive is proper. Convinced that I have a clear perception of what the public service requires on these rivers, and having its interests at heart, I have no hesitation in declaring my belief in my fitness for the control, and anyone who should assist to place me in that position would illy understand the spirit that actuates me were he to do so without sharing the conviction that renders me hardy to apply for the position, that in doing so he consults the good of our country in this terrible struggle.[8]

Phelps's campaign to win command of the flotilla was coming together. He solicited powerful senators like Wade of Ohio and Grimes of Iowa, and Governors Tod and Oliver P. Morton of Indiana. Influential friends like Professor J. P. Kirtland from Cleveland, whose son was fourth master on the *Conestoga,* wrote to Welles, backing Phelps for command. New York connections along with Whittlesey, whom Lincoln had brought back as comptroller of the Treasury, solicited Secretary of the Treasury Salmon P. Chase in their efforts.

Flag Officer Foote, still on crutches, had recovered sufficiently to report to Washington. The command of a fleet by one who only a few weeks before was only a lieutenant was of sufficient sensitivity that Foote circumspectly wrote:

I will work in the good cause . . . you may depend upon my doing all in my power. . . . You are the man to have an important command in these times. Davis has well expressed my views in this respect and when he reaches Washington, and even before I will put my shoulder to the wheel. I want to see [Assistant Secretary of the Navy Gustavus V.] Fox before I can even come to a settled plan for consummating your views and wishes.

Even though Foote was a lifelong friend of Welles, he was concerned enough about the sensitive nature of this campaign to add, "In these stormy times I must inch cautiously as this note may fall into wrong hands."[9]

Leaving the campaign to his friends in Washington, Phelps returned to the flotilla and turned over command of the *Benton* to William Gwin. It had taken seven months, but the *Eastport* was finally finished.

When the boat had arrived at Paducah in February, it was found that Isaac Brown had constructed an interior bulkhead four to five feet from the outer hull to protect the engines and boilers. After the *Eastport* had been towed to Mound City in the middle of March and taken on the ways, Brown's plan was scrapped and a plan designed by Phelps and Capt. Alexander Pennock was adopted. The decision to make her into a ram added to her length, giving her greater speed and less draft.

The new flotilla flagship was a much longer craft than the *Benton*, having a length of 260 feet, a breadth of forty feet, and a depth of hold of eight and a half feet. The four boilers, each thirty-two feet in length and forty-two inches in diameter, were located ten inches below the waterline and were surrounded by coal bunkers, minimizing the risk of being punctured by shot. The boilers fed two high-pressure engines, each having twenty-six-inch cylinders with eight-foot stroke. The engines stood on the main deck but were situated so as to lessen their vulnerability. Like the other ironclad boats, she carried a separate pumping engine and auxiliary steam apparatus for repelling boarders. Each engine drove one of the twenty-eight-foot side wheels with twelve-foot buckets.

The casemate was constructed of heavy gum timber and covered with iron plate that extended four feet below the waterline. The thickness of the iron plate was kept confidential. Her sharp prow rose five feet above the waterline and contained the wrought iron ram, which weighed fifty-seven hundred pounds and was shaped to strike an opposing vessel at the waterline first. The massive ram was set against solid timbers, crossed and bolted together into a compact mass extending back thirty-four feet. These in turn were backed by three fore-and-aft bulkheads that ran the length of the vessel. Cross-braced watertight bulkheads added to the strength and divided the boat into twenty-eight watertight compartments. It was felt that it was almost impossible for the *Eastport* to sink and that, running at ten miles an hour, she could pulverize solid rock.

The open main deck was set back forty feet from the bow and ended thirty feet forward of the stern. The sloping casemate was set at the standard forty-five degrees and was pierced for eight guns, two on the bow and stern and two on each side.

The pilothouse was a six-sided cone, built at a forty-five degree angle with iron-plated timber.

All the decks were covered with three-quarter-inch iron plate. The wheelhouses were sheeted with iron on the sides to a line even with

the hurricane deck, and the ends were protected by extra iron casemates having the same inclination as the sides of the vessel.

The quarters for the officers and men were on the main deck. The
officers' messes were located aft of the wheelhouses. The crew hung
their hammocks on the gun deck, forward of the wheelhouses. Two
rows of cabins were built between the wheelhouses, one on each side.
These included the flag officer's, captain's, first officer's, and paymaster's quarters. Also located there were the kitchens, closets, and
pantries.

Painted black, with her bow and stern rising five feet above the
water and two and a half feet amidships, the graceful *Eastport,* with
her anticipated speed of twelve knots, was the most impressive vessel
on the rivers.[10]

More than a year had passed since Rodgers, Phelps, Stembel, and
Bishop had been sent west to aid the army in the construction and
conversion of a fleet of riverboats into fighting craft. What was
clearly now a naval force, however, was still under the command of
the army. Cooperation among the local commanders varied considerably and made the overall situation awkward at best. Gideon Welles
and Gustavus Fox, along with their allies in Congress, finally rectified
the problem in August with a law that would transfer command of
the flotilla to the navy on October 1.

The flotilla was to be known as the Mississippi Squadron. With
Davis slated to leave for the Bureau of Navigation, the new squadron
commander had not yet been chosen. In fact, Welles and Fox had no
one clearly in mind. Phelps, however, had one strike against him. His
successful lobbying efforts in Congress with regard to the restoration
of returning officers and the vote of thanks for the lower fleet had not
endeared him to the Navy Department. "However great his merit, it
will not do," Fox wrote to Davis. "I am in favor of passing down the list
for a good man in an important command as you know, but for over-
sloughing even one good officer to reach him we should ignore the
whole list. Check his ambition, it is selfish."[11] Fox suggested instead
that Davis stay on until a commander could be selected, and Davis was
agreeable until he could avenge the Vicksburg debacle.

Phelps received his answer in a personal letter from Gideon
Welles, dated September 18, 1862.

USS *Eastport*—After Phelps captured her from the Confederates in early 1862, she was rebuilt into the finest gunboat in Union service. (Cincinnati Public Library)

I deem it proper to address you a letter, partly official, partly personal. No person perhaps better knows or more highly appreciates your services than myself. They have been invaluable to the country and honorable to you and in every proper way I should not only be happy to acknowledge these services but consider it my duty to do so.

One of the highest and most important duties devolving on the Secretary of the Navy is that of faithfully sustaining and bringing forward true merit wherever it exists. Talent, capability, courage and fidelity are each deserving qualities and when they are combined the country has an officer who should be cherished and promoted. It gives me pleasure to accord to you the qualities enumerated and to acknowledge they have been made available in many scenes of conflict when the honor of the flag and the reputation of the Navy have been gallantly supported and successfully maintained. I am proud of your services and am glad to thank you for them. While I am connected with the Department it shall be my endeavor that no opportunity shall pass unimproved to bestow upon you all fitting and proper reward.

But while I would do you this justice, I cannot do injustice, knowingly to others whatever may be your merits. I cannot in the faithful and honest administration of this Department confer honors on you at the expense of others who are also meritorious and worthy.

There are, I am happy to say, many very brave men who are your seniors in the service capable of adorning any position and discharging any duty the Department may require and whom, on sober and deliberate reflection, you would not I am convinced wrong and humble, if by any undue and improper influence you could be elevated to a position to which they are entitled.

It is the proper consideration of this subject which prompts me to address you this letter. I do it with some hesitation because it is unusual but the occasion is also unusual.

Some extraordinary influences have been brought to bear upon the Department with a view of influencing its action in relation to the command of the Western Flotilla. In various ways and from various quarters I have been importuned to confer that important command upon you and I regret to say that these importunities have their origin in a great degree with yourself.

Is it because you have not confidence in the justice, ability, or rightful discrimination of the Department that these indirect influences are put in motion, or is it an attempt by illegitimate means to induce the Department to do injustice to others to gratify your desire for official distinction? I apprehend you have not fully and maturely considered this subject in all its bearings, for could your outside influences so wrong the good and gallant officers who are your seniors it would carry but little gratification with it.

A consciousness of the wrong would obscure all the glory of the position. You would soon as obtained by such means regret that you had resorted to them. Stimulated by zeal you have I am confident acted without full consideration.

Gideon Welles—Lincoln's secretary of the navy, Welles oversaw the rapid expansion of the Union navy after its initial setbacks in the spring of 1861. (National Archives)

Let me say to you also what I have had occasion to say to one other officer, that the Department disapproves the efforts of any officer to influence its actions by outside political influences. I desire that the intercourse between the Department and the officers may be frank and direct. Local and party appeal for promotion and command are the usual resorts of inferior minds and I regret that one so capable and who has rendered such eminent service should adopt them.

There are among your juniors, men of merit who have rendered service but whatever may have been their desires I could not think of giving them position above you and the same considerations must prevent me from giving you a command that by every principle of usage and right, belongs to others.

In selecting another I shall in no way disparage you while by placing you in command of the Flotilla I should perpetuate a wrong on some of the noblest spirits in the service. Thus your own good sense and instincts will condemn and it is ungenerous to these gallant spirits as well as to the Department to stimulate political or local pride with a view of warping or preventing the action of the Department from a strict and faithful administration towards all.

I have written this letter in a spirit of friendly regard which I hope may be justly appreciated. I feel that I personally and the whole country owe you a debt of gratitude for your courage, skill, fidelity and untiring and devoted industry and perseverance in trying and responsible positions. The honors thus earned are all your own. No place or position can gild them and let no aspiration tarnish them. The path of honorable ambition is in the line of your profession and not in the byways of partisans. They cannot help you and you need not their help if they could. With whatever emotion this letter may now be received I am confident that if your life is prolonged the time will arrive when you will be convinced it is prompted by the best of motives to yourself as well as for the service.

Wishing you every success, personally and professionally, I am

> Very respectfully,
> Gideon Welles
> Secretary of the Navy[12]

The blow to Phelps's pride was such that both Foote and Davis felt real concern that he would do something rash. Everyone was stunned by the appointment of Comdr. David Dixon Porter to command the squadron. Ever the philosopher, Davis wrote to Phelps:

This is one of those sudden events that take place in the naval world—like earthquakes in the physical, not only creating surprise, but bringing in great waves, and stirring up howling eddies, in which great ships, as much as little boats, get tossed about in the most disturbing and perplexing manner. . . . In this naval state of affairs I am more troubled on your account than my own. I am a member of a society of which the motto is, philosophy is the guide of life. . . . I think my influence with you is sufficient to justify and demand a word of counsel on this occasion.

This is one of the turning points and governing moments of your future life. If you undertake to oppose this action of the Department, to set yourself a second time in opposition to its wish & judgement, you will not only forfeit its confidence but you will naturally provoke its ill will, the more especially as your motive is the promotion of your own advancement. And, further, you will, by such a course disable your friends.

If on the contrary you accept this new condition of things quietly & cheerfully you may count with certainty upon being Porter's successor and that too, probably, without any longer waiting than you would have had to encounter if I had remained. . . . Wait, then for I say, wait and trust . . . you will have plenty of time to swallow down your disappointment before you see me again. Don't leave your station or communicate your first thoughts to anyone. I have written you somewhat in the style of a parent or like a book in a red cover, but it comes from the right place. I feel the most sincere interest in your progress and I shall labor to advance it as I would that of a relative.[13]

Andrew Foote wrote from Washington, explaining Gideon Welles's decision:

The Department took the ground that while the law authorized the range of all Captains and Commanders in the selection of Flag Officers of squadrons, it has no authority to go down the list to Lieuts. This was the correct one and had the Sect. deviated from it the appt. would have been annulled at the next session [of Congress] while the Sect. would have been censured for acting contrary to law.

I have therefore been anxious and have done all in my power to have you promoted as a Commander when you would have been eligible to the command of a squadron and I shall still work to that end. In the meantime I have strongly recommended you as Commander of one of the divisions on the rivers.

The Dept. fully appreciates your services & merit. . . . I suspect no act of yours is unappreciated or unfavorably considered if perhaps I except the strong political move of you getting command of the flotilla which the Dept. by law could not give to any but a Capt. or Comdr. Mr. Welles fully assented to my opinion of you. I will do all I can as you know in your case.

Two weeks later, Foote wrote:

[Samuel] Dupont is here and dined with [Horatio] Bridge & myself yesterday. [David D.] Porter & [John] Dahlgren also helped to make up the party and [Gustavus] Fox not least was giving us the benefit of his naval & diplomatic experience of Navy and war news. . . . I have already talked to him [Porter] about you and shall do still more to put you right with him. In fact your name & deeds are already history. . . . You must bide your time, as it will come to one so well qualified for every & all positions.[14]

Phelps, confident in his assessment of his own qualifications, had underestimated Gideon Welles. Welles had been through this political pressure before, although not in the form of an organized campaign. Earlier that year President Lincoln had broadly hinted to Welles that Comdr. John Dahlgren, a personal favorite, should command the New Orleans expedition. Lincoln had openly urged that Dahlgren be promoted to captain, and with all that implied, Welles had to be careful. Dahlgren, a junior commander, was a noted ordnance specialist who had spent much of his career in Washington. Welles relied on seniority to avoid offending the president and hurting the morale of his officers. He chose instead a nearsighted, sixty-year-old captain who had been passed over for squadron command three times: David Glasgow Farragut.[15]

The new law passed in August allowed, for the first time, the appointment of captains and commanders to squadron commands on the basis of qualifications and ability. It also added grades, which meant that the new rank of lieutenant commander prevented Phelps from a promotion to commander. Still, Phelps loosely interpreted the new law to mean captains of ships were eligible.

Ironically, although Welles felt he could not pick a new lieutenant commander as an acting admiral, he did something almost equally bold: he appointed a junior commander—David Dixon Porter—to command the new Mississippi Squadron.

The selection of Porter sent rumblings through the navy. Unlike Phelps, Porter was well known to Welles, which made the selection all the more surprising, considering that Porter had embarrassed Welles more than once.

The name Porter was legendary in the navy. The Porters had served the nation at sea through five generations. Before the Revolution, Alexander Porter had commanded a merchant ship out of Boston. His son David commanded the privateers *Delight* and *Aurora* against the British, and was appointed a sailing master in the newly created United States Navy. Grandson David became something of a legend in his own time. First in the war with Tripoli, then as the terror of British shipping during the War of 1812, David Porter brought prizes and glory to the infant navy.

David Dixon Porter was born June 8, 1813, and first went to sea at the age of eleven with his father, fighting West Indian pirates. After his father's court-martial and resignation from the U.S. Navy, David Dixon followed his father and joined the Mexican navy, serving on the armed brig *Guerrero* under another relative, John H. Porter. Captured by the Spanish after a fearsome fight in which John Porter and eighty of his men were killed, the young Porter was soon released and returned to the United States, where he received an appointment as a midshipman on February 2, 1829.

As captain of the *Spitfire* during the Mexican War, Porter made a name for himself at Veracruz and Tuxpan. After the war he received a furlough and commanded the mail steamers between New York and the isthmus of Darien. Even as a civilian, he showed audacity. When the Spanish closed Havana Harbor, Porter sailed the mail steamer *Crescent City* past the guns of Morro Castle and into the harbor, stating that he carried the U.S. flag and the U.S. mail, and by the eternal he was going to enter the harbor.

Welles's relationship with Porter made his appointment almost as shocking as would have the selection of a young lieutenant commander. Porter was one of those whose loyalty was questioned by Welles when he became navy secretary. It was well known in Washington that Porter was courted by Jefferson Davis and other avowed secessionists in early 1861.

On April 1, 1861, Welles received a paper signed by President Lincoln with a postscript written by Porter, that requested the appointment of Capt. Samuel Barron to the Bureau of Detail. At the urging of Secretary of State William Seward, Lincoln had signed the paper without reading it, unaware that Barron had accepted an appointment, five days before, as a commodore in the Confederate States navy.

Welles went to see Lincoln in such a rage that when he entered the president's office, Lincoln immediately said, "What have I done wrong?"[16] Welles suspected Porter's loyalty, and was upset that Porter helped Seward meddle in naval affairs.

The articulate Porter survived all of his schemes. Welles later stated:

> President Lincoln believed the attempt to thrust Barron on the Navy Department was the fault of Porter rather than Seward, and he never thereafter reposed full confidence in Porter, though not insensible to his professional ability. . . . When from time to time I availed myself of Porter's qualities and gave him commands and promotion, the President expressed his gratification that I retained no resentment.

Although Phelps was not chosen, the arguments he made in his own behalf had a telling effect on Porter's selection. Welles's description of Porter in his diary also described Phelps:

> [He] is fertile in resources, has great energy, excessive and sometimes not over scrupulous ambition, is impressed with and boastful of his own powers, given to exaggeration in relation to himself . . . is not generous to older and superior living officers, whom he is too ready to traduce, but is kind and patronizing to favorites who are his juniors. . . . His selection will be unsatisfactory to many, but his field of operation is peculiar, and a young and active officer is required for the duty to which he is assigned.[17]

For Phelps the appointment of Porter concluded an intense year that had begun with a second-rate assignment. The Mississippi Squadron, with Phelps as one of its primary architects and occasional de facto commander, had aided the Union in some of the few successes of 1862. Unlike Foote and Davis, with whom he developed almost a father–son relationship, Porter was cut from the same cloth as Phelps. Although friendly, they would never become close.

ↄ

Flotilla Overhaul

P HELPS HAD kept his fleet constantly engaged since his appointment as acting fleet captain and had spent little time on administration. Now that he had been denied command of the flotilla, he
turned his full attention to overhauling the gunboats. Frustrated
over his rejection, he was determined to make a difference. While
still fleet captain pro tem at Helena, Phelps was determined to bring
the flotilla up to his standards while he had the chance. The two men
he came down on first were Benjamin Dove and Egbert Thompson.
Davis had assented to Phelps's opinion that the two men should be
relieved, and said he would have them reassigned when he had re-
placements. Phelps was not satisfied with their transfers. He wanted
examples made of all those officers he deemed incompetent.

Changes were urgently needed among the gunboat crews, starting
with the captains. A number of gunboats were a shambles. The *Cincinnati* was useless. Her engines had been permitted to run down,
and she had numerous leaks. Out of 147 men on board, only 47 were

fit for duty. Phelps wrote to Flag Officer Foote that before Lieutenant Commander Gwin had transferred to the *Benton,* the *Mound City* was

worth more than Winslow's, Dove's, Bryant's and Thompson's vessels together. The former has been in no action. Dove's has been banished from the scene of active service most of the time because inefficient. Commodore Davis' experience with the last two at Fort Pillow and Memphis caused him to station them about Fort Pillow for the same reason. Walke is a brave man and a reliable one when minutely directed as to what is expected of him. He made a fatal error in judgement in the Yazoo when he met the *Arkansas.* Had he kept head to the enemy the *Carondelet* & *Tyler* would have destroyed him where they met. It was no lack of determination on Walke's part. Younger men are wanted who have the physical energy and habit which will lead them to drill & exercise and discipline their officers and men personally and constantly.

Kilty, Stembel and Paulding are gone and Walke is the only fighting captain of yours who remains among the ironclads. . . . With the loss of the three I have named, the fighting element of the ironclads was gone and they soon ran down for one cause or another, till the *Benton* remained almost alone. The *Cairo* and *Pittsburg* never have been of use; the *Louisville* hardly better, and, like them, most of the time banished to unimportant points away from the active field. The *Cincinnati* just off the ways leaked badly. The *Carondelet* was cut up by the *Arkansas* & sent for repairs while the *Mound City* was without a crew, and the *St. Louis,* at Memphis not efficient under your Boston friend [Winslow]. Gwin took the *Mound City* with the *Tyler*'s crew and has made her a very efficient vessel. [Byron] Wilson now has her and Gwin the *Benton.* Those two with the *Eastport* are the only efficient ironclads now on the river.[1]

One captain whom Phelps no longer had to worry about was Winslow. Upset that Porter had been promoted over him, Winslow asked to be transferred. With $9,662 worth of prize money stolen from his gunboat and disloyal remarks attributed to him by the *Baltimore American*—that he was glad to see General Pope defeated at the Second Battle of Bull Run (Manassas) and hoped the Rebels "would bag old Abe"—Welles was only too happy to send him to command the steam sloop *Kearsarge,* chasing Confederate raiders.[2]

To provide the evidence he needed, Phelps ordered a round of inspections on the boats. For Dove's *Louisville* he sent William Gwin, Joshua Bishop, and Byron Wilson to hold a survey. He specifically directed them: "Be careful to indicate in your report those of the officers who appear to you not to be sufficiently conversant with the divisional exercises and the routine of a man of war—as well as those who from age, want of education or other cause appear not to be adapted for the Naval Service."[3]

Their report was just what Phelps had expected. With the exception of the hold and engine room, the *Louisville* was in a "disgraceful and dirty condition." Her executive officer, two masters, and surgeons were found incompetent; the crew was demoralized and seldom exercised at any of their duties. When they were called to general quarters, confusion prevailed. Instead of being ready in three to four minutes, thirteen minutes passed from the first beat of the drum until the boat was reported cleared for action. The inspection party then found the magazines were not ready, the men at the guns were without any arms at all, the repel boarders detail was without their cutlasses, and the supply and reserve crews were unprepared.

Phelps's report on the Ram Fleet was equally damning. He wrote to Davis:

> As the matter now stands, there are disputes in every vessel where the Col. is not present, as to who commands; there are troubles, disputes, dissatisfaction and a life in common entirely subversive of all discipline. The natural result follows; wherever they land plundering and stealing is the chief aim and the crews have extensively engaged in enticing negroes from plantations. The rams recently returned from the Yazoo were chief parties in plundering the town of Millikensville and I am told that the *Switzerland* has furniture, household clothing, trunks etc. on board taken from there.

Complaints were made to me several times of outrages committed by Naval vessels, but I invariably found on investigation that the acts were committed by the rams. When I discovered attempts at plundering I put them down at once.

My feelings towards Col. Ellet are one of the kindest description, and I feel assured that he is a reliable, honest man and I know of no one who would more gallantly command a ram in a fight. His want of knowledge in the matter of organizing his vessels is no reflection upon him. . . . Could not the Col. be assigned by the War Dept. for duty in the Flotilla; the ram fleet be turned over to the Navy, the officers to be appointed by you?

I have always felt, that the Ram Fleet is a standing insult offered by the War Dept. to the Navy. I cannot rid myself of the feeling and it is one very prevalent among our people. I now feel that the public interests demand a change.[4]

Phelps suggested that the ram fleet be designated as a division of the flotilla and placed under Ellet. The status of the Ram Fleet should have been resolved with the pending transfer of the gunboats to the navy, but the ambiguous wording of the congressional legislation left Ellet's boats in limbo. Since the rams did not carry any cannon, they were not technically gunboats, so both the army and the navy claimed authority. President Lincoln finally stepped in and ordered that the rams be placed under the command of the Navy Department. Ellet was promoted to brigadier general, and his rams were designated the Mississippi Marine Brigade.

Phelps's aggressive reorganization worried Davis, who was in Cairo preparing for the transfer of the squadron to the Navy Department and Flag Officer Porter. Davis wrote:

Your public course, cutting off people's heads, destroying their reputations, bucking the fallen, ordering inspections and courts of inquiry, and playing the Devil generally, alarms and troubles me as much as your private notes gratify me.

I have a feeling of relief that poor Thompson is out of your reach, or you would pluck him like a feather as you have poor Dove. You have acted fully up to the severe maxim of vae

Lt. Col. Alfred W. Ellet—Ellet commanded the Ram Fleet after the death of his brother and later was placed in command of the Mississippi Marine Brigade. (U.S. Naval Historical Center)

victis—"Alas! for the fallen." . . . The thing is notorious—what reason can I give for asking of the Department the immediate dismissal of these two men, only yesterday, as it were, reported for appointments.

I am amused, if nothing else, at the tone of the report. The three captains who made it appear to have drunk Aconite—passion glitters in every line. The calmness and dignity of an official paper are totally wanting. The *animus, diabolo sundentes,* (excuse the Latin, but it is better than swearing) appears to be a gleam of fire on the page and makes it luminous. Pray my dear captain, remember that I have not yet left the squadron & that in matters of life and death like this—in capital cases—I will temper the zeal of the young with a little of the sedateness of age. It is an interesting fact, and one worthy of a moments reflection to those who are disposed to be hasty, that one of the earliest official acts of Captain [Richard W.] Meade (who . . . falls on poor Dove's track with all the ardor of a sportsman) renders him liable to a court martial.

Neither you, nor any commander of the squadron, seem to take in the ideas of my having reported a certain existing state of things to the Department, and that the changes you make, or propose to make, by dismissals, leaves of absence, etc. render this report inaccurate—to the extent—and again, that the squadron being transferred to the Navy, I have no longer the authority I had before; but must refer these questions to the Secretary of the Navy.

Pray, let things remain in status quo, as far as possible.[5]

Phelps gave free rein to his young captains. Along with Gwin and Shirk, these included Thomas Selfridge, an 1854 graduate of the Naval Academy, who replaced the ill Bryant on the *Cairo,* and Richard W. Meade, class of 1856 and nephew of Gen. George G. Meade, who replaced Dove as captain of the *Louisville.* Phelps allowed the new captains to purge their boats of anyone who did not meet their standards.

Davis had given Phelps a great deal of latitude but now felt he was going too far. He wrote to Phelps, "I must decline accepting any resignations or granting any leave of absence; I ask of you the special favor not to forward such papers. It would seem as if some of the young officers intended to dismantle their ships. . . . I feel the same horror for resignations that Macbeth did for reports. 'Bring me no more reports!!!'"[6]

Benjamin Dove was transferred to the naval rendezvous at Baltimore, and Egbert Thompson was sent to the rendezvous at Philadelphia. For almost two years the men were kept on unofficial suspension, doing recruiting duty. Dove went so far as to appeal to Maj. Gen. Lew Wallace for help in returning to active service. He felt his refusal of the surrender at Fort Donelson was behind his removal from command. In 1864 Dove was finally transfered to the North Atlantic Blockading Squadron, and Thompson was given command of the steamer *Com. McDonough* with the South Atlantic Blockading Squadron.

Phelps's overhaul was effective. The efficiency of all the ironclads improved under the command of the younger captains. For new Acting Master's Mate Henry Coffinberry, the new regime was a shock. Reporting aboard the *Louisville* in mid-October, Coffinberry noted:

> I have never in my life worked any harder than I have for the last week. We are not allowed to set down on our watch not even to rest for a minute. When on deck we have exclusive charge of all the ship's crew and have to see that all the ship's duties and routine is carried out in the strictest style possible. Besides our watch on deck we have to go to quarters twice a day and drill the men at the big guns half an hour every day. . . . Our Captain is an educated naval officer and he makes no allowance for anybody and if you ain't just so you will get an overhauling.[7]

On October 9, 1862, the admiral's flag was hauled down from the *Eastport* at Helena, and raised on the *Carondelet* at Cairo, for the change-of-command ceremony on the fifteenth. For Phelps the loss of his status as fleet captain pro tem ironically coincided with the deterioration of what had stood him in good stead for the last year—his health.

Phelps at first ignored his illness, for the *Eastport* and her new crew needed attention. His illness clashed with his stubborn streak, however, to the point that Davis, who was still in Cairo, felt compelled to urge him to take a medical leave. Seeing a chance to get Phelps a much-needed rest and out of Porter's way for a while, Davis played to Phelps's ambition and sense of duty.

> a medical survey now will not impair your reputation for usefulness. It will say "slightly disordered by exposure in line of duty," for example, recommend a change of air, and promise a certain and speedy recovery. Such a survey, or report, is a certificate of service, when drawn up by a friend and sensible surgeon like Dr. [Edward] Gilchrist. What if the examination and report are deferred to a later period, the latter may be necessarily injurious. . . . Now, your attack is acute, easily controlled, thought nothing of—by the by, it will be talked of as constitutional, if suffered to go on. Health is the one essential condition of usefulness—think of that.[8]

Although Phelps was not yet ready to take a leave of absence, the illness and activities of the past weeks had tempered his outlook. It had been three weeks since Gideon Welles had written to Phelps, and now, finally, he sat down to pen his reply:

> I have frequently reperused the unofficial letter you did me the honor to address me and have, I trust, done so with profit to myself. . . . I [have not] been disposed to make haste to answer the charge of seeking advantages at the expense of my seniors through partisan means. . . . I desired time to study my motives & to consider how far I might be answerable to such a charge as well as to fully appreciate the spirit of your letter. Perhaps no officer ever received before, from the head of a great dept. of the gov't., a letter at once so flattering and so cutting to his sensibilities. While I feel the injustice of the charge made the character of your letter such that I can only feel hurt at being so misunderstood and although it has cost me some bitterness that has passed away and I have to thank you for what has given

me in the end more satisfaction than pain. Indeed, believing that I know the integrity of my purpose, I draw from your letter matter to encourage a self confidence that had nearly failed in so high an aspiration. I must ask your patience.

For six months before the Flag of Commander in Chief regularly floated upon the Mississippi, I was cruising upon the Ohio, the Cumberland and the Tennessee and the Mississippi itself, while we possessed it so far, to New Madrid. My vessel was as fleet as the winds and while daily meeting with adventure in our increasing activity, I, with my whole heart in the cause I serve, studied the physical and the military and naval characteristics of the rivers and the nature of the country lying upon them till I was familiar with every turn, every road, every feature. I was an apprentice to a new & strange navigation and only gradually released myself from dependence on others by becoming myself what is usually termed a river man. The knowledge I gained in that active & venturesome service, the like of which no naval officer has experienced, has given me to this day advantages over all other officers on the river. From it too I have learned that no inexperienced officer, however clever in his profession is prepared to take command of this flotilla. Till he has had months of experience he, necessarily, is dependent upon the opinions of others and cannot act independently. This view is adopted sooner or later by all who come on the station. It is a service peculiar and distinct from ordinary experience in naval life and is therefore rather to be regarded as apart from the general service.

You will understand from this why my conscience finds nothing of the reproach of seeking distinction at the expense of my seniors. I had been educated & prepared by the rough experience of the whole war for a service I regard as distinct & not wisely to be brought under all the rules governing ordinary naval service where the experience of one squadron is that of all others. What I myself would have regarded as madness on the coast, here under other circumstances becomes a different act.

There were but two officers afloat in the flotilla senior to me (a third had not been promoted). One of these had seen no service & the other, a brave officer, of long service . . . neither would the Dept. select to command a squadron. Both were captains with commands beneath their rank and a junior to both has now been selected for chief command. I therefore did not seek to do them injustice and the idea of doing naval officers elsewhere wrong, unprepared as they are . . . for this service did not enter my thoughts any more than it did those of Admirals Foote and Davis or other naval as well as army officers and the private gentlemen who were aware of my steps.

Up to the 1st of September beyond talking it over with the officers on the station, I had spoken to no one of my views, to that time I had not felt the conviction in my ability to advance the public service that thought and reflection then had given me. I then consulted with Admiral Davis and thus learned of a confidential letter written by him shortly before to the Dept. I beg you will set that aside as having no part in the subsequent acts as he knew nothing of my thoughts when it was written. I consulted others. I had an interview for the first time in my life with Mr. [Senator] Grimes. My own impulse was to go to you direct and say "experience has educated me & given me confidence for this service. . . . My heart and all my thoughts are in it. If you have confidence I can do so give me command of the flotilla for I believe I can increase its efficiency and give the Gov't satisfaction. My friends said nay, you cannot apply for it but we can place you before the Department. I acquiesced because of their experience. I wrote to Admiral Foote who in his reply seconded me warmly.

I saw three gentlemen besides Mr. Grimes, old friends of my boyhood. I enclosed two letters given me [and] wrote to Mssrs. Wade & Whittlesey, old friends of my father & myself. Besides these I saw two Generals, also old friends in service, who had frequently spoken to me of the command. These are all the persons to whom I have written or spoken. I have many Republican friends & relatives in high positions to whom I might have applied if I had aimed at partisan aid.

I [have] never cast a vote or felt interest in politics. . . . My own wish was simply to convey to the Dept. the idea that men whose position in the North West would give weight to their opinions & who had themselves felt interest in the flotilla, had confidence in me and would be pleased to see me placed in command. It was something to counterbalance the inertia of "the old Navy" which I felt would be against me. I could find no legal objection to my appt. since the law of last session embraced all commanding officers then known to the service.

The spirit of the act must therefore be the rule of construction. I tried always to hold up this one idea simply of the confidence of the North West from whence our officers & many of our men are drawn. If my friends have departed from this, I know it not. . . . You now are acquainted with all I believe that I myself know of my motives and acts. If you have been importuned I regret it and it was not my wish. If you have been written to & thus harassed I am sorry that it should have been and certainly is contrary to my judgement.

Now, Sir, I look into my heart and try to discover all the impulses that have operated with me, well knowing how illy we know ourselves, how often we are deceived as to the true motives actuating us, but I find more thought of my country & her service in these sad days of extreme peril than I do selfish purpose of personal interests. I have honestly believed I sought her interests quite as much as my own, but I have not now to reproach myself ambitions & hopes indulged in from which I have to reap bitterness in their frustration. I thank God that such was the singleness of purpose that possessed me that I have not felt the pang of a single disappointment in learning that so fine an Officer & Gentleman had been selected for the command. I have no thought but to serve on to the end of the flotilla. Once more permit me to thank you for the high appreciation you express for my services & abilities. I trust I shall not disappoint you.

> I have the honor to be respectfully &
> very truly yours,
> S. L. Phelps[9]

Senator Grimes wrote to Phelps that Secretary Welles was gratified by his letter.

> I am very glad that you made the reply to Mr. Welles that you did. It will be for the better for you & for all concerned than if you had exhibited more temper. I am satisfied that he entertains the warmest feelings for you. The probability is that he was committed to the appointment of some other officer & the [case] made by your friends for your selection was so strong that he was constrained to make out a case of official etiquette & discipline in order to prevent your selection being made over his head. Mr. Welles is not boundless in wisdom but he is a man of correct purpose and I am convinced he would not intentionally wrong any man.[10]

Phelps's continued illness was compounded by the condition of the *Eastport*. Having struck a sandbar, the *Eastport*'s bottom was found to have given way fifteen feet in one place, with the keel arching up to just under the boilers. With everything seeming to unravel at once, Phelps summoned Dr. Gilchrist. Gilchrist examined him and recommended an immediate change of climate for what he diagnosed as a severe case of chronic disease of the liver.

Phelps became so sick during the trip home that he had to stop and rest several times. Having taken four days to travel from Cairo to Chardon, he arrived home so ill that he had to rest for thirty minutes just to get the strength to go upstairs and see Lizzie, who also was ill. Lizzie wrote to Whittlesey:

> The next day he was very sick, and I did not see him till Sunday morning when I insisted on going to him. His disease, which was of a decidedly intermittent form, he being better one day & the paroxysm of pain and nausea recurring regularly continued till Tuesday night when he became totally unconscious & alarmingly worse & for 48 hours he was just as ill as he could be. Thursday night was the crisis & after this our intense anxiety was relieved for he was most decidedly better.[11]

The worst of the crisis having finally passed, Phelps's convalescence was aided by his tornado of a daughter, Sally, and three-month-old Lucy Ledyard. He had always been amazed at how Sally adapted. Whether learning to speak Italian, or competing with neighborhood boys, eight-year-old Sally was in many ways just like her father. Phelps felt, however, that a proper young lady should be well educated, and took the opportunity to gently remind her that playing should be secondary to her studies. Little Lucy also shared something in common with her father: they both slept a lot.

By early December, Phelps had recovered sufficiently that he was summoned to Washington to help the Navy Department sort out what was becoming a constant headache—the question of prizes. While there, he found himself appointed to a special board to review the case of Comdr. George H. Preble. While in command of the Union blockading force off Mobile, Alabama, Preble had allowed the Confederate blockade runner *Oreto,* flying the British flag, to run past his ships into Mobile Bay, and Gideon Welles was furious. Although he believed Preble was a loyal officer, Welles felt that he was timid and had worried too much about causing an international incident. He decided to make an example of Preble and went to President Lincoln, who promptly said, "Dismiss him. If that is your opinion, it is mine. I will do it."[12]

Preble's dismissal created a political firestorm. Petitions from Preble's home state of Maine descended upon Welles. "One mistake amidst a thousand useful and brilliant deeds," one petition said, "let not an honorable name be perpetually disregarded."[13] A poignant letter from Preble's wife, Suzan, to Lincoln, asking for an investigation, along with direct requests from various politicians, prompted Welles to offer Preble a deal. Since Preble was already out of the navy, Welles would appoint an informal board to review his case and make a recommendation that would be submitted to Lincoln. Welles appointed Admiral Foote, Commodore Davis, and Phelps, and left the matter up to them. Deciding the fate of the nephew of Commodore Edward Preble, who battled the Barbary pirates at the turn of the century, was a disagreeable duty, but working with Foote and Davis again made it somewhat more palatable. After reviewing

Preble's reports on the affair, the board reported that he had failed to do his whole duty. Welles immediately went to Lincoln, who gave the report his approval.

Preble did not give up, however. In February 1863, Lincoln reluctantly agreed to return Preble to duty. He was exiled to Lisbon, in command of the *Jamestown*, hunting Confederate raiders. In the spring of 1864 Preble, meeting the CSS *Florida* in the neutral port of Funchal, Madeira, refused to engage her. Had he captured or sunk the notorious *Florida* with his old-fashioned sloop, he might have caused a controversy but would have redeemed himself and become a national hero. Ironically, the *Florida* was the new name for the *Oreto*, the ship that Preble let pass at Mobile.[14]

With his temporary duties in Washington finished, Phelps returned to Cairo and command of the *Eastport*. The news of the impending attack on Vicksburg made him anxious to speed her repairs.

Confederate control of Vicksburg and Port Hudson still blocked Union access to the sea, and had generated great political concern in Washington. Western grain and meat had to be shipped east by rail or via the Great Lakes, and unscrupulous businessmen had sent freight rates skyrocketing. This price gouging was increasing antiwar sentiment in the Northwest, and Lincoln was worried that unless the Mississippi River was opened, Westerners might recognize the Confederacy or, worse, entertain the idea of independence for themselves. In the fall of 1862, Lincoln pressed for a renewed effort to take Vicksburg, but the necessity of using troops to rebuild railroads in northern Mississippi and western Tennessee, along with renewed Confederate activity, prevented any action.

By early November, General Grant was ready to move his army south. He planned to advance on Grenada, Mississippi, thus drawing Confederate forces to him. This would allow William Sherman to move downriver from Memphis and, with navy support, take Vicksburg by storm or move inland and surround the city. Grant's army quickly advanced south, seizing Holly Springs, Mississippi, where he established his base of supply. Grant then continued farther south to the town of Oxford, but the Confederates now spoiled his plans. Thirty-five hundred Confederate cavalry under General

Earl Van Dorn swept into Grant's rear and captured Holly Springs. Grant's army was now cut off from their supplies, deep in enemy territory.

In the meantime, Sherman had arrived north of Vicksburg and, looking over the formidable defenses, decided against a frontal attack. He chose instead to penetrate the Yazoo River with its swamps and bayous north of the city, and take the high ground known as Walnut Hills.

To keep the Confederates from constructing batteries on the Yazoo, Acting Rear Admiral Porter sent Walke and several of the iron-clads to patrol the river. The Confederate defenders, under the command of Isaac N. Brown, had planted torpedoes in the river, and for the first time, one worked. The *Cairo,* under her new commander, Lt. Cdr. Thomas Selfridge, sank quickly. Porter saw the sinking as one of the fortunes of war and gave Selfridge command of Phelps's old boat, the *Conestoga.*

Meanwhile, Grant had decided to withdraw from Oxford. With his supply base destroyed and Confederate cavalry under Nathan Bedford Forrest rampaging through western Tennessee, Grant was in no position to continue south. Confederate forces were now free to turn their attention to Sherman, who was unaware of Grant's withdrawal.

When the combined Union expedition arrived at the mouth of the Yazoo River, the first days were spent with armed men in cutters dragging the narrow river for torpedoes and exchanging fire with sharpshooters in the nearby woods. After the gunboat crews finally removed the torpedoes, Sherman's troops began landing at Chickasaw Bayou on December 26.

The gunboats began their supporting bombardment on December 27. With the *Benton* leading the way through a river wide enough for only two boats, large guns once again erupted at each other. William Gwin stood outside the pilothouse of the *Benton,* directing her guns. Confederate cannon responded by pounding away at the slow-moving giant. During the next two hours the *Benton* was struck twenty-four times and in return disabled two Confederate guns. Shells bounced off her forward armor plate, but plunging shells penetrated her decks several times. Suddenly a fifty-pounder cannonball struck Gwin in the right shoulder, tearing away the muscles of his arm and breast. With their captain critically wounded, and the executive officer, Lt. George P. Lord, also severely wounded, the *Benton,* along with the other gunboats, withdrew downriver.

While Gwin lay critically wounded on board Porter's new flagship, the river steamer *Black Hawk,* Sherman's forces began their attack. For two days they tried but failed against fourteen thousand dug-in Confederates. With more than seventeen hundred casualties, Sherman finally called it quits. The Confederate bastion at Vicksburg still stood.[15]

While the gunboats were supporting Sherman, Phelps was in Cairo, trying to get the *Eastport* back in action. With his boat still not ready, Porter used Phelps as a troubleshooter. His first assignment was to travel to Springfield, Illinois, and meet with the U.S. attorney for the district court to which navy and Treasury claims over seizures had been assigned. One of the first prizes to be fought over was the steamer *New National.* Secretary of the Treasury Salmon P. Chase had issued an order releasing her to her owners even though the district court had ruled that Phelps's seizure had been legal. Phelps intended to contest Chase's authority in court, but Porter had a better solution. "I settled the '*New National*' business in short order," Porter wrote to Phelps, "sent the claimants off to Jeff Davis."[16]

The *Eastport* was still on the ways at Mound City, having eighteen-foot-long, fourteen-inch-thick beams placed in her bottom. Phelps recommended that they be braced with thwartship hog chains, but was assured by the contractor that the chains were not needed. The new timbers would be strong enough. With messages arriving almost daily from Admiral Porter, asking when the *Eastport, Lafayette,* and other gunboats would be ready to join him, Phelps was anxious to see the *Eastport* completed, so he did not insist that the hog chains be installed.

The news from Memphis about Gwin had been somewhat encouraging at first, but Phelps had a bad feeling. "Poor Gwin," he wrote, "I do not know what to hope for in his case, but I now fear the worst." Several days later those fears were borne out.

I am too sad to write at any length today—Sunday though it be, for poor Gwin is no more. The intelligence came this

forenoon. I had come down from Mound City and learned that
Mrs. Gwin had arrived, went up to see her and found the little
woman wonderfully cheerful over the good news last had. The
day being bright and warm as spring weather, I invited her to
walk a little. I continued the walk around the square and
brought the young widow back to the hotel, where her father
who had learned the news, with his eyes that too truly told their
tale to escape the quick eye of his daughter. I heard & immediately turned away and left them.[17]

Later Phelps visited Mrs. Gwin.

I feel the greatest desire to do what I may to direct her thoughts
from her affliction. I told her, or tried to tell her that I trusted
she would retain a place in her memory for me and think of
me as a friend, for my attachment & esteem for her husband
rendered it impossible to me to regard her otherwise than with
the deepest interest & solicitude. . . . It is better that she leave
here where everything reminds her of the Navy and her loss. It
is, my dear wife, a time which tries men and when those meet
who learned in the hours of danger and adventure to rely on
each other, the friendship and esteem that springs up is of a
generous and warm kind that endures long.[18]

The loss of Gwin was deeply felt throughout the flotilla. Davis
wrote from Washington:

Poor Gwin! I shall grieve for him as long as I live. I saw a great
deal of him during the last month I was down the river and
when you where away, and became very much attached to him.
And that attachment was increased by our short intercourse
here after he was married. He often expressed his thankful-
ness for having the *Benton*, not fearing death and looking for
honor. . . . Persons at my age have few opportunities of adding
to the number of their friends and such a friend as Gwin—
warm-hearted and affectionate, brave, honorable, hightoned,

gentlemanly and well-bred and accomplished, is not picked up everyday.[19]

Funeral services for Gwin were held at Cairo on January 20, 1863. A damp, cold fog hung over the snow-covered naval cemetery as Phelps, Walke, and the officers and men of the flotilla listened to Scriptures and extolled their fallen messmate. Upon completion of the services, Gwin's flag-draped coffin was escorted to the railroad depot for his last trip home.

January also brought sadder, if not unexpected, news. Elisha Whittlesey died after a long illness. As a mentor, confidant, and politically powerful friend, Whittlesey had looked after Seth Phelps's life and career for almost forty years. This loss was yet another blow, both personally and professionally, in a few short months. For Phelps, dreams of command faded and the task of just getting on with the war became his ambition.

The station at Cairo was under the command of fifty-year-old Capt. Alexander Pennock. Years of duty in the Lighthouse Inspection Service had given him the organizational and administrative talents that made him invaluable to the flotilla. Pennock had become ill, however, as the result of a broken tooth, and left Phelps temporarily in command of the station while he traveled to St. Louis to have the problem attended to.

Progress on the boats had been stalled by a severe snowstorm on January 18, "such as I have not witnessed in this part of the country," Phelps wrote to Porter, and "has set us back in all kind of work. Laborers will not work and three days have been almost entirely lost."[20]

Another move on Vicksburg was expected, and Porter was anxious to have the *Eastport*, *Lafayette*, and *Choctaw* join him as soon as possible. "I shall be glad to see you down in the *Eastport*," Porter wrote prophetically. "I hope you have made her so strong that she won't bend double any more."[21]

Phelps did receive some good news for a change. Porter had divided the gunboats downriver into two divisions for the assault on Vicksburg. Phelps was to have the Second Division and Walke the First.

After the *Eastport*'s new bottom was finally finished, her launching was badly handled. The workmen "let her stern down first, so that she twisted the forward cradles to pieces, and, broke 120 of the trucks on which they ran. A common river boat would have been broken in the middle."[22]

While Phelps waited for the *Eastport* to be completed and take on her new battery, an example of what was becoming a dirty and exhausting guerrilla warfare took place at Harpeth Shoals on the Cumberland River. After Confederate cavalry had stopped the hospital ship *Trio*, several supply steamers, and the tinclad *W.H. Sidell*, a group of drunken Southerners boarded the *Trio* and proceeded to make off with everything not tied down. The vessels were then put to the torch.

Lt. Comdr. Leroy Fitch was already patrolling the Tennessee, Cumberland, and Ohio rivers, but his three tinclads were stretched to the limit. In response to the *Trio* incident, Phelps was dispatched with the *Lexington* to inspect the situation. Maj. Gen. William S. Rosecrans's Army of the Cumberland was at Murfreesboro, Tennessee, licking its wounds after the bloody but indecisive battle at Stone's River; the Cumberland River was the cheapest and easiest means for keeping it supplied.

Heading back to his old stomping grounds, Phelps came upon a transport that had been fired on by Confederate artillery twenty miles above Clarksville. He went to that point and burned a storehouse used for cover during the attack. Proceeding to Clarksville, Phelps found Fitch with his three tinclads escorting thirty-one steamers and numerous barges in tow, bound for Rosecrans's army. Steaming ahead of the convoy, the *Lexington* was fired on by two Confederate guns and struck three times. Phelps returned fire with his big cannon and dispersed the Rebels. Returning to the convoy, he led the fleet of boats to Nashville without so much as a single musket being fired. For Phelps the lesson was obvious. The enemy didn't mind taking on the lightly gunned tinclads but would not engage the big guns of a gunboat. He recommended that the *Lexington* be transferred to Fitch and that no transport be allowed beyond Forts Henry and Donelson without a gunboat for an escort.

Phelps returned to Cairo and once again resumed his efforts to get the *Eastport* ready. With all the delays he was able to spend some time attending to the details of his cabin. He wrote to Lizzie:

I am going to have as pretty a cabin as has been seen. A new Brussels Carpet is being made which will make the thing complete. No officer in the Squadron will have such quarters. You ought to be here to share them to give the finish. I judge the Admiral will not be much on board the *Eastport*. He has a river steamer [*Black Hawk*] on board which he lives and I doubt not will continue to live on board of.

I live pretty much here on the wharf boat with Capt. Pennock. It is very charming to be where I can take my meals with such pleasant people as the Capt. & wife are. . . . Will you believe my wife that I weighed 176 today. I never before passed above 157 . . . and owe part of my good condition to the generous fare & pleasant social circle.[23]

It was still a somewhat lonely existence, however.

I have a Gibraltar Steward, a Negro cook and Michael for my family. My boy of whom I thought to make something—the contraband from Vicksburg you remember, I have had to dismiss. He is so careless that I could not afford to keep him. If I charged the broken china to him, it would have been more than all the pay he received. He broke $10 worth at one dash.

Phelps was also attending to more than decorating his cabin or the social life at Cairo. After the events of the preceding months, he once again was seriously considering leaving the Navy: "I do not contemplate staying long in these waters. Four months hence I shall apply to be detached unless something new turns up—something I cannot now foresee."[24]

Phelps had hoped to mount the *Eastport*'s 100-pounder Parrott guns on pivot carriages, but there was not enough room on the forward gun deck. Instead, he mounted them on modified nine-inch gun carriages. As it was, there was little enough room, for when they were "run in," the guns nearly reached the forward broadside nine-inch guns.

After finally taking on her new battery, the *Eastport* departed Cairo on February 2, 1863, in convoy with the *General Lyons* and *New National,* bound for Vicksburg. With the swift current the *Eastport* was making good time, when suddenly she came to a crashing halt. Water began pouring into her hull, and a quick inspection showed ten timbers, fourteen inches thick, broken "as if they had been pipe stems." Phelps moved her to the riverbank, for her bottom might give way at any moment, taking all down with her. Once the *Eastport* was safely tied to the bank, Phelps sent the other two boats on to Memphis. The next morning the towboat *Collier* was spotted coming upriver with empty coal barges in tow. Phelps hailed it and had his boat lightened by transferring shot, shell, and other heavy articles to the empty coal barges.

A dejected Phelps returned to Cairo with the *Eastport* under tow. Upon examination, it was determined that the *Eastport* would need another new bottom. "I have hardly the heart to write to you or to propose to do anything with this vessel," he wrote to Porter. "It seems to me as if bad luck had come, condensed into three or four months time. . . . I can't divest myself of the prejudice belonging to our calling so as to shake off the idea of ill luck being the attendant of this vessel."[25]

Almost a year to the day from her capture, the *Eastport* had seen only a few weeks' service and no action. Phelps, determined to see her in service, proposed not only new boilers and engines but also a new double-planked bottom. "My pride is somewhat touched with respect to the bottom of this vessel, and with your permission it shall be made to hold, even to jumping bars, as I used to do with the *Conestoga.*"[26]

As with Selfridge and the loss of the *Cairo,* Porter was understanding. "Faint heart never won fair lady," he wrote to Phelps, "so you must not get faint hereafter over the broken bottom of the *Eastport.* Go ahead and try it again. You will yet be in time for the grand finale."[27]

Several weeks earlier, Porter had offered Phelps the *Choctaw* if he wanted her, but Phelps had declined. With the *Eastport* now laid up for weeks, if not months, Phelps examined the *Choctaw* but felt too subdued to make an issue of getting her:

> I think her a more staunch ship than this one [*Eastport*] and if free in the matter of choice would select her. I am aware how-ever that Mr. [Thomas] Pattison has applied for the *Choctaw*. He is my senior . . . and I would not embarrass you in any way and ask that you will dispose of his application according to your views of the interests and propriety of the service. . . . I rec-ognize fully his claim of seniority and withdraw all pretension to any command other than this. . . . I am always ready for ser-vice anywhere and in any capacity.[28]

CHAPTER FOURTEEN

ᡄᢣᡅ

Station Duty & Guerrilla War

AFTER SHERMAN's abortive attempt to get behind Vicksburg in December 1862, various schemes were tried but abandoned. By mid-March 1863, Admiral Porter and General Sherman were at it again, this time attempting to work their way through the narrow, flooded bayous north of the city to get behind the now heavily fortified Snyder's Bluff, which anchored the Confederates' northern defenses.

In the meantime Phelps was ordered to St. Louis to investigate the construction of the *Choctaw* and *Lafayette*. Porter was clamoring for more gunboats, but construction had been terribly slow and expensive, and the contractors were blaming each other.

Porter needed those gunboats to replace the *Queen of the West* and the *Indianola*, lost below Vicksburg. He had succeeded in running the two boats past the batteries at Vicksburg, but the *Queen of the West* had been captured by the Confederates after running aground. The Confederates then used the *Queen*, along with their ram *Webb*, to run down and capture the *Indianola*. The *Indianola* was the only Union ironclad to be surrendered during the war, and Porter was furious.

Porter told Phelps to "get that *Choctaw* out of the hands of the Israelites. If she has steam and guns and casemates plated let us have her here. I must have something to make up for the loss of the *Indianola*. I want the ram power and don't care about the iron, I intend to take half of it off as soon as I get hold of her."

Porter also emphasized the need to keep the boats as light as possible. While the *Eastport* was considered fast even with her old engines, the *Choctaw* was expected to be a lumbering behemoth. "Keep all the iron off of her that you can," he wrote, "the late experience of the Ram *Queen of the West* and the *Webb* taking the *Indianola* proves that rams should be quick active vessels."[1]

Walke had arrived at Vicksburg in command of the *Lafayette*, and Porter was disappointed with this latest addition to his fleet.

> I have examined the *Lafayette* closely, she is a great failure—has no speed and cannot handle . . . she is a mass of iron . . . any two quick working vessels would soon knock her to pieces. I am taking everything out of her I can to bring her up, but she will always be a failure. . . . The *Lafayette* is ironed in places where a shot would not likely hit once in a century . . . [she] has double allowance of anchors and chains [and] her bell is enormous. No note seems to have been taken of all these things.
>
> Get [the *Choctaw*] to me with her iron on board and I will do more work in a day on her here than they will do in three up above. I have a way of making these mechanics work. When they get slack I put them in irons and stop their pay. They seem to understand me very well. Walke's carpenters put on airs when they came down here but I told them what would happen to them and they get along quite decently. Like everybody else in the world that class of people want discipline applied to them.[2]

Phelps's investigation of gunboat construction at St. Louis found that James Lanning, the civilian contractor, was doing his best. Pointing a finger directly at William "Dirty Bill" Porter, Phelps wrote:

Had he [Lanning] followed out the designs and instructions of Commodore Porter both vessels would have sunk long ago at the dock with over weight. The fact appears to be that . . . things were very loose while Commodore Porter was there. When he left, Hall [P.] was ordered there to superintend the construction & then [Wilson] McGunnegle; the former was drunk all the time and the latter sick, so that Mr. Lanning was left to his own resources.[3]

Besides investigating the *Lafayette* and the *Choctaw,* Phelps was detailed to find steamers that could be converted to light-draft gunboats. With increasing Confederate guerrilla activity, it was essential that the navy obtain boats that could operate in small streams and during low water. Pennock had already purchased and converted a number of riverboats into tinclads, and this had sent steamboat stock soaring. A frustrated Phelps recommended seizing what was needed, if necessary, getting a proper appraisal, and paying the owners accordingly. "People have gone mad in regard to steamboat stock," he wrote. "The Ferry Boat *James Thompson,* owned in Louisville, is just the boat for a staunch light clad. In December the owners asked $25,000. She cost between $19,000–$20,000, would now cost $24,000. The price now demanded is $35,000!"[4]

Phelps located three reasonably priced steamers he felt would make good light-draft gunboats and paid a total of $35,000 for the lot. Porter was not particularly pleased, however. "The vessels you bought are very cheap," he wrote. "I hope they are not too cheap—I never buy a cheap thing, I am always afraid of it."[5]

In April, Phelps once again relieved an ill Pennock as commander of the station at Cairo. "I believe 'ways' are a chronic disease with me," he lamented.[6]

On April 15, Phelps received word from Porter to take command of the Tennessee River from Leroy Fitch. After the bloody battle at Stone's River at the beginning of the year, the situation in Tennessee had been quiet while both sides regrouped. General Rosecrans had become alarmed, however, that Confederates under Braxton Bragg were preparing to attack his Cumberland River supply route. Rosecrans went directly to President Lincoln, asking that Fitch's gunboats be placed under his local commanders. This breach of military etiquette went nowhere, but Porter felt that Fitch needed to focus his attention on keeping Rosecrans supplied. Porter sarcastically noted, "Rosecrans seems to be doing nothing but depending upon the Navy." Porter later added, "This thing of hanging around Murfreesboro strikes me as not the way to manage an army. I have never understood yet whether Bragg were blockading Rosecrans or Rosecrans blockading Bragg."[7]

The day after Phelps was given command of the Tennessee River, Porter succeeded in running part of his fleet past the batteries at Vicksburg. Sherman's corps had again failed to get through the swamps north of the city, so Grant had decided on a huge gamble. He would march his army down the west bank of the Mississippi, then, with eight gunboats and seven transport steamers, recross the river to high ground south of the city and attack Vicksburg from the rear.

Once safely on the east bank, and against the advice of all his generals, Grant moved inland, foresaking a supply line. There would be no Holly Springs this time; his troops would move fast and live off the land. Grant quickly neutralized the Confederates at Jackson, Mississippi, on May 14, then turned west and surrounded Vicksburg.

Even though Vicksburg was now under siege, Confederate Lt. Gen. John C. Pemberton still had 32,000 troops and 172 cannon. Grant tried frontal assaults, but Pemberton beat them back. Instead of losing more men, Grant decided to bombard the city while his engineers dug trenches close to Confederate lines. Porter helped by providing two nine-inch guns taken from the *Cincinnati,* which had been sunk.

With all the support the navy was providing, Porter was upset that the press was portraying the campaign as an entirely army affair: "You will not hear of anything but about the army," he wrote to Phelps. "Had it not been for us they would have been no where. I have three naval batteries on shore in the rear of Vicksburg. Selfridge commands one. . . . They are being fired by horse marines. They are knocking the earth about at a great rate and put to shame the pygmy guns of the army."[8]

With all the time that Phelps had been spending in Cairo, he decided to have Lizzie and the girls join him. It took several weeks, but Lizzie and Mrs. Pennock finally located a nice house to share in Mound City.

Pennock was not well enough until early May for Phelps to leave and assume command of the Tennessee Division. Intelligence that the Confederates were "doing something" along the Duck River led Phelps and Fitch to believe that a decisive battle might be brewing, and that their gunboats would play a vital role in cutting off a Confederate retreat should Rosecrans take the offensive.

Rosecrans, despite President Lincoln's urging, stayed in Murfreesboro, depending upon Fitch's Cumberland River convoys that often stretched for five miles. With no major campaign forthcoming, Phelps set out on May 5 to reestablish his presence on the Tennessee. With a fleet of five tinclads, "I . . . proceeded up this river, destroying on the way every kind of boat that could serve the rebels to cross the river."[9]

Confederate guerrilla activity along the river had consisted chiefly of forcibly conscripting Union sympathizers. Phelps had learned that a Rebel raiding party was located at Linden, Tennessee. He arranged with Lt. Col. W. K. M. Breckenridge and fifty-five men of his First West Tennessee Cavalry Regiment to rendezvous at Decaturville Landing on May 11. After dark he crossed Breckenridge's men over to the east bank and then had his tinclads take up blocking positions along the river. Breckenridge moved inland twelve miles and arrived at Linden just before dawn. Confederate pickets were surprised and managed only a few shots before fleeing. After a brief fight at the town's courthouse, in which three butternuts were killed, Breckenridge's men captured the unit's commander, Lt. Col. William Frierson, along with five officers, thirty men, and ten conscripts. After burning the county courthouse, Breckenridge rode back to the river and the safety of the tinclads.

Phelps was pleased with how the combined operation had worked, and suggested that with Breckenridge and three hundred of his West Tennesseans, he could have an effective, fast-moving striking force.

Activity along the Tennessee quieted down for a short period in mid-May, with only occasional sightings of Nathan Bedford Forrest's cavalry along the east side of the river. Phelps, however, kept his division constantly on the move. "Don't ask me how I live," he wrote to Lizzie about the living conditions aboard the tinclads, "because I had rather not tell you, lest you should get alarmed by my peck of earth coming too soon. . . . I am scattered, divided & split up." One bright spot for Phelps, however, was that "all of my sweethearts up the river are flourishing."[10]

After a short visit to Cairo in late May, Phelps hurried back up the Tennessee River to support Col. Florence M. Cornyn and fifteen hundred cavalry who had been crossed over to scatter Forrest's men. Cornyn fought his way down the east side of the river to Florence, Alabama, and was now fighting his way back to his initial crossing point. In a long letter to Lizzie, Phelps wrote that Cornyn's troops

> had burned cotton mills, forges, blacksmith shops, mills, corn, fodder, etc . . . all of which plunder destroyed, captured, stolen & otherwise disposed of, is estimated at $2,000,000.
>
> I pushed up as fast as circumstances and a "heavy tow" would permit, waiting, however, half a day on the promised delivery of the *Champion* [the tinclad would be under the command of Alfred Phelps] from the affectionate embrace of those Paducah cradles. . . . [I was] hugely disgusted and more than half disposed to carry off Messr's Gwin, Haynes & Co. [the contractors] on a voyage for their health up the Tennessee. I left the poor wee craft to her fate and the tender mercies of secessia.

Phelps pressed upriver with the tinclad *Silver Cloud* and arrived at Savannah, Tennessee, on May 30. The *Covington* had crossed over 150 cavalry to harass Confederates who were trying to cut off Cornyn from the river and were now themselves in danger of being isolated. "The 150 men had been doing well," Phelps wrote, "but on the 29th, when bringing in a lot of fine live stock, the commander found a large rebel force disputing his return. Abandoning the stock our people got around the rebs & reached the cover of the *C*'s guns."

With the small cavalry detachment safely aboard a transport, Phelps moved upriver twelve miles to Hamburg Landing, to rendezvous with Cornyn.

It was evident, the rebels had made every possible exertion to cut off Col. Cornyn and heavy forces were gathering about him. His orders were peremptory to return at once to Corinth and so I crossed him over. Some skirmishing, a little brisk, happened while this crossing was effected, and Col. Cornyn was evidently relieved to find himself with the men safely over. In the morning the rebels, who had filled the woods and must have felt very sore to see our people cross the stream safely because of the dreaded & much detested gunboats, were still there, and we treated them to a pyrotechnic display of shell which had the effect to dislodge them and no doubt to turn their attention to more safe & pleasant quarters.

Union sympathizers at Savannah were sufficiently alarmed at the Confederate reaction to Cornyn's raid that they asked Phelps to take them north.

More than all Savannah was scared out of its wit, and more than half, having been in all its troubles loyal to the old & somewhat stricken Uncle in Washington—the old gentleman with the "black tongue" otherwise known as "nigger on the brain"— were anxious to migrate and so I left three gunboats, and a barge to bring them off.

A sweet load of truck that old "barge" contains! Judging by the children I should guess there were fifty families, but counting noses among the marriageable females I arrive at the conclusion there cannot be more than twenty mothers. The fathers don't count in this country seeing that every other house is the home of a "widow." And these little beings which are so bewitching in our own snug homes, have not much of that which would remind one of the little cherubs in that other world or induce one to desire positive contact in this one. So they go down the beautiful river, thinking little of the eye beauty on every hand, but rather of the land to which they are bound, hoping for peace & quiet. While I think of the multiplied evils these poor people may meet with, with the many mouths to feed and the absolute want of every necessity of life, I cannot but feel grateful to the giver of all when my thoughts turn to the weak ones dependent upon me and remember how comparatively well it is with them.

As a sign of how the war was changing, Phelps, who two years earlier would not have dreamed of profiting from the war, accepted a gift from the booty of a grateful Colonel Cornyn. "I have the honor to send a specimen, for the use of the 'Mound City indigent Naval Officer's [*sic*] family retreat' ladies, in the shape of a fancy buggy, & a harness, which the gallant Col. gave me. Col. Breckenridge says he will capture a horse for the turn out." It was Admiral Porter, however, who, upon hearing of the buggy, quickly had a horse sent to Cairo.

As Phelps headed north on the *Silver Cloud* he noted:

As I passed Carrollville that nice lady, who sends me flowers & milk (thus approaching me, man as I am, by the weak road to a man's heart) was standing on the porch of her house and that rebel husband with her, both completely surprised. But I had promised Breckenridge to cross him over, I could not afford the time to stop to capture him [the husband]; and then would I so distress the sweet little woman who is so troubled at her husbands doings? I have put that off on another party & trust that I shall hear of his capture & so have a chance to condole with clean hands in the matter with the wife & promise his release etc. etc. which she will not desire, nor I intend to comply with; and so will go on carrying out the world's play of humbug, for did I not promise her not only to capture him but to hold him captive for the war?[11]

While Phelps was supporting Breckenridge's cavalry, who were raiding Confederate tanneries and filling the gunboats with smelly hides, he received a message from Admiral Porter offering him the *Eastport* and the second division at Vicksburg. Back on the Tennessee, Phelps was in his element, but he was reluctant to give up the *Eastport*. He also was worried about his health, should he return to Vicksburg.

I am warned that having once barely escaped with my life from the effects of congestive chills, I am more liable than before to attacks, and it is probable a return would prove fatal. . . . This consideration makes me hesitate in deciding, preferring, as I do otherwise, the second division. I am much inclined to the belief that "What is, is for the best," and am indisposed to try and shape the course of events from any calculation of probable consequences. I must, therefore, ask you to decide where I am to serve. . . . I shall feel a proper pride in the command of any one of the divisions of your fleet.

Porter decided to leave Phelps in command of the Tennessee Division and gave him command of the Mississippi as far south as Helena, Arkansas, as well. The *Eastport* was finally launched, safely this time, on June 15, and would be Phelps's flagship on the upper Mississippi.

After her first voyage, Phelps was elated.

I came down with the *Eastport* yesterday, making 7 miles in 36 minutes. I consider her a great success, and she is a better-looking craft than ever. The guns are being put on board, and I shall very soon be on the cruising ground between here [Cairo] and Helena. . . . Her speed and light-draft will enable me to use her effectively on this long stretch of river. . . . I should regret the *Eastport* [not being in service earlier] now more than ever.[12]

The sudden death of Admiral Foote at the end of June stunned not only Phelps but the entire squadron. Foote had been detached from his bureau and was on his way to assume command of the South Atlantic Blockading Squadron when he became ill at the Astor House in New York City. For a week Foote lingered, lapsing in and out of consciousness. His friend of twenty years, John Dahlgren, and his brother were by his bed until the end. Foote, resigned to his fate, said that he had seen the last of this world and that his earthly duties were closed. At 10 P.M. on June 26, he passed away. The naval surgeon who was attending him told his brother, "Your brother has literally worn himself out in the public service. He is truly a victim of this war as if he perished on the battlefield."[13]

Late June also brought reports from Confederate deserters that Lt. Gen. Theophilus H. Holmes was marching an army from northeast Arkansas toward the Mississippi, in an effort to relieve Vicksburg. Acting Rear Admiral Porter was concerned enough about these reports that he sent the gunboats *Tyler, General Bragg,* and *Hastings* to Helena to support the garrison under Maj. Gen. Benjamin Prentiss. While at Memphis, Phelps had heard of these reports and, having spent a good deal of time at Helena, suspected something might happen there. "I had felt uneasy about Helena, but I called upon General [Stephen] Hurlbut, who assured me that Price's [Maj. Gen. Sterling Price, passed over for command and now a division commander] movements were known and that he did not think an attack upon Helena was contemplated by the enemy; on the contrary, that he was bound to Milliken's Bend."[14]

Desperately wanting to get the *Eastport* in on any major engagement that might develop at Helena or any location along the river, Phelps resisted requests that he steam north to New Madrid to support a move against the Confederates in that region. An exasperated Hurlbut finally had to order Phelps to New Madrid on July 3: "Our navy officers are so tenacious of orders that I question if any gunboat would leave her station without formal orders from proper authority."[15]

Early on July 4, the same day that Vicksburg surrendered and General Robert E. Lee began his withdrawal from Gettysburg, some ten thousand Confederates threw themselves at Prentiss's thirty-five hundred troops at Helena. Despite poor coordination, the Rebels managed to overrun Battery C on Graveyard Hill, at the Union center, and Battery D, to the south, after hard fighting. Having fought past lines of rifle pits fronted by steep ravines, however, the Confederates were spent. Meanwhile, misunderstandings among the Confederate commanders cost them valuable time and allowed General Prentiss to maneuver his outnumbered forces to keep his defensive line intact.

After pounding the Confederate artillery south of Helena, Capt. James M. Prichett moved the *Tyler* into a position where he could turn his attention to the enemy attacking Helena from Graveyard Hill. With his eight-inch and 30-pounder Parrott guns, Prichett fired on the slopes and enfiladed the ravines. Southern troops attacking down the hill were slaughtered by the rapidly falling shells. Panic quickly set in, and the butternuts retreated. Prentiss counterattacked and, supported by the *Tyler*'s guns, the retreat soon turned into a rout.[16]

It was not until July 6 that dispatches reached Phelps at New Madrid, informing him of the attack on Helena and an expected renewal of the assault. Phelps rushed downriver and found a devastating scene. Union troops had already buried 380 Confederates, and there were 1,100 wounded and 1,100 prisoners. Union scouts found places where the Confederates had buried their own, and reported numerous dead and wounded in the nearby countryside.

Phelps was astonished to find that General Prentiss had anticipated an attack by an overwhelming force for several days. An angry Phelps wrote to Porter, "I can not feel altogether satisfied that a jealousy said to exist between the commanding generals [Prentiss and Hurlbut] should interfere with a common interchange of knowledge of the enemy's movements to such an extent as to needlessly peril great military interests."[17]

For the third time in less than two years, the *Tyler* had helped save a Union army from pending disaster. First at Belmont, then at Shiloh, and now at Helena, the *Tyler*'s big guns played an important part in snatching victory from defeat.

The Union victories in early July were cause for great celebration in the North. Among the honors that were forthcoming was the promotion of Porter to rear admiral. Perhaps with a sense of irony, considering Phelps's attempt to gain command, Porter wrote to him: "This being promoted so fast makes me feel very much like an old fogy. Imagine my associates [Louis] Goldsborough, [William] Shubrick, [Joseph] Smith, [George] Storer, [Francis] Gregory, [Samuel] Breese, and [Hiram] Paulding. Imagine what their horror would be, were the young admiral to offer to skylark with them! Especially Goldsborough." Then in a note of consolation, Porter added, "I hope soon to see some younger than myself crawling up. It must come."[18]

With the surrender of Port Hudson on July 9, the Mississippi River was in Union hands. Now, instead of great battles with opposing fleets or impregnable forts, Phelps found himself trying to catch guerrillas swimming across rivers.

[Rebels] were crossing the Tennessee despite the watchful care of the gunboats using flood wood, etc. to float over [and] have caused great commotion in all the country west of the river. The people have been plundered on all sides. Herds of cattle and horses have been driven away to Bragg's army. A man striding a drift log paddles across the river, leading an old ox or well trained horse swimming, and the herd, driven into the stream, follows the lead across. Horsemen above and below give an hour's warning of the approach of a gunboat.[19]

Livestock was not the only commodity that the gunboats found themselves trying to police. The *Covington* discovered two white women trying to smuggle two hundred of their slaves into Arkansas from Mississippi. The *Covington* managed to capture both of the women and fourteen of the contrabands.

Those contraband slaves, along with many others, were given the opportunity to enlist in the Union cause. With the heat of the summer taking its usual toll in sickness, and a number of sailors completing their enlistments, the squadron was short of firemen and coal heavers. The navy was now enlisting former slaves as apprentice seamen, to haul on the side tackles of the big guns.

In late June, General Rosecrans had finally gone on the offensive and launched a brilliant attack against General Bragg in Middle Tennessee. So quickly did Rosecrans's army advance, that Bragg decided to fall back all the way to Chattanooga. It was as important as Vicksburg, for through it passed the railroads linking the Confederacy through the Cumberland Mountains.

After a pause to repair rail lines in his rear and build up his supplies, Rosecrans resumed his advance on August 16, causing Bragg to abandon Chattanooga on September 8. Bragg was far from finished, however. Reinforced by troops who had evacuated Knoxville, and with two divisions of Lt. Gen. James Longstreet's veterans from the

Army of Northern Virginia, Bragg counterattacked. Eight miles southeast of Chattanooga, on the west fork of Chickamauga Creek, the two armies hurled themselves at one another in what would be the costliest battle in the western theater.

Bragg and Longstreet pushed Rosecrans back to Chattanooga but were unable to exploit their victory when Maj. Gen. George H. Thomas rallied Federal troops and stemmed the Confederate advance. Instead, Bragg had to settle for investing Chattanooga and trying to starve Rosecrans out. With Rosecrans's army besieged, it was imperative that help arrive quickly, for Union troops were soon on half rations.

William T. Sherman received orders from General in Chief Halleck to move his corps from Vicksburg upriver to Memphis upon receipt of news of the defeat at Chickamauga. Sherman then sent his corps by rail from Memphis to Corinth, Mississippi. East of Corinth, his troops were to repair the Memphis and Charleston rail line as they marched toward Chattanooga. With Brig. Gen. Peter J. Osterhaus's division in the lead, Sherman's corps inched toward Iuka, Mississippi, and the Tennessee River.

In the meantime, General Rosecrans was replaced by General Thomas after Grant was dispatched to take overall command. Twenty thousand reinforcements from the Army of the Potomac, under General Joe Hooker, had arrived but were not enough. After Grant arrived on the scene, he decided he could not wait for Sherman to finish his railroad repairs, so he wired Sherman to drop everything and come at once.

The Tennessee River was currently at a low stage, and Sherman hoped it would remain so long enough to ford his corps. Not taking any chances, however, he sent a letter to Admiral Porter asking that some gunboats be spared to assist him. On October 20, the steamer carrying Sherman's letter arrived alongside the *Black Hawk* at Cairo. Porter was surprised by Sherman's request, for he was usually informed of such movements but in this case had heard nothing. Porter ordered Phelps to depart at daylight the following morning and provide Sherman with what help he could.

Phelps did not wait to coal but took a barge with four thousand bushels and departed with the light-draft gunboats *Hastings* and *Key*

West. Both vessels were shorthanded; the *Hastings* had only fifty of her normal crew of eighty, of whom twelve were sick and "as many more utterly worthless."[20]

Even though the light-draft gunboats had a reputation that "they could run on heavy dew," Phelps had a difficult time at first with low water on the Ohio and then the Tennessee. Several times he resorted to a technique learned from his early days on the *Conestoga*. The two gunboats, which came to be nicknamed "grasshoppers," were each fitted with long spars on their bows, and when they came to a narrow shoal, the spars were fixed firmly in the bar. With their boilers threatening to explode, each gunboat used all her power to move ahead and literally vaulted herself forward. Each boat repeated this process until the bar was passed.

Progress was later slowed by dark and stormy nights that necessitated anchoring after the moon had set, so as not to run aground. The rains, along with heavy downpours in the mountains of East Tennessee, caused a rise in the river, which helped the tinclads but blocked Sherman as he arrived on the west bank of the Tennessee River.

Sherman had his men make several attempts to cross, but they were futile; the river was rising at a rate of twenty inches an hour. Sherman was "very much disgusted with everything" and rode back to his headquarters at Iuka. With his corps stopped by the river, an already ill Sherman lay on his cot and "felt as if he had a thirty-two pound shot in his stomach."[21]

Early the next morning, October 24, 1863, Sherman heard the pounding hoofs of a dozen of his cavalrymen. Peering from his tent, saw them coming at a full gallop toward his tent. As they waved their caps, they yelled out music to Sherman's ears: the gunboats had arrived. Sherman dispatched an officer with a horse and escort, and instructions that Captain Phelps join him at his headquarters.

There was rejoicing among Sherman's troops at the arrival of the two gunboats. An aide to General Osterhaus remarked that "effery soltier ought ter garry a gun-poat mit his bocket!" Sherman was so happy to see Phelps that he "almost shook his arm off."[22]

Phelps offered to cross over Sherman's corps, which was stretched some thirty miles along the railway from Iuka to Tuscumbia,

Alabama. Crossing the men on the gunboats would be easy enough, but "it is those cursed wagons and mules that bother us," wrote Sherman. "It is not 'villainous saltpeter' that makes our life so hard, but grub and mules."[23] To cross over the wagons and mules, Phelps suggested that the coal barge be covered and turned into a ferry. Sherman agreed, and ordered his engineers to deck over the barge. Soon his men and equipment were being ferried across.

Sherman invited Phelps to spend the night with him at his headquarters. "We talked over matters generally. Of course we get along together elegantly." A grateful Sherman added, "All I have he can command, and I know the same feeling pervades every sailor's and soldier's heart. We are as one."[24]

Sherman arrived near Chattanooga in mid-November and joined Grant along with General Joseph Hooker's twenty thousand men, who, in a remarkable logistical feat, had traveled more than twelve hundred miles by rail from Warrenton Junction, Virginia, to Bridgeport, Alabama, in less than one week. The reinforced Federals attacked and won a stunning victory at Missionary Ridge on November 25. The Union army was now at the doorstep of Atlanta.[25]

Having seen Sherman's corps on its way to Chattanooga, Phelps returned to policing the rivers. The illicit trade that had flourished in the name of allowing citizens loyal to the Union to conduct business was keeping Confederate guerrillas regularly supplied. Under Treasury Department permits that excluded naval participation, more cotton was reaching the North along the rivers than the blockade runners were getting to Great Britain. In October 1863 the Treasury regulations were modified to allow local army commanders to endorse Treasury permits, and Phelps seized on this to try and get the necessary authority to control illicit trade. "The river is everywhere thronged with guerrillas, and it is useless for us to patrol it and destroy skiffs, flats, &c., to prevent crossing the stream, when a steamer is permitted by the custom-house authorities to be on trading voyages."[26]

Phelps suggested to Sherman that he use his authority to allow permits only to vessels that would be in the escort of a gunboat and to land only where the navy said it was safe and proper to do so. Even this authority failed to stem the illicit trade, for soon it was suspected

that a number of army officers were involved in the cotton specu-
lation.

The regulations were openly ignored, and vessels were often returned to their owners unless the evidence was undeniable. Admiral
Porter was particularly unimpressed by the new regulations: "The
Mississippi, I am sorry to say, is infested with guerrillas who are being
amply supplied with everything they require, by the late Treasury
regulations."[27]

By the summer of 1864, the situation was so out of hand that General Sherman complained that Cincinnati was furnishing more supplies to the South than Charleston, and Maj. Gen. Cadwallader C.
Washburn, then commander of the Memphis district, stated that
Memphis had been of more value to the Confederacy since its capture than Nassau.

Sometimes even the presence of a gunboat was not enough to
deter the more audacious Southerners. Early on the morning of
November 7, 1863, while Phelps was aboard the *Hastings* tending to
his Tennessee Division, the steamer *Allen Collier* received permission from Acting Master Lyman Bartholomew, executive officer commanding the *Eastport*, to land for cotton at Whitworth Landing on
the Mississippi. Shortly after the *Allen Collier* had tied up along the
bank in a thick undergrowth of cottonwood, Bartholomew took a
cutter with a crew consisting of three black sailors and a white boy,
and boarded the steamer. Forty-five minutes later the watch on the
Eastport reported fire aboard the steamer, and shortly she was enveloped in flames. Soon a small boat was spotted drifting downriver.
In it was the young boy, who reported that guerrillas had sneaked
aboard the steamer and taken everyone, including Bartholomew,
prisoner.

Porter felt Bartholomew got what he deserved. "That stupid fellow
Bartholomew," he wrote to Phelps, "has got himself captured, and
the steamer burnt, owing to a disobedience of my orders. . . . I don't
regret his loss, and hope he may have a hard time of it." Porter then
added, "I assert that no accident can happen, in any case, if my
orders are carried out."[28]

In the West the winter months of late 1863 and early 1864 were
quiet, with only the occasional irritating guerrilla activity providing

any relief for the monotonous days of escorting steamers loaded with cotton to Northern markets. Although the Treasury agents and some army officers were rumored to be enriching themselves, all the cotton seized by the navy was taken to Cairo as a prize, to be adjudicated by the district court. "When the cotton is marked C.S.A.," Porter wrote to Phelps, "it is a prize, otherwise don't interfere with the trade."[29]

This hint from Porter soon blossomed into reality, for the sailors quickly made their own stencils with the markings C.S.A. for suspect cotton. The navy was the chief facilitator for getting cotton to market, and Porter was determined that he and his men would share in what was already an accomplished fact.

The trade in cotton had taken on a life of its own. All efforts to stop it were futile, and finally it became the motivating factor behind the Red River campaign.

CHAPTER FIFTEEN

ↇ

Red River

TEXAS RECEIVED scant attention during the first years of the Civil War. By 1863, small Union forces had some success in occupying parts of the lower Texas coast but also suffered outright disasters at Galveston and Sabine Pass. For some in the North, however, Texas was still a prize worth going after.

The fall of Vicksburg and Port Hudson in the summer of 1863 put the Mississippi River in Union hands from Cairo to the Gulf and for the first time allowed some flexibility for Union commanders. Farragut, Grant, and Maj. Gen. Nathaniel Banks were in favor of capturing Mobile, Alabama. Halleck and Sherman supported an invasion of Texas along the Red River. Politics and economics, rather than sound military strategy, became the deciding factors.

Cotton, or the lack of it, had sent prices skyrocketing. By the fall of 1864, cotton was selling for an unbelievable $1.90 a pound in Boston. Capturing Texas and flooding it with immigrants could produce a huge cotton-growing area independent of the Confederacy. In addition, huge quantities of cotton lay trapped in central and northern Louisiana and southern Arkansas. Bringing this cotton to market would quiet the howls of New England mill owners and bring millions into the Treasury. With Louisiana and Arkansas cut off from the rest of the Confederacy, it would also deprive the Confederacy's now autonomous Trans-Mississippi Department of the commodity that paid for its war effort.

The French occupation of Mexico added another element that made Texas a prime objective. In June 1863, France had invaded Mexico and overthrown the government of Benito Juárez. This blatant flouting of the Monroe Doctrine while the United States was preoccupied made President Lincoln and the State Department very uneasy. France's recognition of the Confederacy and its annexation of Texas, Louisiana, and Arizona were alarming possibilities.

Thus the Red River expedition, through the heart of Louisiana's cotton country to East Texas, was conceived. A strong force would proceed up the Red River to Shreveport, Louisiana, and from there into East Texas. A swift operation would, in addition, allow for an assault on Mobile.[1]

The expedition was given to Maj. Gen. Nathaniel P. Banks, former governor of Massachusetts and speaker of the House of Representatives. As a political general, Banks was most notably known as an impeccable dresser: "He wore yellow gauntlets high up on his wrists, looking as clean as if they had just come from the glove-maker," wrote Admiral Porter. "His hat was picturesque, his long boots and spurs were faultless and his air was that of one used to command."[2] Banks had replaced another political general, Benjamin "Beast" Butler, as military commander of New Orleans, where his political charms replaced the iron fist of Butler and earned him the nickname of "dancing master." Although Banks's political skills were an asset for the Union, his military experience was limited. His efforts along the Texas coast and at Port Hudson were lackluster, and Stonewall Jackson had humbled him in the Shenandoah Valley.

Supporting Banks would be an army under Maj. Gen. Frederick Steele, which would move southwest from Little Rock, Arkansas. Together they would form a pincer on Shreveport. Twenty of Admiral Porter's gunboats, led by the *Eastport*, would support Banks and keep him supplied by river.

For most of the year the Red River was navigable only by small boats and shallow-draft vessels. Even veteran rivermen had a difficult time predicting what the river would do. Sherman was as knowledgeable about the river as many rivermen, for he had been superintendent of the Louisiana State Seminary of Learning and Military Academy, located on the river opposite Alexandria, before the war. He was emphatic that twelve feet of water at the falls in Alexandria was needed to operate. He felt the river should be navigable by the gunboats from March until June. With luck, the water would rise from the late winter and spring rains, as it had in the last twenty years except 1855.

Porter did not like the idea of taking his fleet past Alexandria but acquiesced when Banks pointed out that if he stayed behind and the expedition failed, the blame for the failure would be his. Porter had been as far as Alexandria when it had been captured the year before, and was confident that he could get even his heavier ironclads at least that far. Getting above the falls at Alexandria and up the narrow river to Shreveport was another matter.[3]

While preparations were under way to mount the expedition, Phelps was relieved of the Tennessee Division by Lt. James Shirk. Now he would concentrate on his part of the Mississippi and on the coming campaign.

In January there was little activity in the squadron. Morale was at an all time low. Many men had served for two years with no leave, knowing their only chance of going home would be the result of becoming sick or wounded. The morale problem exploded in Admiral Porter's face when he learned of the activities of the *Mound City*. While Byron Wilson, her captain, was away, the executive officer and second master perpetrated a number of outrages. They briefly turned the gunboat into a pirate ship, pillaging and stealing along the river and brutalizing those crewmen who objected. Porter was incensed and made their court-martial an example to his command.

Phelps's division was not immune either.

One of my gunboats had been having fine doings. I had ordered her to a point to protect some coal barges. Instead of going there the commanding officer went to Commerce, having on board some ladies of Memphis. A certain Mrs. Hudson and some half dozen fast friends . . . there in Commerce they had high old doings, playing the devil on board and threatening all the citizens in the country about who happened to be Mrs. Hudson's enemies, for she originated in that neighborhood. Some of the threats signed by the commanding officer of the gunboat have been sent to me. Such doings I am happy to say are rare in the Navy but the possibility shows what war brings in its train.[4]

Early in February, while everyone was concerned with the level of the Red River, Phelps managed to take a few days to return to Chardon to see to the sale of his home. His parents, especially his father, were not well, and a move to Cleveland was contemplated. Phelps was unhappy with the tenant farmer who was looking after his family's 197-acre farm, so he and his father decided to offer it for sale for $7,700. Lizzie and the girls had gone to Washington to be with her parents, so with his business concluded, Phelps decided not to attend a grand party given by a neighbor, and returned to Cairo.

Lizzie also had not been well, and Phelps was worried.

Do let me prevail upon you to be strictly careful in the treatment prescribed by Dr. [Henry] Mixer. You do not know what a world of trouble & affliction is in store for the woman who neglects herself, and allows disease of the kind to become constitutional. Look about you at the infinite number of invalid American women and know that they too have the same disease and did as you are given to do, neglected themselves, when alone it was cured in the earlier stages. Imagination does not fail to point to me more than I wish a home with a care worn, thin & weakly wife, instead of the well and usually happy one past years have accustomed to think so great a blessing.

Sally's success in school was a source of pride for Phelps, and he was fond of Lucy: "What shall I say? Ah me, I expect if [Alexander] Pennock and I were together you would hear of many sighs for her."[5]

By late February, Phelps found himself up the White River in Arkansas, aboard the tinclad *Silver Cloud,* supporting General Steele's buildup preparatory to the Red River campaign.

It is at best I fancy a Godforsaken country, but now, after the desolation of war has brought to its hearths, it is sad, sad country to look upon. The weather was pretty cold for two or three days which made the land appear still more dreary. Yet there are here and there beautiful farms which have comparatively escaped war. That section of Arkansas is suffering greatly from bands of deserters who have organized for plunder and are committing every conceivable outrage.[6]

General Steele had requested that convoys be sent up the Arkansas River to supply his army, and Phelps at first declined. He had consulted a number of men familiar with the river and was satisfied that it was not a reliable route. Instead, he recommended the indirect but safer route along the White River. A rise on the Arkansas River suddenly presented an unusual opportunity to meet Steele's demands, so on February 15, Phelps reluctantly dispatched a convoy that made it as far as Pine Bluff. Unfortunately, the river fell as fast as it rose, and a steamer struck a snag and sank. The tinclad *Naumkeag* went to the aid of the steamer, also struck a snag, and began taking on water. A box was built around the hole in her hull, and filled with clay from the riverbank, stemmed the leak enough to get her afloat. The tinclad *Linden* was not so fortunate. After hitting a snag, she sank and had to be lightened of all her provisions, guns, and casemates. After a week of backbreaking work, the river finally rose enough for the *Linden* to return downriver.

Admiral Porter was upset that Phelps had given in to Steele: "If we are to be governed by the wishes of importunate officers of the army, who know nothing about the difficulties of navigation, we will meet with serious loss in boats and stores."[7] Porter also recommended the White River and suggested to Steele that the army would do well to repair the rail line leading to Little Rock.

Phelps arrived in Memphis on February 23. "I am now to set myself at work to prepare the *Eastport* for the Red River business," he wrote. "She is now in fine trim, and for once has her compliment of officers . . . but not by means so full of good stout men, still I think there are enough to give a good account of her in the approaching fight." As for the Red River, "We have not the rise there yet, but it cannot fail to come soon."[8]

The *Eastport* left Memphis on February 25 and made her way back to the mouth of the White River. The Red River still showed no signs of rising, so most of the Mississippi Squadron found itself with little to do. Capt. James Prichett of the *Tyler* and his wife, along with the wife of Capt. Thomas Farrell of the recently disassembled *Linden*, visited Phelps aboard the *Eastport* while she was coaling at Caroline Landing. "[We] had a pleasant walk on the island," Phelps wrote, "and then I had them on board to 'tea' and we played 'Muggins' til midnight."

Unfortunately, Phelps found himself in the middle of a domestic squabble between the Prichetts:

> The foolish little flirting thing, good enough of her kind, came down of course to kiss and make up the late quarrel, and she scolds in James hearing largely of the tales that had been told her. . . . Mrs. P. who cares as much for her lawful lord as the old gentleman is supposed to love Holy Water, has had an infinite number of false tales told her with which she is free to entertain one. Happily I had very little to do with this late squabble and intend to have less rather than more. She seems to think I have a very good time and while I look about my nice cabin and above all at my regular 4-poster double bed, and think how ample it all is for the wife, I think myself what a good time I might have in lieu of long and solitary days such as are my portion. . . . I made the evening as pleasant as might be; converted myself to a good humored fellow willing to be a child again for now.

Such rare opportunities to escape from the business of war, even if only to observe the domestic problems between a husband and wife, once again brought into focus for Phelps what his future would bring. A year had passed since he first broached the subject of leaving the navy, and although he had not pursued the idea, he had not rejected it. Sally was now nine years old.

> I am anxious that she shall be a really good musician. It will fill up one of the wants in our household I have much felt. . . . It makes me sad to look forward to those coming years and think of how little of them I am destined to pass beneath my own roof. . . . Do not let Lucy forget her cara papa. The little witch! How quickly she would drive off . . . the sadness that lies in my heart deep, deep down. . . . This is a thing that grows upon me and I dread more and more the thought of a cruise on a foreign station.[9]

Taking his leave of Mrs. Prichett and Mrs. Farrell, Phelps slowly headed the *Eastport* downriver toward Vicksburg, towing a barge of coal. "This ship is running even better than anticipated," Phelps noted, "better, I think than before, owing to turning more by the head with some alterations I made." Arriving at Vicksburg and finding the Red River was still low, Phelps continued downriver to Natchez, which he reached on March 1. The ironclad gunboats were to rendezvous there to await a rise on the Red River.

> The Red River has not yet seen fit to take itself up, but is lower even than it was. No man knows when the expedition can come off for want of water. The old *Benton* is here and I went on board to see the old craft. She bears the marks of her war trials but is staunch and good still for any amount of knocks. It does me good to see the old craft.

Phelps was feeling somewhat under the weather, the result of some caulking coming loose and letting water into his cabin. "I have taken cold in the head and have some stiffness in the neck and shoulders. The end of my nose is sore and what is worse is swollen. . . . My head is like a brick. . . . Do you suppose that I present myself in such plight before the fair of Natchez?"

While waiting for the rise in the Red River, Phelps took the opportunity to tour the city.

Natchez is a very pretty place and very delightful just now with its blooming fruit trees and balmy weather. Already traces of green begin to show themselves along the forest in the bottom lands, and the grass is invitingly green. The splendid plantations are beginning to put on the appearance of spring cultivation. . . . People here have fallen upon sad times. There were families who had their 10 and 20 house servants and their $10,000, $20,000 or more, per an., to spend, who now are fortunate to have a field hand left to do their service and as many hundreds of dollars as they formerly enjoyed thousands. [James] Grier [captain of the *Benton*] tells me that the place is not nearly as pleasant as it was. Many of those who contributed most to make it agreeable are gone north or elsewhere. Still some remain.

Phelps managed to look up several old friends of his family who had moved to Natchez before the war. He looked forward to seeing George Smith, but of Orrin Metcalf, he was not sure. "Orrin Metcalf's place was marked out to me and perhaps I may go there before leaving," Phelps wrote Lizzie, "altho' I suppose he is too great a secesh to care to see any bloody Yankee, not withstanding that he himself is a double dyed one of the worst type, having been born in Connecticut I believe. I will first enquire about him, and if he is as bad as I have heard I shall make the masonic sign and pass him by."[10]
Things turned out well.

I went to dine with George Smith today, and also called on Mrs. Metcalf. Mrs. Metcalf I was much pleased with. There was a good deal of cordiality displayed. Mrs. M. spoke of you very pleasantly and so did Mrs. Smith. Miss Lizzie Metcalf is still there and she evidently was very glad to see someone who had recently seen the old place. Mrs. Metcalf had already sent to invite me to spend this evening at her house. The residences of both gentlemen are very pleasant and pretty ones, but like all others in this once charming place show the face of grim war. Mrs. Metcalf lost a daughter last summer, has since had a son killed in battle in [Jeb] Stuart's Cavalry, and has another still in that service. George has a son also in the rebel rank, who is at Mobile, a boy about 19 or 20.

The crew of the *Eastport* was shaping up, and Phelps was confident that they would do well in the approaching expedition. "I like my new first Lieutenant [Acting Ensign Sylvester Poole] very much," he wrote to Lizzie. "He is plain, but a reliable, honest, and shrewd man, ambitious to do his duty well." Phelps added that his paymaster, "Fat Gilman, No. 2, is if anything fatter than ever and the same queer compound." (Fat Gilman, No. 1, was fleet paymaster at Cairo.)[11]

On March 5, Phelps received orders from Porter to hurry down to the mouth of the Red River. The *Eastport* promptly departed Natchez and had covered about thirty-five miles when Phelps ordered the *Eastport* anchored until the moon rose early the next morning. He would not risk running aground when there was no rise on the Red River.

The rendezvous at the mouth of the Red River was crowded with gunboats and steamers of all descriptions. Not since the combined fleets met above Vicksburg had such a powerful fleet gathered on the rivers. Although he was confident that the combined operation would be a success, considering their overwhelming superiority, Phelps remembered that the same feeling was prevalent at Plum Point and Vicksburg. "If they hold us at bay," he wrote in a long letter to Lizzie, "they will deserve well of all rebels and all rebeldom. . . . There can be no question of the superiority of this vessel in most points to the others; the old *Benton* always remaining the best of the floating batteries."

One sad piece of news, especially for Phelps, was that the *Conestoga* had sunk.

The *Conestoga* has made her last trip & fought her last fight. Two or three nights since when she was going up river near Grand Gulf she met the *General Price* coming down. The pilot of the *Price* managed to run into the *Conestoga* and to injure her so badly that she sank in 30 feet of water within five minutes time. Few people escaped except two—the hospital steward and a seaman—but with nothing save the clothes they stood in. Poor old *Conestoga!* A vessel whose good fortune has been a marvel for years has at length met a tragic end. It is a great pity, for there are few vessels whose history is so full of adventure in this war.

This is the third time this kind of thing has happened to Selfridge during this war and by strange co-incidence the vessels lost had their names beginning with the letter C—*Cumberland, Cairo, Conestoga.* Apparently in each case there has been no escape from disaster & no want of precautions, yet when we find such things pursuing one person we must attribute it in a degree to something in the individual which we cannot define and yet which has the effect to attach to him the idea of bad fortune—ill luck. There are men said to be born to ill luck whose bad fortune is traceable to an inherent defect known only to exist because its fruits are witnessed.

While the fleet waited for a rise in the river, many of the captains congregated on the *Black Hawk*. "I have been much aboard the Flag Ship, taking my meals there as often as elsewhere, and I find the Admiral very friendly in his intercourse." One of the topics that arose during the nightly conversations was what the combined fleet would do at the end of the expedition. "It is the plan now, if possible," wrote Phelps, "for all the squadron when we come out of Red River to run down to New Orleans, on a lark. That will be about the best way to finish up the job."

While the *Black Hawk* was tied up at Acklen's Landing, near the mouth of the Red River, one evening, two women came to visit. "There was a widow lady—say 40—and a cousin of hers also widow—say 30—on board the *Black Hawk* last evening," wrote Phelps. Porter later wrote: "These ladies weren't at all put out when they went in to the cabin to find a dozen officers all in uniform. They were both in short hunting skirts, had on high top boots, and carried double barreled guns and fixn's, and each had a pointer dog."[12]

After they had been invited to stay and share some champagne, the purpose of the women's visit soon became clear. "[Mrs. Acklen] has several plantations in this vicinity, and the cotton she has ready for market, notwithstanding that the rebels burned half her crop, is

B-4480

David Dixon Porter—Porter was given command of the Mississippi Squadron even though he had embarrassed Secretary of the Navy Welles more
than once. (National Archives)

worth in New York nearly one million of dollars." Mrs. Acklen made a number of efforts to entice Porter into helping her get her cotton to market, including outright bribes, but Porter would have none of it. "There goes a prize for somebody," Phelps continued, "the pair are ladies and well looking, the younger one [Mrs. Julia Jenkins] possessing the rare attraction of being a capital sports-woman, shooting on the wing with certainty. In the quiet life the war enforces here she has daily found relief in the use of her gun."

Among the boats gathered at the mouth of the Red River was the steamer *Champion,* under the command of Phelps's younger brother Alfred. Phelps learned that Alfred had recently submitted his resignation and was soon to be discharged from the navy. Over the past two years, he had used his influence to get Alfred a command, and now he was leaving the navy with no idea of what he would do for a living. Phelps was disappointed with his brother and upset with Porter. "The Admiral has never spoken to me of him," he wrote. "I am reminded to mention that he (the Adm'l) is not frank about many things. The want of it is a defect in his character. One is always a little suspicious that there is something behind coming out in some round about way at some future time."[13]

The Red River campaign would begin with Banks's army marching on Alexandria from the south to rendezvous with the navy on March 17. The combined force would then move together toward Shreveport, where they would meet Steele's columns. With such a large force everyone expected success. Although Confederate Gen. E. Kirby Smith had an estimated twenty-five thousand troops in the region, it was the level of the river that was the real concern.

On March 10, transports carrying ten thousand hardened troops under Brig. Gen. A. J. "Whiskey" Smith joined the fleet. Smith's men were needed by Sherman for his upcoming march toward Atlanta, and were on loan to Banks until the middle of April.

Two days later the fleet entered the Red River with barely enough water for the larger ironclads to pass over the bar at its mouth. The land on both sides of the narrow river was low for about two miles upriver. There the banks rose to an average height of about thirty-five feet, and all hands kept watch for sharpshooters. The next day the fleet encountered obstructions placed across the river eight miles below Fort De Russy. Porter and Smith decided to turn back and land the troops near the head of the Atchafalaya River. Porter would then take most of his fleet up the Atchafalaya and try to get at Fort De Russy from the rear while Smith went overland.

Porter ordered Phelps to proceed up the Red River and attempt to remove the obstructions placed across it. Phelps took along the tinclads *Fort Hindman* and *Cricket* the river monitors *Osage* and *Neosho,* and the lumbering *Choctaw* and *Lafayette.* The latter two were already experiencing difficulty maneuvering in the narrow, crooked river and were slowing the others.

At 9:30 on the morning of March 14, Phelps boarded the tug *This-tle* and inspected the "bulkhead of trestle work" across the river. He discovered the obstruction to be a row of piles driven into the river bottom. Below this was a second tier of shorter piles on which were bolted braces and ties from the upper piles. Immediately below these was a raft of timber well secured across the river and made of logs that did not float. Finally, hundreds of trees had been cut and floated against the piles from upstream. The branches of the trees intertwined with the piles to form a dam a beaver would have been proud of.

The Confederates failed to take into consideration what was considered the marvel of its day—steam power. After the *Fort Hindman* removed a portion of the raft, which caused a rush of water that carried away part of the right bank, Phelps finally had a chance to put his ram to good use. He drove the *Eastport* into the pilings, after which his sailors threw a nine-inch hawser around the piles and the *Eastport* backed with full power. The hawsers were then cast off and the *Eastport* rammed the pilings again. Again hawsers were thrown around the pilings and the *Eastport* backed up until the pilings pulled free. This procedure lasted until just after 4 P.M., when the river was open. Weeks of work by the Rebels had gained them only a few hours.

The *Eastport,* followed by the *Osage, Fort Hindman,* and *Cricket,* proceeded toward Fort De Russy and arrived at sunset, just as the leading elements of Smith's troops, under Brig. Gen. Joseph Mower, were engaging the fort with their artillery. One of General Smith's officers reached the *Eastport* and informed Phelps that the army was getting into position behind the fort. The line of fire from the gunboats

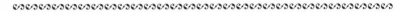

Red River, Spring 1864

would place Smith's men in jeopardy, so Phelps fired a short-fused shell high in the air as a signal; then, to keep the Confederates from realizing that the gunboats were unable to provide gunfire support, he had a rifled shell from one of his 100-pounder Parrotts fired at the lower water battery. The shell burst overhead, forcing the gunners to flee, joining the bulk of the garrison that had earlier withdrawn.[14]

Shortly afterward, a flag of truce was displayed about six hundred yards to the rear of the water battery, and General Mower rode into the fort at the head of his attacking columns.

Porter was having no luck on the Atchafalaya River, so he finally turned around and slowly began the trip back to the Red River.

Learning that Phelps was already at Fort De Russy and that he had no orders to proceed, Porter dispatched the tug *Dahlia* with instructions for Phelps to push on toward Alexandria. The tug was delayed some five hours, especially at the pilings, where a number of trees had floated back into the opening, but finally reached the *Eastport* at 11:30 that night. Wanting to reach Alexandria as quickly as possible, Phelps had sent the swifter *Fort Hindman* and *Cricket* on ahead, just after 9 P.M. With the arrival of Porter's orders, the *Eastport* headed for Alexandria, followed by the river monitors.

The *Fort Hindman* and *Cricket* arrived at Alexandria late on the afternoon of March 15, just in time to see six Confederate steamers escaping above the falls. The steamer *Countess* was torched when it became obvious that she was not going to make it. The *Eastport* arrived a short time later, and Phelps landed a force of 180 sailors and marines, under the command of Lt. Commander Selfridge, now captain of the *Osage*, to occupy the town.

The navy's arrival was ahead of schedule, so while they waited for General Banks, they took advantage of the army's absence to take possession of any Confederate government property. Any cotton marked C.S.A. was considered fair game, and the sailors, with their ever-ready stencils, soon had accumulated a large amount of the valuable commodity. Just so the cotton speculators, who quickly began arriving, would know which bales belonged to the navy, each was also stenciled with U.S.N. as well. The U.S.N.—C.S.A. soon became known as the United States Naval Cotton Stealing Association.

Confederate law required that any cotton about to fall into Union hands be burned. Banks had arranged, however, for payoffs to several Confederate officers who would see that large quantities remained untouched. This connivance in cotton typified the collusion that, in varying degrees, ranged from President Lincoln to Kirby Smith, commander of the Trans-Mississippi Department at Shreveport. Even before the expedition began, agents had been making arrangements to obtain cotton. Former congressman Samuel Casey had already obtained transportation and safe conduct from Lincoln to negotiate with Kirby Smith. When Casey discovered that Porter and the navy would be part of the expedition, he quickly telegraphed

Lincoln: "Do not let Admiral Porter send an expedition up Red River until you hear from me again. If he should he will defeat all my plans."[15] The navy was in an ideal position to insert itself in the middle of the enterprise, and Casey did not want a partner.

"Whiskey" Smith's troops were the first soldiers to arrive in Alexandria on March 18, after mopping up at Fort De Russy. They traveled light and were "rough, brawny-looking fellows, dark as Indians and hard as steel—such men Caesar led into Germany and Gaul and with which he conquered the world."[16]

Banks needed Smith's men, and the message Banks received upon his arrival placed an unfortunate limitation on how long he could use them. Smith's divisions were required by Sherman, and Grant (now lieutenant general commanding) reminded Banks that he could have them only until April 25, "even if it leads to the abandonment of the main object of your expedition."[17] The time constraints placed on Banks added to the urgency with which he needed to proceed, but despite his delay in reaching Alexandria, he still had twenty-six days to reach Shreveport.

After Banks arrived, Phelps kept the *Eastport* at Pineville, opposite Alexandria, for the "political generals are not of my stamp and in fact I have such a big disgust from the doings of the army that I avoid all intercourse possible, not going over to Alexandria at all except on duty."

While the fleet was waiting for the water to rise, the ravages of war were daily brought to Phelps's attention.

> A lady came in on horse back this morning crying bitterly and related to me that her house had been burned during the night by four rebels. It appears that her husband had reported where these men were hidden when they were escaping from the conscription by desertion. One of those betrayed by him was shot for desertion two weeks since. Now has come the hour of retaliation. The rebel soldiery prowling through the country burning cotton and wherever there are families whose members have resisted conscription in any form, they are committing all sorts of excesses.

Phelps found himself in big trouble with Louis, his cook, for giving away too much of his mess stores, especially coffee, "to the needy of which class there are many and the little they had has been robbed from them by our vagabond soldiery." Somewhat coldly, Phelps added, "I have ceased to think the report of thousands killed in battle is so much of a loss to the country considering the material killed."[18]

Reports were received that the Confederates had built the CSS *Missouri* at Shreveport and that she carried four and a half inches of armor and mounted a powerful battery. Porter was told that he need not worry about the *Missouri*, but there were also the same kind of reports about the *Arkansas*.

To take on this potential threat, Porter chose the *Eastport*. "It was necessary that [Porter] should send a formidable vessel up first," said K. Randolph Breese, flag captain of the *Black Hawk*, "because the information we then had of the rebel iron-clads was very indefinite. . . . The light-draught vessels . . . were not able to cope with the rebel iron-clads."[19]

Porter's Red River pilots objected to the *Eastport* on the grounds that she was too big; underwriters would never insure such a large vessel in peacetime. The river at that point was rising slowly, and Porter felt the *Eastport*'s powerful ram and 100-pounder Parrotts would make short work of the *Missouri*. Phelps was itching to go. The *Eastport* had missed out on the taking of Vicksburg and the battle at Helena and this was her last chance for glory. "I am on my feet from morning till night," he wrote, "never sitting, never stopping, all the restlessness of my nature being aggravated when I am on the war path as I may say, and have to wait for the slow process of rising water in the channel before the end can be reached."[20] That Porter and Phelps were of one mind on this matter was reflected in the rumors that they were related and that Porter had personal reasons for wanting the *Eastport* in the advance.

The pilots were unanimous in their opinion that the *Eastport* should not go first; she might become stuck and block the other vessels. Porter told them, "I want you to go on board and take her over the falls."[21] Sure enough, no sooner had the *Eastport* started above the falls than the river began to fall and she became stuck. Now the fleet was delayed until the smaller boats, with as little as six inches of clearance, could maneuver outside the channel and get above the falls. The hospital steamer *Woodford* ran aground and wrecked on the rocks. For three days, tugs and tinclads struggled with the *Eastport* until she finally made it. With the *Eastport* and *Osage* leading the way, the navy headed for Grand Ecore, about halfway to Shreveport.

Soon the sky was black from smoke so thick that the sun "appeared as though seen through a smoked glass." Those Rebels who were not part of the arrangement were burning all the cotton within ten miles of the river as they withdrew before the Union advance. On Sunday morning, April 3, 1864, Phelps spotted a man waving a white handkerchief from in front of a handsome house. He and Selfridge went ashore to see what the man wanted.

> He told us his name was Colhoun, that he was a brother of Captain [Edmund R.] Colhoun of the United States Navy; that, being over age, he had taken no part in the conflict, but had remained at home cultivating his plantation. With tears in his eyes he told us that night his cotton pile, of 5000 bales, had been set on fire, and his ginhouse, costing $30,000, destroyed. He was a rich man the night before, and the morning found him penniless.

The fleet had used up its supply of coal, so each evening, about two hours before sunset, the fleet tied up to the riverbank and all of the crews, along with Smith's troops, scoured the countryside for fence rails. Each man was expected to return with two rails, and soon the countryside was stripped of fences as far as the eye could see. "So dependent were we upon these rails for fuel," Selfridge noted, "that it was a saying among the Confederates that they should have destroyed the fences and not the cotton."[22]

As the fleet pushed its way toward Grand Ecore, it was obvious that the *Eastport* was still slowing things down. Phelps sent the lighter boats on ahead as he struggled with tugs at each end of his boat pushing and pulling her around the narrow bends.

Banks's army had departed Alexandria on March 27 and was concentrated near Natchitoches by April 3. The gunboats and twenty-six transports with General Smith's corps had arrived at Grand Ecore, four miles away, the same day. New orders arrived reinforcing the original timetable for the return of Smith's troops, but since Shreveport was only four days' march, it was agreed to press ahead.

Porter had remained in Alexandria, so Phelps was temporarily in command of the squadron at Grand Ecore. That cotton was still a primary objective was demonstrated when the three barges that Porter had sent to be used to bridge the river were turned over to the army. Porter had intended for the navy to fill the barges with cotton when the expedition was over, but troops were already bringing in the remaining cotton from the surrounding countryside. Phelps reported this to Porter, who was delighted. "Let [them] do it," Porter said, "we will capture it when the flatboats are full."[23] General Banks intervened with Porter after Phelps seized the barges, and he was forced to return the barges and cotton to the army.

After Smith's divisions had landed, the expedition resumed its march toward Shreveport. Inexplicably, Banks chose to stay on the west side of the river instead of crossing over and taking the road that followed the Red River all the way to Shreveport. The road Banks chose soon diverged from the river and took him twenty miles away from the navy's big guns and his supplies.

Porter arrived from Alexandria and realized that although the *Eastport* had gotten above the shoals at Grand Ecore, the water was still so low that only his light-draft gunboats could proceed any farther. Porter departed Grand Ecore on April 7 with a force of river monitors, tinclads, and transport steamers, leaving Phelps behind, in command of the heavier boats.

In the meantime, Banks was walking into a trap. Without gunboat support and stretched out along a single, narrow road through pine forests and broken wilderness, his army approached a place called Sabine Cross Roads (Mansfield). Eleven thousand Confederates, under Maj. Gen. Richard Taylor (the son of Zachary Taylor) lay in wait, commanding a clearing twelve hundred yards long and nine hundred yards wide, through which ran a deep ravine.

After some sharp skirmishing, both armies began to maneuver for a battle they expected to take place on April 9. Late on the afternoon of the eighth, however, the Rebels saw their advantage and charged the head of the Union column. Quickly the Union troops were driven back upon their supply wagons, which were too close to the head of the column. Union troops fled, leaving more than 400 mules, 250 wagons, and 18 pieces of artillery. Taylor's troops pressed the attack until Banks withdrew.

Fortunately, Banks's division commanders slowed Taylor's advance and allowed the remaining Union army an orderly retreat to Pleasant Hill, fifteen miles to the southeast.

> On the 2nd day, [Gens. William B.] Franklin and Smith were allowed to have their way pretty much and they chose a fine field where all say the prettiest and probably the most fierce battle of the war took place. The whole field of battle was in sight being a perfect panorama and Franklin says that it was a perfect picture and the only time he has seen lines of infantry at close quarters pouring volley after volley into each other approaching to within 60 yards. The result of this fight was a decided repulse of the enemy.[24]

General Kirby Smith, Taylor's commander, arrived on the scene at the close of the battle and ordered Taylor to withdraw to Mansfield, Louisiana, in preparation for a move against General Steele in Arkansas.

Banks was at first in favor of pressing ahead the next day, but on the evening of April 9 he called a council of war at which it was decided not to continue toward Shreveport. His generals, except Smith, who was not at the meeting, had been bloodied and had no stomach for another battle under Banks's command. With Smith's divisions due to be recalled to Georgia, the decision was to abandon the expedition and withdraw toward Grand Ecore.[25]

When General Smith heard the news, he pleaded with Banks to resume the advance, but Banks refused. Smith then went to General Franklin, Banks's second in command, and proposed that he relieve Banks of his command and press on toward Shreveport. Franklin, hurting from a wound suffered at Sabine Cross Roads, asked, "Smith, don't you know this is mutiny?"[26] Realizing Franklin was not in favor of seizing command, Smith let the matter drop.

Porter had reached Springfield Landing on April 10. The river at that point was blocked by the large steamer *New Falls City*, which had been sunk across the channel, her bow and stern lying in the woods on each side. "An invitation in large letters," wrote Porter, "to attend a ball in Shreveport was kindly left stuck up by the rebels, which invitation we were never able to accept."[27]

While attempts were being made to remove the sunken steamer, a courier arrived with word that the army was retreating toward Grand Ecore. Porter assembled his captains and informed them that they had to go back. The gunboats were placed at intervals among the thirty transports, and the *Osage* brought up the rear.

With the river still falling, the ponderous fleet slowly made its way downstream. Soon a large Confederate force was spotted in the woods about three miles away by the pilot of the transport *Blackhawk* (not to be confused with Porter's flagship), who had an elevated position and could see over the riverbank. Lieutenant Commander Selfridge sent the *Lexington* downriver to wait for the attack and open an enfilading fire.

Confederate Maj. Gen. Thomas Green, a veteran of Texas's fight for independence and the Mexican War, had his cavalry dismount as they approached the small fleet. Protected by the high banks, Green's troops approached in columns and opened a withering musket fire at a distance of one hundred yards.

For forty-five minutes the sound of twenty-five hundred rifle-muskets mixed with the roar of the huge naval guns of the *Osage* and *Lexington*. It was a decidedly one-sided affair. Using all his grape and canister, and finally shells with fuses cut to one inch, Selfridge slaughtered Green's troops.

As the battle was winding down, Selfridge noticed an officer about two hundred yards below the troops and aimed one of his eleven-inch guns at him. A canister ball struck General Green over the right eye and carried away the top of his head. The death of the "Napoleon of the West" was a shock to his men and particularly to General Taylor, who was an old and dear friend.

When the battle was over, Selfridge estimated more than four hundred Confederates lay dead at the riverbank. The woodwork of the *Osage* and *Blackhawk* was so pitted with bullet holes that "one

could not place the hand anywhere without covering the shot-mark."
Despite the incredible musket fire, Selfridge reported only a handful
of wounded men.[28]

On April 15, the fleet was safely back at Grand Ecore along with
Banks's army. The river was still falling, however, and unless the fleet
withdrew to Alexandria, there was a real possibility that it would be
trapped at Grand Ecore. The *Eastport* was already having great difficulty getting back below the Grand Ecore shoals, but after much difficulty she finally made it. It was quite apparent that the return
journey would be long and difficult, and would require the army to
keep the riverbanks clear of Confederates.

Porter had gone to Banks, barging past his sentries, and urged
him to resume his advance, fearing a retreat would place his fleet in
jeopardy. He used the argument that a retreat would allow Kirby
Smith to turn his full attention to Steele, who was unaware of
the Union withdrawal. Since communications with Steele were extremely slow due to the long, circuitous route involved, Banks was
under the impression that Steele had failed, and thus was not concerned. Banks reassured Porter that he would not abandon the navy
but reiterated that his orders to return Smith's troops precluded an
advance. His order to withdraw stood.

Porter felt he could not trust Banks, so he went to Smith, who
promised to stand by the fleet until it was safely out of the Red River.
Porter wrote to Sherman:

> The safety of this army and my whole fleet depends on his stay-
> ing here. His is the only part of the army not demoralized, and
> if he was to leave there would be a most disastrous retreat. . . .
> You know my opinion of political generals. It is a crying sin to
> put the lives of thousands in the hands of such men, and the
> time has come when there should be a stop put to it.[29]

Porter ordered the *Eastport* and the heavier ironclads to return to
Alexandria immediately while he managed the transports and tinclads over the Grand Ecore shoals.

After waiting for the *Ozark* to clear the channel, the *Eastport* began
the slow trip downriver on April 15. With scarcely more than a foot of

water beneath her keel, the gunboat drifted lazily down the center of the channel. With a northwest breeze pushing the *Eastport* along, the helmsman maintained headway even though the wheels were not turning, and the crew went about their duties without the incessant chug-chug-chug from her engines. Just after four o'clock, Phelps was in his aft cabin, when, about eight miles below Grand Ecore, he felt a peculiar trembling sensation. His first impression was that the boat had probably struck another snag, except that its headway had not changed.

The noise of the crew being called to quarters followed as Phelps was informed that the boat had struck a torpedo. As he worked his way forward, he was told that a powerful explosion under the bow had nearly thrown his leadsman overboard. Water was rapidly filling the forward holds, so Phelps ordered the *Eastport* moved to the nearby bank where she would not block the river. The *Eastport's* damage control parties quickly set up the steam siphon pump and three hand pumps on the forecastle. Those crewmen not assigned to operate the hand pumps were put to work in bailing parties.

The pumps did not seem to have any effect on the water in the forward holds, so Phelps dispatched a tug to Alexandria to fetch the two steam pump boats. An hour after the explosion, the *Lexington* came alongside and ran a hose from her steam pump into the *Eastport.*

As soon as Porter received word that the *Eastport* was sinking, he ran down in the *Cricket* to see what needed to be done. So far the *Eastport's* and *Lexington's* pumps were having little effect as the bow settled lower and lower. Finally, after five hours, just as water covered the forward gun deck, the bow came to rest on the river bottom. After consulting with Phelps, Porter ordered that the *Eastport's* battery and all ammunition be removed while he went to Alexandria to hurry up the steam pump boats.

Down in the bow of the *Eastport,* crewmen tried to discover the source of the leak. With a bulkheaded double hull and numerous "watertight" compartments, it was all but impossible for the repair crews to isolate the damage. The wooden bulkheads, which were originally thought to make the gunboats almost invulnerable, only served to get in the way of stopping the leak.

Crewmen from the *Eastport* began passing ammunition to the *Ozark* as other crews began the laborious job of removing the port blinds in preparation for removing the huge guns through the gun ports. Working parties from the *Lexington* were assigned to the aft nine-inch guns, which were transferred to the *Ozark*.

The remaining battery and ammunition were placed on a flatboat brought alongside the *Eastport*'s port quarter. The tinclad *Fort Hindman* tied up next to the flatboat and rigged booms for transferring the hundred-pounder Parrott guns. After using block and tackle to drag the guns up the sloping deck to the open gun port, they were removed from their carriages and, in a skillful corkscrew movement, hoisted through the gun port to the flatboat. Seeing an opportunity to make his tinclad a more formidable vessel, Capt. John Pearce of the *Fort Hindman* got permission from Phelps to keep one of the Parrotts, which he placed on his starboard bow.

Twenty-four hours after the *Eastport* first took on water, the last of the battery had been removed while parties still toiled at removing the tons of ammunition from the magazines and shell rooms. The *Lexington* and the tinclad *Juliet* alternated using their steam siphon pumps in what was so far an unsuccessful attempt to refloat the *Eastport*.

Porter reached the falls at Alexandria just in time to see the steam pump boat *Champion No. 5*, followed about an hour later by the steam pump boat *New Champion* (also known as *Champion No. 3*), headed upriver. At 9:15 A.M., on April 17, *Champion No. 5* tied up alongside the *Eastport* and began pumping with her ten-inch and twenty-inch steam pumps. The water slowly began to recede.

After interminable delays getting upriver, the *New Champion* also reached the *Eastport* and put her large pumps to work. As the water level dropped in the bow, Phelps had his carpenters go to work building another bulkhead in an attempt to seal off the leak. Under the direction of Acting Master George Rodgers, who had come over from the *Pittsburg*, the carpenters, often working chest deep in water, began constructing the bulkhead.

For Phelps, naval tradition and personal pride dictated that the *Eastport* would not be given up without a fight. His crew and men from the other gunboats were determined that the *Eastport* would not fall into Confederate hands. The *Eastport* was not a riverboat but a U.S. Navy man-of-war, and the training and discipline that Phelps had instilled in his crew would now be tested. Their efforts finally paid off when, at 5 P.M. on the twentieth, the bow began to lift off the bottom. Although still somewhat down at the bow, enough of the *Eastport*'s hull was visible to confirm that her bottom was once again shattered.

The *Fort Hindman* came alongside, took a hawser from the *Eastport,* and attached it to her capstan. She then moved to the opposite shore and tied up to trees along the bank. Once secured, the *Fort Hindman* began to groan as her steam-powered capstan slowly pulled the hawser tight. After what seemed an eternity, the *Eastport* finally began to move into the center of the river.

One of the steam pumps from the *New Champion* was transferred to the forecastle of the *Eastport* for the trip to Alexandria. The *Eastport*'s furnaces then were fired and steam was raised in the boilers, which enabled her to power the additional steam pump and use her wheels if necessary. *Champion No. 5* tied up alongside the *Eastport* and, with the tinclads *Fort Hindman* and *Juliet* and the admiral's flagship *Cricket,* the little fleet began slowly making its way downriver just after noon on April 21.

The movement of the *Eastport* precipitated a serious misunderstanding between Porter and Banks. Although primed to withdraw to Alexandria, Banks had remained at Grand Ecore while efforts to float the *Eastport* continued. Porter was still suspicious of Banks's intentions, however, especially after General Franklin and others had warned him that Banks intended to leave.

On the afternoon of the twenty-first, General Banks sent Col. W. S. Albert to inform Porter that the army was prepared to move if Porter was ready. Albert found the *Eastport* gone, and was told by Porter that he was ready to move and had made preparations to protect his boats. Satisfied that Porter would take care of himself, Banks ordered his army, including Smith, to evacuate Grand Ecore. The plodding fleet was quickly left behind.

The *Eastport* had made twenty miles down the winding river by late afternoon when *Champion No. 5* had trouble controlling the 260-foot boat; she floated out of the channel and ran aground.

USS *Cricket*—The tinclad served as Admiral Porter's flagship during the abortive Red River campaign in the spring of 1864. (U.S. Naval Historical Center)

Pickets were sent ashore to watch for the enemy, for they were now unprotected by the army.

Rodgers's carpenters continued trying to stem the leak. Working in water up to their waists, often going underwater with hammer, chisel, and caulking, the carpenters slowed the intake of water but were never able to stop it. On the forecastle other crewmen worked the hand pumps in shifts, day and night. Attempts were made to strip off the armor plating, but without the proper tools, the task was impossible.

Lines were run to the *New Champion*, *Champion No. 5*, and *Fort Hindman*, which then tied up to the bank downriver. All three then began pulling with their steam capstans. Other lines, using block and tackle, were run out and manned by the crew. Around the clock on April 22, lines groaned, men cursed, and the *Eastport* moved only half her length. Finally, at 3 A.M. on the twenty-third, the *Eastport* floated free and, with the *New Champion* alongside, again started downriver.

The *Eastport* traveled about five miles, then ran aground again. The *Fort Hindman* ran alongside her stern, took a line, and tried to pull her upriver, where she could get a better position to pass the bar. That effort failed, so the three boats once again took lines from the *Eastport,* ran downriver, and began pulling. All day they pulled with little success. At 8 P.M., Phelps called a temporary halt to give some of his crew their first rest in a week. An hour later the *Eastport* felt light enough that Phelps had the *Fort Hindman* come up and take a line to pull her stern around. Finally, at 10:15 P.M., she was afloat again. All hands were awakened to scavenge for fence rails to supply the boiler fires.

Shortly after midnight the *Eastport* got under way and traveled two miles before she again ran aground. This time the *Fort Hindman* pulled her free, and after taking some time to repair the rudder, the *Eastport* continued a short distance until she grounded on sunken logs near the small town of Montgomery. Once again, the routine of trying to drag the *Eastport* across the bar began. Rodgers asked that a detail be sent ashore to gather clay, which he hoped would serve as caulking for the bulkhead. At 6 P.M. on the twenty-fourth, the *Eastport* floated free, only to swing around and ground again. Later that evening a six-inch hawser was run around a large tree on shore and back to the steam capstan of the *Eastport,* then over to the steam capstan of *Champion No. 5.* After hours of pulling, the *Fort Hindman* took a line from the *Eastport's* stern, and the combination pulled her free. At 7:40 A.M. on the morning of April 25, the *Eastport* started again.

So far Phelps and Porter had been lucky. The Confederates were following General Banks in his retreat to Alexandria and took little notice of the gunboats. Their scouts most likely reported that the gunboats were going nowhere quickly, and there would be time to attend to them later. The Rebels attacked Banks's rear guard, under General Franklin, at Monett's Ferry on the Cane River, but were repulsed. Looking for easier pickings, they turned their attention to the small fleet making its way downriver.

Expecting an attack at any moment, gunners on the *Fort Hindman,* the *Juliet,* and the admiral's flagship *Cricket* constantly scanned the riverbanks for signs of the enemy. The *Fort Hindman's* gunners were directed to train their guns either ahead or behind the *Eastport,* but to be careful not to fire into her. Captains were told that in case of attack, they should immediately drop into the center of the river. Marines under Lt. Frank Church patrolled the riverbanks, skirmishing with Confederate scouts who seemed to buzz around the fleet like flies. The *Eastport's* crew kept their small arms at hand.

After the *Eastport* had traveled a short distance, she grounded once again. With the pumps still "vomiting" water from her forward hold and Rodgers's carpenters trying to stop the incessant leak, the *Eastport* was dragged across the bar until, just after 3 P.M., she was free again. She floated a little way downriver, then ran aground in five and a half feet of water. While the crew went about what had become routine, Phelps sent his pilot to sound the river below. This time, after hours of pulling, of pouring water on the hawsers around the capstans for cooling and better friction, the *Eastport* had not moved an inch. The pilot's report was even more discouraging. Only a few hundred yards farther downstream lay another bar of sunken logs in less water.

"For the first time hope left me," wrote Phelps. "My crew was worn out beyond its power and endurance."[30] The *Eastport* had moved sixty miles, and in another sixty would be safely at Alexandria, where Banks's army was just arriving. Both Porter and Phelps were now aware that the Confederates would turn their full attention to the small fleet.

After consulting with Porter, Phelps decided to blow up the *Eastport.* Porter wrote to Phelps:

> The time has come at last, when we must perform the most painful duty that can [befall] an officer of the Navy—viz.— destroy the ship he has so long commanded and connected with are so many associations. You have done all that a brave & zealous officer could do to save your vessel.[31]

Phelps replied to Porter:

The command of the *Eastport* has been to me a source of great pride, and I could not but deplore the necessity for destroying her. The act has been the most painful one experienced by me in my official career. She was the finest vessel of your squadron and one of the best possessed by the Government. Your order to me to proceed to destroy her . . . not only relieved me from all responsibility, but was also grateful to my feeling, both as a man and officer. I desire further to express to you my grateful sense of your forbearance in ordering the destruction of the vessel, when yourself convinced of the impossibility of saving her, yielding your judgement to my natural anxiety to exhaust every means that seemed to offer a hope of success. I fear that your forbearance led to greater risks both for your squadron and yourself than even the saving of the *Eastport* would justify.[32]

At 2 A.M. on April 26, Phelps had the crew mustered on the gun deck. After commending their efforts to save the boat, he informed them that she would have to be blown up. Everything of any value to the Rebels would be transferred to the other boats. Time was running out, so the crew, along with parties from the other boats, quickly went to work.

Sunrise the next morning, April 27, revealed increased Confederate activity along the banks of the river. The crews worked frantically to finish clearing out the *Eastport*. A two-hundred-pound can of powder connected to an insulated wire, and eight barrels of cannon powder, were placed beneath the forward casemate. The wire was run ashore by an army lieutenant and attached to a galvanic battery. Just after ten that morning, as the last of the *Eastport*'s officers boarded the *Fort Hindman*, a large enemy force opened up on the fleet and attempted to rush the *Cricket*, which was tied up to the right bank. With most of the crew ashore gathering fence rails, the two officers and twenty men aboard the *Cricket* opened up with shrapnel and grape. Seeing that the Confederates were close to boarding, one of the *Cricket*'s crew grabbed an axe and ran to the hawser holding the boat to the riverbank. Under heavy musket fire the man cut the line, and the *Cricket* floated away from the bank. With a heavy cross fire from the *Juliet* and *Fort Hindman,* the butter-nuts withdrew after a one-hour fight.

When Phelps gave the word, the army lieutenant tried once, twice, three times, but the galvanic battery would not work. Phelps then decided to transfer more powder from the *Fort Hindman* while the wires were torn out, and cotton trains were laid through the *Eastport.* More than three thousand pounds of powder was placed beneath the after casemate and around the machinery, and combustibles were poured on the wooden decks. Just after 1 P.M. the *Fort Hindman* took aboard the remaining crew and stood downriver. Phelps remained behind with four men in a cutter, to fire the trains when the boats were clear. The train was divided in the wardroom, where it crossed some scattered powder. Phelps had scarcely touched the match to the cotton train when the loose powder ignited, throwing embers toward the charges. He sprang through the smoke to a gun port and sprinted across the deck, leaping into the cutter as it pulled away. With the cutter less than fifty yards away, the *Eastport* began blowing up. The after casemate erupted, followed by the grand stern magazine, which ripped her apart and sent huge pieces of casemate hurtling into the air.

> Hidden by the smoke, the captain had not been seen to escape the boat and but four could be distinctly made out in her, and for a moment intense anxiety was felt on board the *Fort Hind-man.* Then a little veer of the boat showed to the watchers with glasses that five sitters were in her. He is there! All could see that the fragments had fallen and the boat still pulled for the ship. That she passed through those falling timbers and plates of iron untouched, was one of those mysterious happenings which we ascribe to the especial providence of God.[33]

A few minutes later—for the powder train had been partially blown away by the first explosions—the forward casemate blew up, tearing off the bow as the stern had been before. After a series of seven explosions, fire quickly began consuming what was left.

As Phelps and Porter returned and rowed around the burning hulk, the remaining iron plates began collapsing as the wood supports burned away. The *Eastport* was "as perfect a wreck as ever was made by powder."[34]

The small fleet needed to hurry, for the force of the explosion, contained by the high banks, was powerful enough to bend the nearby trees and shook the countryside for miles around. There was no doubt that this would surely bring the Rebels running. To keep the tinclads cleared for action, it was decided that the five hundred contrabands who had sought refuge with the fleet at Grand Ecore should go aboard the two pump boats. They would be safer there as well, for it was felt the Confederates would concentrate on the gunboats.

The fleet quickly started downriver, with Admiral Porter in his flagship, the *Cricket,* in the lead, followed by the *New Champion,* the *Juliet,* and *Champion No.5,* which were lashed together. The *Fort Hindman,* with Phelps in command, brought up the rear.

Scouts reported the departure of the fleet, so orders were passed for Confederate units to form an ambush at the confluence with the Cane River. Capt. Thomas Benton moved his six-pounder smoothbore battery into position above Deloache's Bluff and, along with several hundred infantry, waited for the fleet.

Porter sat in a chair on the deck of the *Cricket,* his eyes scanning the bushes along the banks. After having traveled about twenty miles, he spotted movement on the bluff ahead. "Give those fellows in the bushes a two-second shell," he yelled to the *Cricket*'s captain.[35] The shell exploded in the bushes, and the riverbanks erupted. Within what seemed like moments, the *Cricket* was staggered by nineteen artillery shells. Before her crew could fire another gun, she was underneath the masked battery. With her stern facing the battery, the *Cricket* received another nineteen direct hits from artillery now only twenty yards away. Raked fore and aft with shells that often penetrated, the *Cricket* next took volley after volley of rifle–musket fire. Suddenly her engines stopped. Porter, who had been momentarily stunned by a solid shot that penetrated the pilothouse, recovered to find not only the *Cricket*'s engines stopped but her guns silent. As she drifted slowly toward the lower riverbank, the

Confederates gave three cheers and turned their fire to the *Juliet* and the pump boats; the *Cricket,* they felt, was theirs.

The *New Champion* began backing furiously to get away from the *Cricket* and hit the *Juliet,* smashing her bow. While they were scrambling to pull themselves apart, shells penetrated the *New Champion,* punctured her boilers, and let loose a torrent of live steam among the hundreds of contrabands. They were scalded to death by the score. Those able to jump overboard were mowed down by the riflemen on the banks. The tragedy on the *New Champion* proved to be, however, the salvation of the *Cricket.* With Henry H. Gorringe, her captain, wounded but still at the wheel, Porter went below to see what could be done with the engines and his guns. As he made his way aft, he spotted a soldier running along the bank, firing at him. He grabbed a musket but then realized that shooting people was not his job—directing others to shoot people was his job—so he gave the musket to a crewman and ordered him to shoot the Confederate. The sailor fired and the man fell, one of the few butternut casualties of the fight.

Going below, Porter came upon a shocking scene. Twenty-four people, including the wife of the boat's steward, were dead or wounded on the gun deck. Porter reorganized the mostly black crewmen to man the guns, which they called "bulldogs," with orders not to worry about aiming, just load and fire, to let the enemy know they weren't dead yet.

Down in the engine room Porter found the engineer dead, his hand on the throttle valve. He was answering commands from the pilothouse when he was killed, and as he fell, he turned off the steam. Porter opened the valve, and the *Cricket*'s engines once again came to life. It was a short, decidedly one-sided fight, but the *Cricket* finally was safely out of range.

Aboard the *Fort Hindman,* Phelps cursed the boats in front of him. The three boats had turned sideways in the river and blocked his gunners from opening fire. Phelps watched helplessly as the *Cricket* drifted around the bend and out of sight. With her wheel stopped and her guns silent, Phelps felt great anxiety that Porter was dead or wounded.

With the *Cricket* out of sight, Phelps turned his attention to the *Juliet* and *Champion No. 5.* The *New Champion,* enveloped in steam, had drifted against the bank right in front of the Confederate battery and could not be helped. The *Juliet*'s steam pipe and tiller ropes had been shot away. When the steam cloud cleared, Acting Master John S. Watson, captain of the *Juliet*, discovered that the captain and pilot of *Champion No. 5* had abandoned the pilothouse and were cutting the lines holding the two boats together. With only one line remaining, Watson aimed his pistol and threatened to kill the next man who attempted to cut it. Those crewmen who tried to abandon ship found themselves driven back by musket fire from the *Fort Hindman* as Phelps yelled through his trumpet that deserters would be shot. William Maitland, one of the *Juliet*'s second-class pilots, then braved the intense small arms fire to dash across to *Champion No. 5*, where he turned her around and headed upstream, towing the *Juliet* out of danger.

As the *Juliet* and *Champion No. 5* began to move upriver, Phelps steered the *Fort Hindman* around them to cover their retreat. The gunners on the *Fort Hindman* were by now panic-stricken, so Phelps descended to the gun deck, where "I found it necessary to lay my hand upon my revolver & caution them that the first man who should flinch from his gun would receive its contents." During the withdrawal upriver, Lieutenant Church was wounded in the leg and Sylvester Poole, the *Eastport*'s executive officer, and Joseph Scott, a black seaman, were killed. The three vessels finally ran alongside the bank safely out of range; there Phelps and his captains discussed their options.

"I had not slept but one night from the 15th to the 26th and had been on my feet 48 successive hours," Phelps wrote, "when I found myself cut off from the Admiral with the *Hindman, Juliet* & *Champion No. 5* on my hands." With the possibility that thousands of Confederates lined the high banks, the prudent decision would be to run past after dark. Examination of the *Juliet* and *Champion No. 5* showed, however, that basic repairs would take all night. The *New Champion* was secured by the enemy to the bank, narrowing the river considerably, and it was felt likely that they might sink her across the channel to block it. After weighing the options, and determined not to abandon the three vessels, Phelps decided to run past the battery the following morning. He felt the Confederates couldn't miss at such close range even in the dark, and it would be safer to have daylight to navigate around the obstacles.

All night, while pickets watched for an attack that might come at any moment, "I worked preparing for the morning's contest," Phelps wrote, "putting my own men & officers at the guns, only filling up with the *Fort Hindman*'s men who had in the evening fight by no means done themselves credit." Crews toiled to repair what damage they could. They also transferred thirty bales of cotton from the *Juliet* to the *Fort Hindman*, where they were placed around the pilothouse and casemate. Occasionally Phelps had a shell fired at the *New Champion* to disrupt any attempt by the Southerners to sink her across the channel.

The captain and crew of *Champion No. 5* proposed abandoning her and running the battery on board the tinclads. Phelps would have none of it. *Champion No. 5,* with all her cotton, was as safe as the tinclads, and he declared she was going through. To make sure, he relieved the captain and placed Maitland, who had volunteered, in command and left his personal effects aboard. "Although I had nearly a day in which to remove my things to the *Fort Hindman*, I would not touch them and in doing it admit that I was forcing men into perils in which I was not willing to risk my property."

Just after 9 A.M. on April 27, the *Juliet*, her steering still disabled, made fast alongside the *Fort Hindman*'s port side, and the trio started downriver. About thirty minutes later the *Juliet* struck a snag that punctured her below the waterline. Capt. John Watson ordered preparations begun in case she had to be abandoned. Seeing that the *Juliet* was rapidly taking on water, Phelps ordered the *Fort Hindman* about, and the two boats headed back upriver. Using mattresses and planks, Watson stopped the leak, and the boats once again made their way downriver.

Phelps had the two gunboats shell the woods where he knew the Confederates were waiting for them. The Rebels held their fire until the boats were about five hundred yards from the bend, then opened up from their masked battery. Soon a shot passed through the pilothouse of the *Fort Hindman*, carrying away her tiller rope and wounding Lt. John Pearce. With their steering now gone, the two gunboats drifted in circles with the current. The gunners fired at whatever

USS *Fort Hindman*—Phelps took command of the tinclad during the navy's attempt to fight their way out of the Red River in 1864. (U.S. Naval Historical Center)

target spun into view. Bouncing off one bank and then the other, the two tinclads were riddled by Rebel gunfire. The *Fort Hindman*, in addition to having her pilothouse shot to pieces, was holed at the waterline, had a shell just miss the steam pipe, and one penetrate the magazine, breaking open several barrels of powder. "It seemed as if Providence turned the shot through crowds that it should do no harm. I saw them traverse her crowded decks and cannot understand how so little harm came of them."

The *Juliet* had her rudder shot off, and one shell struck her port crankshaft, cutting it off, which knocked out both cylinder heads on the port engine.

Phelps had hoped to blast the *New Champion*, but was happy, under the circumstances, just to miss her as "we drifted past the enemy—waltzing as I may say."[36] With the tinclads unable to aim their guns effectively to keep the Confederate gunners' heads down,

Champion No. 5 took a fearful pounding. As she passed the battery, she caught fire in the hold. Maitland, wounded eight times, stayed at the helm and guided her to the opposite bank, next to her sister boat, then he and his crew scrambled ashore. After about thirty minutes of being blasted by 6-, 12-, and 24-pounders, along with countless muskets, the two gunboats finally drifted out of danger. There were still numerous sharpshooters along the bank who were "very annoying," according to Phelps. Twelve miles below the battery, the two boats spotted the *Neosho*, which had been sent upriver by Porter. For the first time in almost two weeks, Phelps could breathe easy. He had lost his boat, but he had brought the two tinclads through with surprisingly few casualties.[37]

At 10:30 on the morning of April 28, funeral services were held at Alexandria for Ensign Poole. In a separate ceremony the black sailors of the *Fort Hindman* buried their shipmate Joseph Scott. The following morning, Phelps had the crew of the *Eastport* mustered for the last time aboard the *Fort Hindman*. Thanking them for their efforts, he informed them that they would be transferring to other vessels to fill out their complements. Wishing them good luck and Godspeed, he said his farewell and departed the boat. Phelps soon left Alexandria and returned to his northern Mississippi district.

The efforts to save the *Eastport* prompted Porter to write:

> I don't think I ever witnessed harder work than was performed by the officers and crew of the *Eastport,* and it seemed to be the determination of all on board that she should not fall into the hands of the enemy. . . . S. L. Phelps had done all that man could do to save his vessel and felt it a matter of pride to get her to Alexandria. She had grounded eight times badly, and each time under circumstances where it was very doubtful if she would come off, but the commander's confidence never deserted him, and I could not help but admire his coolness and faith in getting his vessel to Alexandria. . . . He worked with almost superhuman efforts to accomplish the object in view, sleeping apparently neither night nor day. Everybody worked and went through privations of all kinds, and I must say that, mentally, I never went through so much anxiety in my life.[38]

In a letter to General Sherman, Porter criticized Phelps for forgetting to put canvas under the bottom of the *Eastport*—which, he claimed, would have saved her from sinking. He neglected to mention, however, that he was on the scene before she finally touched bottom and, if canvas would have helped, he also forgot.

The situation at Alexandria was still confused. Due to the low water level, all of the larger boats were stuck above the upper falls. Some of the tinclads, with as little as eighteen inches of water, scraped over the rocks and made their way to the wharves where they found numerous steamers loading cotton. The army held the surrounding countryside for about six miles, but General Banks still intended to withdraw to New Orleans. When he asked Porter which boats he would have to destroy, Porter angrily told Banks that if he had to wait two years for a rise in the river, he would not abandon his fleet.

General Franklin reminded Porter of a visit he had at Grand Ecore with Lt. Col. Joseph Bailey, Banks's chief engineer. Bailey had suggested damming the river below the *Eastport* to help her get started. Porter did not think much of the plan at the time and declined the offer. This time Porter was willing to try anything. An engineer and lumberman by trade, Bailey had experience in damming streams in order to move lumber to the mills. Still, the task seemed all but impossible. The river was more than seven hundred feet wide at the point where Bailey proposed building the dam, and the water would have to be raised a minimum of three feet. With support from Banks, however, more than three thousand soldiers and sailors began work on April 30.

A number of experienced lumberjacks from the 4th Wisconsin went to work opposite the town, felling the numerous trees to build a dam. On the other side of the river, soldiers built cribs that were filled with bricks and stones, along with machinery from houses and mills that were torn down. Quarries were opened nearby, and flatboats were built to transport the rock to the cribs.

While the army was busy building the dam, sailors were offloading their boats. Guns, coal, and ammunition were taken ashore, where they were hauled below the falls by wagons. Armor plate from the heavier ironclads was stripped off and sunk where the Confederates could not retrieve it.

On May 8 the river had risen five feet, four and a half inches, enough for three of the tinclads to pass the falls. Early on May 9, however, the water pressure began to wash away the sunken barges that were to serve as gates when the time came to pass the dam. Seeing that a week of work might soon be wasted, Porter jumped on his horse and galloped to the falls, where he yelled at George Bache, captain of the *Lexington,* to head for the opening—now. While thirty thousand soldiers and sailors collectively held their breath, the *Lexington* churned toward the water rushing through the break. As she reached the rocks, she rolled back and forth, then suddenly pitched nose down, hesitated, and careened into the water below. A loud cheer went up but quickly subsided as all eyes turned to the *Neosho.*

The *Neosho* did not fare quite so well. Her pilot decided at the last second that he could not make it, and tried to stop by reversing the engine. It was too late. To the spectators on the banks she seemed to sink as her low profile dipped underwater, but the current carried her onto the falls, crashing along the rocks, and finally into the quiet water below. The *Fort Hindman* and *Osage* passed the falls easily. There were still a number of heavier boats stuck above the falls, and moving the barges against the current and back into the breach was ruled out. Instead, Bailey proposed building a series of wing dams above the falls that would serve to raise the level of the river enough for the boats to pass.

Another three days were needed to build the wing dams, and on May 11 there was enough water for some of the gunboats to pass. Several boats still needed another six inches of water, but instead of waiting, it was decided to drag them over. A four-inch hawser was run out, and with an army band playing a lively march, two thousand men stomped their feet to the music as they dragged the remaining boats to freedom. After reshipping their supplies and equipment below the city, the navy set out for the mouth of the Red River.

The final, sad chapter to the Red River expedition was the burning of Alexandria. How it started was unclear, but the wind-whipped fire destroyed a good part of the town. For the hundreds of contrabands vainly hoping for a trip to freedom and for homeowners watching their houses go up in flames, the departure of the Union army and navy brought to a close an unmitigated and unnecessary disaster.

As soon as the fleet reached the Mississippi, Admiral Porter allowed the illness that had plagued him for some time to overtake him, and he collapsed in bed for the trip back to Cairo. Banks was sacked, replaced Maj. Gen. Edward R. S. Canby.

Phelps was philosophical about the loss of the *Eastport*.

I was the first to go up Red River as I was the last in the descent to Alexandria. No amount of pay could induce me to pass through those two weeks of care and labor again. That sense of duty which becomes the dominant tone of a Naval officer, who has had the idea held in every turn before him from boyhood alone could enable one to endure so much. . . . It is a terrible thing to destroy one's ship but while I felt sad I felt no sense of humiliation. We succumbed to the fiat of heaven & not to the power of an enemy. Where there was not water we could not float her. . . . If I never had another decided conviction it is one at least that I am not fit for peaceful life in time of war & yet I am tired enough of war.[39]

$\wp$

Frustration & Resignation

As CONFEDERATE engineers labored to salvage the *Eastport*'s remains that blocked the Red River, Phelps returned to his division and found everything relatively quiet. With the loss of all his personal belongings aboard *Champion No. 5*, he was short of funds to pay for a quick trip to see Lizzie and the girls. He wrote to Lizzie, asking her to see Admiral Davis to arrange orders to Washington, on the pretext of discussing the question of prizes.

While waiting to see if Lizzie could pull a few strings, Phelps received the tragic, if not totally unexpected, news of the death of his father. The hoped-for dispatch directing him to report to the Navy Department arrived several days later, and Phelps stopped in Chardon to comfort his mother before proceeding to Washington.

The prospect of vast amounts of Red River cotton being condemned as a lawful prize for the navy prompted Gideon Welles to send for Phelps to help the department plot its strategy. From the beginning of the war, the navy had been having trouble with the

District Court for the Southern District of Illinois in getting its prize claims settled, and Welles did not want to be shortchanged.

Phelps had dealt with the court before, and urged that the department retain legal counsel to protect its interests. After consulting with Admiral Davis, he recommended that noted attorney Charles Eames look into the matter.

Before Phelps left Washington, Welles invited him to dinner on Saturday night, May 21, to hear firsthand about the Red River fiasco.

> [He has] given me many interesting details concerning the Red River expedition and the incompetency of General Banks. Among other matters he relates some facts in regard to cotton speculations by persons connected with General Banks—some of his staff that are exceedingly discreditable. Among others whom he specially mentions is one Clark from Auburn, New York who appears to be managing director of the cotton operations.[1]

After an all-too-brief reunion with his family, Phelps returned to Cairo and the war. His advice to the Navy Department soon bore fruit, for within a few days after his arrival at Cairo, Marshal D. L. Phillips handed over sixty thousand dollars to the navy from the district court. There was no breakdown as to which prizes the money represented, but obviously Mr. Eames knew how to shake a few trees. Porter was so impressed with Eames's success that he directed Phelps to offer him the job of representing the squadron in connection with their Red River prizes, on a contingency fee basis.

The sixty thousand was a trifling amount compared with the two-and-a-quarter million dollars' worth of cotton before the district court. Treasury agents were making all sorts of claims that the cotton was under their jurisdiction, and people were coming out of the woodwork to claim the cotton as their own. Out of the seven thousand bales that the navy had seized, it had yet to realize a cent. Legal talent was one thing; what was really needed was political power.

Meanwhile, the problem of trying to restrict trade along the rivers, only to be thwarted by people with permits issued by the Treasury

Department, was worse than ever. On June 14, George Bache and the *Lexington* seized three steamers engaged in trading with Confederate troops. The steamers would make handsome prizes, but the business of protecting the people with these permits infuriated Phelps. "Manifestly the safety of our light gunboats is greatly endangered by thus placing boats engaged in the cotton traffic at the disposition and control of the enemy."[2]

While Phelps was fighting both the Confederates and the Treasury Department, he received the shocking news in June of the death of his younger daughter, Lucy. Not yet two years old, the little girl had come down with the measles shortly after he left Washington the month before.

> There will be one void never to be filled in this world. I here realize to the full the loss of our Lucy. It was here that my thoughts of home ever so full of her and now I am conscious that the attraction she gave it has fled forever, & I fear no child of mine can ever fill the place she occupied. . . .The heart can never forget the little arms that have been stretched in mute plea to be taken; now I know what they mean who tell us that the vacant place of a lost child is never taken.[3]

Conflicting thoughts about his wife and surviving daughter, and of his future in the navy, once again tore at Phelps's conscience. In the meantime, plans for returning home were postponed because of Confederate activity in Arkansas.

> I had hoped to be with you and draw you to my heart. You would not have me neglect an urgent public duty any more than I would be likely to do it for personal pleasure. I cannot even now tell you when I will go to you, because it is a matter over which I have no control and about which no one can project. It is the enemy alone who interferes and no one can guess when he will let me up. I already feel the necessity there is for me to go home as respects yourself. What you cannot conceal is as patent as possible in every line you write. You

are not well and not happy. I shall make preparations for you having that in view and what I am to do heaven only knows. If not practicable otherwise you must come to Memphis to live and if this can be afforded in the double households to be kept up, I must apply for a leave of absence and when it has expired go to sea. Duty in Washington is out of the question while the place is so expensive. I had hoped that a reasonable arrangement like that in Cleveland would have answered well.

If matters continue on White River as they are I shall insist on some one being sent to relieve me for a time so I can go home. This is the best I can promise now.[4]

Activity on the White River flared up on the morning of June 22 when three hundred Confederates of the Tenth Missouri Cavalry crossed the Arkansas River in small boats and attacked the Union garrison at the mouth of the river. After the assault was beaten back, Brig. Gen. Napoleon Buford saw an opportunity to trap the Confederates. He went to Phelps at Helena, and they quickly embarked eight hundred troops on the tinclad *Hastings* and two ferryboats, and sailed for the White River cutoff.

Finding no sign of the enemy at the cutoff, Phelps headed up the Arkansas River ten miles. Too late to catch the butternuts, he balked at taking the steamers farther up the narrow river. He pointed out to Buford that the crowded ferries would be easy targets for Brig. Gen. John S. Marmaduke's Confederate troops, who were reported to be within ten miles of the river. Buford agreed, and the small force returned to the mouth of the White River.

Confederate activity in Arkansas in the summer of 1864 was increasingly worrisome for Phelps. Brig. Gen. Joseph O. Shelby was reported to have twenty-five hundred men, Marmaduke to have eight thousand, and General Sterling Price was thought to be moving on Little Rock with a force of eighteen thousand. Phelps realized that his tinclads would be hard pressed to stand up against strong batteries placed along the narrow rivers, so he went to Memphis and, on his own authority, borrowed the *Carondelet*.

Heading down the White River on board the tinclad *Hastings* on July 4,

> I was cogitating upon the day and how I should make a noise in the way of celebration, when the rebs saved me all trouble by opening a sharp fire of musketry upon us at about 20 yds. distance and then and there we opened a ball and fired a grand 4th Jubilee. I do not see how our people escaped unhurt as they did for many were exposed. A bullet lodged in my secretary, another in my bedstead and a third managed to make no less than 6 holes through a pair of pants.

Remembering the 64-pounder shot from the *Arkansas* that took the nap of his coat two years before, Phelps added: "The rebs have a special spite against my clothes."[5]

In mid-July, Phelps received a letter from his friend Capt. Allan McLane of the Pacific Mail Steamship Company. McLane offered the prospect of commanding one of the company's steamers making the Panama–San Francisco run, at five thousand dollars a year, in gold. Phelps felt that living in San Francisco would be delightful; however, the voyage to Panama and back averaged thirty-four days, and there would be only a six-day layover between trips. Since he could expect to be home only about three months out of the year, he left the decision to Lizzie. She was not enthusiastic, so Phelps replied that the prospect of long family separations prevented him from accepting.

Phelps could only shake his head when he received the news about what happened off Cherbourg, France.

> Do you see that the *Kearsarge* (old Winslow who was relieved from here in disgrace on account of the condition of his vessel) has become a great man by the capture of the *Alabama*. The fight appears to have been a lame affair, the vessels not doing much on either side. The *Kearsarge* was not hurt much and although the *Alabama* sunk, it appears to have been a lucky & accidental shot that did it. Hardly a week passes but some vessel in this squadron goes through with more exposure to shot in five minutes than the *Kearsarge* did in more than an hour.[6]

A lithograph of Seth Phelps taken from an 1873 photograph. (U.S. Naval Historical Center)

Phelps's reaction to Winslow's fame paled in comparison, however, with his reaction to what resulted from the fight between the USS *Sassacus* and the Confederate ironclad ram *Albemarle* on the North Carolina coast. Lt. Francis A. Roe, captain of the *Sassacus*, had courageously closed with the *Albemarle* and rammed her, causing considerable damage but not sinking her. As a reward for his gallantry, Roe was advanced five numbers on the Register, which placed him above Phelps. Phelps exploded. He wrote to Secretary Welles and reminded him of his commitment to seniority, then added:

> I feel sad and embittered as well as humiliated at the idea that more than three years of active service, in which I have given all my energies and freely risked my life, count for nothing. It is so many years of labor, trouble, exposure to battle, risk of the guerrilla's assassin bullet, and the evil influence of a destructive climate, absolutely thrown away except in the consciousness of having done my duty. I was perfectly satisfied so long as no promotions were made in my grade, and was glad to see that some of those advanced in the higher grades were receiving merited rewards. I was content with promotion by seniority and the professional repute gained and more than once had occasion to check measures being taken by friends with a view to procure my promotion. I now see one of my class placed above me. I must conclude that service on the coast is most highly esteemed.
>
> I have served here to see all my successive Commanders in Chief promoted to the highest grades, viz. Com Rodgers, & Admirals Foote, Davis & Porter. With two of these I served as Flag Captain and as well doing the duty of Fleet captain, both of whom confided largely in me. I can point with pride to the reports and opinions of all these high officers. Bearing in mind the rules of the Naval services of the world, it may be presumed that such an instance of service under such circumstances is without parallel in any Navy."[7]

Phelps was also upset when he learned that Congress had passed a law stating that captures on inland waterways would not be regarded as maritime prizes.

> This is the result of the combined efforts of the War Department, Mr. [Salmon P.] Chase and his friends the cotton speculators. It is another proof that our service is considered as second-

ary, or perhaps more justly that Congress don't care a fig what becomes of us if the votes are only secured. Upon the whole, I am much inclined to say to Capt. McLane, secure me a command and I will resign in minutes. The idea of service on to the end of this interminable war is fast going from me . . . leaving me to be used as a tool by which public men may help themselves to climb. My belief in our country is shaken, or rather in the patriotism of our Gov't; as it is. The mass who serve as food for slaughter in the war which rabid & designing politicians are & have been rendering interminable for their own ends, are patriotic; they and they alone.[8]

The approaching presidential election held little promise that anything would change.

Let us hope for the best to our poor country. One believes little in the pretense of either party struggling for power, they are all alike—corrupt. Yet one cannot well see how Mr. Lincoln can make peace being commited as he is to a policy that creates a barrier that keeps him from breaking through. I hope for, I had near said "pray for," the solution that makes our country what it once was. Two things I certainly *pray for,* that Charleston may be destroyed and that a universal draft may force every able bodied man in the North into the field. The lesson would not be lost or thrown away.

With all his bitterness, however, Phelps still was not ready to give up his career. In early August he requested to be detached from the squadron and, after a leave, to be assigned to the coast blockade, where he might command a ship and distinguish himself.

A month passed, and Phelps did not receive an answer to his request; "the direct effect will be to keep me here."[9] On September 22, Secretary of the Navy Gideon Welles ordered Porter to assume command of the North Atlantic Blockading Squadron in place of David G. Farragut, who was in poor health. Command of the Mississippi Squadron would go to Samuel Phillips Lee, whom Phelps thought little of. In addition, Phelps was not among those officers

Porter chose to take with him. Being left out of a chance for command of a ship in taking Fort Fisher, the last great Confederate coastal stronghold, was the final straw.

Two years previously Phelps was at the pinnacle of success. For months, while Foote was ill and Davis was learning the rivers, he was, in all but name, commander of the Western Flotilla. Now he felt his career was over.

Phelps made his decision after receiving another letter from Allan McLane, this time offering him the position of agent at the company's coaling station at Acapulco, Mexico. After twenty-three years of service, Lt. Comdr. Seth Ledyard Phelps submitted his resignation and was released from the navy on October 27, 1864.

ↄ

Steamships, Canals,
& Diplomacy

P HELPS SPENT only a short time with his family before traveling to
Acapulco, where he found himself in the middle of more fighting. Mexican partisans, led by Benito Juárez, were waging a guerrilla
war against the French occupation, and there were freqent skirmishes in and around the town.

Indeed, the Juaristas had become so emboldened that at Phelps's
first contact with them, they demanded duties from the company's
concession. The French had been collecting the duties, but it was an
open secret that they were about to leave. To make matters worse, it
was rumored that after the French left, the Juaristas would consider
any remaining foreigners traitors, and they would be shot.

Phelps quickly wrote to his company, asking that they request
a U.S. Navy warship to look after the port. In the meantime, most
foreigners, along with many natives, fled the town. "I left Acapulco
in trouble," Phelps wrote, "and very likely to be sacked, but that will
be all over before Lizzie can get out to join me."[1] Phelps traveled to

Mexico City, making his way through "contending parties," until things settled down.

The withdrawal of the French from Acapulco allowed Phelps to negotiate a settlement with the Juaristas, and send for Lizzie and Sally. Life in the little seaside town was, for a short time, idyllic. Seth and Lizzie enjoyed the wonderful climate and beautiful beaches while watching their daughter learn her third language.

Phelps was not content to run a small outpost, however. After the Civil War, the Pacific Mail Steamship Company began to expand greatly. In 1865 it purchased Commodore Vanderbilt's New York–Aspinwall line, giving it a monopoly on the Panama route to the West Coast. In addition, steamship service to the Far East meant that more men and ships were needed.

The company directors knew that completion of the transcontinental railroad in 1869 would seriously cut into their traffic, so diversification became paramount. Service to Japan and China was to become the backbone of the company. A mail contract was obtained in 1865, and construction of steamers was begun in order to commence operations on January 1, 1867. Phelps was promoted and, in the early 1870s, traveled to the Far East on a number of occasions to attend to the myriad details of the semimonthly service.

Phelps eventually was promoted to vice president, but his success was incomplete. The voyages to the Far East, South America, and Europe on company business meant that Lizzie and Sally saw as much of him as if he were still in the navy.

A career in politics was probably the last thing Phelps envisioned for himself, but it offered a solution and a new challenge. He had never taken much interest in politics except when it could advance his career, but in 1874 an opportunity arose when Congress overhauled the District of Columbia's government. Lizzie was particularly enthusiastic, and called on her many influential friends in Washington. They submitted Phelps's name to President Grant, who was to appoint a three-member Board of Commissioners to replace the District's government.

Phelps's father had been active in Republican politics in Ohio, so, through Lizzie's prodding and his acquaintance with Grant, Phelps received the appointment.

The new Board of Commissioners was created to stem the abuses and inefficiency that had plagued past administrations. Especially nettlesome was the District's Board of Public Works. Under the direction of Alexander Shepard, sewers and water mains were laid, streets were paved, and parks were planted. Modern Washington, D.C., was created, but at three times the cost that had been promised. Also troubling to Congress was "Boss" Shepard's patronage system. Abetted by black suffrage, Shepard controlled local elections with the promise of jobs and contracts. Congress held three investigations in three years and finally decided to abolish the old system.

The mid-1870s was a propitious time for Phelps to be working in Washington. His experience along the Central American coast drew him into the government's growing interest in constructing a canal to join the oceans.

In 1872 President Grant appointed an Interoceanic Canal Commission to study the feasibility of a canal. By February 1876 the commission recommended, instead of a Panama canal, a canal route across Nicaragua. In 1879 Phelps joined with Rear Adm. Daniel Ammen, Maj. Gen. George McClellan, and financier Levi Morton to found the Provisional Interoceanic Canal Society. With a concession from Nicaragua and support from Grant, Ammen and Phelps reorganized the society into the Maritime Canal Company of Nicaragua.

Their plans called for a canal just over fifty miles long that would follow the San Juan River along the southeastern edge of Nicaragua, cross Lake Nicaragua, and cut through a steep but narrow range of mountains along the Pacific coast, using about a dozen locks. Phelps and Ammen estimated the cost of the canal at ninety-three million dollars.

The Nicaragua canal was in direct competition with two rival groups. After his success building the Suez Canal, Ferdinand de Lesseps had turned his attention to building a canal across the Isthmus of Panama. He estimated that his sea-level canal would cost three hundred million dollars. A third group, led by James B. Eads, proposed to construct a ship–railway across the Isthmus of Tehuantepec in southern Mexico. Eads's design called for a multitrack railway using cradles to carry fully loaded ships from the Gulf of Mexico to the Pacific.

De Lesseps had attracted a hundred thousand shareholders, and began work on his Panama canal in February 1881. Meanwhile, Phelps and Ammen locked horns with Eads in an effort to get American investors, and especially Congress, to underwrite their projects. Both groups asked Congress to guarantee their profits during the first years of operation. Phelps and Ammen asked for a guarantee of 3 percent for twenty years on a hundred-million-dollar capitalization; Eads asked for 6 percent for fifteen years on fifty million dollars.

In January 1881, a special House committee held hearings on the two proposals. The lobbying was intense. Both groups attacked De Lesseps but went to greater lengths to discredit one another. Phelps testified that carrying ships overland was sheer lunacy. He claimed the trip would take a week, and a good gust of wind could blow the whole concern over on its side. Eads responded that not one reputable engineer had come forward to dispute his plan.

The committee favored Eads's proposal, but Ammen and Phelps's supporters blocked any congressional action and the matter died for the time being. Neither side could muster the necessary votes.

By late 1882, the State Department, with an eye to the strategic implications of a Nicaraguan canal, began to maneuver for control of the project. Until a policy was in place, however, Secretary of State Frederick T. Frelinghuysen utilized the Maritime Canal Company's concession to forestall any European interest.

Hoping to salvage something of his company, Phelps agreed to help the State Department negotiate with the Nicaraguan government. Frelinghuysen sent him on an informal mission to establish coaling stations on Lake Nicaragua, in the middle of the proposed canal route. While he was in Managua, rumors about Phelps's mission culminated in a violently anti-American article in a nationalist newspaper. Phelps responded with an article denying any designs on Nicaraguan sovereignty by the United States.

In 1883, with his canal project floundering, Phelps received an offer from U.S. President Chester Arthur to be minister to Peru. The foreign service was at that time, according to John Hay, "like the Catholic Church, calculated only for celibates,"[2] and ministers had to be independently wealthy or go into debt to take the job. Service to his country had dominated Phelps's life, and this would be no different.

Phelps arrived in Lima during the summer of 1883. The chief problems facing him were the culmination of the War of the Pacific and a local civil war. The War of the Pacific, involving Peru, Chile, and Bolivia, had been going on since 1879 and was by now largely settled. Chile emerged as the strongest of the three and was in the process of dictating terms. The United States had injected itself into the conflict by attempting to mediate an end to the war, but to no avail. The war deprived Bolivia of its outlet to the sea and Peru of one of its richest provinces. All three countries resented American interference and were suspicious of territorial ambitions. Diplomatic damage control became Phelps's primary mission.

In early June 1885, Phelps traveled into the Andes on a hunting trip and apparently contracted Oroyo fever. The disease became pernicious in the following weeks, but Phelps refused to let it affect his work. At 11:45 A.M. on June 24, Phelps was at his desk in Lima when he suddenly collapsed and died. Ceremonies were held at the legation, followed by a procession of members of Peru's cabinet and members of the diplomatic corps to the vault where his body was interred, awaiting transportation to the United States. Seth Phelps was accompanied home by a U.S. Navy escort aboard the Pacific Mail steamer *City of Iowa*.

Phelps is buried at Oak Hill Cemetery in Washington, D.C. His epitaph simply states that he served in the Mexican and Civil wars, as a commissioner of the District of Columbia, and as minister to Peru. That simple statement underscores a larger legacy, however. In many respects the Western campaigns determined the outcome of the American Civil War. Union victory in the West depended on control of the rivers, and as the "pioneer" in Mississippi and Alabama, and the "active spirit" of Island No. 10, Fort Pillow, and Memphis, Seth Phelps influenced that victory.

Seth Ledyard Phelps's twenty-three-year career in the U.S. Navy was short by the standards of the day, and he quickly faded into historical obscurity. After the turn of the century and through World War II, the navy commissioned hundreds of destroyers and destroyer escorts, and named many after naval heros of the Civil War.[3] Phelps was not included. He never had a ship named after him, but those who sought his advice and looked to him for leadership, did.

e⁄ɔ

Epilogue

LIZZIE MAYNADIER PHELPS. Lizzie lived in Washington, D.C., until her death on May 27, 1897.

SALLY PHELPS BROWN. Sally married Sevellon Alden Brown on February 5, 1880, in Washington, D.C. She had five children: Sevellon, Anne, Phelps, Gertrude, and Maynadier. Sally died on January 25, 1916, in Washington, D.C.

TIMOTHY BENHAM. Benham was promoted to commander on February 5, 1848. He was placed on the Reserve List on September 14, 1855.

USS *BENTON*. The *Benton* was sold at auction at Mound City, Illinois, on November 29, 1865, for three thousand dollars. Her iron plating was sold separately.

HEZEKIAH (HAL) G. D. BROWN. During the Civil War, Brown organized an artillery company known as the Seven Stars Artillery. Later he was captain of the local Copiah County defense unit. The Foster Creek Rangers was a twenty-seven-man cavalry company.

Isaac N. Brown. With the remnants of the *Arkansas*'s crew, Brown performed shore duty at Port Hudson and later along the Yazoo River, where his torpedoes sank the ironclads *Cairo* and *Baron de Kalb*. After the fall of Vicksburg, Brown was ordered to Charleston, South Carolina, to command the Confederate ironclad *Charleston*. He was paroled on May 22, 1865, and returned to his Mississippi plantation without a dollar. He worked his land for twenty years before moving to Corsicana, Texas.

Henry L. Chipman. Chipman resigned from the navy on September 19, 1846, one day after being arrested for drunkenness and disobedience.

Charles H. Davis. Davis was promoted to rear admiral and commanded the Brazilian Squadron from 1867 to 1869. In 1870 he was named superintendent of the Naval Observatory, where he remained until his death on February 19, 1877.

Benjamin Dove. In November 1863, Dove was ordered to the North Atlantic Blockading Squadron. He died at Key West on December 19, 1868.

James B. Eads. One of America's foremost engineers of the nineteenth century, Eads's greatest feat was his construction of jetties at the mouth of the Mississippi River. This allowed deep-draft vessels access to the heart of the United States. Eads died at Nassau on March 16, 1887.

Alfred W. Ellet. Ellet resigned from the army on December 31, 1864. He worked as a civil engineer and railroad developer. He died on January 9, 1895.

James Melville Gilliss. After being placed on the Reserved List, Gilliss worked for the Smithsonian Institution until the outbreak of the Civil War. After Maury fled south, he was appointed to head the Naval Observatory. Gilliss was promoted to captain and died in Washington, D.C., on February 9, 1865.

AUGUSTUS KILTY. Kilty lost his left arm as a result of the explosion on the *Mound City*. He recovered and was assigned to ordnance duty at Baltimore, followed by command of the frigate *Roanoke* with the North Atlantic Blockading Squadron. He was promoted to rear admiral on July 13, 1870, and died November 10, 1879.

MATTHEW F. MAURY. After his attempts at designing torpedoes, Maury was sent to Great Britain by the Confederacy. After the war he served for a time with Emperor Maximilian in Mexico. In 1868 Maury was offered a professorship of physics at Virginia Military Institute in Lexington, Virginia, where he died on February 1, 1873.

ARCHIBALD McRAE. McRae committed suicide on board the Coast Survey schooner *Ewing* at San Francisco on November 17, 1855.

DAVID DIXON PORTER. After the Civil War, Porter was appointed superintendent of the Naval Academy, which he enlarged and improved. In 1870, he was promoted admiral of the navy after Farragut's death. He wrote numerous books and continued to work for the navy after his retirement, until 1890. Porter died on February 13, 1891, in Washington, D.C.

WILLIAM PORTER. Porter was promoted to commodore in July 1862. In September 1862, he was ordered to New York to answer charges made by Charles Davis and to explain to Welles a letter he wrote attacking the Navy Department. Porter saw no further action and died on May 1, 1864.

THOMAS O. SELFRIDGE, JR. Selfridge led expeditions to survey the Isthmus of Panama in the 1870s and sided with De Lesseps against Phelps's company. He was commander in chief of the European Squadron from 1895 to 1898. Selfridge retired on February 6, 1898, and died on February 4, 1924.

JAMES W. SHIRK. Shirk commanded the 7th Division on the Mississippi as well as the gunboat *Tuscumbia* during the assault on Vicksburg. After the war, he commanded the steam frigate *Franklin* with the European Squadron and performed special duty with the Navy Department in Washington, where he died on February 10, 1873.

CHARLES F. SMITH. Smith fell and skinned his shin while boarding a yawl at Savannah. He died of infection on April 25, 1862.

RODGER N. STEMBEL. Stembel recovered from his wound and commanded the steam sloop *Canandaigua* with the European Squadron from 1865 to 1867. He was given command of the Pacific Fleet in 1872 and promoted to rear admiral in 1874. Stembel died in New York City on November 20, 1900.

EGBERT THOMPSON. After the Civil War, Thompson commanded the steam sloop *Dacotah* with the South Pacific Squadron from 1866 to 1867. He was promoted to captain on July 26, 1867.

HENRY WALKE. Walke was promoted to commodore in 1866 and commanded the naval station at Mound City, Illinois, until 1870. He was promoted to rear admiral and retired in 1871, but continued to serve on the Lighthouse Board until 1873. An accomplished artist, Walke died on March 9, 1896, at Brooklyn, New York.

LEWIS WALLACE. Wallace was president of the court that tried Henry Wirz, the commandant of Andersonville. He was also a member of the commission that tried the Lincoln conspirators. After practicing law, Wallace was appointed governor of New Mexico Territory in 1878, and minister to Turkey in 1881. Most notably known as the author of *Ben Hur*, Wallace died at Crawfordsville, Indiana, on February 15, 1905.

GIDEON WELLES. Welles continued as secretary of the navy until 1869, when he retired. He died in Hartford, Connecticut, on February 11, 1878.

∞

Prize Money Awards

THE PRIZE LAW of the U.S. Navy was adapted from that of the British navy. Originally all prizes were divided equally between the captors and the government. In 1798, Congress amended the law so that any capture of a vessel of equal or greater strength belonged wholly to the capturing crew. The proceeds were divided into twenty equal shares. The captain received three shares, two were split between the lieutenants and masters, two between the Marine and warrant officers, three between the midshipmen and chief petty officers, three among the lesser petty officers, and seven among the ordinary seamen and marines.[1]

Pay in the navy was in many respects at not much more than a subsistence level. For example, in 1861, Phelps's pay as a lieutenant commanding was $2,250; with his promotion, it had risen to $2,343 by 1864. A rich prize could add hundreds, if not thousands, to a captain's purse. During the Civil War, the capture of heavily loaded blockade runners was extremely lucrative. For example, the capture of the

Lady Sterling netted $494,909.29, shared by her two captors, and $510,914.07 was awarded for the capture of the steamer *Memphis*.

Determining the amount of prize money to be awarded depended on many factors, such as the courts involved, appraisals, and just plain luck. Phelps's richest prize, the *Fair Play*, was valued by Davis at between $300,000 and $500,000, but the district court at Springfield set the prize value at $35,546.62.

Prize money awarded for gallantry in action was another source of income that was very subjective. It depended largely on the estimated monetary loss suffered by the enemy. For example, Lieutenant William Cushing and his small band were awarded a total of $282,857 for their daring raid and sinking of the Confederate ram *Albemarle*. Cushing received a total of $46,056.27, and each crewman, $4,019.40. Conversely, Lieutenant Worden and the crew of the *Monitor* did not receive a cent for their engagement with the *Virginia*.

For her part in the capture of Memphis, the crew of the *Benton* was awarded $18,527.42. The money was divided as follows:

Charles H. Davis	$3,715.52
Seth Phelps	$1,465.34
Pilots	$397.44
Henry Maynadier	$248.40
Gunners	$56.77
Boatswains	$56.77
Cooks	$54.50
Seamen	$40.89

The cotton recovered during the Red River expedition was fought over for years. The *Eastport* was initially awarded $11,618.39 out of the squadron's share of $225,751.08. Over the years the amount was revised upward at least four times. Phelps's first check, issued on November 14, 1865, was for $496.51. Subsequent checks were issued for $10.56, $42.43, $168.06, and $142.85.[2]

Squadron commanders were by far the biggest winners, for they shared in the success of all their ships. Admiral S. P. Lee was the winner, with $109,689.69, followed by David Porter with $91,528.98, including $12,372.77 from his share of Red River cotton.

NOTES

1. Robert W. Daly, "Pay and Prize Money in the Old Navy, 1776–1899," *U.S. Naval Institute Proceedings* 74 (Aug. 1948): 967–70.

2. RG 217—Fourth Auditor, NA.

∾

Phelps's Gunboat Plans

Louisville, KY July 12, 1861

Commander John Rodgers, US Navy
Cincinnati, Ohio

Sir:

I enclose a tracing of a plan for a river war steamer of iron and shot proof. Will you submit it for consideration by those who are to adopt plans for gun-boats for service on the western rivers?

The boat is 175' long, 40' beam, draught 6½ feet, two propellers 8 feet diameter, with two engines, geared, and each acting independently upon one shaft. The engines and boilers to be in the stern of the boat, the casemate being placed sufficiently forward to balance the weight. The center of displacement in the model, submitted herewith, is one foot forward of the center section.

The casemate is formed of sides of 4½ inch iron plates, at an angle of 45°, springing from the water line, and backed by wood or iron frames, both of which are sketched in cross sections. The

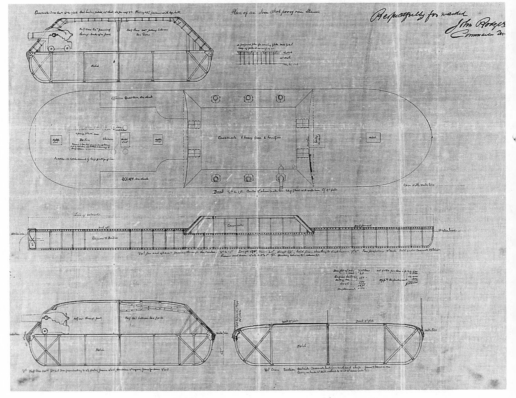

Phelps's gunboat design. (National Archives)

backing of 12 inch oak would be the simplest if not the best method. The timbers on end and perfectly in contact at the sides, extend the whole height of the sideplates and their ends rest upon the ends of the timber supporting the roof of 2 inch plates and which is also of oak 8" by 12". Iron knees—4" x 2" secure each side timber to the corresponding roof timber and is bolted through to the side and top plating. Athwartships of the casemate these knees bolt across the roof timber. Iron bars—2" x 1"—run horizontally around the inside of the side timbers, and underneath, on the roof timbers, through which the bolts, securing the plates to the timber, pass; thus, with the external plates and the internal bars, the timber is bound in one solid mass one foot thick at the sides and eight inches under roof. Knees of iron will secure the sides at the angles of the casemate. The foot of the side or "glacis timbers," besides resting upon the deck at a sharp angle is further supported by a triangular piece on deck bolted both ways. The gun deck (within casemate) is flat, on a level with the water line, of 2 inch plank over $\frac{1}{4}$ inch iron plates to which the T beams are to be riveted. Posts as shown in the tracings, form further supports to the inclined sides. Iron stanchions 3" square, at 5' intervals, resting over beams similarly supported below, sustain the center of the casemate roof and have iron knees fastened to them and to the oak above.

Outside the casemate the deck springs also from the water's edge and rises in an arch two feet high in the center and is of 2" plate, to be secured directly to the beams. It is supposed that tap bolts may be used effectively in securing plating wherever designed to resist shot. In the sides of the casemate the bolts, passing through the iron bars & oak, might penetrate the $4\frac{1}{2}$" iron $2\frac{1}{2}$" and leave the exterior surface without a bolt hole to the depth of 2". Plates extending from 2'6" below the water line to the roof of the casemate and $2'7\frac{1}{2}$" wide could be forged, and 4 such would fill the space from edge to edge of two adjoining ports. Three rows of bolts to each plate would be sufficient. If the thread of large sized bolts is sufficiently strong certainly the chance of bolts being driven through and of rivet heads doing the execution of bullets is greatly reduced. I have sketched a plan for placing the plates with angular edges.

The frames and beams are estimated for the proportions T— 4"x $\frac{3}{4}$"x 5"x 1"—4"x $\frac{3}{4}$" and 5"x 1"—the weight of which will admit of modifications of forms, and at 12 inches apart center to center. The cross of the beams may be bolted with tap bolts to the deck plating leaving its surface uncut to the depth of $\frac{1}{2}$" or 1". No shot can strike it except at a very obtuse angle and would be easily turned from line of flight.

Strong iron beams run fore and aft amidships on underside of deck beams and upper side of bottom frames, which rest in forks of stanchions 3" square, at 5' intervals, being double forked at right angles so as to receive also the beams and frames to which they are bolted, the ends shouldering upon the cross of the T. In the wake of the boilers the midship stanchions and fore & aft pieces will be impossible; rows upon either side as close as possible must be substituted. As the frames and beams outside the casemate section form one piece, the boilers must be placed before the stern frames are in position, or other provision made. For a width say of 8' or 9' and 18' or 20' in length immediately over the boiler place, an opening can be made, the coaming being made very heavy and well secured & shored up. Fore and aft bars of iron—3" x 5", of the length of the hatch, secured at either end by heavy bolts and supported by cross bars at 2' intervals, also bolted to coamings under side, the bars to be at 2½" apart, would at once resist shot, or prevent their falling below and give light and ventilation. If well secured the strength of the vessel would not be materially effected. Each hatchway should have heavy iron gratings. The bends of the boat are cased with 6" plates at water line, decreasing to the thickness of sheathing at 2½' below this line. Systems of stanchions and diagonal ties and braces are shown in the tracings, and will be necessary to give strength to bear the weight of iron and resist the shock of shot. These are 3" x 3" & 3" x 2".

The ends of the beams within the casemate, where they are at right angles with the frames, can be secured by two iron plates each of 2" thickness of the form in the tracings, and, shouldering upon the cross of the T frames and beams, be bolted firmly to them and embrace the end of the diagonal ties at that angle. The side ports admit of 15° and 60° lateral range. The end ones give 30° elevation. If greater elevation is required, triangles of 10° angle can be kept in readiness rather than weaken the sides to a greater extent. The portholes are left open for 5° elevation and 20° lateral range, the remainder being closed by oval ports of 4½" plates in two vertical sections turning on hinges sunk in the lower side of the plates so as to leave an unbroken joint and 2" of iron covering the hinges. The ports when closed and secured will present an arch to resist compression or being driven in, while flat ones would depend upon the fastenings for stability. A lighter plate— 2½"—to resist shell and grape shot can be hinged underneath the port so as to be forced out by the gun, when being run out, to a horizontal position and can close by action of a spring when the gun comes in, or lanyards could be used. There must be a hole through it to receive the rammer handle.

The casemate should have small round iron ventilators screwed to the roof plating and be made of tough, heavy plates. The same kind of ventilations will be required over the furnaces and engine room.

A bulwark of light iron—$\frac{1}{4}$ inch—boiler iron, passes all around the vessel, except where the glacis is, and quarters for officers with movable bulkheads are to be placed either side abaft the casemate, while the galley, water closets, etc. can be placed forward. The roofs of all being made permanent as they will not interfere in firing aft or forward. The bulwarks, both forward and abaft, around the bow & stern, to be made to let down. The casemate will furnish ample berth room for the crew, and, with awnings fore and aft, a no more comfortable vessel of the size is built for the service anywhere.

The deck immediately over the propeller should be raised one foot to admit of the free passage of the flanges. The casing on the side of the propeller may reach to the water, but abaft must be left open.

Vessel 175' long; 40' beam; 6½' draft; Disp±1000 tons
Estimated weights—

Glacis—sides—80 tons.   Oak backing—sides—27 tons
   "   ends—48   "   top—12   "
   "   roof—38   "   Knees, bars, posts etc.—10.5 "
                                      bolts — 2   "
_____
              166 tons +   51.5 tons   = 217.5 tons
Deck in casemate—iron 10 tons; plank 4 tons   =   14.0 tons
Outside of casemate—
           forward @ 75934 lbs; aft 105654 lbs. = 162.0 tons
Frames & Beam   = 216.5 tons
Sheathing—
       $\frac{5}{8}$ inch outside = 81 tons
       $\frac{1}{4}$ inch inside = 29 tons   = 110.0 tons
Casing of bends   =   46.0 tons
Bulwarks, bolts & not enumerated   =   30.0 tons
Ties, stanchions etc.   =   25.0 tons
                                              _____
                                              821.0 tons

Engines, boilers, implements, water in boilers,
shaft & propellers   =   100.0 tons

Battery, etc.   =   <u>50.0 tons</u>

     Total without coal   971.0 tons

     Displacement about   1100.0 tons

Cost approximately—

     821 tons iron less 46 tons wood

     <u>-46</u>

     775 tons iron at 180 per ton is $139,500

         Engines, boilers & machinery   12,000

         Wood & carpenter work   <u>2,000</u>

                             $153,500

         Respectfully,

         S.L. Phelps

         Lt. U.S.N.[1]

NOTE

1. RG 92—U.S. Quartermaster Corps, Gunboat File, NA.

သ

Notes

CHAPTER ONE: DESTROYING A FLEET

1. Ivan Musicant, "The Fires of Norfolk," *American Heritage* 41 (Mar. 1990): 63.

2. Seth Phelps to Elisha Whittlesey, Feb. 17, 1858, Elisha Whittlesey Collection, Western Reserve Historical Society, Cleveland, Ohio (hereafter cited as EWC).

3. Rebecca Paulding Davis, *The Life of Hiram Paulding, Rear-Admiral, USN* (New York: Baker & Taylor, 1910), 241.

4. Musicant, "Fires of Norfolk," 59.

5. For a description of naval ordnance see Spencer Tucker, *Arming the Fleet: U.S. Navy Ordnance in the Muzzle-Loading Era* (Annapolis: Naval Institute Press, 1989).

6. Seth Phelps to his father, Alfred Phelps, May 4, 1864, Kate Fowle Collection, Washington, D.C. (hereafter cited as KFC).

7. *Official Records of the Union and Confederate Navies in the War of the Rebellion*, 30 vols. (Washington, D.C.: GPO, 1895–1929), ser. 1, vol. 4:295 (hereafter cited as *ORN*).

8. *New York Times*, Apr. 26, 1861.

CHAPTER TWO: "REEFERS"

1. Maynadier Brown, "Out of a Sea Chest" (unpublished manuscript, 1968). This chapter is based on Brown's account of Phelps's early career and, unless otherwise

noted, is quoted from it. A grandson of Seth Phelps, Maynadier Brown drew on letters in the Kate Fowle Collection and recollections of his mother and grandmother.

2. Phelps to A. G. Riddle, Apr. 30, 1842, Huntington Library, San Marino, California.

3. Ibid.

4. Ibid.

5. Frederick J. Bell, *Room to Swing a Cat: Being Some Tales of the Old Navy* (New York: Longmans Greenard, 1938), 129.

6. Charles O. Paullin, *Paullin's History of Naval Administration, 1775–1911* (Annapolis: Naval Institute Press, 1968), 198.

7. Capt. Charles Morgan to Secretary of the Navy Abel P. Upshur, Oct. 29, 1842, Record Group 45, National Archives (hereafter cited as NA).

8. William H. Parker, *Recollections of a Naval Officer 1841–1865* (New York: Charles Scribners' Sons, 1883), 14.

9. Morgan to Upshur, Oct. 30, 1842, RG 45, NA.

10. Phelps to Whittlesey, June 11, 1843, EWC.

11. Ibid.

12. Parker, *Recollections of a Naval Officer*, 21.

13. Ibid., 24.

14. Phelps to Whittlesey, Jan. 21, 1844, EWC.

15. Log of the USS *Jamestown*, July 29, 1845, NA.

16. Bell, *Room to Swing a Cat*, 133–36.

17. For an account of the resettlement of American slaves to Africa, see James Wesley Smith, *Sojourners in Search of Freedom: The Settlement of Liberia by Black Americans* (Lanham, Md.: University Press of America, 1987). Major Hicks was probably N. W. Hicks, a former slave and favorite servant of Chauncy Whittlesey, who practiced law in New Orleans for a number of years. Upon returning home to Connecticut, Whittlesey gave Hicks his freedom, whereupon Hicks settled in Philadelphia before emigrating to Liberia. Like many colonists, Hicks gave himself a title; and although an influence in the colony, he was known more for being the local hotel keeper.

CHAPTER THREE: *BONITA*

1. Phelps to his father, June 15, 1846, KFC.

2. Records of the District Courts of the United States (South Carolina), RG 21, NA.

3. Phelps to his mother, May 30, 1846, KFC.

4. Phelps to his father, June 15, 1846, KFC.

5. Ibid.

6. Parker, *Recollections of a Naval Officer*, 65.

7. Phelps to his mother, Aug. 9, 1846, KFC.

8. Ibid.

9. Phelps to his father, Oct. 6, 1846, KFC.

10. K. Jack Bauer, *The Mexican War 1846–1848* (New York: Macmillan, 1974), 115; Parker, *Recollections of a Naval Officer*, 78.

11. Phelps to his mother, Oct. 5, 1846, KFC.

12. Lt. Timothy Benham to Commodore David Conner, Oct. 16, 1846, RG 45, NA.

13. Phelps to his father, Oct. 5, 1846, KFC.

14. K. Jack Bauer, *Surfboats and Horse Marines: U.S. Naval Operations in the Mexican War* (Annapolis: Naval Institute Press, 1969), 46.

15. Ibid., 50–55.

16. Phelps to his father, Dec. 25, 1846, KFC.

17. Bauer, *Surfboats and Horse Marines,* 79.

18. Ibid., 80.

19. Ibid., 90.

20. Parker, *Recollections of a Naval Officer,* 104.

21. Bauer, *Surfboats and Horse Marines,* 114–20.

CHAPTER FOUR: BETWEEN WARS

1. Charles Todorich, *The Spirited Years: A History of the Antebellum Naval Academy* (Annapolis: Naval Institute Press, 1984), 55.

2. Parker, *Recollections of a Naval Officer,* 118–19.

3. Todorich, *Spirited Years,* 48.

4. Ibid., 55.

5. Ibid., 58.

6. James Gillis to Matthew Maury, Sept. 28, 1850, RG 78, NA.

7. Phelps to Whittlesey, Sept. 24, 1850, EWC.

8. Ibid., Sept. 25, 1850.

9. Ibid., Sept. 24, 1850.

10. Ibid., Jan. 24, 1851.

11. Ibid., Mar. 21, 1851.

12. Ibid., July 24, 1851.

13. Ibid., Jan. 24, 1852.

14. Ibid., May 23, 1853.

15. Phelps to his father, Oct. 2, 1853, KFC.

16. James Russell Soley, *Admiral Porter* (New York: D. Appleton, 1903), 87–88.

17. Paullin, *History of Naval Administration,* 238–43. For a different perspective on the retirement board, see Frances Leigh Williams, *Matthew Fontaine Maury: Scientist of the Sea* (New Brunswick, N.J.: Rutgers University Press, 1963), 269–308.

18. Phelps to his father, Sept. 14, 1855, KFC.

19. Ibid., Mar. 9, 1856.

20. Phelps to Lizzie, May 5, 1856.

21. Ibid., May 21, 1856.

22. Ibid., May 7, 1856.

23. Ibid., May 8, 1856.

24. Ibid., May 21, 1856.

25. Ibid., May 8, 1856.

26. James M. McPherson, *Battle Cry of Freedom* (New York: Ballantine Books, 1988), 110–16.

27. Phelps to Whittlesey, May 16, 1856, EWC.

28. Ibid., June 18, 1856.

29. Ibid., Oct. 2, 1856.

30. Ibid., Mar. 6, 1857.

31. Ibid., Mar. 22, 1857.

32. For a complete account of the transatlantic cable, see Henry M. Field, *The Story of the Atlantic Telegraph* (New York: Arno Press, 1972).

33. Phelps to Whittlesey, June 1, 1857, EWC.

34. Ibid., Aug. 26, 1857.

35. Phelps to Lizzie, Aug. 8, 1857, KFC.

36. Phelps to Whittlesey, Dec. 2, 1857, EWC. *The Times* (London) reported in a series of articles on efforts to lay the transatlantic cable in 1857. In its July 24, 1857, edition, it was reported that, after the wire was completed, it was discovered that the twist of the wire manufactured by Newall was opposite that manufactured by Glass & Elliot. Joined in the middle of the Atlantic, they would form a right-hand and left-hand tension that would make the splice dubious at best.

37. Phelps to Lizzie, Aug. 13, 1851, KFC.

38. Phelps to Lizzie, Aug. 20, 1857, KFC.

39. Ibid., Sept. 4, 1857.

40. Ibid., Nov. 2, 1857.

41. Phelps to Whittlesey, Dec. 2, 1857, EWC.

42. *New York Times,* Jan. 14, 1858.

43. Phelps to Whittlesey, Jan. 2, 1858, EWC.

44. Ibid., Feb. 17, 1858.

45. Phelps to Lizzie, Dec. 20, 1857, KFC.

46. Report of the secretary of the navy in answer to a resolution of the U.S. Senate, Senate Executive Documents, 35th Cong., 1st sess., vol. 2, no. 48 (1857–58).

47. Lizzie to Whittlesey, Apr. 18, 1858, KFC.

48. Phelps to Whittlesey, Apr. 28, 1858, EWC.

49. *Congressional Globe,* Mar. 3, 1858, 953.

50. Ibid.

51. Phelps to Whittlesey, May 15, 1858, EWC.

52. Ibid., Dec. 2, 1858.

53. Ibid., Mar. 17, 1859.

54. Phelps to Lizzie, Mar. 14, 1859, KFC.

55. Phelps to Whittlesey, May 2, 1859, EWC.

56. Transcript of the court-martial of Comdr. Robert D. Thorburn, Apr. 27, 1859, RG 45, NA.

57. Phelps to Whittlesey, May 2, 1859, EWC.

58. Ibid., Aug. 29, 1859.

59. Ibid., Dec. 10, 1859.

60. Ibid., Apr. 6, 1860.

61. Ibid., July 2, 1860.

62. Ibid., Nov. 13, 1860.

63. Ibid., Feb. 12, 1861.

CHAPTER FIVE: MONGREL SERVICE

1. George B. McClellan, *The Civil War Papers of George B. McClellan,* ed. Stephen W. Sears (New York: Ticknor and Fields, 1989), 37.

2. Ibid., 22.

3. Rodgers to Welles, *ORN* 22:283.

4. Welles to Rodgers, ibid., 285.

5. Rodgers to Welles, ibid., 286.

6. George McClellan to John Rodgers, June 26, 1861, John Rodgers Collection, Manuscript Division, Library of Congress (hereafter cited as JRC).

7. Phelps to Whittlesey, July 13, 1861, EWC.

8. Phelps to Rodgers, June 30, 1861, JRC.

9. Ibid., *ORN* 22:290–92.

10. Phelps to Lizzie, July 5, 1861, KFC.

11. Phelps to Whittlesey, July 13, 1861, EWC.

12. Phelps to Rodgers, July 13, 1861, JRC.

13. Ibid.

14. *Cincinnati Daily Gazette,* Jan. 16, 1862.

15. Rodgers to Welles, *ORN* 22:302.

16. Frémont to Montgomery Blair, ibid., 297.

17. Phelps to Foote, ibid., 325.

18. Ibid.

19. Phelps to Whittlesey, Oct. 10, 1861, EWC.

20. Virgil C. Jones and Harold L. Peterson, *U.S.S. Cairo: The Story of a Civil War Gunboat* (Washington, D.C.: National Park Service, 1971), 44.

21. Myron J. Smith, Jr., *The U.S. Gunboat Carondelet 1861–1865* (Manhattan, Kans.: MA/AH Publishing, c. 1982), 72.

22. Ibid., 73–74.

23. E. J. Huling, *Reminiscences of Gunboat Life in the Mississippi Squadron* (Saratoga Springs, N.Y.: Sentinel, 1881), 41–42.

24. Thomas Lyons Diary, Manuscript Division, Library of Congress.

25. Phelps to Whittlesey, Oct. 10, 1861, EWC.

26. Phelps to Foote, *ORN* 22:379–83; Phillips to Lt. Col. August Mersy. ibid., 381–82.

27. Phelps to Whittlesey, July 30, 1861, EWC.

28. Ibid., Nov. 16, 1861.

29. Lizzie to Whittlesey, Oct. 25, 1861, EWC.

30. Phelps to James Everlith (Lizzie's brother), U.S. Army Engineers, Nov. 24, 1861, EWC.

31. Lizzie to Whittlesey, Oct. 25, 1861, EWC.

32. Phelps to Everlith, Nov. 24, 1861, EWC.

33. *Cincinnati Commercial,* Nov. 25, 1861.

34. Phelps to Whittlesey, Oct. 10, 1861, EWC.

35. Foote to Phelps, Nov. 26, 1861, Seth Ledyard Phelps Letter Book, Missouri Historical Society Archives, St. Louis (hereafter cited as SPLB).

36. Lizzie to Whittlesey, Dec. 30, 1861, EWC.

37. Phelps to Foote, Jan. 21, 1862, RG 45, NA.

38. *ORN* 22:501.

39. Ibid., 510.

40. Foote to Phelps, Jan. 24, 1861, SPLB.

ᴄᴐ

CHAPTER SIX: FORT HENRY AND THE TENNESSEE RIVER RAID

For a complete account of the Federal assault against Forts Henry and Donelson, see Benjamin Franklin Cooling, *Forts Henry and Donelson: The Key to the Confederate Heartland* (Knoxville: University of Tennessee Press, 1987).

1. Lew Wallace, *An Autobiography* (New York: Harper & Brothers, 1906), 357–64.
2. *New York Daily Tribune,* Feb. 12, 1862.
3. Benson J. Lossing, *Pictoral History of the Civil War,* 3 vols. (Philadelphia: G. W. Childs, 1866–68), 1:202.
4. Foote to his wife, Feb. 6, 1862, RG 45, NA.
5. Ira Merchant to Henry Yates, Feb. 26, 1862, Illinois State Historical Library, Springfield.
6. Foote to his wife, Feb. 6, 1862, RG 45, NA.
7. *Memphis Daily Appeal,* Feb. 12, 1862.
8. Virgil C. Jones, *The Civil War at Sea* (New York: Holt, Rinehart, Winston, 1960), 369.
9. Phelps to Foote, *ORN* 22:572.
10. Virgil Carrington Jones, *The Civil War at Sea,* 370.
11. *Cincinnati Daily Gazette,* Feb. 20, 1862.
12. *The War of the Rebellion: A Compilation of the Official Records of the Union and Confederate Armies,* 128 vols. (Washington D.C.: GPO, 1880–1901), ser. 1, vol. 17:867 (hereafter cited as *OR*).
13. Phelps to Foote, *ORN* 22:573.
14. *Cincinnati Daily Commercial,* Feb. 15, 1862.
15. Ibid., Feb. 17, 1862.
16. *New York Times,* Feb. 13, 1862.
17. *Tuscumbia Constitution,* quoted in *Memphis Daily Appeal,* Feb. 13, 1862.
18. John B. Jones, *A Rebel War Clerk's Diary,* ed. Earl Schenck Miers (New York: Sagamore Press, 1958), 110.

CHAPTER SEVEN: FORT DONELSON

1. Henry Wise to Foote, Feb. 10, 1862, RG 45, NA.
2. Henry Walke, *Naval Scenes and Reminiscences* (New York: F. R. Reed, 1877), 82.
3. *Cincinnati Daily Commercial,* Feb. 17, 1862.
4. *Cincinnati Daily Gazette,* Feb. 17, 1862.
5. *New York Times,* Feb. 22, 1862.
6. Foote to Welles, *ORN* 22:571.
7. Walke, *Naval Scenes and Reminiscences,* 68.
8. Foote to his wife, Feb. 6, 1862, RG 45, NA.
9. Foote to Phelps, Feb. 13, 1862, SPLB.
10. Henry Walke, "The Western Flotilla at Fort Donelson, Island Number Ten, Fort Pillow and Memphis," in *Battles and Leaders of the Civil War,* ed. Robert Underwood Johnson and Clarence Clough Buel, 4 vols. (New York: Century, 1884), 1:433.

11. *Cincinnati Daily Gazette*, Feb. 18, 1862.

12. Walke, "The Western Flotilla," 436.

13. McPherson, *Battle Cry of Freedom*, 402.

14. Wallace, *An Autobiography*, 430–31.

15. Phelps to Whittlesey, Feb. 26, 1862, EWC.

16. Ibid.

17. Foote to his wife, Feb. 26, 1862, RG 45, NA.

18. Phelps to Whittlesey, Feb. 26, 1862, EWC.

19. Lizzie to Whittlesey, Mar. 1, 1862, EWC.

20. Foote to his wife, Feb. 18, 1862, RG 45, NA.

21. Ibid.

22. *New York Times*, Mar. 4, 1862.

23. Foote Proclamation, Feb. 20, 1862, RG 45, NA.

24. Phelps to Whittlesey, Feb. 26, 1862, EWC.

25. Foote to his wife, Feb. 22, 1862, RG 45, NA.

26. Ibid., Feb. 17, 1862, RG 45, NA.

CHAPTER EIGHT: ISLAND NO. 10

1. Phelps to Whittlesey, Mar. 4, 1862, EWC.

2. *New York Tribune*, Nov. 14, 1861; Phelps to Whittlesey, Feb. 26, 1862, EWC.

3. James B. Eads, "Recollections of Foote and the Gun-Boats," in *Battles and Leaders* 1:340–41.

4. Phelps to Whittlesey, Feb. 26, 1862, EWC.

5. Ibid.

6. Foote to his wife, Mar. 9 and 12, 1862, RG 45, NA.

7. Symmes Browne to his wife, no. 31, Symmes Browne Collection, Ohio Historical Society, Columbus (hereafter cited as SBC).

8. Ibid.

9. Phelps to Whittlesey, Mar. 27, 1862, EWC.

10. Halleck to Foote, *ORN* 22:700.

11. *ORN* 22:685.

12. Eads, "Recollections of Foote and the Gunboats," 343–45.

13. Foote to his wife, Mar. 17, 1862, RG 45, NA.

14. Phelps to Whittlesey, Mar. 27, 1862, EWC.

15. Walke, *Naval Scenes and Reminiscences*, 117.

16. Colonel Bissell to Senator Benjamin Wade, *ORN* 22:734.

17. Foote to Pope, Apr. 6, 1862, RG 45, NA.

18. Walke, "Western Flotilla," 441.

19. Symmes Brown to his wife, Mar. 31, 1862, SBC.

20. Frederick Stansbury Haydon, *Aeronautics in the Union and Confederate Armies* (Baltimore: Johns Hopkins University Press, 1941), 392–96.

21. Phelps to Foote, Sept. 7, 1862, RG 45, NA.

22. Walke, "Western Flotilla," 442.

23. Ibid., 444.

24. Junius Brown, *Four Years in Secessia* (Hartford: O. D. Case, 1865), 124–27.

CHAPTER NINE: FORT PILLOW AND THE
BATTLE OF PLUM POINT BEND

1. Robert D. Whitesell, "Military and Naval Activity Between Cairo and Columbus," *Register of the Kentucky Historical Society* 61 (1963): 110–11.

2. Robert Suhr, "Gunboats on the River," *America's Civil War* 1 (July 1989): 20.

3. Phelps to Whittlesey, Apr. 29, 1862, EWC.

4. Walke, *Naval Scenes and Reminiscences,* 194, 245.

5. *ORN* 23:63.

6. Ibid.

7. Phelps to Whittlesey, Apr. 29, 1862, EWC.

8. *New York Tribune,* May 16, 1862.

9. Phelps to Whittlesey, May 6, 1862, EWC.

10. Junius Brown, *Four Years in Secessia,* 165–66.

11. Ibid.

12. Phelps to Whittlesey, Mar. 27, 1862, EWC.

13. *New York Tribune,* May 16, 1862.

14. Eliot Callender, "What a Boy Saw on the Mississippi," in *Military Essays and Recollections,* papers read before the Commandery of the State of Illinois, Military Order of the Loyal Legion of the United States, vol. 1 (Chicago: A. C. McClurg, 1891), 61.

15. Symmes Browne to his wife, May 12, 1862, SBC.

16. Callender, "What a Boy Saw on the Mississippi," 63.

17. William Van Cleaf to his mother, May 15, 1862, William Van Cleaf Collection, Special Collections and Archives, Rutgers University Library, New Brunswick, N.J. (hereafter cited as WVCC).

18. The account of the Battle of Plum Point Bend was compiled from J. Thomas Scharf, *The Confederate States Navy* (New York: Fairfax Press, 1977) 253–56; Walke, *Naval Scenes and Reminiscences,* 251–67; *ORN* 23:14–19.

19. *ORN* 23:19.

20. Phelps to Foote, May 28, 1862, RG 45, NA.

21. Ibid., May 31, 1862, RG 45, NA.

22. Phelps to Foote, quoted in James Mason Hoppin, *Life of Andrew Hull Foote, Rear-Admiral United States Navy* (New York: Harper Brothers, 1874), 320.

23. Phelps to Foote, May 31, 1862, RG 45, NA.

24. Foote to Phelps, June 6, 1862, SPLB.

25. Phelps to Foote, May 31, 1862, RG 45, NA.

26. David L. Voluska, *The African American in the Union Navy: 1861–1865* (New York: Garland, 1993), 33.

27. *New York Tribune,* May 16, 1862.

28. Foote to Phelps, May 27, June 6, 1862, SPLB.

29. *ORN* 23:100–101.

30. H. Allen Gosnell, *Guns on the Western Waters: The Story of the River Gunboats in the Civil War* (Baton Rouge: Louisiana State University Press, 1949), 22.

31. Phelps to Foote, May 31, 1862, RG 45, NA.

CHAPTER 10: MEMPHIS AND THE *MOUND CITY* DISASTER

1. *Cincinnati Daily Commercial,* June 11, 1862.

2. Ibid.

3. Ibid.

4. Letter by unnamed relative, quoted in Mrs. E. O. Wells, "When Memphis Surrendered," *Confederate Veteran* 35 (Dec. 1927): 465.

5. Walke, *Naval Scenes and Reminiscences,* 293.

6. Phelps to Foote, *ORN* 22:136.

7. Ellet to Edwin Stanton, ibid., 133.

8. Wells, "When Memphis Surrendered," 465.

9. *Chicago Tribune,* June 10, 1862; Phelps to Foote, *ORN* 22:136.

10. *ORN* 22:121.

11. Walke, *Naval Scenes and Reminiscences,* 291.

12. *Cincinnati Daily Commercial,* June 11, 1862.

13. Hoppin, *Life of Andrew Hull Foote,* 325.

14. *ORN* 22:224.

15. Phelps to Whittlesey, June 23, 1862, EWC.

16. *ORN* 22:147.

17. Alfred W. Ellet, "Ellet and His Steam-Rams at Memphis," in *Battles and Leaders* 1:458.

18. Foote to Phelps, June 9, 1962, SPLB.

19. Ibid., June 20, 1862.

20. Ibid., June 14, 1862.

21. *ORN* 22:223.

22. James Russell Soley, "Naval Operations in the Vicksburg Campaign," in *Battles and Leaders* 1:551–55.

23. John D. Milligan, ed., *From the Fresh Water Navy 1861–1864* (Annapolis: Naval Institute Press, 1970), 96.

24. *Cincinnati Daily Commercial,* June 20, 1862.

25. Phelps to Foote, *ORN* 22:223.

26. Phelps to Whittlesey, June 23, 1862, EWC.

CHAPTER ELEVEN: VICKSBURG

1. Charles Lee Lewis, *David Glasgow Farragut* (Annapolis: Naval Institute Press, 1943), 107.

2. *New York Tribune,* July 11, 1862.

3. Phelps to Foote, quoted in Hoppin, *Life of Andrew Hull Foote,* 340.

4. Phelps to Whittlesey, July 9, 1862, EWC.

5. *Cincinnati Daily Commercial,* July 12, 1862.

6. Charles H. Davis, *Life of Charles Henry Davis, Rear Admiral* (Boston: Houghton Mifflin, 1899), 258.

7. Phelps to Foote, July 6, 1862, RG 45, NA.

8. Phelps to Whittlesey, July 9, 1862, EWC.

9. David D. Porter, *The Naval History of the Civil War* (1866; rpt., Secaucus, N.J.: Castle, 1984), 235–41.

10. Phelps to Foote, quoted in Hoppin, *Life of Andrew Hull Foote*, 341.

11. Phelps to Whittlesey, July 9, 1962, EWC.

12. Phelps to Foote, July 6, 1862, RG 45, NA.

13. *New York Tribune*, July 23, 1862.

14. Ibid., July 11, 1862.

15. Phelps to Whittlesey, July 9, 1862, EWC.

16. *Cincinnati Daily Commercial*, July 17, 1862; William Van Cleaf to his mother, Aug. 8, 1862, WVCC.

17. Phelps to Whittlesey, July 19, 1862, EWC.

18. Lewis, *David Glasgow Farragut*, 107.

19. *New York Tribune*, July 23, 1862.

20. Phelps to Whittlesey, July 9, 1862, EWC.

21. Phelps to Foote, July 6, 1862, RG 45, NA.

22. Isaac N. Brown, "The Confederate Gun-Boat *Arkansas*," in *Battles and Leaders* 1:572.

23. Phelps to Whittlesey, July 19, 1862, EWC.

24. Isaac N. Brown, "Confederate Gun-Boat *Arkansas*," 572.

25. C. W. Read, "Reminiscences of the Confederate States Navy," *Southern Historical Society Papers* 1 (May 1876): 353.

26. Scharf, *Confederate States Navy*, 310–11.

27. Read, "Reminiscences of the Confederate States Navy," 354.

28. Isaac N. Brown, "Confederate Gun-Boat *Arkansas*," 575.

29. Gosnell, *Guns on Western Waters*, 114.

30. Ibid., 114–15.

31. Charles H. Davis, *Life of Charles Henry Davis*, 263.

32. Phelps to Whittlesey, July 19, 1862, EWC.

33. Isaac N. Brown, "Confederate Gun-Boat *Arkansas*," 576.

34. Phelps to Whittlesey, July 19, 1862, EWC.

35. Isaac N. Brown, "Confederate Gun-Boat *Arkansas*," 576.

36. Phelps to Whittlesey, July 19, 1862, EWC.

37. Isaac N. Brown, "Confederate Gun-Boat *Arkansas*," 576.

38. Phelps to Whittlesey, July 19, 1862, EWC.

39. *New York Tribune*, July 26, 1862.

40. Phelps to Foote, *ORN* 19:56.

41. Phelps to Whittlesey, July 19, 1862, EWC.

42. Scharf, *Confederate States Navy*, 320.

43. Phelps to Whittlesey, July 19, 1862, EWC; Phelps to Foote, *ORN* 19:56.

44. Phelps to Whittlesey, July 19, 1862, EWC.

45. Phelps to Foote, *ORN* 19:56.

46. Gosnell, *Guns on the Western Waters*, 125.

47. Isaac N. Brown, "Confederate Gun-Boat *Arkansas*," 577.

48. Phelps to Whittlesey, Aug. 7, 1862, EWC.

49. Phelps to Foote, *ORN* 19:57; Davis to Farragut, July 17, 1862, RG 45, NA.

50. Phelps to Foote, *ORN* 19:57.

51. *Cincinnati Daily Gazette*, Aug. 2, 1862.

52. Charles H. Davis, *Life of Charles Henry Davis*, 267, 273.

53. Lewis, *David Glasgow Farragut*, 120.
54. Phelps to Whittlesey, Aug. 7, 1862, EWC.
55. Phelps to Foote, *ORN* 19:58.
56. *Cincinnati Daily Gazette*, Aug. 2, 1862.
57. Charles H. Davis, *Life of Charles Henry Davis*, 272.

Chapter Twelve: *Fair Play* and Politics

1. Phelps to Whittlesey, Aug. 7, 1862, EWC.
2. *Cincinnati Daily Commercial*, Sept. 2, 1862.
3. Edwin C. Bearss, "The Union Raid down the Mississippi and up the Yazoo—August 16–27, 1862," in *Military Analysis of the Civil War: An Anthology by the Editors of Military Affairs* (Millwood, N.Y.: KTO, 1977), 213–24.
4. *ORN* 22:325.
5. Phelps to Foote, Sept. 7, 1862, RG 45, NA.
6. Phelps to Whittlesey, Sept. 9, 1862, EWC.
7. Phelps to Foote, Sept. 25, 1862, RG 45, NA.
8. Phelps to Whittlesey, Sept. 9, 1862, EWC.
9. Foote to Phelps, Sept. 12, 1862, SPLB.
10. *Cincinnati Daily Commercial*, Aug. 23, 1862.
11. Gustavus Vasa Fox, *Confidential Correspondence of Gustavus Vasa Fox*, ed. Robert Means Thompson and Richard Wainwright (New York: Naval History Society, 1912), 63.
12. Welles to Phelps, Sept. 18, 1862, SPLB.
13. Davis to Phelps, Sept. 27, 1862, SPLB.
14. Foote to Phelps, Sept. 20, 4 Oct. 1862, SPLB.
15. John Niven, *Gideon Welles: Lincoln's Secretary of the Navy* (New York: Oxford University Press, 1973), 383–84.
16. Gideon Welles, *Diary of Gideon Welles*, vol. 1, ed. Howard K. Beale (New York: W. W. Norton, 1960), 17.
17. Ibid., 36, 157–58.

Chapter Thirteen: Flotilla Overhaul

1. Phelps to Foote, Sept. 7, 1862, RG 45, NA.
2. Richard S. West, Jr., *Gideon Welles: Lincoln's Navy Department* (Indianapolis: Bobbs-Merrill, 1943), 254.
3. Phelps to Gwin, Wilson, and Bishop, Sept. 29, 1862, SPLB.
4. Phelps to Davis, Aug. 31, 1862, RG 45, NA.
5. Davis to Phelps, Oct. 6, 1862, SPLB.
6. Ibid.
7. Henry Coffinberry to his parents, Oct. 29, 1862, Maria D. Coffinberry Collection, Western Reserve Historical Society.
8. Davis to Phelps, Oct. 12, 1862, SPLB.
9. Phelps to Welles, Oct. 10, 1862, SPLB.
10. Grimes to Phelps, Oct. 29, 1862, SPLB.

11. Lizzie to Whittlesey, Nov. 4, 1862, EWC.

12. Beale, ed., *Diary of Gideon Welles,* 141.

13. Petition to Welles, RG 45, NA.

14. Abraham Lincoln, *The Collected Works of Abraham Lincoln,* vol. 6, ed. Roy P. Basler (New Brunswick, N.J.: Rutgers University Press, 1953), 102; Charles H. Davis, *Life of Charles Henry Davis,* 302–3.

15. Bruce Catton, *Grant Moves South* (Boston: Little, Brown, 1960), 324–46; Porter, *Naval History of the Civil War,* 287.

16. Porter to Phelps, Feb. 14, 1863, SPLB.

17. Phelps to Lizzie, Jan. 11, 1863, KFC.

18. Ibid., Jan. 16, 1863, KFC.

19. Davis to Phelps, Jan. 12, 1863, SPLB.

20. *ORN* 24:178.

21. Porter to Phelps, Jan. 18, 1863, SPLB.

22. Phelps to Porter, *ORN* 24:313.

23. Phelps to Lizzie, Jan. 25, 1863, KFC.

24. Ibid., 22, Jan. 31, 1863.

25. *ORN* 24:314, 316.

26. Ibid., 314.

27. Porter to Phelps, Feb. 14, 1863, SPLB.

28. Phelps to Porter, Feb. 7, 1863, SPLB.

CHAPTER FOURTEEN: STATION DUTY AND GUERRILLA WAR

1. Porter to Phelps, Mar. 4, 1863, SPLB.

2. Ibid., Mar. 6, 1863.

3. Phelps to Porter, Mar. 14, 1863, SPLB.

4. Ibid.

5. Porter to Phelps, May 2, 1863, SPLB.

6. Phelps to Lizzie, May 14, 1863, KFC.

7. Porter to Phelps, Apr. 15, June 14, 1863, SPLB.

8. Porter to Phelps, June 14, 1863, SPLB.

9. Phelps to Lizzie, May 6, 1863, KFC.

10. Ibid., May 24, 1863.

11. Ibid., June 2, 1863, KFC.

12. *ORN* 25:167, 194–95.

13. *The National Cyclopedia of American Biography,* s.v. "Andrew H. Foote."

14. Phelps to Porter, *ORN* 25:261.

15. Hurlburt to Prentise, *OR* 34:354.

16. Robert E. Shalhope, *Sterling Price: Portrait of a Southerner* (Columbia: University of Missouri Press, 1971), 238–42.

17. *ORN* 25:261.

18. Porter to Phelps, July 27, 1863, SPLB.

19. Phelps to Porter, *ORN* 25:322.

20. Ibid., 472.

21. David D. Porter, *Incidents and Anecdotes of the Civil War* (New York: D. Appleton, 1885), 210.

22. Ibid., 211.
23. Sherman to Porter, *ORN* 25:474.
24. Ibid.
25. Bruce Catton, *Grant Takes Command* (Boston: Little, Brown, 1968), 22–62.
26. Phelps to Sherman, *OR* 43:798.
27. Porter to Phelps, Nov. 2, 1863, SPLB.
28. Ibid., Nov. 12, 1863.
29. Ibid., Jan. 11, 1864.

CHAPTER FIFTEEN: RED RIVER

1. For an excellent account of the Red River campaign and especially the role that cotton played, see Ludwell H. Johnson, *Red River Campaign: Politics and Cotton in the Civil War* (Baltimore: Johns Hopkins Press, 1958; rpt., Kent, Ohio: Kent State University Press, 1993).
2. Porter, *Incidents and Anecdotes*, 219.
3. Ibid., 213.
4. Phelps to Lizzie, Feb. 12, 1864, KFC.
5. Ibid., Feb. 21 and 23, 1864.
6. Ibid., Feb. 21, 1864, KFC.
7. Porter to Col. L. B. Parsons, *ORN* 25:704.
8. Phelps to Lizzie, Feb. 24, 1864, KFC.
9. Ibid., Feb. 28, 1864.
10. Ibid., Mar. 2, 1864.
11. Ibid., Mar. 5, 1864.
12. Ibid., Mar. 9, 1864; Porter, *Incidents and Anecdotes*, 331.
13. Phelps to Lizzie, Mar. 9, 1864, KFC.
14. Phelps to Porter, *ORN* 26:30–31.
15. Johnson, *Red River Campaign*, 72.
16. Porter, *Incidents and Anecdotes*, 219.
17. *OR* 46:610.
18. Phelps to Lizzie, Mar. 24, 1864, KFC.
19. *Report of the Joint Committee on the Conduct of the War,* vol. 2 (Washington, D.C.: GPO, 1865), 282.
20. Phelps to Lizzie, Mar. 24, 1864, KFC.
21. *Report of the Joint Committee*, 290.
22. Thomas O. Selfridge, "The Navy in the Red River," *Battles and Leaders* 4:363.
23. Porter, *Incidents and Anecdotes*, 231.
24. Phelps to Lizzie, Apr. 14, 1864, KFC.
25. Johnson, *Red River Campaign*, 163.
26. Ibid., 164.
27. David D. Porter Journal, Manuscript Division, Library of Congress.
28. Porter, *Naval History of the Civil War*, 515.
29. Richard S. West, Jr., *The Second Admiral: A Life of David Dixon Porter 1813–1891* (New York: Coward-McCann, 1937), 255.
30. Phelps to Porter, *ORN* 26:79.
31. Porter to Phelps, Apr. 25, 1864, SPLB.

32. *ORN* 26:79.

33. *Philadelphia North American,* quoted in the *Jeffersonian Democrat* (Ohio), June 17, 1864. The story of the sinking of the *Eastport* and efforts to save her was compiled from reports in *ORN* 26:68–79 and from the logbooks of the *Eastport* and *Fort Hindman.*

34. Porter to Welles, *ORN* 26:74.

35. Porter, *Incidents and Anecdotes,* 241.

36. Phelps to Lizzie, May 3, 1864, KFC.

37. Reports of participants in *ORN* 26:80–85; Porter, *Incidents and Anecdotes,* 240–44.

38. Porter to Welles, *ORN* 26:72–73.

39. Phelps to Lizzie, May 3, 1864, KFC.

CHAPTER SIXTEEN: FRUSTRATION AND RESIGNATION

1. Beale, ed., *Diary of Gideon Welles* 2:37.

2. Phelps to Porter, *ORN* 26:393.

3. Phelps to Lizzie, June 9, 1864, KFC.

4. Ibid., June 21, 1864.

5. Ibid., July 4, 1864.

6. Ibid., July 5, 1864.

7. Phelps to Welles, July 29, 1864, KFC.

8. Phelps to Lizzie, July 26, 1864, KFC.

9. Ibid., Sept. 13, 1864.

CHAPTER SEVENTEEN: STEAMSHIPS, CANALS, AND DIPLOMACY

1. Phelps to his mother, Nov. 30, 1864, KFC.

2. David M. Pletcher, *The Awkward Years* (Columbia: University of Missouri Press, 1962), 19.

3. USS *Davis,* DD65, DD395, DD937; USS *Fitch,* DD462; USS *Foote,* DD169, DD511; USS *Gwin,* DD71, DD433, DD772; USS *Kilty,* DD137; USS *Meade,* DD274, DD602; USS *Prichett,* DD561; USS *Porter,* DD59, DD356, DD800; USS *Selfridge,* DD357; USS *Shirk,* DD318; USS *Stembel,* DD644; USS *Walke,* DD416, DD725. The USS *Phelps* was named after Lt. Com. Thomas S. Phelps, who served on the coastal blockade.

ↄ

Glossary

ABAFT: Toward or at the stern

ABEAM: On a line at right angles to a ship's keel

ATHWARTSHIP: Running across at an oblique angle to fore and aft

BARBETTE: A mound of earth or a protected platform from which guns fire over a parapet

BERTH: The place where a ship lies when at anchor or at a wharf; a place to sit or sleep on a ship

BILGE: The lowest point of a ship's inner hull

BOATSWAIN: A petty officer in charge of the hull maintenance and related work

BONNET: An additional piece of canvas laced to the foot of a jib or foresail

BOWDITCH: The popular name for the book *American Practical Navigator,* by Nathaniel Bowditch

BOWSPRIT: A large spar projecting forward from the stem of a ship

BRACE: A rope passed through a block at the end of a ship's yard to swing it horizontally

BRAIL: A rope fastened to the leech of a sail and run through a block for hauling the sail up or in

BREECHING: A sturdy hawser attached to the rear of a gun and secured to either side of the gun port, to limit recoil

BULWARK: The side of a ship above the upper deck

BUTTERNUT: A soldier or partisan of the Confederacy, so named for their homespun overalls, dyed brown with a butternut extract

CANISTER: A short-range antipersonnel projectile consisting of a light sheet metal case and small iron balls. The case was designed to open just beyond the muzzle of the gun, allowing wide dispersal of the iron balls

CAPSTAN: A machine for moving or raising heavy weights by winding cable around a vertical, spindle-mounted drum driven by steam or hand power

CARLINE: A fore-and-aft member supporting the deck of a ship

CARRONADE: A short, light, iron cannon used mostly as a broadside gun where long range was not needed

CASEMATE: An armored enclosure on a warship from which guns are fired through an opening

COAMING: A raised frame around a hatchway on the deck of a ship, to keep out water

COLUMBIAD: An ambiguous term that goes back at least to 1807, probably referring to cannon cast at the foundry in the District of Columbia. The first American shell gun, the columbiad was originally designed as an alternative to the carronade, but by the Civil War the term usually was applied to the smoothbore army coast defense cannon. Made of cast iron, it was longer, thicker, and much heavier than the regular coast howitzer.

CORDAGE: The ropes in the rigging of a ship

COURSE: The lowest sail on a square-rigged mast

CROSSJACK: Square sail spread by the yard of the same name, or the lowest yard on the mizzenmast

DAHLGREN GUN: Named after Rear Adm. John Dahlgren, who invented a series of guns resembling a soda bottle to take into account the higher pressures generated at the breech

DAVIT: A crane that projects over the side of a ship for raising and lowering boats, anchors, or cargo

DEADEYE: A rounded wood block that is encircled by a rope or an iron band and pierced with holes to receive the lanyard, used to set up shrouds and stays

DEPTH OF HOLD: Distance from inside the planking at the keel to the top of the gunwale, measured amidship

ENFILADE: Gunfire directed from a flanking position along the length of an enemy battle line; to fire in such a way

FALL: A hoisting tackle rope or chain, especially the part of it to which the power is applied

FANTAIL: A counter or overhang of a ship shaped like a duck's bill

FIREMAN: An enlisted man who works with engineering machinery, one who tends or feeds the boiler fires

FLAG CAPTAIN: The captain of a vessel that serves as headquarters for a fleet commander

FORECASTLE: The part of the upper deck of a ship forward of the foremast

FRIGATE: A three masted, square-rigged ship typically carrying thirty-six to forty-four guns.

FUSE: The mechanism by which fire is transmitted to the charge in a shell. It consists of combustible material enclosed in a wood, paper, or metal case, and is inserted into the shell before firing. Since wooden fuses deteriorated in the damp conditions aboard ship, they were replaced by metal fuses in the 1850s. To prevent the corrosive combustible material from reacting with the metal case, the composition was cased in paper and inserted in the fuse when ready for use. Fuses came with five-, ten-, and fifteen-second burn times, but could be cut for quicker detonation if necessary.

GIG: A long, light, ship's boat designed for speed rather than work

GLASSIS: A slope that runs downward from a fortification

GRAPE: A cluster of iron balls, usually nine, held together by plates, rings, and a connecting rod. In flight, the balls would spread

GRAPPLINGS: Instruments with iron claws used to fasten an enemy ship alongside before boarding

GUARD: Railing erected in the absence of bulwarks at a ship's side

GUN DECK: A deck below the spar deck on which guns are carried

GUN PORT: Opening in a ship's side through which a gun's muzzle is pointed in firing

GUNWALE: The part of a ship where the topside and deck meet

HALF DECK: The deck next below the upper deck or spar deck

HAWSER: A large rope for towing, mooring, or securing a ship

HOG CHAIN: Iron rod an inch to two and a half inches thick running the length of the boat. These combined with vertical wooden braces to keep the bow and stern from dropping and the midships from raising.

HOLYSTONE: A soft sandstone used to scrub a ship's deck

HURRICANE DECK: The upper deck of a ship

JEER: A pair of heavy tackles or any combination of tackles for raising and lowering a topsail or lower yard

JIB: Triangular sail set on a stay leading from the bowsprit to the head of the foremast

KEDGE: A small anchor

KEEL: A longitudinal timber extending along the center of the bottom of a ship and projecting from the bottom

KEELSON (KILSON): A reinforcing structural member laid over the floors, parallel with, and through-bolted to, the keel

LARBOARD: Port or left. On February 18, 1846, the U.S. Navy officially substituted the word "port"

LOCK: The mechanism for exploding the charge of a firearm

MAINSAIL: The principal sail on the mainmast

MASTER MATE: Petty officer who acts as an assistant to the master or captain

MASTHEAD: The top of a mast

MATCH: A chemically prepared wick or cord used in firing firearms or powder

MIDWATCH: The watch from midnight to 4 A.M.

MIZZENMAST: The mast aft or next aft of the mainmast on a ship

MOLE: A massive work, formed of masonry and large stones or earth, laid in the sea as a pier or breakwater

MORTAR: A muzzle-loading cannon having a short tube in relation to its caliber that is used to throw projectiles with low muzzle velocities at high angles

MOULDED BEAM: The extreme width of a ship at the widest part

NECK OF THE CINCH (CASCABEL): Place where breeching is attached to the rear of a cannon

OCTANT: A reflecting astronomical instrument of the same character as the sextant but adopted for measuring an arc not greater than 90°

ORLOP DECK: The lowest deck in a ship of four or more decks

PAIXHANS GUN: A large-bore cannon named after Colonel Henri Paixhans of the French artillery, who demonstrated that by placing the fuse toward the muzzle, exploding shells could be fired like solid shot. Since exploding shells were much more destructive than solid shot against wooden hulls, the shell gun quickly became the standard of the day

PARROTT GUN: A muzzle-loading, cast iron rifled cannon named after U.S. Army Capt. Robert Parrott. Made with a wrought iron band shrunk around the breech for extra strength, it was effective and cheap, but plagued by failures, especially in the larger pieces. It was abandoned after the Civil War.

PENDANT: A short rope hanging from a spar and having at its free end a block or spliced thimble

PERPENDICULARS: The length between the forward and aft reference lines, used to determine the vessel's length

PILOTHOUSE: A forward deckhouse for a boat's helmsman containing the steering wheel, compass, and navigating equipment

PIVOT GUN: A large cannon mounted on a carriage, usually capable of traversing at least 180°

PORTFIRE: A quick-burning composition of gunpowder, saltpeter, and sulfur moistened with linseed oil that burned like a flare

PRIMING WIRE: A piece of wire used to clear the vent of a gun

QUARTERGUNNER: A petty officer whose duty was to assist the ship's gunner—appointed one for each four guns

QUARTERMASTER: The ship's petty officer who attends to a ship's helm, binnacle, and signals

QUOIN: A wedge placed under the breech of a gun to elevate or depress the muzzle

RAKE: The overhang of a ship's bow or stern

RAZEE: A ship that has had one or more upper decks removed

RECEIVING SHIP: A naval vessel; usually one laid up or unfit for service, used as a station for admitting recruits

REEFER: Lower deck colloquial name for a midshipman

RIFLED GUN: A gun where the barrel is given a series of spiral grooves in the surface of the bore, causing a projectile to rotate along its longer axis

RIGGING: The distinctive shape, number, and arrangement of ropes, sails and masts of a ship

RIVER MONITOR: An armored vessel designed with a low freeboard and mounting one or more revolving gun turrets

ROUNDHOUSE: A cabin on the stern of the quarterdeck

ROYAL: A small sail on the royal mast immediately above the topgallant sail

SABOT: A thrust-transmitting carrier that positions a projectile in a tube

SCHOONER: A fore-and-aft rigged ship having two masts with a smaller sail on the foremast and with the mainmast located nearly amidships

SHEAR: An action resulting from applied forces that causes two contiguous parts of a body to slide relative to each other in a direction parallel to their plane of contact

SHEET: A rope or chain that regulates the angle at which a sail is set in relation to the wind

SHIP OF THE LINE: A warship large enough to have a place in the line of battle, usually superior to a frigate

SHIP'S LIEUTENANT: A ship's executive officer or second in command

SLOOP: A light cruiser that ranked below a frigate and carried eighteen to thirty-two guns on one deck

SNAG BOAT: A boat used to remove sunken riverboats and logs

SPANKER: The fore-and-aft sail on the mast nearest the stern of a square-rigged ship

SPAR: A stout, rounded piece of wood used to support rigging

SPARDECK: The top, main or weather deck

SQUARE-RIGGED: A sailing ship in which the sails are bent to the yards carried athwart the mast and trimmed with braces

STERNPOST: The principal member at the stern of a ship, extending from the keel to the deck

STROKE: The movement, or distance of the movement, of the piston rod in either direction

SUPERSTRUCTURE: The structural part of a ship above the main deck

TACK: The direction of a ship with respect to the trim of her sails

32-POUNDER: Artillery piece with a bore of 6.4 inches

TILLER: The lever used to turn the rudder of a boat from side to side

TORPEDO: The nineteenth-century term for what is now refered to as a mine. The torpedos used at Fort Henry consisted of a stout sheet of iron rolled into a cylinder and pointed at both ends. They were about five and a half feet long and a foot in diameter. In the interior was a canvas bag containing seventy pounds of powder. Connected to the upper end was an iron lever, three and a half feet long, armed with prongs designed to catch the bottom of a passing boat. The passage of the boat was expected to work the lever, which was attached to an iron rod on the inside of the cylinder that triggered a percussion cap, exploding the powder. The torpedo was anchored to the riverbed by two ropes and contained an air chamber to give it buoyancy. Later torpedos used five-gallon glass demijohns as a container and were detonated by friction primers or galvanic wire

TRUCK: A small wooden cap at the top of the masthead

THWARTSHIP BAR: Bar placed across the hull for support

VEDETTE: A mounted sentinel stationed in advance of pickets

WAYS: An inclined structure upon which a ship is built or supported in launching

WHEELHOUSE: The structure enclosing a riverboat's paddle wheel

WHITWORTH GUN: A large, rifled cannon, made in England, with wrought iron bands shrunk around a cast iron core. It featured a bore with a hexagonal spiral c/ɔ

Bibliography

LETTERS, DIARIES, MANUSCRIPTS

Browne, Symmes   —Ohio Historical Society, Columbus (microfilm)
Coffinberry, Maria D.   —Western Reserve Historical Society, Cleveland,
                          Ohio
Foote, Andrew H.   —Library of Congress, Manuscript Division, Na-
                          tional Archives, Record Group 45
Lyons, Thomas   —Diary, Library of Congress, Manuscript Division
Phelps, Seth L.   —Kate Fowle Collection (private), Washington,
                          D.C.
                         —Huntington Library, San Marino, California
                         —Missouri Historical Society, St. Louis (microfilm)
                         —National Archives, Record Group 45
Porter, David D.   —Journal, Library of Congress, Manuscript Divi-
                          sion
Rodgers, John   —Library of Congress, Manuscript Division
Van Cleaf, William   —Special Collections and Archives, Rutgers Uni-
                          versity Library, New Brunswick, New Jersey

{ 431 }

Wade, Benjamin   —Library of Congress, Manuscript Division
Welles, Gideon   —Library of Congress, Manuscript Division
Whittlesey, Elisha   —Western Reserve Historical Society, Cleveland, Ohio

Books and Articles

Adams, Herbert B., ed. "The City of Washington." *Johns Hopkins University Studies* 3 (1885).

Andrews, J. Cutler. *The North Reports the Civil War*. Pittsburgh: University of Pittsburgh Press, 1955.

Battles and Leaders of the Civil War. Ed. by Robert Underwood Johnson and Clarence Clough Buel. 4 vols. New York: Century, 1884.

Bauer, K. Jack. *The Mexican War 1846–1848*. New York: Macmillan, 1974.

———. *Surfboats and Horse Marines: U.S. Naval Operations in the Mexican War*. Annapolis: Naval Institute Press, 1969.

Bearss, Edwin C. "The Construction of Fort Henry and Fort Donelson." *West Tennessee Historical Society Papers* 21 (1967): 24–47.

———. "The Fall of Fort Henry, Tennessee." *West Tennessee Historical Society Papers* 17 (1963): 85–107.

———. "A Federal Raid up the Tennessee River." *Alabama Review* 17 (Oct. 1964): 261–70.

———. *Hardluck Ironclad*. Baton Rouge: Louisiana State University Press, 1966.

———. "The Ironclads at Fort Donelson." *Register of the Kentucky Historical Society* (Jan., Apr., July 1976).

———. "The Union Raid down the Mississippi and up the Yazoo—August 16–27, 1862." In *Military Analysis of the Civil War: An Anthology by the Editors of Military Affairs*. Millwood, N.Y.: KTO, 1977.

Bell, Frederick J. *Room to Swing a Cat: Being Some Tales of the Old Navy*. New York: Longmans Greenard, 1938.

Brown, Junius. *Four Years in Secessia*. Hartford: O. D. Case, 1865.

Brown, Maynadier. "Out of a Sea Chest." 1968. Unpublished manuscript.

Burrow, Clayton R., Jr. *America Spreads Her Sails: U.S. Seapower in the 19th Century*. Annapolis: Naval Institute Press, 1973.

Callender, Eliot. "What a Boy Saw on the Mississippi." In *Military Essays and Recollections*. Papers read before the Commandery of the State of Illinois, Military Order of the Loyal Legion of the United States. Vol. 1. Chicago: A. C. McClurg, 1891.

Carrison, Daniel J. *The Navy from Wood to Steel 1860–1890*. New York: Franklin Watts, 1965.

Catton, Bruce. *Grant Moves South*. Boston: Little, Brown, 1960.

———. *Grant Takes Command*. Boston: Little, Brown, 1968.

Chapelle, Howard Irving. *The History of the American Navy*. New York: Bonanza, 1949.

Christy, David. *The Rise of the Republic of Liberia and the Progress of African Missions*. Cincinnati: Rickey, Mallory and Webb, 1857.

Church, Frank L. *Civil War Marine: A Diary of the Red River Expedition, 1864*. Edited and annotated by James P. Jones and Edward F. Keuchel. Washington D.C.: Historical Branch, USMC, 1975.

The Confederate Veteran Magazine. 43 vols. 1893–1932. Wilmington, N.C.: Broadfoot, 1990.

Cooling, Benjamin Franklin. *Forts Henry and Donelson: The Key to the Confederate Heartland*. Knoxville: University of Tennessee Press, 1987.

Dahlgren, Madeleine V. *Memoir of John A. Dahlgren*. Boston: James R. Osgood, 1882.

Daly, Robert W. "Pay and Prize Money in the Old Navy, 1776–1899." *U.S. Naval Institute Proceedings* 74 (Aug. 1948): 967–70.

Davis, Charles H. *Life of Charles Henry Davis, Rear Admiral*. Boston: Houghton Mifflin, 1899.

Davis, Rebecca Paulding. *The Life of Hiram Paulding, Rear-Admiral, USN*. New York: Baker & Taylor, 1910.

Derthick, Martha. *City Politics in Washington D.C.* Cambridge: Joint Center for Urban Studies of MIT and Harvard, 1962.

Dorsey, Florence L. *Road to the Sea and the Mississippi River: The Story of James B. Eads*. New York: Rinehart, 1947.

Ellet Family. *History of the Ram Fleet and the Mississippi Marine Brigade*. St. Louis: Buschart Brothers, 1907.

Field, Henry M. *The Story of the Atlantic Telegraph*. New York: Arno Press, 1972.

Foltz, Charles S. *Surgeon of the Seas*. Indianapolis: Bobbs-Merrill, 1931.

Fowler, William M. *Under Two Flags: The American Navy in the Civil War*. New York: W. W. Norton, 1990.

Fox, Gustavus Vasa. *Confidential Correspondence of Gustavus Vasa Fox*. Edited by Robert Means Thompson and Richard Wainwright. New York: Naval History Society, 1912.

Gosnell, H. Allen. *Guns on the Western Waters: The Story of the River Gunboats in the Civil War*. Baton Rouge: Louisiana State University Press, 1949.

Haydon, Frederick Stansbury. *Aeronautics in the Union and Confederate Armies*. Baltimore: Johns Hopkins University Press, 1941.

Hoppin, James Mason. *Life of Andrew Hull Foote, Rear-Admiral United States Navy.* New York: Harper Brothers, 1874.

Huling, E. J. *Reminiscences of Gunboat Life in the Mississippi Squadron.* Saratoga Springs, N.Y.: Sentinel, 1881.

Johnson, Ludwell H. *Red River Campaign: Politics and Cotton in the Civil War.* 1958. Reprint, Kent, Ohio: Kent State University Press, 1993.

Johnson, Robert Erwin. *Far China Station: The U.S. Navy in Asian Waters 1800–1898.* Annapolis: Naval Institute Press, 1979.

———. *Rear Admiral John Rodgers 1812–1882.* Annapolis: Naval Institute Press, 1967.

Jones, John B. *A Rebel War Clerk's Diary.* Edited by Earl Schenck Miers. New York: Sagamore Press, 1958.

Jones, Virgil Carrington. *The Civil War at Sea.* New York: Holt, Rinehart, Winston, 1960.

Jones, Virgil Carrington, and Harold L. Peterson. *U.S.S. Cairo: The Story of a Civil War Gunboat.* Washington, D.C.: National Park Service, 1971.

Kemble, John H. *The Panama Route 1848–1869.* New York: Library Editions, 1970.

Lewis, Charles Lee. *David Glasgow Farragut.* Annapolis: Naval Institute Press, 1943.

Lincoln, Abraham. *The Collected Works of Abraham Lincoln.* Vol 6. Edited by Roy P. Basler. New Brunswick, N.J.: Rutgers University Press, 1953.

Lossing, Benson J. *Pictorial History of the Civil War.* 3 vols. Philadelphia: G. W. Childs, 1866–68.

Mahan, Alfred Thayer. *The Gulf and Inland Waters.* New York: Charles Scribner's Sons, 1883.

McClellan, George B. *The Civil War Papers of George B. McClellan.* Edited by Stephen W. Sears. New York: Ticknor and Fields, 1989.

McPherson, James M. *Battle Cry of Freedom.* New York: Ballantine, 1988.

Merrill, James M. "Captain Andrew Hull Foote and the Civil War on Tennessee Waters." *Tennessee Historical Quarterly* 30 (Spring 1971): 83–93.

———. *DuPont: The Making of an Admiral.* New York: Dodd, Mead, 1986.

Milligan, John D., ed. *From the Fresh Water Navy 1861–1864.* Annapolis: Naval Institute Press, 1970.

Millington, Herbert. *American Diplomacy and the War of the Pacific.* New York: Columbia University Press, 1948.

Musicant, Ivan. "The Fires of Norfolk." *American Heritage* 41 (Mar. 1990): 63.

The National Cyclopedia of American Biography. New York: James T. White, 1897.

Niven, John. *Gideon Welles: Lincoln's Secretary of the Navy.* New York: Oxford University Press, 1973.

Parker, William H. *Recollections of a Naval Officer, 1841–1865*. New York: Charles Scribner's Sons, 1883.

Paullin, Charles O. *Paullin's History of Naval Administration, 1175–1911*. Annapolis: Naval Institute Press, 1968.

Parrish, Tom Z. *The Saga of the Confederate Ram Arkansas*. Hillsboro, Tex.: Hill College Press, 1987.

Perry, Milton F. *Infernal Machines*. Baton Rouge: Louisiana State University Press, 1965.

Pletcher, David M. *The Awkward Years*. Columbia: University of Missouri Press, 1962.

Porter, David D. *Incidents and Anecdotes of the Civil War*. New York: D. Appleton, 1885.

———. *The Naval History of the Civil War*. 1866. Reprint, Secaucus, N.J.: Castle, 1984.

Pratt, Fletcher. *Civil War on Western Waters*. New York: Henry Holt, 1956.

Read, C. W. "Reminiscences of the Confederate States Navy." *Southern Historical Society Papers* 1 (May 1876): 331–62.

Reed, Rowena. *Combined Operations in the Civil War*. Annapolis: Naval Institute Press, 1978.

Sandburg, Carl. *Abraham Lincoln: The War Years*. Vol. 1. New York: Charles Scribner's Sons, 1939.

Scharf, J. Thomas. *The Confederate States Navy*. New York: Fairfax Press, 1977.

Shalhope, Robert E. *Sterling Price: Portrait of a Southerner*. Columbia: University of Missouri Press, 1971.

Smith, George W., and Charles Judah, eds. *Chronicles of the Gringos*. Albuquerque: University of New Mexico Press, 1968.

Smith, James Wesley. *Sojourners in Search of Freedom: The Settlement of Liberia by Black Americans*. Lanham, Md.: University Press of America, 1987.

Smith, Myron J., Jr. *The U.S. Gunboat Carondelet 1861–1865*. Manhattan, Kans.: MA/AH Publishing, c. 1982.

Soley, James Russell. *Admiral Porter*. New York: D. Appleton, 1903.

Still, William N., Jr. *Iron Afloat: The Story of the Confederate Armorclads*. Nashville: Vanderbilt University Press, 1971.

Suhr, Robert. "Gunboats on the River." *America's Civil War* 1 (July 1989).

Todorich, Charles. *The Spirited Years: A History of the Antebellum Naval Academy*. Annapolis: Naval Institute Press, 1984.

Tucker, Spencer. *Arming the Fleet: U.S. Navy Ordnance in the Muzzle-Loading Era*. Annapolis: Naval Institute Press, 1989.

Voluska, David L. *The African American in the Union Navy: 1861–1865*. New York: Garland, 1993.

Walke, Henry. *Naval Scenes and Reminiscences.* New York: F. R. Reed, 1877.

Wallace, Lew. *An Autobiography.* New York: Harper and Brothers, 1906.

Ward, W. E. F. *The Royal Navy and the Slavers.* New York: Pantheon, 1969.

Wells, Mrs. E. O. "When Memphis Surrendered." *Confederate Veteran* 25 (Dec. 1927).

Welles, Gideon. *Diary of Gideon Welles.* Vol. 1. Edited by Howard K. Beale. New York: W. W. Norton, 1960.

West, Richard S., Jr. *Gideon Welles: Lincoln's Navy Department.* Indianapolis: Bobbs-Merrill, 1943.

————. *The Second Admiral: A Life of David Dixon Porter 1813–1891.* New York: Coward-McCann, 1937.

White, Lonnie. "Federal Operations at New Madrid and Island Number Ten." *West Tennessee Historical Society Papers* 17 (1963): 47–67.

Whitesell, Robert D. "Military and Naval Activity Between Cairo and Columbus." *Register of the Kentucky Historical Society* 61 (1963): 107–21.

Williams, Frances Leigh. *Matthew Fontaine Maury: Scientist of the Sea.* New Brunswick, N.J.: Rutgers University Press, 1963.

Government Documents

Congressional Globe. Washington, D.C. Mar. 31, 1856 (reprint of a speech by Senator John Slidell of Louisiana); Mar. 3, 1858, 948–55.

Official Records of the Union and Confederate Navies in the War of the Rebellion. 30 vols. Washington, D.C.: GPO, 1895–1929.

Report of the Joint Committee on the Conduct of the War. Vol. 2. Washington, D.C.: GPO, 1865.

Senate Executive Documents, 35th Cong., 1st sess. Vol. 12, no. 48 (1857–58).

The War of the Rebellion: A Compilation of the Official Records of the Union and Confederate Armies. 128 vols. Washington, D.C.: GPO, 1895–1929.

Logbooks

USS *Independence*	USS *St. Mary's*
USS *Columbus*	USS *Benton*
USS *Jamestown*	USS *Eastport*
USS *Susquehanna*	USS *Fort Hindman*

NEWSPAPERS

Chicago Times	*Missouri Republican*
Chicago Tribune	*New York Herald*
Cincinnati Daily Commercial	*New York Times*
Cincinnati Daily Gazette	*New York Tribune*
Jeffersonian Democrat (Ohio)	*New York World*
Memphis Daily Appeal	*Philadelphia North American*
Missouri Democrat	*The Times* (London)

Index

INDEX

Porter, William, 104, 133, 254, 327–28, 399; vs. *Arkansas*, 275, 276, 280; Battle of Fort Henry, 157, 160
Portsmouth (USS, sloop), 25, 27–28, 139
Potomac (USS, frigate), 61
Preble, George H., 316–17
Preble (USS, sloop), 16, 39
Prentiss, Benjamin, 335–36
Price, Sterling, 335, 385
Prichett, James M., 149, 335–36, 348
Princeton (USS, screw steamer), 58

Queen, Lt. Henry, 96–98
Queen of the West (ram), 326–27; vs. *Arkansas*, 261, 263, 265, 267, 274–75, 277; Battle of Memphis, 236–37
Quinby, Isaac, 231

Red River, Federal expedition, 344–45, 347–48, 349, 351, 354–81
Red Rover (sidewheel steamer), 197
Reed, G. W., 239
Reefer (USS, schooner), 47, 49–50, 56–58, 64
Retirement Board, 76–78, 99–101, 102–4, 106–7
Richmond (USS, screw sloop), 251, 258, 268, 278
Riddle, A. G., 11, 16
Riley, F. A., 179
Robert Wilson (slave ship), 41–44, 47
Robey, Francis M., 245
Rocket (steamer), 283
Rodgers, George, 366, 368, 369, 370
Rodgers, John, 2, 4–7, 189, 294, 388, 406; creating a flotilla, 113, *114*, 115–16, 118–19, 121; relieved of command, 124
Roe, Francis A., 387–88
Rose, Frederick, 98, 99
Rosecrans, William S., 322, 328, 330, 337–38
Rowan, Stephen, 2

Sabine Cross Roads, Louisiana, 361–62
St. Charles Hotel (Cairo, Illinois), 123

St. Louis (Baron de Kalb) (USS, ironclad), 138, 149, 243, 249, 305; Battle of Fort Donelson, 176–79, *181*, 182; Battle of Fort Henry, 152, 155, *156*, 159, 161; Battle of Memphis, 236; Island No. 10, 200–202, 224, 226
St. Mary's (USS, sloop), 51–52, 86, 101–3, 105,106
Salley Wood (sternwheel steamer), 167, 170–71
Sam Kirkman (sternwheel steamer), 167–69
Sampson (ram), 283
Samuel Orr (steamer), 162–63
Sands, Joshua, 56, 60, 86–87, 89, 96–98; Phelps's description of, 80, 82, 92, 94
Sanford, Joseph, 215–16
San Juan de Ulloa, Mexico, 51, 61–62, 64, 82
Santa Anna, Antonio Lopez de, 58, 59
Saratoga (USS, sloop), 94–95
Sarranac (USS, sidewheel steamer), 102, 106
Sassacus (USS, sidewheel steamer), 387
Savannah, Tennessee, 165, 170,
Scorpion (USS, sidewheel steamer), 67
Scott, Joseph, 375, 378
Scott, Thomas, 212
Scott, Winfield, 9, 61–63, 65, 67
Scourge (USS, screw steamer), 65, 66
Sebastian, John, 170
Selfridge, Thomas, 309, 318, 324, 399; Red River, 357, 360, 363–64
Seward, William, 302
Shelby, Joseph O., 385
Shepard, Alexander, 393
Sherman, William T., 143, 151, 195, 338–40, 343, 345, 358, 364, 379; attempts to take Vicksburg, 317–19, 326, 329; opinion of Phelps, 341
Shiloh, Tennessee, see Pittsburg Landing
Shirk, James W., 159; and Tennessee River Raid, 170, *171*, 193, 289, 309, 345, 400
Shirley, Paul, 81, 83, 96
Shirley, S. W., 117

{ 447 }

Ironclad Captain
was composed in 10/13 ITC New Baskerville
on a Macintosh Quadra 700 system using QuarkXPress
by Books International;
printed by sheet-fed offset on 50-pound Glatfelter Supple Opaque stock
(an acid-free recycled paper),
notch case bound over 88-point binder's boards
in ICG Pearl Linen with 80-pound Rainbow endpapers,
and wrapped with dust jackets printed in three colors
on 100-pound enamel stock finished with matte film lamination
by Thomson-Shore, Inc.;
designed by Will Underwood;
and published by
The Kent State University Press
KENT, OHIO 44242